MATERIALS IN TRIAL ADVOCACY

PROBLEMS AND CASES

ASPEN COURSEBOOK SERIES

MATERIALS IN TRIAL ADVOCACY

PROBLEMS AND CASES

Eighth Edition

THOMAS A. MAUET
Director of Trial Advocacy
and Milton O. Riepe Professor of Law
University of Arizona James E. Rogers College of Law

JUDGE WARREN D. WOLFSON
Distinguished Visiting Professor of Law
DePaul University College of Law

STEPHEN D. EASTON
Professor of Law
University of Wyoming College of Law

Photography by
Amanda Merullo

About Wolters Kluwer Law & Business

Wolters Kluwer Law & Business is a leading global provider of intelligent information and digital solutions for legal and business professionals in key specialty areas, and respected educational resources for professors and law students. Wolters Kluwer Law & Business connects legal and business professionals as well as those in the education market with timely, specialized authoritative content and information-enabled solutions to support success through productivity, accuracy and mobility.

Serving customers worldwide, Wolters Kluwer Law & Business products include those under the Aspen Publishers, CCH, Kluwer Law International, Loislaw, ftwilliam.com and MediRegs family of products.

CCH products have been a trusted resource since 1913, and are highly regarded resources for legal, securities, antitrust and trade regulation, government contracting, banking, pension, payroll, employment and labor, and healthcare reimbursement and compliance professionals.

Aspen Publishers products provide essential information to attorneys, business professionals and law students. Written by preeminent authorities, the product line offers analytical and practical information in a range of specialty practice areas from securities law and intellectual property to mergers and acquisitions and pension/benefits. Aspen's trusted legal education resources provide professors and students with high-quality, up-to-date and effective resources for successful instruction and study in all areas of the law.

Kluwer Law International products provide the global business community with reliable international legal information in English. Legal practitioners, corporate counsel and business executives around the world rely on Kluwer Law journals, looseleafs, books, and electronic products for comprehensive information in many areas of international legal practice.

Loislaw is a comprehensive online legal research product providing legal content to law firm practitioners of various specializations. Loislaw provides attorneys with the ability to quickly and efficiently find the necessary legal information they need, when and where they need it, by facilitating access to primary law as well as state-specific law, records, forms and treatises.

ftwilliam.com offers employee benefits professionals the highest quality plan documents (retirement, welfare and non-qualified) and government forms (5500/PBGC, 1099 and IRS) software at highly competitive prices.

MediRegs products provide integrated health care compliance content and software solutions for professionals in healthcare, higher education and life sciences, including professionals in accounting, law and consulting.

Wolters Kluwer Law & Business, a division of Wolters Kluwer, is headquartered in New York. Wolters Kluwer is a market-leading global information services company focused on professionals.

SUMMARY OF CONTENTS

CONTENTS

I V

91

EXHIBITS

IMPEACHMENT AND REHABILITATION

VI

351

EXPERTS

VII

485

ADVANCED DIRECT AND CROSS-EXAMINATION

VIII

737

CLOSING ARGUMENTS

IX

753

TRIALS

PREFACE

This book presents a progressive series of problems, cases, and trial files. They can be utilized for semester courses in trial advocacy as well as in post-graduate programs for trial lawyers. The problems are organized to parallel the various stages of a jury trial. Each chapter contains a mix of civil and criminal problems of increasing difficulty, allowing for substantial assignment selection. The problems present situations that commonly occur during civil and criminal trials. They are designed to develop basic trial skills. Chapter 7 contains a dozen cases involving two opposing witnesses that can be used as advanced direct and cross-examination problems, as opening statement and closing argument exercises, and as short trials or hearings. The last chapter, Chapter 9, contains overviews of 14 trial files, each having two to four witnesses per side, that can be used during the semester or as a final trial at the end of the course. The trial files are in the Companion Website that accompanies the book. Each trial file can be effectively tried to a jury in approximately three to four hours.

The organization and design of the problems are a result of our experiences as trial lawyers, judges, and trial advocacy teachers. In our view, some of the other available trial advocacy teaching materials are too lengthy and complex. Often these materials base problems on complete case files, requiring the reading of an entire case to prepare one problem. This results in assignments being an exercise in reading and memory, not in trial techniques. The problems in this book, on the other hand, have two principal characteristics. First, they are efficient and self-contained, often being only two or three pages long. Second, each problem emphasizes a specific trial skill that is essential to every competent trial lawyer.

Many of the problems, cases, and trial files are based on actual cases that we have tried during our years as trial lawyers or as judges or those that otherwise have come to our attention. In redrafting the materials for this book, we have converted the actual dates into a now commonly used system of stating dates based on their relationship to the present year. For example, "[-1]" means one year ago, "[-2]" means two years ago, and so on. For example, this year being 2015, the date of "6/15/[-1]" is June 15, 2014; "August 1, [-2]" is August 1, 2013. Through this device the dates can be kept realistic.

Finally, we must point out difficulties created by the mock trial setting. Obviously, testimony in that setting gets shaped and at times created by the students. There is perhaps a danger that students will confuse the mock world with the real world. In a mock trial, lawyers cannot know what the truth is because there is no truth: Everything is made up. In the real world, lawyers often know what the truth is and do the best they can to deal with it. Those attempts should lead to serious and important discussions about the nature of the adversary system and a lawyer's ethical obligations and sense of morality.

This book is designed to help teach trial techniques to people who want to learn them and who eventually might have to use them. We do not want to discourage discussion about the lawyer's role and duties in the real trial world; nor do we want our purpose diluted by a confusion of the mock with the real. We rely on the teachers to point out the differences.

What's New in the Eighth Edition

Materials in Trial Advocacy has been used for over 30 years. Since 1981 we have received numerous suggestions for additions, deletions, and modifications. We always welcome these suggestions and have incorporated many of them over the years, so that the present edition is substantially different from the first. The principal changes in this eighth edition are listed here:

First, we replaced essentially all of the photographs with new photographs, which were taken by skilled photographer Amanda Merullo. Frankly, some of the images were starting to get a bit dated, so it was time for a comprehensive update. Thanks to Amanda's efforts, you now have photographs of modern cars, buildings, and exhibits.

Next, we replaced most of the other graphics with new versions. University of Wyoming College of Law students Jeff Van Fleet and Skyler Bagley did the work of creating the new images. We are grateful for their many hours of effort and their talent.

Whenever possible, we changed the names of witnesses to gender-neutral names. This should make it easier for those of either gender to play most of the witness roles.

Finally, we added two new problems. One, Problem 7.12, involves a police officer's seizure of a cell phone during a search incident to arrest. The other, Problem 4.27, involves the admissibility of a social media post. The latter is actually several problems, because we have created over two dozen contexts for this problem.

The intent, in all instances, was to modernize the book while retaining and advancing the core concept of presenting real world problems that raise the kinds of issues that arise in actual trials. We hope you will be pleased with the additions and changes in this eighth edition.

Acknowledgments

We would like to thank John Mollenkamp, who developed the 9.14 files with one of the co-authors at the University of Missouri School of Law. We would also like to thank Ms. Shannon Snow for her assistance in researching and drafting the medical records for Jennifer Smith v. Kelly Davis, M.D. (9.12). We would also like to thank Professor Mary Rita Luecke of DePaul College of Law for contributing supplemental material, including the drawings in Problems 7.2, 7.6, and 7.9, as well as the defense file memo for Problem 7.7 that is included in the Teacher's Manual. We also would like to thank Professor Tawnya Plumb, Electronic Services Librarian at the University of Wyoming College of Law's George W. Hopper Law Library, who provided invaluable research assistance and University of Wyoming Professor Elaine Welle, who provided guidance about the law. Finally, we would like to thank Joe Bevington and Skyler Bagley, students at the University of Wyoming College of Law, for their amazing technical assistance in updating the graphics and Amanda Merullo for her diligence and skill in finding and photographing the assorted items in the problems and trials.

Thomas A. Mauet
Tucson, Arizona

Warren D. Wolfson
Chicago, Illinois

Stephen D. Easton
Laramie, Wyoming

January 2015

I

JURY SELECTION

INTRODUCTION

The problems in this chapter represent common types of civil and criminal cases that are routinely tried to juries. They present recurring issues about which a trial lawyer must reach decisions before and during the jury selection process. In addition, the two-witness cases in Chapter 7 may be used.

For each problem assigned, you should be prepared to make all necessary preliminary decisions and resolve any procedural uncertainties before the jury selection process actually begins. You must be thoroughly familiar with the applicable substantive law, your jurisdiction's procedural rules, and your judge's particular practices during jury selection.

Your instructor may modify the assignments and make specific additional assignments for these exercises.

The suggested background reading is Mauet, *Trial Techniques and Trials*, Chapter 3.

1.1 CIVIL: AUTOMOBILE NEGLIGENCE

This is a negligence action brought by Sharon Howard against James Walton arising out of a vehicle collision that occurred two years ago during the evening of May 2.

At the time, Howard was driving southbound in the inside lane of Main Street, a four-lane street with two lanes of traffic in each direction. Suddenly, another car, driven northbound in the inside lane by Walton, turned left without signaling and cut in front of Howard. Howard slammed on her brakes but couldn't avoid hitting Walton's car.

Walton maintains that he was driving northbound on Main Street, that he decided to turn left, and that the oncoming car driven by Howard was speeding and crashed into him before he could complete the turn. Walton says he was stopped in the inside southbound lane of Main waiting for a break in the outside lane traffic, so he could finish the turn, when the other car struck him.

The police at the scene gave Walton a Breathalyzer test because they smelled liquor on his breath. The test showed some alcohol but in an amount below the legal presumption-of-intoxication level. The police gave Walton a citation for failing to signal a left turn. The charge was dropped at a later date.

Both drivers were taken to a nearby hospital. Walton was examined and released. Howard was admitted with a broken nose, concussion, and facial cuts. Today she still has visible scarring on her nose and cheeks and complains of periodic headaches. She is 22 years old and single.

Plaintiff's occurrence witnesses are two girls, ages 11 and 12, who were sitting on their front lawn across from where the collision occurred. They will support plaintiff's version of the event, including Howard's claim that she was not speeding.

1. Prepare a juror profile of favorable and unfavorable jurors.
2. Conduct a voir dire examination of prospective jurors and make appropriate cause and peremptory challenges for the plaintiff or defendant.

3. Submit a written list of supplemental questions you wish the court to ask the prospective jurors if the court will conduct the entire voir dire.

1.2   CIVIL: PRODUCTS LIABILITY

This is a products liability case brought by Susan James against the ABC Manufacturing Company.

Three years ago, at a local supermarket, James purchased a standard metal can opener manufactured by the defendant. When purchased, the can opener was in a plastic and cardboard package. The back of the package contained the following words: "WARNING: Use only for opening bottles and cans." James did not read the back of the package at any time.

On May 2, two years ago, James used the can opener to pry open a sticky kitchen drawer. The tip of the can opener broke off and flew into her left eye, resulting in a total loss of vision in that eye.

At the time of the accident, James was 53 years old, married, and had three adult children no longer living with her. She is not formally employed outside of her house, though she is a potter who sells her work at art and craft fairs.

The ABC Manufacturing Company, a Japanese corporation located in Tokyo, defends on the basis of product misuse and the adequacy of the written warning contained on the package. ABC manufactures numerous kitchen utensils and appliances, principally for importation to the United States. It has been in business since 1948. There are several products liability cases pending against ABC based on alleged defects in the can opener, but none has yet been settled or tried.

1. Prepare a juror profile of favorable and unfavorable jurors.
2. Conduct a voir dire examination of prospective jurors and make appropriate cause and peremptory challenges for the plaintiff or defendant.
3. Submit a written list of supplemental questions you wish the court to ask the prospective jurors if the court will conduct the entire voir dire.

1.3   CIVIL: MEDICAL MALPRACTICE

This is a medical malpractice case brought by Juan Gonzalez against Mercy Hospital.

On May 2, two years ago, Gonzalez fell down the stairs of his apartment and fractured his ankle. He was taken to the Mercy Hospital emergency room, where he was examined and treated by the emergency room personnel.

An intern employed by the hospital set the fracture and placed the lower leg in a cast. The next day Gonzalez began to complain of swelling and numbness in the leg, was examined periodically by the hospital staff, and was assured repeatedly by the hospital staff that his complaints were not unusual in injuries of that type.

Five days after the accident the cast was removed and the leg was found to have significantly impaired circulation. Gangrene had set in. Despite remedial measures, the condition worsened, and the leg eventually had to be amputated just below the knee.

Gonzalez at the time of the accident was 35 years old, married, and the father of two small children. He was employed as a carpenter by a local construction company, but he has not worked at that job or any other since the accident. His employer's health and disability insurance has covered his medical and lost income expenses to date.

Gonzalez, a Mexican national, was a lawful resident alien when the accident happened.

Mercy Hospital, a not-for-profit charitable institution, has been owned and operated for many years by the Jesuits, a Catholic order.

1.   Prepare a juror profile of favorable and unfavorable jurors.
2.   Conduct a voir dire examination of prospective jurors and make appropriate cause and peremptory challenges for the plaintiff or defendant.
3.   Submit a written list of supplemental questions you wish the court to ask the prospective jurors if the court will conduct the entire voir dire.

1.4 CIVIL: WRONGFUL DEATH

This is a wrongful death and survival action brought by William Smith, administrator of the estate of Jennifer Smith, deceased, against the defendants, Frank Jones and the ABC Construction Company.

On May 2, two years ago, Jennifer Smith, age 6, was playing with several other children in the schoolyard of her grade school shortly after school had let out for the day. At the same time, Frank Jones, a 62-year-old carpenter, was driving down the street by the schoolyard in a truck owned by his employer, ABC Construction Company, on his way to a job site.

The school zone is marked with signs. Jones was driving within the posted speed limit. The schoolyard is separated from the street by a fence, which has periodic openings in it.

Jennifer then spotted an ice cream truck parked across the street from the schoolyard. Its lights and music were on. Jennifer suddenly ran through an opening in the fence and across the street toward the truck.

Jones saw the ice cream truck and then saw Jennifer running across the street. He slammed on his brakes and turned his steering wheel but was unable to stop in time. The truck knocked Jennifer down on the pavement.

Jennifer was taken to a nearby hospital where she died five days later without ever regaining consciousness.

1. Prepare a juror profile of favorable and unfavorable jurors.
2. Conduct a voir dire examination of prospective jurors and make appropriate cause and peremptory challenges for the plaintiff or defendants.
3. Submit a list of supplemental questions you wish the court to ask the prospective jurors if the court will conduct the entire voir dire.

1.5 CRIMINAL: ARMED ROBBERY AND AGGRAVATED BATTERY

This is an armed bank robbery and aggravated battery case brought against the defendant, William Hill.

On May 2 of last year, two persons, one of whom was armed with a handgun, robbed the Second Federal Savings and Loan Association. Two tellers and the branch manager were in the bank at the time. Approximately $16,000 was taken.

During the robbery, one of the tellers, Helen Lee, age 37, married, with two teenage children, was shot in the foot. She was taken to a nearby hospital and treated. Today her left leg is slightly smaller in the calf area than the right leg, and she has a noticeable limp.

The police, who obtained the license plate number of the getaway car from a passerby, arrested the defendant one hour later. The defendant, a 20-year-old high school dropout who had been unemployed six months when arrested, had been previously arrested twice for robbery and burglary. The robbery charge was dismissed; the burglary charge is still pending.

Following his arrest, the defendant was placed in a lineup with several other persons. One of the tellers positively identified the defendant as the robber. Helen Lee and the branch manager were unable to make any identification.

The money and handgun were never found. The second offender was never arrested or charged.

1. Prepare a juror profile of favorable and unfavorable jurors.
2. Conduct a voir dire examination of prospective jurors and make appropriate cause and peremptory challenges for the prosecution or defense.
3. Submit a list of supplemental questions you wish the court to ask the prospective jurors if the court will conduct the entire voir dire.

1.6 CRIMINAL: SEXUAL ASSAULT

This is a criminal sexual assault prosecution brought against the defendant, William Jackson.

The victim, Mary Rice, age 22 and single, will testify that she worked as a bartender at Butch's, a local spot popular with college students and young working persons. On May 2 of last year, she left work at 2:00 A.M. and walked to her apartment building one block away. A man followed her onto the elevator and exited on her floor. As she opened her apartment door, the man grabbed her from behind, pushed her into the apartment, told her he had a knife, and sexually assaulted her.

Immediately after the man left, Rice called the police. When they arrived she told them that she had seen the man previously at Butch's. (Based on this and other information, the police arrested the defendant several days later.) The police took Rice to a hospital, where she was examined and released.

When arrested, the defendant told the police that he had accompanied Rice to her apartment, that she had invited him in, and that they had voluntarily engaged in sex.

The defendant, age 22, who is African American, has a prior conviction for burglary. The victim is white.

1. Prepare a juror profile of favorable and unfavorable jurors.
2. Conduct a voir dire examination of prospective jurors and make appropriate cause and peremptory challenges for the prosecution or defense.
3. Submit a list of supplemental questions you wish the court to ask the prospective jurors if the court will conduct the entire voir dire.

1.7   CRIMINAL: TAX EVASION

This is an income tax evasion case brought against the defendant, Joseph Church.

The indictment charges that for the tax year ending December 31, two years ago, the defendant, a physician specializing in orthopedic surgery, intentionally and knowingly understated his gross income. It charges that his unreported gross income for the year was $293,000, resulting in an underpayment of tax in the amount of $70,000.

Church admits that he underreported his gross income in the amounts alleged but denies that this was intentionally and knowingly done. His defense is that he delegated all the financial aspects of his practice to his bookkeeper (since fired), who, he later discovered, was sloppy and did inaccurate work. He claims that he personally had no idea what his gross income for the tax year was when he signed the return.

The bookkeeper will testify that the doctor was satisfied with her work until his tax difficulties began and that she merely did the billings and paid the office expenses. She contends she never did accounting or tax work for the doctor.

1. Prepare a juror profile of favorable and unfavorable jurors.
2. Conduct a voir dire examination of prospective jurors and make appropriate cause and peremptory challenges for the prosecution or defense.
3. Submit a list of supplemental questions you wish the court to ask the prospective jurors if the court will conduct the entire voir dire.

1.8   CRIMINAL: MURDER

This is a murder case brought against the defendant, William Barnes.

On May 2 of last year the victim, Fred Silver, was found in his apartment by police, who were called to the scene by a neighbor who complained of loud voices and noises coming from Silver's apartment. When police arrived, they found Silver already dead, with numerous stab wounds in the neck, chest, and back. At the time of his death, Silver was age 42, single, and worked for an advertising agency.

Following an anonymous tip, two homicide detectives went to the defendant's home. After a lengthy interrogation, the defendant finally admitted killing Silver, a social friend, after an argument.

The indicated defense is insanity. The defendant's proof will show that during the past five years, the defendant has been admitted two times on a voluntary basis to psychiatric institutions for paranoid schizophrenia. A defense psychiatrist who examined the defendant after his arrest concluded that the defendant was suffering from the same condition at the time of the stabbing. The prosecution has an expert with a contrary opinion.

1. Prepare a juror profile of favorable and unfavorable jurors.
2. Conduct a voir dire examination of prospective jurors and make appropriate cause and peremptory challenges for the prosecution or defense.
3. Submit a list of supplemental questions you wish the court to ask the prospective jurors if the court will conduct the entire voir dire.

II

OPENING STATEMENTS

INTRODUCTION

The trial files summarized in Chapter 9 and included in full on the Companion Website, prepared for use as full trials, may also be used here as representative civil and criminal cases on which to base separate opening statement assignments. In addition, the two-witness cases in Chapter 7 may be used for additional opening statement assignments.

For each problem assigned you should be prepared to present an opening statement that is logically organized and persuasively delivered to the jury. Your instructor may modify the assignments and make specific additional assignments for these exercises.

The suggested background reading is Mauet, *Trial Techniques and Trials,* Chapter 4.

III

DIRECT AND CROSS-EXAMINATION

Introduction

III

DIRECT AND CROSS-EXAMINATION

INTRODUCTION

The problems in this chapter represent the kinds of recurring problems routinely encountered during the direct and cross-examinations of common types of witnesses. Each problem focuses on a specific kind of skill, the mastery of which is essential to present the witness's testimony effectively in the courtroom. This chapter focuses on occurrence witnesses, the most common and important witnesses in personal injury and criminal cases. The advanced direct and cross-examination cases in Chapter 7 have a number of witnesses in commercial transactions settings.

You should prepare your specific assignment for each problem as though the case were actually on trial. Accordingly, you should determine whether any admissibility issues exist and anticipate the objections and arguments your opponent is likely to make. In addition, you should structure and execute your direct or cross-examination so that you will effectively present that witness's testimony to the jury.

Most of the witnesses do not have background information. Be prepared to develop realistic, credible backgrounds for them.

Your instructor may modify the assignments and make specific additional assignments for these exercises.

The suggested background reading is Mauet, *Trial Techniques and Trials*, Chapters 5 and 6.

3.1 CONVERSATIONS AND TELEPHONE CALLS

1. The charge is extortion. Jess Smith is the complaining witness. The defendant is Ed Crosby. Smith has worked with Crosby at Ajax Machine Works for the past five years. They spoke on several occasions, at the plant.

Smith will testify that on January 15 of last year, at 6 P.M., in the 14' by 20' Ajax Machine Works coffee room, Crosby said that unless Smith paid him $1,000 by the end of the week, he would put sugar in the gas tank of Smith's new Cadillac. No one else was in the coffee room at the time. Ajax is located at 322 W. Vernon Street.

For the prosecution, call Smith as a witness and put the conversation in evidence.

2. Use the same facts as in No. 1 above, except that the conversation occurred when Crosby called Smith at Smith's home. Smith lives at 3110 S. Crawford Avenue.

For the prosecution, call Smith as a witness and put the telephone conversation in evidence, assuming:

(a) they had talked on the phone many times before January 15 of last year; or

(b) they had never talked on the phone before January 15 of last year.

3. Assume that Crosby and Smith had never met or spoken before January 15 of last year. Smith will testify that Crosby telephoned him/her at home on January 15, at about 6:00 P.M., and made the threat contained in No. 1 above. Crosby did not give his name during the call. One week later Crosby walked up to Smith outside Smith's house, at 2:15 P.M., and said: "I'm the one who called you last week. Do you have the $1,000?"

For the prosecution, call Smith as a witness and put both conversations in evidence, assuming:

(a) when they talked in front of Smith's house, Smith recognized Crosby's voice; or

(b) when they talked in front of Smith's house, Smith did not recognize Crosby's voice.

4. For the defense, in each of the above situations, oppose the testimony and cross-examine Smith.

3.2   CONVERSATIONS AND TELEPHONE CALLS

A new client, Kennedy Smith, came to you one year ago today and told you the following story:

One month ago I decided to purchase a new car, so I checked the yellow pages of the telephone directory and called Ace Motors. A man answered, said he'd be happy to talk to me, and said I should come in so they could show me the various models and accessories.

The next day I went to Ace Motors and met a salesman, Tim Bonner. I looked at several cars and the accessories, got price quotes, and finally placed my order for a new sports car. I gave him a check for $2,000 as a down payment. The full price of the car was $36,000.

The next day I had second thoughts about the sports car. I decided that it was not the right car for me and that what I really needed was a minivan. I called Ace again and a woman answered. I told her I had ordered a car but wanted to switch my order to a minivan I had looked at the previous day with the same accessories I ordered for the sports car. She asked my name and put me on hold for a few minutes. When she came back she said everything was taken care of; they'd call when the minivan came in. She said the price would be $28,000.

Two weeks later the phone rang. I picked it up and said, "Hello," and the voice said, "Hi, it's Tim Bonner at Ace—your sports car arrived and is ready for pickup." I told him I'd changed the order, and he said he didn't know anything about it. He said I'd better come in.

The next day I went again to Ace Motors and talked to Charles Locker, the owner and manager. He said he had no written record of any order change. In any event, he said, none of the women working for him were sales personnel, and only salespeople were authorized to either write purchase contracts or modify existing orders. Hence, he said, he could only deliver the sports car in accordance with the terms of the written contract.

The next day I called Ace Motors and talked to Mr. Locker again. I demanded that he obtain the minivan for me. He refused. I then demanded that he return my $2,000 deposit. He refused, stating that he couldn't return my money since it was a deposit for a sports car, and they were ready to deliver a sports car.

You have brought suit to enforce the oral modification of the contract or, alternatively, for the return of the $2,000. The case is now on trial.

1. For the plaintiff, conduct a direct examination of Smith.
2. For the defendant, cross-examine Smith.

3.3 REFRESHING RECOLLECTION AND RECORDED RECOLLECTION

On February 15, [-1], there was a burglary at the Ace Hardware Store, located at 1050 North Main Street.

At about 3:00 A.M. that day, Logan Stone was walking on the sidewalk in front of the store on the way home from the nearby plant where s/he worked the night shift, 5:30 P.M. to 2:30 A.M. Stone saw a man run out of the store and jump into a large black sedan. The car sped away.

Stone, from about ten feet away, saw the license plate number of the car, ZQB-437, as it pulled away from the curb. S/he ran to his/her locked car, which was parked a half-block away, found a pencil and piece of paper in the glove compartment, and wrote down the license plate number. Stone then used a cellular telephone to call the police and report what s/he had just seen. Later, s/he gave Officer Arthur Jones the scrap of paper containing the license plate number.

Now, Fred Miller, the registered owner of the black car, is on trial for the burglary. Stone is called by the prosecution to testify about the license plate number on the black car that left the scene.

1. On direct examination, Stone is unable to remember the license plate number. Use the piece of paper to refresh Stone's memory of the number.

2. On direct examination, Stone cannot remember the license plate number, even after being shown the piece of paper. Get the paper or its contents in evidence.

3. For the prosecution, be prepared to conduct the entire direct examination.

4. For the defense, cross-examine Stone.

5. Assume that Stone testifies that the car s/he saw was a large *white* car. The defendant owns a white Lincoln Continental. For the defense, cross-examine Stone using Jones's police report.

ZQB-437

33

POLICE REPORT

Re: Burglary at 1050 North Main Street
To: Commanding Officer
From: Patrolman Arthur Jones

Reporting officer arrived at scene of reported burglary at 3:20 A.M. (2/15/[-1]). Interviewed witness Logan Stone. Said witness told reporting officer s/he saw a man run out of the Ace Hardware Store, 1050 North Main, at about 3 A.M. Witness further said the man jumped into a large black car and said car then sped away. S/he did not see the face of the man, but did note the number on the car license plate. Stone said s/he then ran to his/her own parked car and wrote down the license plate number. S/he gave the reporting officer the piece of paper with the license plate number on it.

Arthur Jones
Star number 1424

2/15/[-1]
600 hours

3.4 REFRESHING RECOLLECTION AND RECORDED RECOLLECTION

This is a contract action. Plaintiff, the Oregon National Bank, is suing Smith Brothers Car Sales, a small local car dealer, alleging that the dealership violated its contract with the bank. The contract provided for recurring loans to the dealership each time it bought a new car. When the car was sold, the dealership was required to pay the bank the loan amount on the car, and the bank would then release its lien on the car.

In June, two years ago, the bank's president, Mortimer Jones, suspected that the dealership was selling cars "out of trust"—that is, was selling cars without using part of the proceeds to pay off the bank's loans. He sent one of the loan officers, Mel Jenkins, to the dealership to take a physical inventory of the cars on the lot so that Jones could then compare it with the bank's loan and lien records.

On June 30, two years ago, Jenkins went to the dealership and conducted the inventory and prepared a written record of the inventory results. Based on a comparison of the inventory with the bank's records, Jones directed the bank's attorneys to file this action.

The case is now on trial. The bank calls Jenkins as a witness. Jenkins, before coming to court today, went to the bank's loan records and pulled the inventory sheet, which s/he brought with him/her.

1. On direct examination, Jenkins is unable to remember the number of cars s/he saw on the lot during his/her inventory. Use the inventory sheet to refresh Jenkins' recollection.

2. On direct examination, Jenkins is unable to remember the car models, years, and vehicle identification numbers, even after being shown the inventory sheet. Get the sheet (or its contents) in evidence.

3. For the defendant, cross-examine Jenkins.

OREGON NATIONAL BANK

To: Mortimer Jones, President

The following are the results of the floor and lot inventory I conducted at Smith Brothers Car Sales on June 30 at your request:

Car Model	Year	VIN
Chevrolet sedan	[-0]	YX43307J
"	"	BZ66237Q
"	"	YX56987J
"	"	GJ44512Q
"		GJ98002Q
Chevrolet wagon	"	K4439856
"	"	K6742381
"	"	K9012376
"	"	K4438705
"	"	K6745001
Chevrolet Corvette	[-1]	J22341BX
Ford Mustang	[-2]	FX4409821
Buick Le Sabre	[-2]	B2341821Q

Mel Jenkins,
loan officer

3.5 HOMICIDE VICTIM'S WIDOW

This is a manslaughter prosecution. The manslaughter charge arises out of a tavern argument that turned into a brawl, during which the victim was killed when he was stabbed in the chest. The defense is self-defense.

The case is now on trial. To prove the identity of the victim and to show that the victim had no preexisting medical condition that could have caused his death, the prosecution will call the victim's widow, Mary Jones. Mrs. Jones can testify on direct examination that she last saw her husband, Frank Jones, the morning he was killed, May 15 of last year. At that time he was in perfect health. She next saw him late that evening in the county morgue. At that time he was dead.

1. For the prosecution, conduct a direct examination of Mary Jones.
2. For the defense, cross-examine Mary Jones as necessary.
3. For the prosecution, conduct any necessary redirect examination.

3.6 ALIBI WITNESS

This is a criminal case. The defendant, Elmer Barnes, is charged with robbery. The defense is alibi. The defendant claims that at the time of the robbery, June 15 of last year at 10:00 P.M., he was at home, about one-half mile from the scene of the robbery. He claims he didn't feel well that evening and had gone to bed around 9:30 P.M. The defendant, age 17, has no brothers or sisters. One of his parents is deceased. He was arrested and charged on July 3, [-1].

The case is now on trial. To support his alibi defense, the defense intends to call the defendant's mother/father, Peyton Barnes. Mr./Mrs. Barnes can testify that on the night in question, s/he was home all evening. Elmer came home about 7:00 P.M., watched television with him/her in the living room for a while, and went to bed shortly before 10:00 P.M. S/he went to bed a few minutes after he did, after the 9:00 P.M. news program ended.

Peyton Barnes has not previously told this to anyone other than the defense attorney. Police investigators attempted to interview him/her shortly before trial, but s/he told them s/he did not wish to talk to them.

1. For the defense, conduct a direct examination of Peyton Barnes.
2. For the prosecution, cross-examine Peyton Barnes as necessary.
3. For the defense, conduct any necessary redirect examination.

3.7   WITNESS TO CAR COLLISION

This is a personal injury case arising out of an automobile intersection collision that occurred on June 15 of last year. The plaintiff claims that he was driving eastbound on Main Street toward Elm Street, entered the intersection, and was struck by a car, driven by the defendant, that was going northbound on Elm. Plaintiff claims that the defendant ran the red light and was speeding.

The case is now on trial. Plaintiff calls Skylar Howard, who testified as follows, on July 15, [-1], at the Traffic Court case arising from this accident:

I was driving eastbound on Main Street toward the intersection of Elm Street on June 15, [-1], at approximately 8:30 A.M. I was on my way to work, about three miles away. It was the morning rush hour. The car and pedestrian traffic was normal for that time of day. Main Street is a commercial street with four lanes of traffic, two in each direction. Commercial stores and office buildings line Main and Elm.

As I was driving on Main Street, in the outside lane, there was another car ahead of me, perhaps half a block away. Both I and the other car were going perhaps 20 mph. As the car in front of me, a tan Ford sedan, the plaintiff's car, entered the intersection, the light turned yellow. As the Ford reached the far side of the intersection, another car, a beige Toyota, the defendant's car, going from right to left, suddenly entered the intersection and slammed into the right rear side of the Ford. The light was still yellow for Main Street at the moment of impact. The Toyota was speeding as it went into the intersection. I can't tell you how fast the Toyota was going in exact miles per hour, but it was going very fast.

I had worked for my present employer for five years, and my expected work hours were 8:30 A.M. to 5:00 P.M.

1.   For the plaintiff, conduct a direct examination of Skylar Howard.
2.   For the defendant, cross-examine Howard.

3.8 PEDESTRIAN AT CAR COLLISION

This is a negligence action brought by Leslie Morse against Frieda Smith. Morse gave the following written statement to Smith's insurance company investigator one month after the accident.

On January 15 of this year, at 9:30 P.M., I was walking on the sidewalk on the east side of Main Street northbound toward the intersection of Elm Street. The intersection is controlled by traffic signals.

Both Main Street and Elm Street have one lane of traffic in each direction and parking on both sides of the street. There are walk lights on each corner of the intersection, which is in a single-family residential neighborhood.

As I reached the southeast corner of the intersection, the traffic lights were green for the Elm Street traffic. I waited on the corner looking at the walk lights. When the lights changed and the walk light turned green, I started to cross Elm Street.

Suddenly I heard a loud screech, looked west, and saw a car driven by Smith skidding through the intersection. I tried to jump out of the way, slipped on the pavement, and was struck in the back by the front of Smith's car as I fell. The car was about five feet from me when I first saw it.

It had snowed slightly earlier in the day. At the time of the accident the streets were still wet, and the temperature was approximately 20 degrees.

I was coming from the grocery store, where I bought a quart of milk. I live at 2005 Main Street, about three blocks north of Elm.

Signed

Leslie Morse

_____

Leslie Morse

Date: February 15, [-2]

47

James Lavery

James Lavery

Acme Insurance Co.

Investigator

1. For the plaintiff, conduct a direct examination of Morse.
2. For the plaintiff, conduct a direct examination of Morse, using the attached diagram of the intersection.
3. For the defendant, cross-examine Morse.

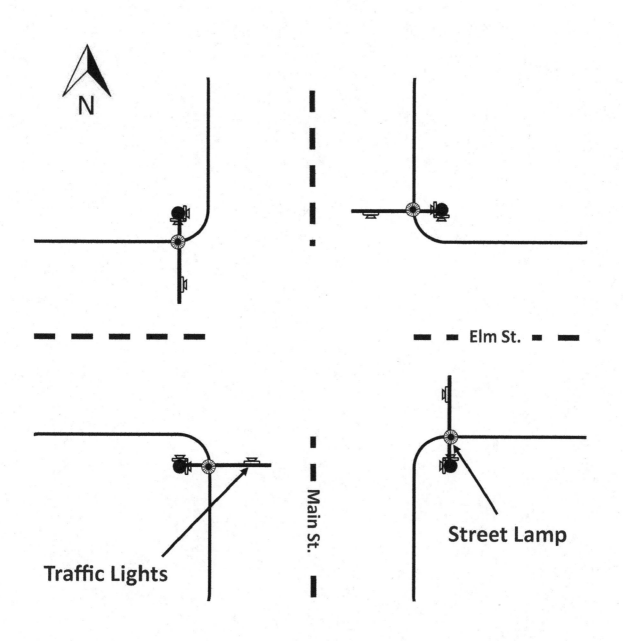

N

Elm St.

Main St.

Traffic Lights

Street Lamp

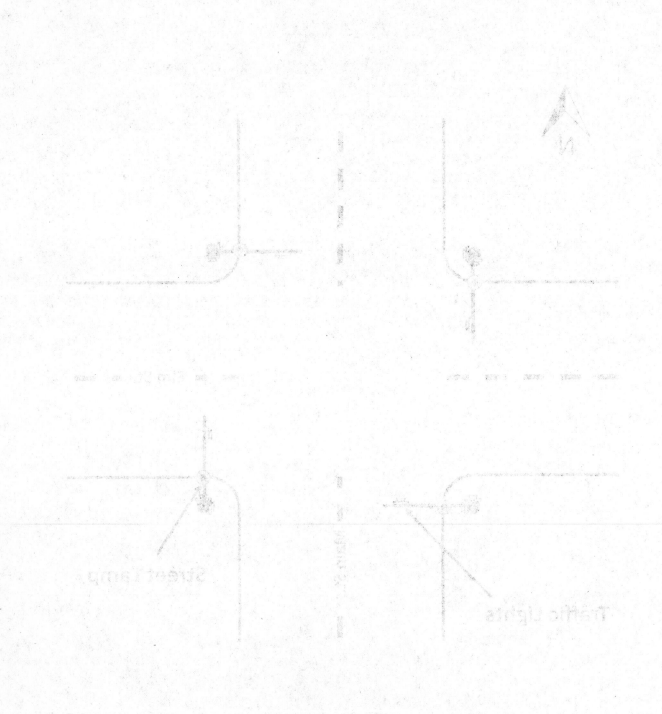

3.9 POLICE OFFICER ON SURVEILLANCE

*[handwritten note: * not hearsay — R. 803(6) records of a regularly conducted activity (5) recorded recollection]*

This is an attempted burglary case brought against the defendant, Frank Johnson. The events on which the charge is based occurred on January 15 of last year. The principal evidence against the defendant was developed during the surveillance conducted by Officer Tony Barlow. Barlow's report states in pertinent part:

[handwritten note: Barlows police report = Principal evidence]

REPORT OF EVENTS: On 1/15/[-1], on midnight shift, assigned to surveillance of Jones's Electronics, a radio and TV repair shop located at 4318 N. Broadway. Store has been burglarized several times in past month, with entry always in the rear. Store is in high-crime area and backs up to large public housing project. Today received tip that another attempt would be made on store.

[handwritten note: You were assigned to surveillance on Jan. 15? why was the particular store surveilled? where is the store located?]

Arrived at location at 0045 hrs. in unmarked car, parked across street directly in front of store. Streets were lighted, traffic average. (Store is standard small store, with plate glass front, one light on inside. Other similar stores on either side. Narrow alley to left of store, leading to larger alley behind store.) At 0215 hrs. a black Ford sedan, older model, pulled up near front of store, two occupants. They talked for a few minutes, then passenger got out, sedan drove to next corner, lights and motor off. Driver remained in car. Passenger, a male, stood in front of store, apparently casing it, looked around to see if anyone was watching, then turned and walked down an alley adjacent to store, and disappeared behind it. A few minutes passed, then a burglary alarm went off. Moments later the passenger came running down the alley, looked around for the car, ran to the same car still parked on the corner, and jumped in.

[handwritten note: what did he do when he stood in front of the store? After he cased the joint what did he do? After the burglary alarm went off what happened?]

Reporting officer made a U-turn, following sedan as it pulled away from the corner. A block later put on siren and lights, sedan speeded up, taking obvious evasive action by ducking down side streets and alleys. Finally curbed sedan at 4700 N. Pearl, arrested two occupants, who said nothing. Passenger identified himself as Frank Johnson, age 17. Driver was juvenile. Car had several empty beer cans on back seat.

51

Both offenders handcuffed, placed in rear of car, and returned to scene of burglary. Inspected rear of store; window broken, apparently setting off alarm. No other persons in area at time.

INVESTIGATION CLEARED AND CLOSED.

Officer Barlow has been a police officer for 12 years, the last 6 as a burglary detective.

1. For the prosecution, conduct a direct examination of Officer Barlow.
2. For the defense, cross-examine Officer Barlow.

And when you returned to the scene of the burglary — what did you see?

Headlines:

52

3.10 POLICE OFFICER AT SEXUAL ASSAULT SCENE

This is a criminal case that involves the alleged aggravated sexual assault of the victim, Darlene Smith, by the defendant, James Hill. The attack occurred on January 15 of last year. The issue in the case is the accuracy of Ms. Smith's identification of the defendant. Ms. Smith was the prosecution's first witness. She positively identified the defendant as her assailant. She said there was enough light from a nightlight to recognize him. Officer Sean Connors is now called to testify.

You have the police report of Officer Connors. The narrative portion of the officer's report states the following:

NARRATIVE OF EVENTS: On 1/15/[-1] at approx. 0415 hrs., while on routine patrol, received flash message "Rape at 901 Main, 2nd Floor." Proceeded to location, up to 2nd floor of two-story flat (outside doors unlocked), knocked on door, no answer. Pushed door open, saw a woman, now identified as Darlene Smith of same address, sitting on couch. Victim was dressed in nightgown, obviously distraught. As I walked in, she looked up, realized I was a police officer, and immediately said: "I've just been raped." I attempted to comfort the victim, called for an ambulance, and did a quick search of apt.

Victim stated that she was sleeping in her bedroom, heard a noise, looked up, and saw someone moving in the room. She said, "Who's there?" and was suddenly grabbed by the throat. A man with a deep voice said, "Just do as I say and you won't get hurt." She said she saw the man's face for about 30 seconds just after he grabbed her throat. Victim said that the man then sexually assaulted her and ran out the front of the apt. After a few minutes, she got up and called the police from the living room phone.

Ambulance attendants arrived, took victim to St. Mary's Hospital ER. Conducted search of bedroom after turning on overhead light; victim's bed was messed up, obviously the scene of a struggle. A window was broken out on the kitchen door leading to the back porch. (The apt. has a living room off the front stairs, a bedroom, bath, with kitchen in rear.) The kitchen door was the apparent point of entry.

On 1/18/[-1] did follow-up interview of Ms. Smith at her apt. Noted dark blue bruise marks on her neck and face, and moving head carefully. Victim stated the bruises came from the offender grabbing her. She further stated that the hospital discharged her the next morning and that the tests were positive for the presence of semen. She was also positive that she could identify the man if she ever saw him again.

INVESTIGATION CONTINUES. . . .

Officer Connors has been a police officer for six years, always in the patrol division. On the night of the assault s/he was working the first watch (midnight to 8:00 A.M.) on routine patrol in a police car.

1. For the prosecution, conduct a direct examination of Officer Connors.
2. For the defense, cross-examine Officer Connors.

Do we have to introduce narrative of events?

3.11 ROBBERY VICTIM

Δ – Charles Tucker
π – Corey Johnson

This is an armed robbery and aggravated kidnapping prosecution brought against the defendant, Charles Tucker. In this jurisdiction, an aggravated kidnapping is a kidnapping committed while the perpetrator is armed with a dangerous weapon. The complainant is Corey Johnson. The alleged crimes occurred on June 15 of last year. You have the police report of the investigating officer, Robert Jones. The narrative portion of his report states the following:

11:30p

NARRATIVE OF EVENTS: On 6/15/[-1] at approx. 2330 hrs., the victim, Corey Johnson, was walking northbound on the east side of Elm Street. Area is residential w/street lights—victim had left a neighbor's house, where s/he had been playing cards, and was on the way home 2 blocks away.

drinking anything? were you doing anything else x's play playing cards.

Suddenly s/he sensed someone behind him/her and started to turn. As s/he turned, s/he saw the offender's face for two or three seconds. That was the only time s/he saw his face, but s/he had a "good look" at him. The offender (later identified as Charles Tucker) grabbed him/her around the neck, choking him/her. S/he tried to scream, but couldn't. The offender said he had a knife and told him/her not to scream or he'd stab him/her. Victim felt a cold hard object pressed against his/her neck. Offender then forced him/her down an alley, still holding him/her by the neck with one hand, to the rear of an adjoining building. (There were no lights in the alley, but victim states that there was enough light from street lights to see the assailant.) Offender ordered victim to lie face down and not move.

only able to see the assailants face only time? for how long?

But did you see the knife? But did you see the cold hard object?

But I thought you only saw assailants face once?

Discredit witness: so was it once or did you see them again in the alley?

Offender threatened to kill him/her if s/he called the police, took victim's backpack, and walked down the alley to the street. Victim then waited a minute and ran to his/her house, where s/he immediately called the police, stating what had happened and describing the assailant as a white male, approx. 20 yrs. old, 5'8" tall, medium build, wearing dark pants and shirt. Description broadcast.

you got this whole description in 2-3 min?

55

One squad went to victim's house. About same time another squad saw man fitting description on Elm Street about two blocks from where robbery occurred, in opposite direction from victim's home. Victim was transported in squad car to location where man was detained. As that squad car pulled up to location, victim, who was sitting on back seat of squad car, suddenly blurted out, "That's the man who just robbed me!" and pointed to offender, Charles Tucker.

INVESTIGATION CONTINUES. . . .

The case is now on trial.

1.   For the prosecution, conduct a direct examination of Johnson.
2.   For the defense, cross-examine Johnson.

[handwritten margin notes: When you saw him did you see your backpack? was such room. Where's backpack?]

56

3.12   ACCIDENT VICTIM

Two years ago Jayden French came to your office with the following statement s/he had given an investigator for Ralph Jones's insurance company:

(handwritten) ① 2 years ago June 1

On June 1, [-2], at approximately 3:00 P.M., I was driving my car northbound on Clark Street toward Division Street. When I reached Division the light turned yellow, so I stopped at the intersection. Just as I stopped my car, a Honda Civic, I heard a loud screeching sound, like brakes being applied hard. I looked into my rearview mirror and saw a large American make of car almost on top of me. Before I could react, the car ran into the rear of my car.

(handwritten right margin) crash in progress

(handwritten left margin) Yellow light & stopped / After you stopped what did you hear? / what did you see

The force of the crash threw me back against the seat and snapped my head backward. I felt a sharp pain at the base of my neck and was momentarily dazed by the force of the crash. After a minute or so, I got out of my car and talked to the driver of the other car, Ralph Jones. We exchanged our names and other information. I was able to drive my car home.

(handwritten right margin) during crash

(handwritten left margin) what happened the next day?

The next morning my neck was painful and it was too stiff to move. I saw my family doctor, Edmond Gaines, who said I had a classic whiplash injury and prescribed bed rest, heat, and a cervical collar.

(handwritten right margin) next day

For the next week I stayed at home, in bed, applying heat from a hot water bottle at regular intervals. The pain and stiffness prevented me from doing anything and kept me from sleeping. The following week I returned to work, but I still wore the neck brace for two more weeks, and the neck was still painful, especially when I moved it. As the weeks went by the pain gradually decreased in severity, although it still prevented me from doing my usual types of physical activities, such as yard work and sports such as tennis or swimming.

(handwritten right margin) the next week

(handwritten right margin) 2 more weeks

(handwritten left margin) followed Dr's orders / - Stayed @ home for a week - couldn't sleep / - wore neck brace for 2 more weeks after that

Only in the past week or so has the pain generally subsided, so that I'm finally able to return essentially to normal. I'm still cautious in using my neck, since I'm afraid to strain it and have a relapse. I'm still apprehensive about driving my car, since I obviously don't want the same thing to happen twice.

57

As far as my financial losses are concerned, it cost $3,800 to repair my car, I lost $2,200 from being out of work for one week, and my doctor's bill was $1,500.

Jayden French
July 15, [-2]

You have brought suit on behalf of Jayden French against Ralph Jones, charging that Jones negligently operated his automobile and caused French's injuries. Your suit asks for all proper damages. The case is now on trial.

1. For the plaintiff, conduct a direct examination of Jayden French.
2. For the defendant, cross-examine French.

3.13   BATTERY VICTIM: CHANGED TESTIMONY

You are the assistant district attorney prosecuting a battery case against the defendant, Phillip Dunn. The victim, Ann Rodd, was standing in front of her home at 4216 S. Ellis on December 11 of last year, at about 6:00 P.M. At that time a man she had never seen before walked up to her and struck her in the face with his right fist. She screamed. Then he ran away. When the police arrived, minutes later, she described her assailant as being a male, about 30 years of age, medium build, and about 5' 6" tall.

The defendant, Phillip Dunn, was arrested a week later based on a description given to a police artist by Rodd. Dunn is 6' tall, 28 years old, and weighs about 170 pounds. Rodd is 5' 4" tall.

On December 12, the day after the attack, the police prepared a supplementary report on the case, which states:

SUPPLEMENTARY REPORT — CORRECTION: Victim originally described her assailant as being 5' 6" to Det. James Lanners, #2763, who was preparing information to be used for publication in the daily Police Dept. Bulletin. Reporting officer received a telephone call from Mrs. Rodd on December 12 at about 1930 hours, and she stated that upon standing up in her hospital room at the Swedish Covenant Hospital for the first time since the assault in the presence of her husband she realized that the offender was taller than she had advised Det. Lanners. She stated that based on a comparison with her husband, who is 5' 10" tall, the assailant was approx. 6' tall. This change was immediately forwarded, enabling the Graphic Arts Section to make the correction in Bulletin #19-314 for December 14.

1.   For the prosecution, conduct a direct examination of Rodd. How will you handle the change in height description?
2.   For the defense, cross-examine Rodd.

3.14 ACCIDENT INVESTIGATOR AT INTERSECTION COLLISION

On January 15, two years ago, an automobile accident occurred between the plaintiff, Jack Joseph, and the defendant, Charles Frederick, at the intersection of Main Street and Elm Avenue. Plaintiff's insurance company, University Casualty Insurance Company, sent a traffic accident investigator, Willy Snoop, to the site of the accident the moment it heard about it. Snoop's report states:

UNIVERSAL CASUALTY INSURANCE CO.

Accident Report

Date: 1/15/[-2]

Time: 8:30 P.M.

Location: Main and Elm

Insured: Jack Joseph

REPORT OF EVENTS: On above date and time, arrived at above location pursuant to home office radio dispatch. On arrival, parties and police still there and interviewed. Measured intersection, location of cars, prepared attached diagram. Car #1 (Joseph) had extensive damage on front. Car #2 (Frederick) had extensive damage on its right side, from rear door to rear bumper. Damage indicated at least moderate speed at impact. Interviewed drivers: Joseph stated he was going through intersection southbound on Main Street with green light when Car #2 suddenly turned left and cut in front of him. Joseph said he tried to stop but couldn't. Frederick stated he was in the intersection, facing north, the light turned yellow, so he made a left turn onto Elm Avenue but the oncoming car (#1) ran the yellow light. Police officer at scene stated that he'd also interviewed Frederick within minutes of the accident, but Frederick never claimed that the light had turned yellow.

61

Officer gave Frederick ticket for failure to yield right-of-way. (See attached diagram.)

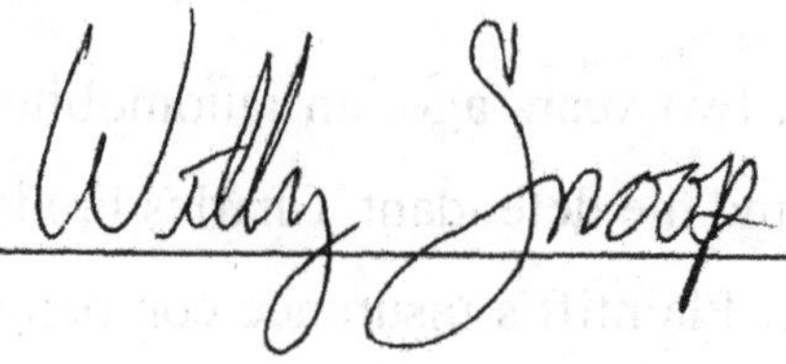

Willy Snoop

_____

Willy Snoop

Snoop, a retired police officer who worked primarily in the traffic division for 18 years, has worked for Universal for three years investigating accidents. The case is now on trial. S/he has no formal training in accident reconstruction.

In this jurisdiction a driver may not enter an intersection on a yellow light. If a driver seeking to make a turn is lawfully in an intersection when the light turns yellow, s/he may complete the turn if s/he can do so safely.

1. For the plaintiff, conduct a direct examination of Snoop.
2. For the plaintiff, conduct a direct examination of Snoop, using the following diagram to illustrate his testimony.
3. For the defendant, cross-examine Snoop.

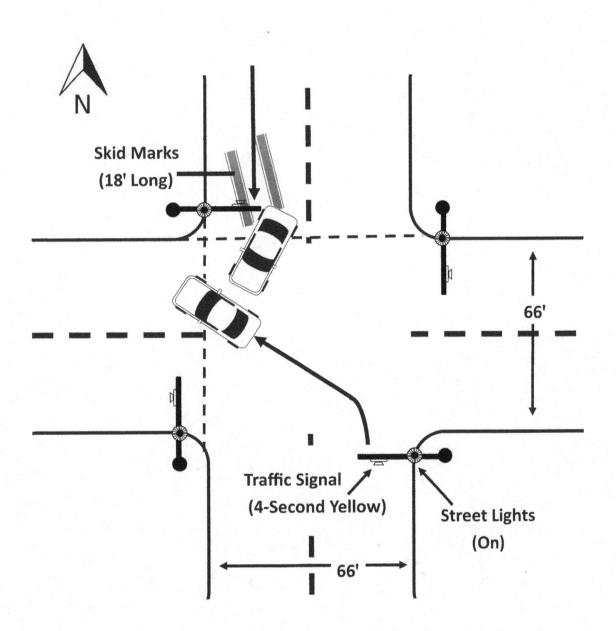

Skid Marks
(18' Long)

66'

Traffic Signal
(4-Second Yellow)

Street Lights
(On)

66'

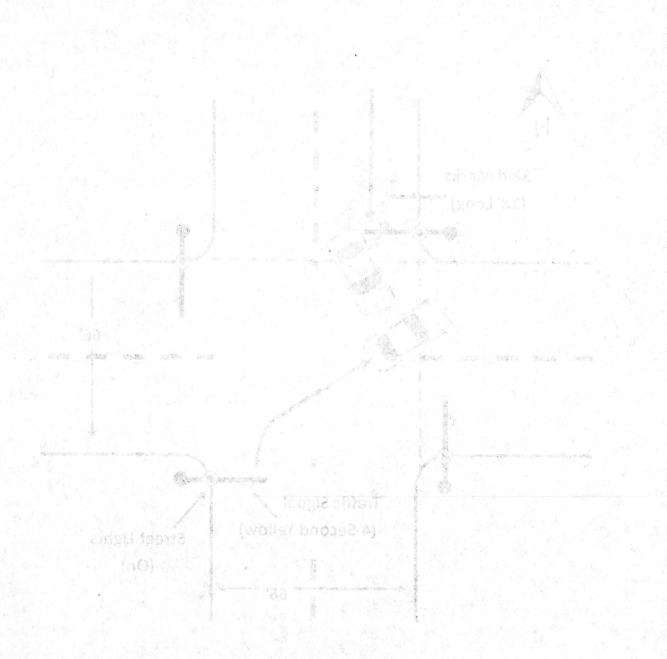

3.15   ROBBERY VICTIM AND BANK DIAGRAM

Avery Stern is the manager of the Second Federal Savings and Loan Association. One year ago today, at about 10:00 A.M., Stern was sitting behind the desk in his/her office in the rear of the bank when s/he heard a gunshot.

S/he jumped up, ran out the door of his office and five feet to the left into the hallway. S/he saw a man with a handgun, whom s/he now identifies as the defendant, Ralph Switzer. The defendant was standing about 20 feet away, at one of the tellers' windows.

Stern says that the defendant turned his head, looked momentarily right at him/her, then turned around and ran through the lobby and out the bank's front door.

1. For the prosecution, conduct a direct examination of Stern.
2. For the prosecution, conduct a direct examination of Stern, using the following diagram to illustrate his testimony. The diagram was prepared under Stern's supervision two weeks after the robbery. It is drawn to scale.
3. For the prosecution, conduct a direct examination of Stern, using the diagram to illustrate his testimony. The diagram was prepared under Stern's supervision two weeks after the robbery. It is not drawn to scale.
4. For the defense, cross-examine Stern.

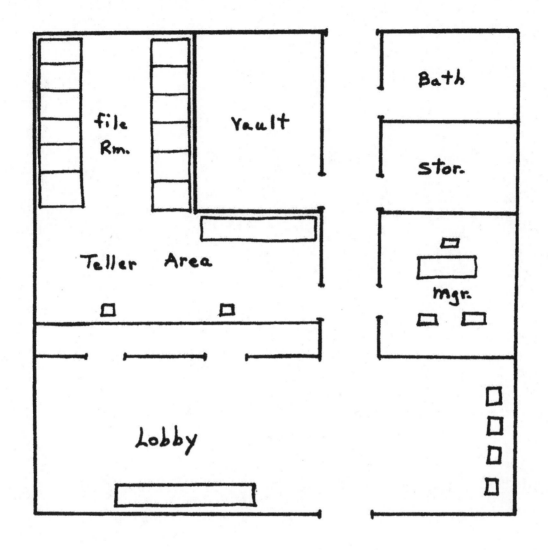

Second Federal Savings and Loan Association

Scale: 1" = 10'

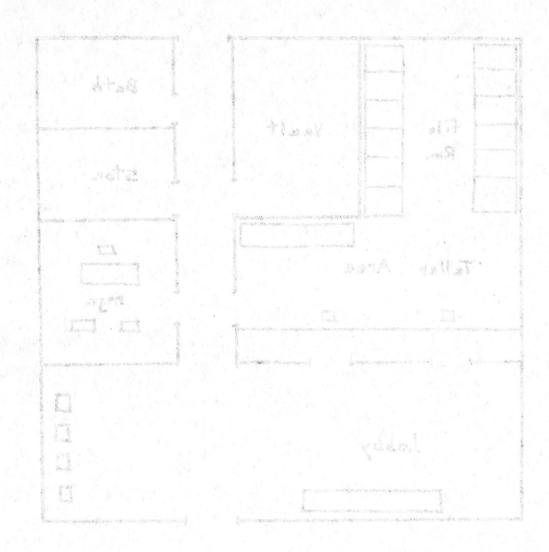

Second Federal Savings and Loan Association

Scale: 1" = 10'

3.16 ROBBERY VICTIM AND LINEUP PHOTOGRAPH

On January 15 of last year, Devon Bradley was robbed of a computer bag by two young men as Bradley was walking at approximately 11:00 P.M. from his/her parking lot to his/her apartment building. The parking lot is next to the building and, while it has no lights of its own, it is illuminated by a street light directly across from the lot.

When the police arrived, Bradley gave them a description of the two men. S/he described each as being about 25 years old, white, approximately 5' 10" tall, 175 pounds in weight, wearing blue jeans and white T-shirts. Neither had a beard, moustache, unusual-looking hair, or other noticeable features.

Three days later the police called Bradley and asked him/her to come to the station to view a lineup. When s/he arrived, Bradley was asked to look at the persons in the lineup and, if s/he recognized anyone as one of his/her assailants, to point him out. After looking at the lineup, Bradley identified the second person from the left, defendant Samuel Jones.

1. For the prosecution, conduct a direct examination of Bradley.
2. For the prosecution, conduct a direct examination of Bradley, using the attached photograph to illustrate his testimony.
3. For the defense, cross-examine Bradley.
4. Assume that Bradley, after viewing the lineup, is unable to identify anyone as the robber. At trial the prosecution on direct examination introduces no evidence about the lineup, although Bradley does identify the defendant in court as the robber. You have the lineup photograph. For the defense, cross-examine Bradley.

is it a fair and accurate depiction of line-up

① I'm handing you what I have marked for purposes of identification as states exhibit Number 1

② Let the record reflect i'm showing the exhibit to opposing counsel

④ lay
⑤ offer into evidence
⑥ use the evidence

69

③ Your honor may I approach the witness

3.17　RECORDS WITNESS AND EXHIBIT

This is a negligence action arising out of an automobile accident on July 27, [-1]. ~how do you know the π?~ As part of the damages aspects of his case, plaintiff Charles Sampson intends to call Blair Jones, the bookkeeper at his place of work, ABC Warehouse Storage Company, to introduce a payroll record.

Prior to trial you interview Jones, who brings the attached payroll sheet. S/he explains that the warehouse supervisor keeps time cards for each employee and sends him/her the time cards at the end of each work week. Jones computes the gross wages for each employee, based on hours worked and hourly wage rate, then enters the amount on the appropriate payroll sheet. While the number of employees at ABC varies, there is an average of around 40 employees at any given time.

Jones has worked for ABC for nine years; two as a clerk, four as an administrative assistant, and the past three years as the bookkeeper. In addition to preparing payroll sheets, s/he maintains the time cards, prepares payroll checks, and does all the bookkeeping for the company's receipts and expenditures.

1.　For the plaintiff, conduct a direct examination of Jones.
2.　For the defendant, cross-examine Jones.

(handwritten annotations:)

① I'm handing you ~what~ This document I have marked for purposes of identification as exhibit No. 1
— what is this document?
— How are you familiar ~are you~ with this document?
(— How long have you worked for ABC Warehouse Storage Co.?
⟨ what do you do for ABC?

② Let the record reflect that I'm showing this document / exhibit to opposing counsel

③ may I approach the witness ✓

④ LAY

73

⑤ offer into evidence

hearsay exception: business record address

hearsay concern is this a record kept in the ordinary course of the business?

ABC Warehouse Storage Company
Business Office: 40 E. Congress
Warehouse: 4318 Broadway

Payroll Sheet, 3rd Quarter, [-1]
(warehouse inspectors)

Week Ending	Tom Fields		Charles Sampson		Ted Smith	
7/5	417.00		424.00			V
7/12	417.00		424.00		410.00	
7/19	417.00		424.00		410.00	
7/26		V	424.00		410.00	
8/2		V		SL	451.00	OT
8/9		V		SL	451.00	OT
8/16	463.00	OT		SL	410.00	
8/23	463.00	OT		SL	410.00	
8/30	444.00	OT		SL	410.00	
9/6	470.00	OT	212.00	PT	410.00	
9/13	453.00	OT	212.00	PT	410.00	
9/20	417.00		424.00			V
9/27	417.00		424.00			V
OV: overtime	PT: part time		V: vacation		SL: sick leave	

3.18 CHARACTER WITNESS

Arthur Bowen has been charged with the crimes of theft and battery. The theft charge is based on Bowen's alleged shoplifting of merchandise from a Sears store. The battery charge is based on Bowen's alleged striking of a Sears security guard, who accused Bowen of shoplifting. These incidents happened one year ago today.

The case is now on trial. Bowen has already testified on his own behalf. He then calls as a witness his next next-door neighbor, Carson Fern, who has known Bowen for six years. Fern has been a social friend and a co-worker of Bowen for those years. Both work as salespeople for Acme Insurance Company.

As next-door neighbors, Fern and Bowen see each other almost every week. They socialize regularly with other neighbors, which includes cookouts in their back yards, going out to dinner at neighborhood places, and being involved in their children's sports events and other school activities. As salespeople for Acme Insurance, Fern and Bowen both work in and out of the office meeting prospective clients and handling established clients' needs. Fern and Bowen are in the office at least one day a week attending sales staff meetings and doing paperwork.

1. For the defense, put in evidence the appropriate character trait of the defendant for each charge. Assume that this jurisdiction has adopted the Federal Rules of Evidence.

2. Use the same information as in No. 1, except that this jurisdiction permits only reputation evidence.

3. For the prosecution, cross-examine Fern.

The prosecution then decides to attack the defendant's testimonial veracity. It calls as a witness Max Palm, another co-worker of Bowen for one year. Palm, also a salesperson at Acme Insurance, has known Bowen for one year.

Palm was assigned to Bowen during his/her probationary training period, which lasted six months. During that time s/he was with Bowen every day, learning how to sell insurance and handle client problems. With the probationary period over, Palm now works on his/her own but still sees Bowen regularly, particularly during the weekly sales staff meetings. S/he believes Bowen is unethical and untruthful. On one occasion, s/he found Bowen had falsified an insurance application in order to earn a commission, but s/he did not report the incident.

4. For the prosecution, put in evidence the appropriate character trait of the defendant. Assume that this jurisdiction has adopted the Federal Rules of Evidence.

5. Use the same information as in No. 4, except that this jurisdiction permits only reputation evidence.

6. For the defense, cross-examine Palm.

3.19   ADVERSE WITNESS

This is a personal injury action brought by Charles Smith against Jamie Watson and the Jacobs Construction Company. Smith was injured when the car he was driving was struck by a truck driven by Watson, a truck driver employed by Jacobs Construction, who was hauling building materials in a company truck to a construction site when the accident happened. The accident occurred June 1, [-2].

Jacobs Construction in its answer admitted Watson was an employee, but denied Watson was on a company job at the time of the accident.

Under the law of this jurisdiction, plaintiff, to establish a prima facie case against Jacobs Construction, must show that Watson was an employee or agent of the company and was working within the scope of his/her employment at the time of the accident. If this is established, any negligence on Watson's part will be imputed to Jacobs Construction.

During discovery, plaintiff took Watson's deposition, part of which is attached. The case is now on trial.

1. For the plaintiff, call Watson as an adverse witness and establish the required proof.
2. For the plaintiff, introduce Watson's deposition for the same purpose.
3. For defendant Jacobs Construction, conduct any further appropriate examination.
4. For defendant Watson, conduct any further appropriate examination.

DEPOSITION OF JAMIE WATSON,

Taken, under oath, on 10/1/[-2]

at office of Frank Tucker,

10 E. Congress St. #500

Jamie Watson, having first been duly sworn, testified as follows:

p. 14

1 Q. (by Thomas Jones, one of the plaintiff's lawyers)

2   Where were you working on June 1, [-2], the day

3   of the collision?

4 A. I was at Jacobs Construction. I'm still there.

5 Q. How long had you worked at Jacobs Construction, as

6   of June 1?

7 A. About five years.

8 Q. What kind of work did you do for the company?

9 A. I was a truck driver supervisor.

10 Q. Was that your job on June 1?

11 A. Yes.

12 Q. What were your hours that day?

13 A. The usual—8:00 A.M. to 4:00 P.M.

14 Q. When did the collision happen?

15 A. Around 3:00 P.M.

16 Q. What were you doing at that time?

17 A. I was delivering some lumber to one of our

18   construction sites.

19 Q. Whose truck was it?

20 A. It was one of the company's flatbed trucks.

21 Q. Who gave you that assignment?

22

23 p. 15

24 A. Bobby Jackson.

25 Q. Who's he?

26 A. He's the dispatcher at the company office that
27   gives out all the jobs for the drivers.
28 Q. Jamie, you no longer work as a supervisor for
29   Jacobs Construction, is that correct?
30 A. Right. I was demoted.
31 Q. When did you stop working as a supervisor?
32 A. June 2.
33 Q. That was the day after the collision?
34 A. Right.
35 Q. Did anyone tell you why they were demoting you?
36 A. Well, Mr. Braverman, he's the head of personnel,
37   told me I was being demoted because "they couldn't
38   afford to keep me as a supervisor anymore."
39 Q. Did anyone else say why they were demoting you?
40 A. Well, the word was that I was going to be the
41   fall guy, to let the other drivers know what would
42   happen if they ever got the company into any
43   lawsuit that would cost it money.
44 Q. Do you know who said that?
45 A. Not really, but I figure somebody in management
46   would have.

3.20 STIPULATIONS

Prepare two written stipulations, in whatever form you consider appropriate, to get the following facts in evidence. You may add any reasonable facts necessary to the stipulation that are not included in the problem. Be prepared to present the stipulation to the jury in the most effective way.

1. Mary Jones has worked in the records department of Rush Hospital for three years. Her job includes filing, retrieving, and copying hospital records.

The records of the hospital are kept in the records department at all times, and include such common records as emergency room reports, progress notes, nurses' notes, reports of operations, and X-ray reports, as well as various laboratory reports. These reports are routinely sent to the records department after they have been prepared at various locations in the hospital.

A subpoena directed to Rush Hospital was sent to Jones. She searched the patient records under "Helen Smith," the name on the subpoena, and found the attached record.

2. Dr. William Burns, a Cook County medical examiner's office pathologist, performed an autopsy on a James Johnson. A copy of his report is attached.

RUSH-PRESBYTERIAN-ST. LUKE'S MEDICAL CENTER 1753 West Congress Parkway

EMERGENCY ROOM / ACUTE CARE

HOSP. # 2

TIME IN: 10:30 (A.M.) P.M. TIME OUT: 1:30 A.M. (P.M.)

PATIENT NAME: Helen Smith

DATE: 2 May (-1)

CLINIC # OR INVOICE #:

ADDRESS: 6000 W. 26<u>th</u>, #100, CITY Cicero, STATE Ill. ZIP CODE

TELEPHONE:

EMPLOYER: 2d federal S + L

BIRTHDATE: AGE: SEX: F RACE: W

CIVIL STATUS: □S □M □W □D □SEP

ADDRESS:

TELEPHONE: INSURANCE (B.C./B.S. OTHER):

INS. OR B.C./B.S. #: PUBLIC AID #: CASE NAME:

NEXT OF KIN OR EMERGENCY ADDRESSEE NAME: TELEPHONE:

ADDRESS: CITY STATE ZIP CODE

BROUGHT IN BY: CFD ambulance

ACCIDENT LOCATION:

POLICE INVESTIGATION: ☒Yes □No

ATTENDING DOCTOR OR SOURCE OF PRIMARY CARE.

□IN AREA □OUT OF AREA

SUBJECTIVE:

Patient stated she was shot in lower left leg near ankle, by the same man who robbed the bank that morning.

OBJECTIVE: T 98.6 P 72 R 18/min. B/P 110/70

Physical Exam:

Pallor, with organsystems (HEENT, h, l, abd) within normal limits.

Open wound (0.5 x 0.5 cm) anterior-lateral aspect distal third left lower leg with venous oozing. Marked tenderness and swelling

CONSULTATION: of wound area with crepitation of bone.

PROBLEM(S):

Gunshot wound distal lower left leg, Fx left tibia and fibula.

PLAN:

Admit.

DIAGNOSTIC STUDIES:

CBC, U/A, EKG, chest X-ray, lytes X-ray, left lower leg

Campbell
Physician's Signature

Nurse's Signature

INSTRUCTION TO: _____ DATE: _____
(Patient's Name) (Hospital #)

NEXT VISIT TO: _____
(Physician or Institution)

IMPRESSION AND INSTRUCTION:

PHYSICIAN'S OR NURSE'S SIGNATURE: _____ PATIENT'S _____

FORM # 3797 3/77 **MEDICAL RECORDS**

85

EMERGENCY ROOM / ACUTE CARE

Helen Smith

5000 W. 25th West, Chicago, Ill.

28 Federal St.

MEDICAL EXAMINER

Ellis Smith, M.D., Medical Examiner

Report of Findings
Name: James Johnson, of 3318 W. Congress
       5'8", 167 lbs., M/W

Identifying witness: Myrna Johnson, 3318 W. Congress,
                                (wife of deceased)

Date of Examination: October 30, [-1, at 1:45 p.m.

Date of Injury: October 28, [-1]

Location: 3318 W. Congress

How occurred: Multiple injuries to head-chest

Nature of injury: Accident____; Suicide____; Homicide__x__;
                  Unknown____.

Death was caused by: a.___Multiple injuries_____

                      b._____

                      c._____

Pathological findings: (external and internal)

        1.   Multiple contusions, face-head-neck-chest
        2.   Multiple fractures, larynx-cricoid
        3.   Multiple fractures, anterior ribs, third through
              eighth
        4.   Multiple contusions, brain
        5.   Subdural and epidural hemorrhage
        6.   Intraorbital hemorrhage, left and right
        7.   Intramuscular hemorrhage, anterior and posterior
              to chest and abdominal areas, extensive
        8.   Multiple contusions, heart

                              Examination performed by:

                              _William Burns_____
                              William Burns, M.D.
                              Forensic Pathologist

87

3.21 JUDICIAL NOTICE

1. Get the following facts in evidence through judicial notice. Assume that each fact is relevant to the issues in the case on trial, which is a civil case.

(a) Broadway in midtown Manhattan is a busy street during rush hour.

(b) In January, the ground in Montana is usually frozen.

(c) On October 5, [-2], the moon was full.

(d) November 11 is a legal holiday on which banks are closed.

(e) The life expectancy of a white male presently 40 years of age is 36.3 years.

(f) On June 1, [-1], the blood alcohol content limit under Illinois law for a driver over the age of 21 was 0.08. (Assume that the trial is in a jurisdiction other than Illinois.)

(g) The government of Kazakhstan has no extradition treaty with the United States.

2. How will you get the judge to inform the jury of the judicially noticed facts?

3. What differences would result if the trial were criminal?

4. As the opponent, oppose the introduction of the facts in each instance.

IV

EXHIBITS

Introduction

INTRODUCTION

The problems in this chapter deal with the kinds of exhibits that are commonly introduced in evidence during civil and criminal trials.

For each problem you should be prepared to establish a foundation that is legally sufficient to admit the exhibit in evidence and that maximizes its persuasive effect. In addition, you should be prepared to introduce the exhibit at a time when it reinforces and complements the witness's direct examination. Finally, you should be prepared to publish the exhibit to the jury at the most advantageous time and in the most persuasive way.

Most of the witnesses do not have background information. Be prepared to develop realistic, credible backgrounds for them.

Your instructor may modify the assignments and make specific additional assignments for these exercises.

The suggested background reading is Mauet, *Trial Techniques and Trials*, Chapter 7.

4.1 GUN

This is an unlawful possession of a concealed weapon prosecution. A police officer, Fran Smith, arrested the defendant, Earl Jones, after a search that produced a revolver from his coat pocket.

Officer Smith recorded the following information about the seized revolver in his/her report: a .38 caliber Smith and Wesson revolver, 2" barrel, stainless steel with wood handle.

Before giving the weapon to the police department's evidence section, Officer Smith placed his/her initials and date on the revolver: "2/8/[-1]—FRS."

1. For the prosecution, get the gun in evidence. (Prepare and bring an appropriate exhibit to class.)

2. Assume that this is an armed robbery prosecution. Officer Smith has testified to the seizure of the gun from Jones. The victim, Sandy Wilson, is now testifying. S/he identifies the defendant as the man who took his/her wallet at gunpoint on February 6, [-1]. The victim describes the defendant's gun as a "shiny revolver with a short barrel" but can only say that the exhibit "looks similar to" the one used by the defendant during the robbery. For the prosecution, get the gun in evidence during Wilson's testimony.

3. For the defense, oppose the offers.

4.2   MONOGRAMMED CARD CASE

This is a burglary prosecution. Someone broke into the home of Dakota Fran Dickinson, the burglary victim, sometime during the day on June 15 of last year. Three weeks later, the police found the attached item in a trash barrel in the defendant's backyard.

When the item was shown to Mahoney, s/he stated that it was a brass business card case with his/her initials monogram on it, given to him/her as a Christmas present two or three years ago by his/her husband/wife. S/he kept it on the dresser in his/her bedroom.

1.   For the prosecution, get the card case in evidence. (Prepare and bring an appropriate exhibit to class.)
2.   For the defense, oppose the offer.

4.3 KNIFE

This is an armed robbery prosecution. On June 15 of last year at about 11:00 P.M., Lee Thompson was robbed at knifepoint in the 1900 block of Clark Street. The robbery occurred on the sidewalk in the middle of the block at the entrance to an alley.

Thompson described the knife to the police as a "small dark pocketknife with a blade about two inches long." Dallas O'Leary, a police officer who arrived at the scene of the robbery, found a knife fitting that description in an open trash barrel in the alley, about 30 feet down the alley from the sidewalk where Thompson told the officer s/he had been robbed. When it was shown to him/her, Thompson stated that this knife looked "just like" the one used to rob him/her, but s/he couldn't say for sure it was the same one. Thompson has identified the defendant, Marshall Harris, as the man who robbed him/her with a knife.

Now, at trial, both Thompson and O'Leary are available as witnesses. Since finding the knife, Officer O'Leary has kept it in his/her locked locker at the police station and has brought it to court today. S/he did not place any labels or markings on the knife.

1. For the prosecution, get the knife in evidence. (Prepare and bring an appropriate exhibit to class.)
2. For the defense, oppose the offer.

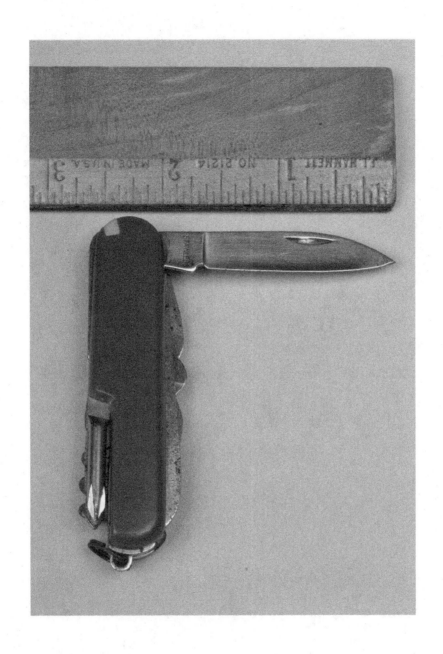

4.4 SEXUAL ASSAULT EVIDENCE COLLECTION KIT

This is a criminal sexual assault prosecution. The defendant is accused of sexually assaulting Phyllis Moore on September 20, [-1], in Springfield, Massachusetts.

After the alleged assault, Moore was treated and examined by Dr. Ralph C. Tucker of Western New England Hospital. Dr. Tucker took a vaginal swab of the victim. He then placed the specimen onto a slide that he sealed into an envelope with the printed kit number 46740, initialed the slide "RCT," and checked the box for "yes" in response to the question, "Was sample collected?"

Dr. Tucker then sealed the envelope into a Sexual Assault Evidence Collection Kit box with the same number, 46740. In response to the "Incident Reported to Police?" question on the kit's cover, Dr. Tucker checked the box for "Yes: If yes, record victim's name here" and wrote the name "Phyllis Moore." He then checked the box for "No" in response to the question "Other evidence (e.g., clothing) submitted in transport bag?" Then he filled in the following information, in his handwriting: For "Hospital/Clinic," he wrote "Western New England Hospital"; for Phone number/ext.," he wrote "(413) 787-2903"; for "Clinicians," he wrote "N/A"; for "Kit sealed by," he wrote "Dr. Ralph Tucker"; for "Placed by," he wrote "Hand delivered to Officer Robert Jacobs"; for "Date," he wrote "Sept. 20, [-1]"; for "Time," he wrote "11:32," and then he circled "P.M."

Dr. Tucker then handed the sealed box to Springfield Police Officer Robert L. Jacobs, who was in the emergency room waiting area. When Officer Jacobs received the sealed box, he wrote the following information on it: For "Received from," he wrote "Dr. Ralph Tucker"; for "Medical Facility," he wrote "Western New England Hospital"; for "Police identification no.," he wrote "Badge No. 4264," which is his badge number; for "Date," he wrote "9/20/[-1]"; for "Time," he wrote "23:32"; for "Received by," he wrote "Off. Robert Jacobs."

Officer Jacobs then drove to his precinct headquarters. At the precinct headquarters, he wrote the phrase "To precinct vault, 9/21/[-1], 0:12 A.M., RLJ" next to "Agency"; then "9/21/[-1]" after "Date," and "0:12" after "Time." He then placed the sealed box in the precinct's locked vault.

On September 27, [-1], Officer Jacobs removed the sealed box from the vault, drove to the State Crime Lab, and delivered it to Dr. Ashton Jones, the laboratory pathologist. Just before handing the sealed box to Dr. Jones, Officer Jacobs wrote the following entries on the outside of the box: For "Received from," he wrote "Officer Robert Jacobs"; for "Medical Facility," he wrote "Springfield P.D."; for "Police Identification No.," he wrote "Badge No. 4264"; for "Date," he wrote "9/27/[-1]"; for "Time," he wrote "9:24."

After receiving the box from Officer Jacobs, Dr. Jones wrote the following entries on the bottom of the box: For "Received by," s/he wrote "Dr. Ashton Jones"; for "Agency," s/he wrote "State Crime Lab"; for "Date," she wrote "Sep. 27, [-1]"; for "Time," she wrote "9:24," then she circled "A.M.:"

After receiving the box, Dr. Jones opened it. S/he then opened the envelope and examined the slide under a microscope. Dr. Jones's examination indicated the presence of semen in the specimen. Dr. Jones had not seen the specimen before September 27. After examining the slide, Dr. Jones put it back into the envelope. S/he kept the envelope containing the slide in his/her laboratory until today, when s/he brought it to court.

Two weeks before this trial began, Officer Robert Jacobs died of a heart attack. No other police officer saw the box in question.

Assume that Dr. Tucker has testified to preparing the vaginal swab and slide and to sealing the slide into the envelope, then sealing the envelope into the box. He says he delivered the box to Officer Jacobs. He does not know what Officer Jacobs did with the box.

There are no other documents concerning this specimen.

The case is now on trial. Phyllis Moore has already testified. The witness is Dr. Jones.

1. For the prosecution, get the tube in evidence, assuming that Dr. Tucker testified he sealed the envelope and box and recognizes the box as the one he delivered to Officer Jacobs on September 20. (Prepare and bring an appropriate exhibit to class.)

2. For the defense, oppose the offer.

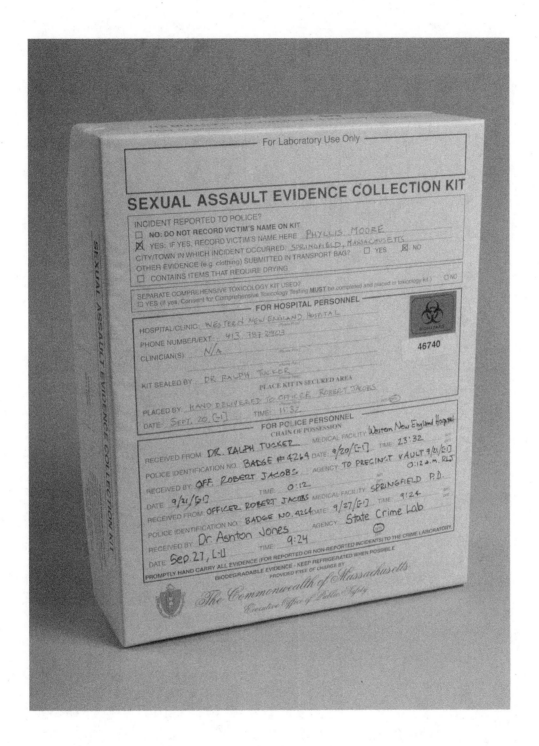

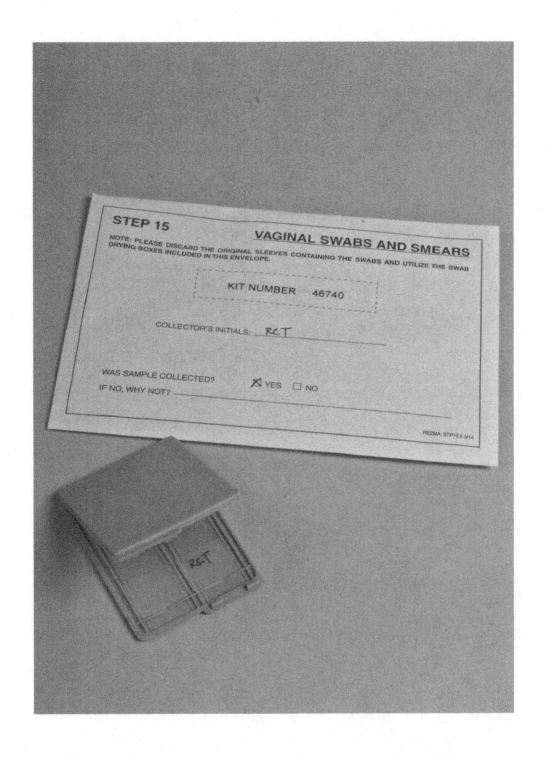

STEP 15   VAGINAL SWABS AND SMEARS

NOTE: PLEASE DISCARD THE ORIGINAL SLEEVES CONTAINING THE SWABS AND UTILIZE THE SWAB
DRYING BOXES INCLUDED IN THIS ENVELOPE.

KIT NUMBER   46740

COLLECTOR'S INITIALS: RCT

WAS SAMPLE COLLECTED?   ☒ YES   ☐ NO
IF NO, WHY NOT? _____

RE2MA: STP15.5 3/14

111

4.5   BRAKE TUBE

This is a products liability action brought against an automobile manufacturer. The plaintiff alleges that a rubber brake hose was defectively designed and manufactured, resulting in a brake failure and accident.

On June 15 of last year, Riley Schmidt, an accident investigator, went to the corner of Maple and Elm Streets, where a collision between two cars had just occurred. S/he prepared the following report:

> I examined one of the two cars involved, a [-3] Ford sedan, Vehicle Identification No. AZ4180772. During my examination I removed a rubber brake hose from the brake assembly of the car's left rear wheel.
>
> After removing the hose, which was about 12" long, I wrapped it in a plastic bag, then placed it in a small cardboard box. I put shipping tape on all the edges of the box, prepared an address label, which I then glued to the box, put proper postage on it, and dropped it in a mailbox.

A few days later Morgan Smith, a professor of chemistry at the University of Illinois, received the box in his/her university mailbox. Professor Smith put the box in his/her desk. Some days later s/he removed the box from her desk, took it to the laboratory, cut open one side of the box, and removed the plastic bag and hose. After examining the hose, s/he cut a 4" section off. The remaining 8" section s/he photographed and put back in the box; s/he then closed the cut side of the box with shipping tape. S/he next put the box back in his/her desk, where it was left until s/he removed it and brought it to court.

On November 1, [-1], Professor Smith performed a variety of microscopic and chemical tests on the 4" section. That section was entirely destroyed during the testing process.

1.   For the plaintiff, get the box and contents in evidence. (Prepare an appropriate exhibit and bring to class.)
2.   For the defendant, oppose the offer.

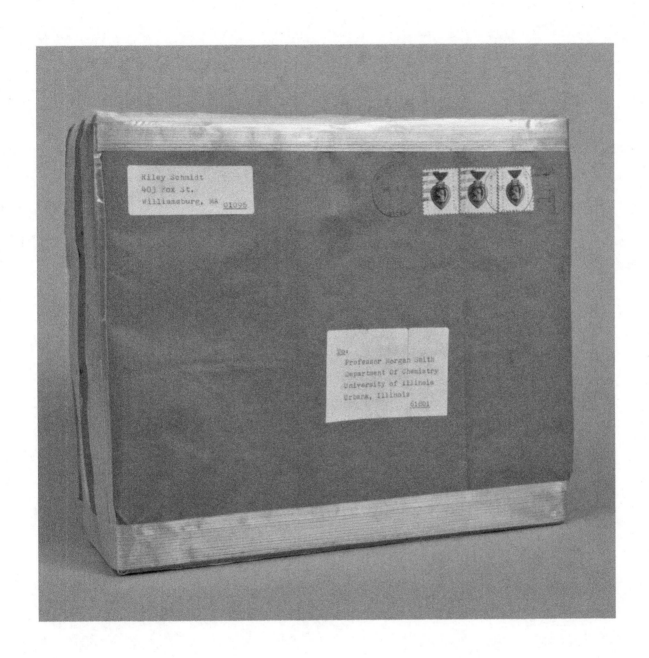

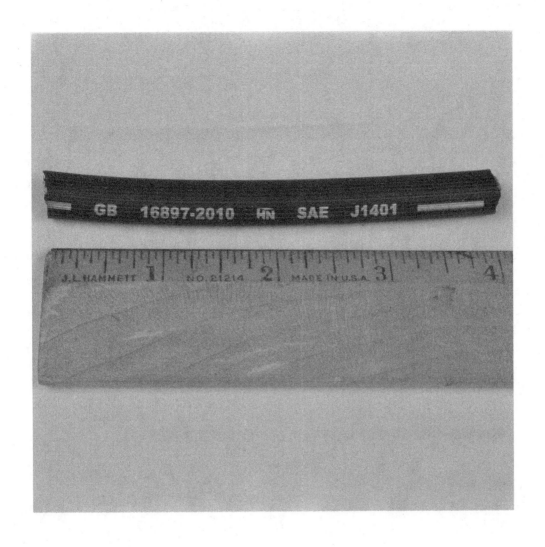

4.6 PHOTOGRAPH OF POLICE OFFICERS AND PLAINTIFF

This is a civil rights action brought against the city police department by Charles Jackson, who was arrested by the police on June 15 of last year. Jackson alleges that the police arrested him on that date without reason and physically assaulted him, depriving him of his civil rights.

Plaintiff's witness, Mickey Mars, was standing on the southeast corner of Clark and Madison Streets at about noon on January 15 and saw police officers on that corner forcing Jackson to the ground. Mars was about five feet away from the scene. The weather was clear and sunny. S/he was on his/her way to lunch from his office, one block south on Clark Street. One of the officers, s/he says, held Jackson while another officer poked his nightstick in Jackson's neck. Jackson then shouted: "Help, they're killing me!"

Mars "did not like what the officers were doing," according to the e-mail s/he sent to Jackson's attorney. Therefore, s/he took out her cell phone and took a picture of the scene. The next day, s/he noticed a story in the local newspaper about the arrest. The story said Jackson was the person being arrested. It also identified his attorney. Mars e-mailed her cell phone photo to the attorney.

1. For the plaintiff, get the photograph in evidence and use it in conjunction with the witness. This is the first time during the trial that the photograph has been mentioned.

2. For the defendant, oppose the offer.

4.7 PHOTOGRAPHS OF ACCIDENT VICTIM

This is a wrongful death action brought by Earl Sanders, executor of the estate of Frances Sanders.

On June 15 of last year, Frances Sanders was struck and instantly killed by a car driven by Karl Schmidt. A police officer, Jules Monroe, can testify that s/he was on patrol duty, received a radio message about the accident, and arrived at the scene moments later, at 2:15 P.M. When s/he arrived, he found Frances Sanders lying motionless on the pavement, as portrayed in the attached photographs taken by police investigators called to the scene by Monroe. Other testimony will show that Ms. Sanders was crossing Main Street at its intersection with Elm Street when she was struck.

1. For the plaintiff, get the photographs in evidence.
2. Assume that Sanders was not killed and has brought a negligence action against Schmidt. For the plaintiff, get the photographs in evidence.
3. For the defendant, oppose the offers.

4.8 PHOTOGRAPH OF BUILDING

This is a burglary prosecution. The condition of the Whiskerz Pub on January 15, two years ago, is an issue in this case. The tavern, located at 1610 Maple, was torn down last year, and the location is now a vacant lot.

You have a photograph of the Whiskerz Pub taken in January of last year. [Note: This photograph is available on the Companion Website that accompanies the book.] In addition, you find a witness, Jaime Mendez, who lived in an apartment above the tavern in January, two years ago.

1. For the prosecution, get the photograph in evidence.
2. Assume that the sign that extends from the building was not there when Mendez lived in the building. For the prosecution, get the photograph in evidence.
3. Assume that Mendez lived in the apartment at the two windows on the left side of the photograph, to the north, at 1612 Maple. S/he has told the police that on the day of the burglary, at about 3:00 P.M. on a sunny day, s/he was looking out the right of the two windows when s/he saw the defendant, Carl Dunn, run out of the Whiskerz entrance, look up at him/her "for a moment," then run north past his/her window. The distance from the window to the place where Dunn was standing when he looked up is approximately 15 feet. For the prosecution, elicit Mendez's identification of the defendant, making use of the photograph.
4. For the defense, oppose the offers.

4.9 PHOTOGRAPH OF BUILDING

This is a burglary prosecution. On June 15 of last year someone broke into Robin Smith's house, located at 1234 Halsted Street. Entry was apparently made through a side door, as shown by pry marks on the frame and door.

Officer Quinn Jackson, who was called to the scene when the owner discovered the break-in, saw the marks and recovered a crowbar lying in some shrubs and grass, approximately five feet from the door. Technician Kaden Jones took the attached photograph later that same day.

1. For the prosecution, get the photograph in evidence via the testimony of either Jackson or Jones, and then use it in any way you deem appropriate.
2. For the defense, oppose the offer.

4.10   PHOTOGRAPH OF BUILDING

This is an armed robbery prosecution. The witness, Bobbie Cleary, saw an armed robbery taking place at about 11:30 P.M. one year ago today. Cleary was standing on the wooden porch in front of 3002-04 Elm Street, the doorway in the left side of the photograph. The armed robber was standing on the wooden porch in front of 3006-08 Elm Street, the doorway in the right side of the photograph. The victim of the robbery was standing just to the right of the robber on the porch of the 3006-08 doorway. Cleary has identified the defendant as the man who committed the armed robbery. The two doorways are approximately 30 feet apart.

1. For the prosecution, get the photograph in evidence, have the witness describe the distance between the doorways, and use the photo in any way you deem appropriate.

2. For the defense, oppose the offer and cross-examine the witness.

4.11   DIAGRAM OF INTERSECTION

A police officer, Emerson Tatum, was in his/her squad car on June 15 of last year at 3:00 P.M. observing traffic at the intersection of Maple and Elm Streets. Tatum had parked in a parking lot on the northwest corner of the intersection, facing southeast. There are no traffic control signals at the intersection.

Tatum saw a pedestrian, Elmer Franks, cross Elm Street, going northbound, on the east side of Maple. As Franks entered the crosswalk, a car driven northbound on Maple by Robert Dixon made a right-hand turn on Elm and failed to stop for Franks. The car's front bumper struck Franks as he was in the crosswalk, knocking him several feet east, where he fell down on the pavement, facing east. The car then stopped at Franks's feet.

Franks has brought a negligence action against the driver of the car. The defense is that the pedestrian was not in the crosswalk at the time of the accident.

Plaintiff now calls Officer Tatum as a witness. Two weeks before trial Tatum went to the intersection, made the necessary measurements, and prepared a diagram of the intersection, which is attached.

1. For the plaintiff, get the diagram in evidence and use it to illustrate Tatum's testimony.
2. For the plaintiff, have Tatum illustrate his/her testimony by making a sketch of the intersection on a blackboard.
3. For the defense, oppose the offer and cross-examine Tatum.

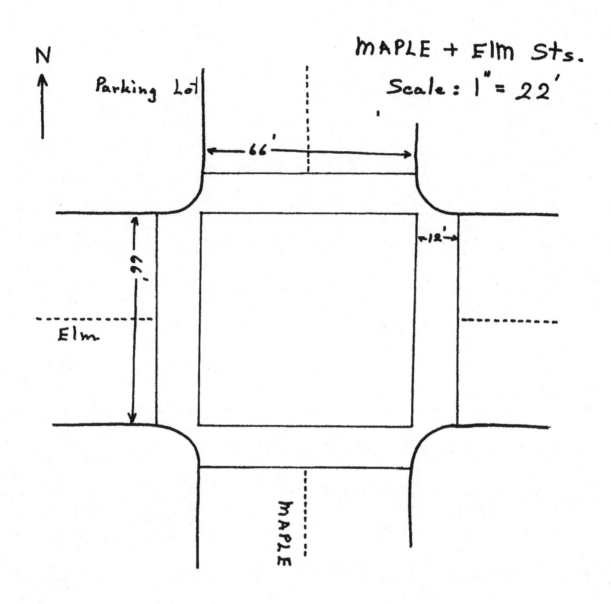

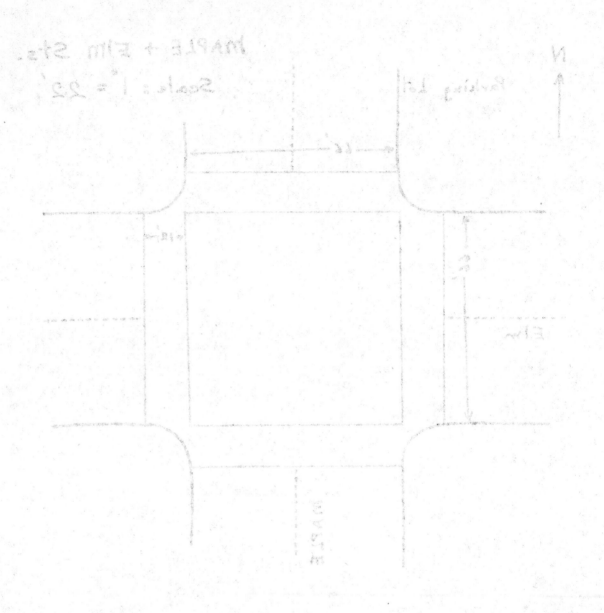

4.12   DIAGRAM OF HOUSE

This is a criminal sexual assault prosecution. The victim, Shirley Rice, was attacked at approximately 2:00 A.M. on June 15 of last year by a man who apparently gained entry to her home through an open living room window.

At the time of the attack, the bedroom lights were off but the lights in the living room and kitchen were on. Rice awoke when she heard a sound in the living room, sat up, and saw a man standing in the doorway to the bedroom. He stood there for about ten seconds. That was the last time she saw his face clearly.

The issue at trial is the identification of the attacker. Rice identified the defendant, Sam Moore, during a lineup one week after the attack.

A police officer, Fred Miller, sketched a diagram of Rice's house that day. The diagram, which is attached, is not to scale.

1.   For the prosecution, use the diagram during Rice's direct testimony in any way you deem appropriate. Confine the examination to the identification issue.

2.   For the defense, oppose the offer and cross-examine Rice.

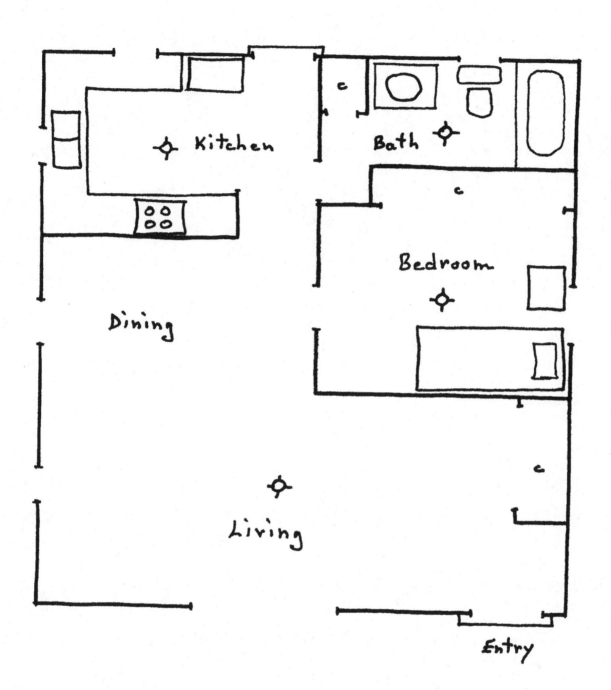

Kitchen

Bath

Dining

Bedroom

Living

Entry

Rice House - 6/15/[-]

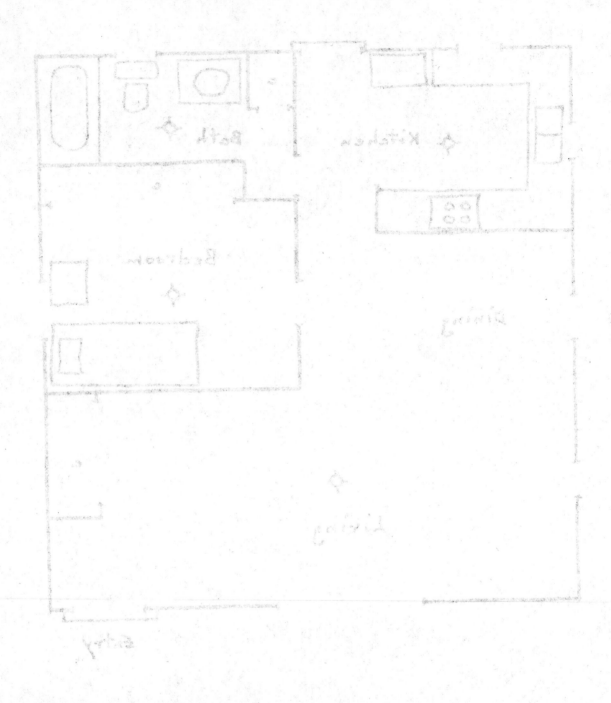

4.13 MAP

This is a robbery prosecution. The defendant is accused of robbing a concession stand in the state capitol in downtown Phoenix at 5:00 P.M. on June 15 of last year. However, evidence will also establish that the defendant "punched in" at his place of work, the dining hall at the Mesa Community College near downtown Mesa, at 5:30 P.M. and that he customarily drives his car to work.

To prove that it is possible to drive from the state capitol to Mesa Community College within 30 minutes, the prosecution calls Madison Wilson, a police patrolman, as a witness. Wilson will testify that s/he took two possible routes from the state capitol to the College: first, south on 19th Avenue and east on Southern Avenue, the local route; second, using Interstate 10 and Highway 360, the expressway route. Both routes are approximately 15 miles long.

Wilson will testify that s/he drove both routes at 5:00 P.M. on the same day of the week as the robbery. S/he drove both routes in a squad car, going as quickly as s/he reasonably could, given the traffic conditions. His/her time for the local route was 35 minutes; the expressway route took 25 minutes.

1. For the prosecution, get the map in evidence and use it to illustrate Officer Wilson's testimony.
2. For the defense, oppose the offer and cross-examine Wilson.

4.14 PROMISSORY NOTE

This case involves a suit brought by Fran Smith on a promissory note allegedly signed by William Burns. Burns denies signing the note.

Your witnesses are Fran Smith, the plaintiff, who says that s/he was present when Burns signed the note, and Reese Jones, who was not present when the note was signed but is familiar with Burns's signature through previous correspondence and business dealings.

1. For the plaintiff, get the promissory note in evidence, using Fran Smith as the witness.

2. For the plaintiff, get the promissory note in evidence, using Reese Jones as the witness.

3. Assume that the promissory note is payable to Household Loan Company and is one of the company's regular forms. Call a custodian of the records from Household to get the note in evidence.

4. For the defendant, oppose the offer(s).

```
                    PROMISSORY NOTE


                            Date:   June 30, [-2]


For value received, the undersigned hereby promises

to pay to Fran Smith the sum of twelve thousand

($12,000.00) dollars on or before December 31, [-2]


                            Signed: William Burns
                                    William Burns
```

4.15   CONTRACT

This is a contract action, brought by Charlie Joiner against Fred Turner, which alleges that Turner failed to perform in accordance with a written contract they had previously executed. The case is now on trial.

According to Joiner, the contract, which is attached, was executed by them in Turner's office on the date shown on the contract. Joiner claims that s/he personally saw Turner sign his name on the contract. Turner denies signing it.

1. For the plaintiff, introduce the contract in evidence, using Joiner as the witness.

2. What other methods can be used to authenticate the contract?

3. Assume that after executing the contract, Turner kept the signed original and gave Joiner an unsigned photocopy of the contract. Assume also that Turner has denied the existence of the contract and has not produced the original. For the plaintiff, get the unsigned photocopy in evidence. (Assume that the attached contract is the unsigned photocopy.)

4. For the defendant, oppose the offer.

CONTRACT

The parties, Charlie Joiner ("Joiner") and Fred Turner ("Turner"), hereby enter into the following agreement:

1. Joiner for the past five years has been in the business of building custom homes, a business that requires substantial amounts of sand and gravel earthfill.

2. Turner for the past five years has been in the business of obtaining and selling sand and gravel earthfill to contractors and other customers.

3. Joiner hereby agrees to purchase, and Turner agrees to sell, all sand and gravel earthfill in such quantities as Joiner will require, for a period of five years from the date of this contract.

4. Joiner will notify Turner, either orally or in writing, of his/her requirements as they shall arise from time to time. Turner will fill the orders and deliver them to any job site within a radius of fifty (50) miles of Turner's present business headquarters, within the shortest practical period of time, and in any event within a commercially reasonable period of time.

5. Joiner will pay Turner in full for any deliveries within ten (10) days of delivery, at a rate that will be identical to the most preferred rate Turner has given to any other customer within ninety (90) days preceding the order, and in any event shall not be higher than the average rate in the industry during the same time period.

Date: 1 June [-1]

Charlie Joiner
_____
Charlie Joiner

Fred Turner
_____
Fred Turner

4.16 PHOTOCOPIES OF CHECK

This is a contract action. Shannon Smith sues Jordan Jones for failure to pay a $2,000 debt. Jones claims s/he paid off the debt through the check that is photocopied in the proposed exhibit. The issue is whether the debt is discharged.

Jones will testify that s/he prepared the check and dropped it off at Smith's place of work, the Hasty Tasty Restaurant at 1400 Main Street. S/he will say that Smith was not there at the time. Jones is not familiar with Smith's handwriting. S/he did not see the check again, but the bank statement that s/he received at the beginning of March [-1] included photocopies of the front and back of the check that s/he now intends to introduce into evidence.

Smith has testified that s/he does not remember ever seeing the check. S/he has admitted that the signature on the back of the (photocopied) check "looks like" his/her signature, but s/he does not recall endorsing the check or doing anything with it. S/he admits to having an account at the Second National Bank.

The plaintiff has rested. Jones is on the stand.

1. For the defendant, get the check in evidence to prove that Jones made the payment and that Smith received the payment.
2. For the plaintiff, oppose the offer.

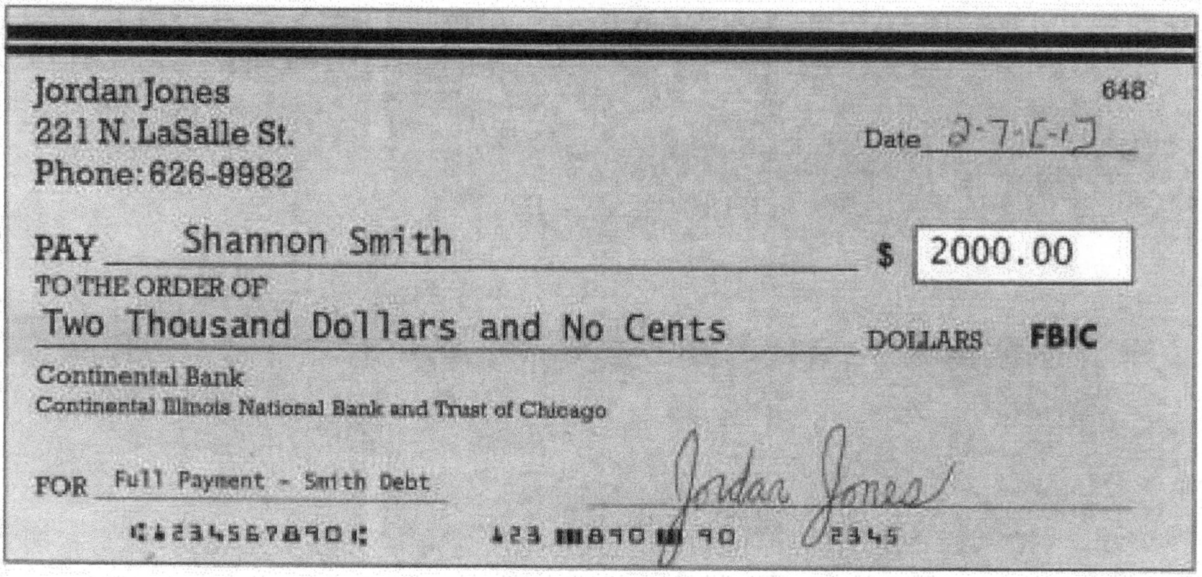

Jordan Jones
221 N. LaSalle St.
Phone: 626-9982

648

Date 2-7-[-1]

PAY TO THE ORDER OF Shannon Smith $ 2000.00

Two Thousand Dollars and No Cents DOLLARS FBIC

Continental Bank
Continental Illinois National Bank and Trust of Chicago

FOR Full Payment - Smith Debt

Jordan Jones

⑆1234567890⑆ 123 ⑈890 ⑈ 90 2345

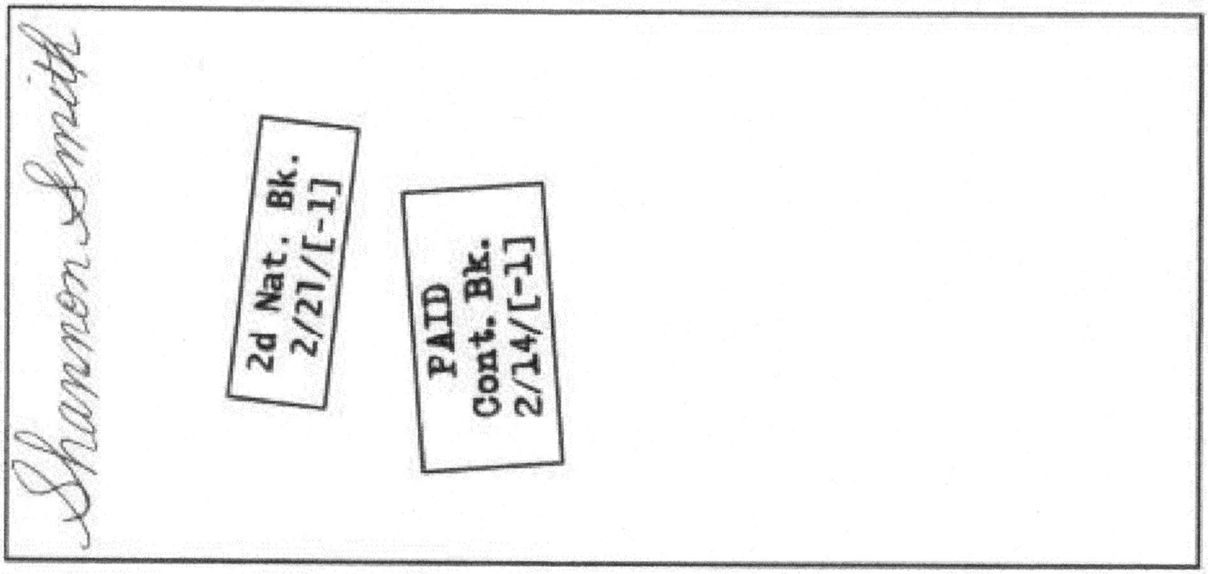

Shannon Smith

2d Nat. Bk.
2/21/[-1]

PAID
Cont. Bk.
2/14/[-1]

4.17   LETTERS

This is a contract action brought by Alex Jones against Fred Neal and Acme Wholesale Distributors. Jones alleges that Neal and Acme violated their agreement when they refused to deliver a quantity of folding chairs.

The alleged contract is contained in the attached letters. Neal's letter is the original received by Jones. Jones's letter is an unsigned photocopy obtained from Jones's files. Neal denies ever receiving the original of Jones's letter.

Assume the following facts:

(a) Hilda Frank, who had been Jones's secretary for 15 years at the relevant time, died before this trial.

(b) Jones cannot testify that s/he is able to recognize Neal's signature, but Jones can recognize Neal's voice from prior conversations.

(c) Jones will say that s/he personally did not mail the August 6 letter, nor did s/he see it mailed.

(d) Jones will say that for the 15 years before August 6, [-1], Hilda would not file an unsigned photocopy until she had mailed the original and that she always mailed the original on the same day it was dictated and signed.

(e) On August 8, [-1], the wholesale price charged by Acme for its metal folding chairs was increased to $30.00 each.

1.   For the plaintiff, conduct a direct examination of Jones and get the two letters in evidence.

2.   For the defendants, oppose the offers and cross-examine Jones.

ACME WHOLESALE DISTRIBUTORS
2933 East Congress

June 15, [-1]

Alex Jones
Ace Office Supply Company
418 E. Broadway
Toledo, Ohio

Dear Alex:

In accord with our phone conversation of last Wednesday, we hereby offer to sell you metal folding chairs (Catalogue item #A-417) at $23.00 each, plus freight charges, carrier of your designation, payable C.O.D., delivery at your place of business within 30 days of your acceptance of this offer.

This offer will remain an open firm offer until August 7, [-1]. Any acceptance must be in writing and our offer will be deemed accepted only when your written acceptance addressed to this firm is duly deposited in the United States mail.

Very truly yours,

Fred Neal

ACME WHOLESALE DISTRIBUTORS

By: Fred Neal

ACE OFFICE SUPPLY COMPANY
418 E. Broadway

August 6, [-1]

Acme Wholesale Distributors
2933 E. Congress
South Haven, Michigan

Att'n: Fred Neal

Dear Mr. Neal:

    In accord with your offer contained in your letter of
June 15, [-1], we hereby order one thousand (1,000) metal
folding chairs (Item #A-417), total price of $23,000.00, on
terms specific in your letter.

    Please give us 48 hours notice of anticipated delivery
so we can make arrangements here.

                              Sincerely,

                              ALEX JONES

4.18 STOCK PURCHASE ORDER

This is a contract action brought by the Zoom Corporation, a creditor of Jamie Z. Wilson. The issue is whether Wilson bought 300 shares of General Foods Organic Products stock on March 1, two years ago. S/he denies that s/he did.

To prove that the transaction took place, you subpoena Andy Jones, district manager of the local office of MWE Investing Services. Your subpoena calls for him/her to produce MWE records that deal with the transaction in question.

Jones comes to court with the attached record. S/he had never seen it before receiving the subpoena and had no hand in its making. S/he will say that the document is referred to at the company as a "purchase order." It is created by the person who takes the order, whether in person, on the phone, or otherwise. After the order is typed, it is sent to the purchase order department, where the actual purchase is made. Once the purchase is made, a copy of the order, along with a request for payment, is sent to the buyer. Jones cannot say who filled out the purchase order. At least 15 people were in the order department in March [-2]. S/he has been unable to locate any other records concerning the transaction.

1. For the plaintiff, conduct a direct examination of Jones and get the document into evidence.

2. Assume that Jones searches the records but cannot find any records showing any transactions concerning Wilson during the year in question. For the defendant, conduct a direct examination of Jones to demonstrate the absence of any such records.

3. Assume that Jones will testify that the company's regular procedure was to destroy original purchase orders after one year, but that at the end of the year the records department feeds the purchase information into its computer records. He brings to court the computer document created when the trial subpoena was received. For the plaintiff, get the document into evidence.

171

4. Assume that the words "Wilson is a liar and a thief" are handwritten on the document, as in the second version of the document included here. Offer it into evidence.

5. For the defendant, oppose all the plaintiff's offers.

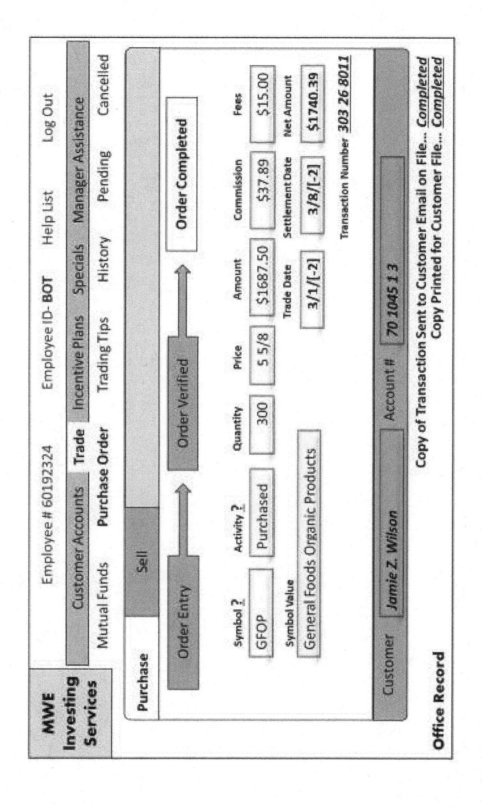

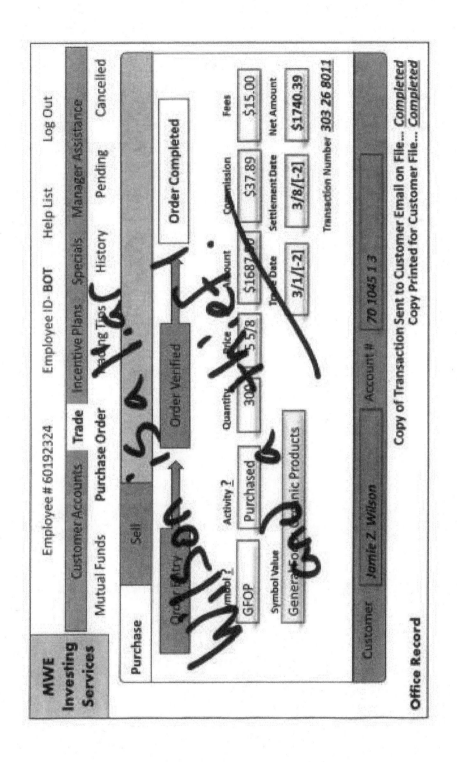

4.19 THEFT REPORT

This is a theft prosecution. The defendant, Fred Riley, is on trial for the theft of Sandra Franklin's car on September 25 of last year. When the trial begins, the prosecution learns that Franklin is somewhere in Europe and cannot be located in time to call her as a witness.

In order to prove the theft of the car and the ownership of the car, the prosecution subpoenas London Maxwell, general manager of the Maxwell Insurance Company. S/he brings the attached form. Ralph Sturdley, the agent who signed the form, cannot be located.

1. For the prosecution, get the form in evidence to prove the theft and ownership of the car.

2. Assume that this is an action by Franklin against Maxwell Insurance on the insurance policy. To prove that she reported the theft on October 1 of last year, Franklin intends to introduce the attached form. For the plaintiff, get the form in evidence for the stated purpose, using London Maxwell as a witness.

3. Use the same information as in No. 2, except that Maxwell Insurance denies Franklin was insured at the time of the theft. For the plaintiff, get the form in evidence to establish that Franklin was insured.

4. For the defense, oppose the offers.

AUTO THEFT REPORT FORM

PERSON REPORTING: Sandra Franklin

DATE OF THIS REPORT: October 1, [1]

INSURED: Sandra Franklin

VEHICLE: Toyota Prius
                                     LICENSE NUMBER 123-899

SERIAL NUMBER: Y257831670

DATE OF THEFT: September 25, [-1]

PLACE VEHICLE TAKEN FROM: Greyhound Parking Lot,
                                     Clark and Lake
                                     Streets, Chicago

WERE POLICE NOTIFIED: Yes

IF YES, DATE POLICE NOTIFIED: September 27, [-1]

MAXWELL INSURANCE COMPANY

BY: *Ralph Sturdley*
Ralph Sturdley, Agent

4.20 ACCIDENT REPORT

This case involves a two-car collision resulting in personal injury and property damage. The collision occurred on July 1, two years ago. The plaintiff, Frank Jones, the driver of the first car, is suing Sharon Walker, the driver of the second car, for negligence in allegedly crossing the center line of a highway on a curve and driving too fast for conditions.

The case is now on trial. Plaintiff calls Sandy Smith, the custodian of records of Acme Casualty Company, the defendant's insurance carrier. Pursuant to a subpoena, Smith brings the attached accident report prepared by one of the company's accident investigators, Charles Franklin, who was at the scene after the accident. Franklin is unavailable for trial.

1. For the plaintiff, get the report in evidence.
2. Assume that the state highway department accident investigator prepared the attached report pursuant to his statutory duty. For the plaintiff, get the report in evidence.
3. For the defendant, oppose the offer.

ACCIDENT REPORT FORM

Acme Casualty Company, Inc.

Date of this report: July 1, [-2]

Investigator at scene: Charles Franklin

Insured: Sharon Walker
Policy: Standard casualty policy, $100,000 max.
coverage
Insured vehicle: [-4] Chrysler sedan Illinois license #
987-654

Date of accident: July 1, [-2]
Time of accident: 4:00 p.m.
Location of accident: Sheridan Road, 1/4 mile N. of Town Rd.,
Glencoe (curve at bottom of ravine)
Parties involved: (1)   insured
(2)   Frank Jones, driving a [-5]
Cadillac Seville
Other witness(s):   (1)   Fred Minelli, Glencoe Police Dept.
Patrolman, at scene after accident.

Condition of vehicle(s): (1)   Walker vehicle had damage to left
front bumper, headlight and wheel
area
(2)   Jones vehicle had damage to left
side of body from front headlight
to rear door.

Accident scene: Sheridan Rd., at accident scene is a
right hand curve, going northbound.
(1)   Walker car stopped at shoulder of
road on east side of road. Skid
marks for approx. 45' from rear of
car. Skid marks for left wheels
crossed center line near point of
origin.
(2)   Jones car stopped at shoulder of
road on west side of road, approx.
60' from Walker car. Skid marks
for 15', beginning in west lane
directly opposite from Walker car
skid marks origin.

Statements: (1)   Walker said she was sorry about the
whole thing, that she wasn't
familiar with the road and the
curve was sharper than she thought.
(2)   Jones said he was driving in his
customary safe manner when he was
hit by the Walker car when it
crossed the center line and veered
into his outside lane.

183

ACCIDENT REPORT FORM

Acme Casualty Company, Inc.

4.21 TIME CARD

This is a criminal prosecution. The whereabouts of the defendant, John Hudson, on February 9 of last year at 10:30 A.M.—the date and time of the crime involved—is the principal issue in the case. Evidence has been presented showing that the robbery occurred three miles from Brenner Metal Works and that it would take about ten minutes to drive between the two places at 10:30 in the morning.

Hudson says he was at work at the time. His lawyer subpoenas Terry Brenner, president of Brenner Metal Works. Brenner brings, as the subpoena commands, Hudson's time card with machine-stamped time entries for the pertinent time period. The time cards are kept in a rack next to the time clock by the employee entrance to the plant. At the end of each two-week period the cards are collected and given to the bookkeeper.

Brenner has no personal knowledge of Hudson or of Hudson's activities on the relevant date.

1. For the defense, conduct a direct examination of Brenner, get the time card in evidence, and present it to the jury in the most effective way.

2. Assume that Brenner brings to court a computer printout of all employees' in and out times for the February 1 to 15 time period. S/he tells you that all time cards are summarized at the end of each quarter on computer memory banks and the time cards are then destroyed. S/he ordered the computer printout from the records department when s/he received the subpoena.

    For the defense, conduct a direct examination of Brenner, getting into evidence the computer printout and testimony about the relevant date. (Use the attached record as if it were the computer printout.)

3. For the prosecution, oppose the offers and cross-examine Brenner.

185

Brenner Metal Works — Employee Time Card

Employee Name: _John Hudson_

Pay Period: _2/1 to 2/14_

Signature: _John Hudson_

Date	2/1	2/2	2/3	2/4	2/5	2/6	2/7
In:	5:58 ☒A.M. ☐P.M.	6:02 ☒A.M. ☐P.M.	6:05 ☒A.M. ☐P.M.	5:58 ☒A.M. ☐P.M.	5:55 ☒A.M. ☐P.M.	☐A.M. ☐P.M.	☐A.M. ☐P.M.
Out:	10:02 ☒A.M. ☐P.M.	10:05 ☒A.M. ☐P.M.	10:02 ☒A.M. ☐P.M.	10:01 ☒A.M. ☐P.M.	10:02 ☒A.M. ☐P.M.	☐A.M. ☐P.M.	☐A.M. ☐P.M.
In:	10:30 ☒A.M. ☐P.M.	10:35 ☒A.M. ☐P.M.	10:30 ☒A.M. ☐P.M.	10:35 ☒A.M. ☐P.M.	10:30 ☒A.M. ☐P.M.	☐A.M. ☐P.M.	☐A.M. ☐P.M.
Out:	2:35 ☐A.M. ☒P.M.	2:35 ☐A.M. ☒P.M.	2:35 ☐A.M. ☒P.M.	2:40 ☐A.M. ☒P.M.	2:35 ☐A.M. ☒P.M.	☐A.M. ☐P.M.	☐A.M. ☐P.M.

Date	2/8	2/9	2/10	2/11	2/12	2/13	2/14
In:	5:50 ☒A.M. ☐P.M.	5:58 ☒A.M. ☐P.M.	5:55 ☒A.M. ☐P.M.	6:02 ☒A.M. ☐P.M.	6:00 ☒A.M. ☐P.M.	☐A.M. ☐P.M.	☐A.M. ☐P.M.
Out:	10:05 ☒A.M. ☐P.M.	9:50 ☒A.M. ☐P.M.	10:02 ☒A.M. ☐P.M.	10:05 ☒A.M. ☐P.M.	10:01 ☒A.M. ☐P.M.	☐A.M. ☐P.M.	☐A.M. ☐P.M.
In:	10:35 ☒A.M. ☐P.M.	10:25 ☒A.M. ☐P.M.	10:31 ☒A.M. ☐P.M.	10:35 ☒A.M. ☐P.M.	10:35 ☒A.M. ☐P.M.	☐A.M. ☐P.M.	☐A.M. ☐P.M.
Out:	2:40 ☐A.M. ☒P.M.	2:30 ☐A.M. ☒P.M.	2:40 ☐A.M. ☒P.M.	2:35 ☐A.M. ☒P.M.	2:32 ☐A.M. ☒P.M.	☐A.M. ☐P.M.	☐A.M. ☐P.M.

4.22 DEPOSIT AND WITHDRAWAL SLIPS

The Valley National Bank was robbed shortly after opening on June 1 of last year. Following the robbery the branch manager, Gale Atkins, performed an audit of the bank to determine the amount of the loss. Included in the audit were the previous day's cash count, the cash count after the robbery, and the records of transactions conducted on June 1. The robbery occurred at one teller station. The previous day's cash count at that station was $3,500. An audit after the robbery showed a cash count at that station of $250. From these figures Atkins was able to compute the cash taken during the robbery.

The only transactions conducted on June 1 before the robbery are represented by the attached documents, which Atkins found in the usual compartments in the tellers' drawers.

1. For the prosecution, get the records in evidence via the testimony of Gale Atkins.
2. For the defense, oppose the offers.

Valley National Bank of Arizona

SAVINGS DEPOSIT

DATE 6-1-[-1]

DEPOSITS MAY NOT BE AVAILABLE FOR IMMEDIATE WITHDRAWL

SIGN HERE IF CASH RECEIVED FROM DEPOSIT

GERALD THEIRS

NAME (PRINTED)

1307 GARFIELD AVE.

ADDRESS

⑈1234567890⑈ ACCOUNT NUMBER 7 9 2 1 - 9 9 6 0

CURRENCEY	100	0	0
COIN			
CHECKS	289	4	3
SUBTOTAL			
LESS CASH RECEIVED			
NET DEPOSIT	389	4	3

Valley National Bank of Arizona

SAVINGS DEPOSIT

DATE 6 - 1 - [-1]

DEPOSITS MAY NOT BE AVAILABLE FOR IMMEDIATE WITHDRAWL

SIGN HERE IF CASH RECEIVED FROM DEPOSIT

Perry Jones

NAME (PRINTED)

TERRY JONES

501 E HAWAII

ADDRESS

⑈1234567890⑈ ACCOUNT NUMBER 3 7 0 1 - 3 3 5 7

CURRENCEY			
COIN			
CHECKS	243	5	7
SUBTOTAL			
LESS CASH RECEIVED	100	0	0
NET DEPOSIT	143	5	7

Valley National Bank of Arizona

SAVINGS DEPOSIT

DATE 6-1-[-1]

DEPOSITS MAY NOT BE AVAILABLE FOR IMMEDIATE WITHDRAWL

SIGN HERE IF CASH RECEIVED FROM DEPOSIT

FRANCIS WINCHESTER

NAME (PRINTED)

1393 E. PINE ST

ADDRESS

⑈1234567890⑈ ACCOUNT NUMBER 8 8 8 1 - 4 3 9 1

CURRENCEY	300	0	0
COIN (bK)	288	0	1
CHECKS	415	3	7
SUBTOTAL			
LESS CASH RECEIVED			
NET DEPOSIT	1,003	3	8

Valley National Bank of Arizona

SAVINGS WITHDRAWAL

DATE O601[-1]   BRANCH ☐ MAIN ST. ☒ UNIVERSITY ☐ $ 127.00

One hundred twenty-seven and no _____ DOLLARS

CHARGED TO BELOW LISTED ACCOUNT

Pat Smith
SIGNATURE

1501 S. Taylor
ADDRESS

⑈⑈1234567890⑈ ACCOUNT NUMBER 8 5 2 1 - 0 6 7 8

Valley National Bank of Arizona

SAVINGS WITHDRAWAL

DATE 6/1/[-1]   BRANCH ☐ MAIN ST. ☒ UNIVERSITY ☐ $ 500 00/100

five hundred no 7/00 _____ DOLLARS

CHARGED TO BELOW LISTED ACCOUNT

Freddie Jackson
SIGNATURE

453 Tenure
ADDRESS

⑈⑈1234567890⑈ ACCOUNT NUMBER 6 2 1 7 - 4 9 8 0

Valley National Bank of Arizona

SAVINGS WITHDRAWAL

DATE 6/1/[-1]   BRANCH ☐ MAIN ST. ☒ UNIVERSITY ☐ $ 100 00

One Hundred dollars and 00/100 _____ DOLLARS

CHARGED TO BELOW LISTED ACCOUNT

Halen Jackson
SIGNATURE

2119 S. Pulaski, AE
ADDRESS

⑈⑈1234567890⑈ ACCOUNT NUMBER 6 2 8 7 - 1 3 4 0

4.23   SUMMARY CHART

This is a warranty action. The XYZ Car Rental Company purchased numerous vehicles from General Motors during the past four calendar years. XYZ claims that the four-speed automatic transmissions that came with some of the cars it bought from General Motors during that time period were defective and is suing for the cost of replacing the transmissions and other consequential damages.

To determine the full extent of the loss, XYZ hired a temporary employee from a secretary service, Kelly Services. For five weeks, from November 1, [-1], to December 7, [-1], the employee, Sammy Sparks, went through numerous records to determine which of XYZ's purchased automobiles had the special four-speed automatic transmission in them. This transmission was the purportedly defective part (General Motors stock item #T33-413).

After going through all the records (order forms, shipping orders, invoices, etc.), Sparks produced the following document and gave it to Wilbur Theis, the general manager of XYZ. (The underlying documents have already been examined by the defendants but have not been introduced in evidence.)

1. For the plaintiff, conduct a direct examination of Sparks and get the document in evidence.

2. Assume that all of XYZ's records are computerized. The exhibit was created by comptroller Hayden Johnson, who conducted a computer search for all vehicle purchases involving GM Stock Item #T33-413. For the plaintiff, conduct a direct examination of Johnson and get the document in evidence.

3. For the defendant, oppose the offer(s).

**SUMMARY OF XYZ CAR RENTAL COMPANY'S PURCHASES OF
VEHICLES FROM GENERAL MOTORS DURING THE
PERIOD 1/1/[-4] THROUGH 11/1/[-1]
DEFECTIVE FOUR-SPEED AUTOMATIC TRANSMISSIONS
(GM Stock Item #T33-413)**

Car Type	VIN	Purchase Date	Invoice Cost
Chevrolet	VX23816	Jan. 1, [-4]	$2,413
Buick	QT31620	May 1, [-4]	2,508
Buick	QT4140	June 30, [-4]	2,508
Chevrolet	VX33016	Aug. 4, [-4]	2,413
Chevrolet	VX33493	Aug. 30, [-4]	2,413
Chevrolet	PX4407	Feb. 1, [-3]	2,483
Chevrolet	PX5996	March 1, [-3]	2,483
Buick	J337	March 10, [-2]	2,543
Buick	J40077	June 1, [-2]	2,543
Buick	J59338	July 1, [-2]	2,543
Buick	J88710	Oct. 15, [-2]	2,543
Chevrolet	AB99-6110	Feb. 1, [-1]	2,576
Chevrolet	AB10-16217	March 1, [-1]	2,576
Chevrolet	AB17-73556	June 15, [-1]	2,576
Chevrolet	AB20-66137	Aug. 1, [-1]	2,576
Total: 15 cars			$37,697

4.24   PRISON LOGBOOK

This is a prosecution for conspiracy to commit three murders. The defendant, Jerry Stone, was an inmate at the Ironside Correctional Center at the time of the acts alleged in the indictment. The prosecution's theory is that the actual killer, Victor Raines, committed the murders on instructions from Stone. The prosecution has the prison visitors' logbook that reflects Raines's visits with Stone one day before each murder. It seeks to introduce the logbook to prove that Raines had in fact visited Stone at the prison on those particular dates.

In order to introduce the logbook into evidence, the prosecution relies on the testimony of Gabbie McMann, the Inmate Records Coordinator at Ironside. An FBI agent interviewed McMann after the murder, and the agent's report contains the following:

> Gabbie McMann has been employed by the Department of Corrections for eight years. S/he is responsible for maintaining and storing the prison visitors' logbook. S/he is familiar with the procedure for admitting visitors and has personally observed the procedure from time to time. S/he states that normal prison procedure is that visitors are required to show identification to the lobby officer and to sign their names and record their addresses on a sheet in the logbook. The lobby officer is required to check a visitor's identification against the entry in the book. McMann has no personal knowledge of whether the lobby officer checks each entry in the logbook against the identification that has been shown to the officer, but s/he can say that lobby officers are required to follow the prescribed procedure. S/he has no personal knowledge of the entries that reflect visits by a Victor Raines.

1. For the prosecution, conduct a direct examination of McMann and get the logbook entries into evidence.
2. For the defendant, oppose the offer and cross-examine McMann.

IRONSIDE CORRECTIONAL CENTER

Date: March 15[2]

Inmate visited: Richard Jefferson
Name of visitor: Sam Everett
Address of visitor: 1642 Thomas   City

Time in: 1045
Time out: 1210

Inmate Visited: Jerry Stone
Name of visitor: Victor Olaine
Address of visitor: 6230 S. White
City

Time in: 1150
Time out: 1410

Inmate Visited: Ralph Henry
Name of visitor: Felix Sampson
Address of visitor: 2017 Hale   City

Time in: 1315
Time out: 1420

201

Date: June 2, [-2]

Inmate visited: Jerry Stone
Name of visitor: Victor Raines
Address of visitor: 6230 S. White
City

Time in: 945
Time out: 1115

Inmate Visited: Sidney Berg
Name of visitor: Ralph Stein
Address of visitor: 400 N. Michigan City

Time in: 1020
Time out: 1215

Inmate Visited: Arthur Blane
Name of visitor: Thelma Bledsoe
Address of visitor: 1640 W. Taylor City

Time in: 1045
Time out: 1340

Date: Aug 7 [-2]

Inmate visited: Sanford Stark
Name of visitor: Louise Stark
Address of visitor: 3630 Belmont City

Time in: 940
Time out: 1145

Inmate Visited: Harry Fields
Name of visitor: Sam Fields
Address of visitor: 4012 W Harper City

Time in: 1015
Time out: 1230

Inmate Visited: Terry Stone
Name of visitor: Victor Raines
Address of visitor: 6230 S. White City

Time in: 1030
Time out: 1045

4.25   E-MAIL AND WEBSITE MESSAGES

This is a breach of contract case arising out of an attempt to purchase a car advertised on a website. On July 14, [-1], defendant Corey Cain placed an ad on the website Jackie's Jalopies offering to sell a [-4] Chevy SUV for $20,000.

On July 19, [-1], plaintiff Alex Abel sent an e-mail to the address listed in the ad offering to pay $18,500 for the SUV. The defendant admits receiving this e-mail. The plaintiff claims that defendant sent a return e-mail accepting the offer on July 20, [-1]. The defendant's deposition is attached.

The key exhibits in this case are the two e-mails, one sent by the plaintiff to the defendant, and the other allegedly sent by the defendant to the plaintiff. Plaintiff claims that s/he printed these two e-mails from his/her computer without altering them in any way.

The case is now on trial.

1. For the plaintiff, introduce the ad and the two e-mails in evidence.

2. For the defendant, oppose the admission of the claimed e-mail from the defendant to the plaintiff.

Web Advertisement

reply below ☐ Prohibited   Posted 07-14 1:54 PM_DT

◀ prev ▲ next ▶

★ **[-4] Chevy SUV $20,000**

A great vehicle at a steal of a price!

Reply to: cuinsept@mmsn.com

LS Sport Utility 4 Door with 4WD
$20,000 firm

This is a terrific deal!! I am headed to grad school in the city and need the money more than a vehicle, otherwise I would keep it.

Chevy	SUV
4WD	

Bluebook value is $22,900 so $20,000 is the lowest price I want to go. I am wiling to transport a reasonable distance upon payment.

Contact Corey Cain at cuinsept@mmsn.com for more information!

Details:
Mileage: 52,000
Engine: 6-Cyl, 4.2 Liter
Transmission: Automatic
Drive Train: 4WD
Color: Silver

post id: 123456789   posted: 7-14   email to friend   report abuse

E-mail from Plaintiff Abel to Defendant Cain

To: Corey Cain <cuinsept@mmsn.com>

From: Alex Abel <aabel@aaol.com>

Re: Vehicle listed for sale on *Jackie's Jalopies*

Date: July 19, [-1]

Time: 2:32 P.M.

I want to buy the Chevy SUV you listed for sale on *Jackie's Jalopies*.

I will pay you $18,500 for it immediately after my mechanic inspects it and finds it to be in proper working order.

You can contact me at aabel@aaol.com.

Alleged E-mail from Defendant Cain to Plaintiff Abel

To: Alex Abel <aabel@aaol.com>

From: Corey Cain <cuinsept@mmsn.com>

Re: Vehicle listed for sale on *Jackie's Jalopies*

Date: July 20, [-1]

Time: 10:47 A.M.

Thank you for your offer to buy my Chevy SUV for $18,500. It's a great vehicle and $18,500 is more than a steal of a price. Although your offer is lower than I wanted to go, I need to complete this transaction now to pay for grad school, so I will accept your offer.

I will contact you soon with details about where and when we can meet to complete this transaction.

To: Alex Abel <aabel@aol.com>

From: Corey Cain <ccainsout@nmail.com>

Re: Vehicle listed for sale on Jackie's Jalopies

Date: June 20, [ ]-11

Time: 10:47 A.M.

"Thank you for your offer to buy my Chevy SUV for $16,500. It's a great vehicle and $18,500 is more than a steal of a price. Although your offer is lower than I wanted to go, I need to complete this transaction now to pay for grad school, so I will accept your offer.

I will contact you soon with details about where and when we can meet to complete this transaction."

Excerpts from Transcript of Deposition of
Corey Cain, Defendant
October 25, [-1]

Conducted at Howard, Fine & Howard, Inc.,
Office of plaintiff's attorney

410 Grand Avenue

Corey Cain, having been first duly sworn, testified
as follows:

p. 3

1 Q. State your name, please.
2
3 A. Corey C. Cain
4
5 Q. What is your e-mail address?
6
7 A. C U IN SEPT @ MMSN.COM
8
9 Q. Do you have any other e-mail accounts?
10
11 A. No, I do not.
12
13 Q. Do you share this e-mail account with anyone else?
14
15 A. No, I do not.
16
17 Q. Do you ever use public computers to send e-mails?
18
19 A. Yes, I use the ones on campus and also the ones in
20   the public library.
21
22 Q. Did you place an ad on the website Jackie's Jalopies
23   offering to sell a Chevy SUV?
24
25 A. Yes, I did.
26
27 Q. Using your cuinsept@mmsn.com e-mail address?
28
29 A. Yes.
30
31 Q. Is Exhibit 1 a copy of the ad you placed?
32
33 A. Yes, it is.

34 Q. And is Exhibit 2 a copy of the e-mail response you
35   received from the Plaintiff, Alex Abel?
36
37 A. Yes, it is.
38
39 Q. Is this the only response you received to the Jackie's
40   Jalopies ad?
41
42 A. No, I received several others over the course of
43   about 10 days after I placed the ad. But all but one
44   were offers for less than the offer from Abel.
45
46 Q. Did you sell the vehicle to one of the people who
47   responded?
48
49 A. Yes, on July 23rd I received an offer for the full
50    $20,000 I asked for and I sold that person the car.
51
52 Q. What about Exhibit 3, the e-mail presented by Abel,
53   saying that you would sell the car to the plaintiff
54   for $18,500?
55
56 A. I did not send that e-mail.
57
58 Q. Is the "from" e-mail address on this correspondence
59   your e-mail address?
60
61 A. Yes, it is, but I never sent that e-mail.
62
63 Q. Did you send any e-mails to the plaintiff?
64
65 A. No.
66
67 Q. You never responded to this offer to buy the car for
68    $18,500?
69
70 A. No. I really didn't want to sell it for less than
71    $20,000. It was worth a lot more than that so I was
72   already losing money with that price and I didn't
73   want to go lower.
74
75 Q. But you didn't reject the offer either?
76
77 A. No, I didn't want to say yes or no right away. I was
78   afraid it might be my only chance to sell the car so
79   I just ignored it hoping I would get a better offer,
80   and I did.
81
82 Q. Did you ever respond to the plaintiff's e-mail?

216

83 A. Not individually. I sent a message via Jackie's
84   Jalopies to everyone who used the ad service saying
85   the car was sold.
86
87 Q. Where do you think this e-mail came from?
88
89 A. I think Alex Abel created a phony e-mail to try to
90   force me to sell the car at the lower price and used
91   my words from the ad to make it sound like me. If I
92   was going to answer a specific e-mail offer, I would
93   have just hit the reply button, not started a whole
94   new message.

This is to certify that I have read the transcript of my deposition taken on October 25, [-1], and that the transcript accurately states the questions asked and the answers given.

_____
                                    Corey Cain

Subscribed and sworn to
Before me on this 14th
day of November, [-1]

_____
              Notary Public

4.26   CHAT ROOM TRANSCRIPT

Defendant, Wade Sampson, is charged with arson and murder. The state alleges that on July 19, [-1], Sampson intentionally started his house on fire, and that the fire killed Nellie Sampson, his daughter. Sampson denies starting the fire and claims that the fire was started by a faulty electrical appliance.

The key evidence in the case is an alleged "Booze Busters" chat room discussion. The police received alleged transcript(s) of this chat room discussion from Mitch Bronson, who says he is a regular participant in the chat room. Bronson says that "Booze Busters" is an Internet group of problem drinkers who support each other through the chat room. The defendant denies making any of the statements in the alleged transcript(s) of the chat room discussion.

Attached are transcripts of interviews of Mitch Bronson and the defendant's girlfriend, Gloria Wilbur, and an alleged printout of the chat room conversation.

The case is now on trial.

1. For the state, introduce the "cut and paste" transcript of the chat room conversation in evidence. For this version of the exercise, assume that the only version of the transcript available is the one with the title "Booze Busters Chat Room Excerpts, November 12, [-1]." Assume that this is the version of the transcript delivered by Mitch Bronson to Detective Shelby Moore. According to Bronson, he produced this version by cutting and pasting the conversation from the chat room to a word processing document, then printing the word processing document. For this version of the exercise, assume that neither Bronson nor Moore made any attempt to produce a screenshot version of the chat room discussion, and that it is no longer possible to produce such a version. In other words, assume that a screenshot version of the transcript does not exist.

2. [As an alternative:] For the state, introduce the screenshot version of the chat room conversation. For this version of the exercise, assume that, after

meeting with Mitch Bronson, Detective Shelby Moore went with Bronson to his home. Bronson printed a screenshot of the chat room conversation and gave it to Moore.

3. For the defense, oppose the offer(s).

20:15:01   <SlamminSammy> Slammin' Sammy here. What's up? Anyone in?

20:15:06   <TheMitchster> TheMitchster here. Not Much. How about you?

20:15:12   <SlamminSammy> I'm way down. I'm mourning the loss of people I've rejected all my life. My sweetheart watched me go to jail twice. And I killed Nellie because her mother stood between us.

20:15:26   <TheMitchster> Sammy, what are you talking about, you killed Nellie? Is this a cold fact? Are you getting help?

20:18:40   <SlamminSammy> I don't know if this is so smart. They could trace this back to me somehow. My handle is no big secret. But I guess everyone here promised each other confidentiality, so I guess I can open up. You might think that I'm flailing myself for some sort of weird self gratification. But this is as real as it gets. After I divorced her mother, I tried to get custody of Nellie, and we agreed to joint custody. She used joint custody to jerk me around, using Nellie to make my life miserable. So the last night when Nellie was still with me, before she had to go back to her mother, I got totally wasted. I just kept thinking that my ex was ruining both my and Nellie's lives. I knew I had to end that. So after Nellie went to sleep, I set the house on fire. I got outside, and made a big show of how distraught I was, so nobody would know what I did. In the emergency room in Piney River, I bawled my eyes out. After a while the booze wore off, and I realized what I had done. They were so worried about me that they flew me to Springfield Hospital. I got released a while ago, and I've been dwelling on it ever since.

20:20:55   <TheMitchster> Sammy, do the cops know you did this?

20:22:05   <SlamminSammy> No, they think the fire was caused by an electrical appliance. At least that's what they said the fire marshal told them. Thank god the fire marshal was such an idiot.

The screenshot version of the chat room dialogue is shown below.

Booze Busters Chat Room

Date:
November 12, [-1]

File   Edit   View   Friends   Help

ADD

SlamminSammy

TheMitchster

20:15:01 <SlamminSammy> Slammin' Sammy here. What's up? Anyone in?

20:15:06 < TheMitchster> The Mitchster here. Not Much. How about you?

20:15:12 <SlamminSammy> I'm way down. I'm mourning the loss of people I've rejected all my life. My sweetheart watched me go to jail twice. And I killed Nellie because her mother stood between us.

20:15:26 < TheMitchster> Sammy, what are you talking about, you killed Nellie? Is this a cold fact? Are you getting help?

20:18:40 <SlamminSammy> I don't know if this is so smart. They could trace this back to me somehow. My handle is no big secret. But I guess everyone here promised each other confidentiality, so I guess I can open up. You might think that I'm flailing myself for some sort of weird self gratification. But this is as real as it gets. After I divorced her mother, I tried to get custody of Nellie, and we agreed to joint custody. She used joint custody to jerk me around, using Nellie to make my life miserable. So the last night when Nellie was still with me, before she had to go back to her mother, I got totally wasted. I just kept thinking that my ex was ruining both my and Nellie's lives. I knew I had to end that. So after Nellie went to sleep, I set the house on fire. I got outside, and made a big show of how distraught I was, so nobody would know what I did. In the emergency room in Piney River, I bawled my eyes out. After a while the booze wore off, and I realized what I had done. They were so worried about me that they flew me to Springfield Hospital. I got released a while ago, and I've been dwelling on it ever since.

20:20:55 < TheMitchster> Sammy, do the cops know you did this?

20:22:05 <SlamminSammy> No, they think the fire was caused by an electrical appliance. At least that's what they said the fire marshal told them. Thank god the fire marshal was such an idiot.

SEND

Transcript of Interview of Mitch Bronson

on November 13, [-1]

at Buffalo Police Department

Statement of Mitch Bronson, age 42, of 414 Maple Street, Buffalo, regarding possible homicide, pursuant to interview by Police Detective Shelby Moore.

1 Q. Please state your name.
2
3 A. Mitch Bronson.
4
5 Q. And your address?
6
7 A. 414 Maple Street, here in Buffalo.
8
9 Q. We just met, Mr. Bronson, but you know that I am
10   Detective Shelby Moore of the Buffalo Police
11   Department, right?
12
13 A. Yes.
14
15 Q. And you came to the police station today of your own
16   free will?
17
18 A. That is correct.
19
20 Q. In fact, you came in on your own, without me or anyone
21   else from the Buffalo Police Department asking you to
22   do so.
23
24 A. Yes. I came to report my concerns about a possible
25   crime. I wish I did not have to be here, but I could
26   not sleep at all last night, so I decided I had no
27   choice but to come to tell you about this.
28
29 Q. Before we get into the reason why you are here, let
30   me cover one more preliminary matter. Mr. Bronson,
31   you have agreed to answer my questions and to have
32   those questions and your answers recorded, so that an
33   electronic transcript can be produced.
34
35 A. That is correct.
36
37 Q. Okay, I think that is all of the preliminary stuff.
38   Tell me why you are here.

39 A. Like I said, I could not get any sleep last night
40   after what happened yesterday.
41
42 Q. What happened yesterday?
43
44 A. Something crazy happened in the chat room.
45
46 Q. Chat room?
47
48 A. You know. A place in cyberspace where people can go
49   to communicate with each other online. Each person
50   can add to the conversation. The chat room that I use
51   is for a group called Booze Busters.
52
53 Q. What is Booze Busters?
54
55 A. It is sort of like Alcoholics Anonymous, only
56   different. All of us in Booze Busters know we have
57   a drinking problem, but we don't agree with the AA
58   folks that you have to give up drinking completely.
59   We know we have a problem, but we believe we can
60   reduce our drinking without totally eliminating it.
61
62 Q. So this chat room is sort of an electronic version of
63   a support group?
64
65 A. Yep. Sometimes I go there when I need help controlling
66   my drinking, like when I am upset. Other times, like
67   yesterday, I go there to support other members of
68   Booze Busters who might need help.
69
70 Q. Is it anonymous?
71
72 A. It is supposed to be. All of us use made-up names,
73   instead of our real names. But some of the made-up
74   names are pretty close to people's real names.
75
76 Q. What is your name in this chat room?
77
78 A. The Mitchster. See what I mean?
79
80 Q. So it is not really all that anonymous?
81
82 A. Well, when you join the group, you promise to never
83   tell anyone outside the group what anybody said in
84   the chat room. That is why I feel so bad about being
85   here talking to you today. But I couldn't live with
86   myself if I did not tell somebody in law enforcement
87   about what happened yesterday, so here I am.

224

88 Q. What happened in the chat room yesterday?
89
90 A. Yesterday evening I was online, checking sports
91   scores, so I decided to log into the chat room for a
92   while. And Slammin Sammy said some things that were
93   really disturbing.
94
95 Q. Who is Slammin Sammy?
96
97 A. Well, I guess I am not supposed to know, because
98   of all that anonymous stuff. But I do know. Slammin
99   Sammy is Wade Sampson.
100
101 Q. How do you know that?
102
103 A. I am the one who invited him into the Booze Busters
104   group in the first place, a couple of years ago. At
105   the time, Wade was my business partner.
106
107 Q. How so?
108
109 A. He and I owned a bunch of sandwich shops together.
110   He had invented a sandwich with roast beef, ham,
111   and turkey that he just loved, so we called it the
112   Slammin Sammy on our menu. When he joined the group,
113   he used that as his group name.
114
115 Q. Why did you invite him to join the group?
116
117 A. Both of us drank too much. He had a better excuse
118   than I did, to tell you the truth, as some bad
119   things happened to him. He went through a horrible
120   divorce in his hometown of Piney River. And then his
121   daughter died in a house fire. I felt really bad for
122   him. Well, I used to, anyway.
123
124 Q. Getting back to yesterday, what happened in the chat
125   room?
126
127 A. I printed out the important part. Here it is.
128
129 Q. And you are handing me a one-page document that says
130   Booze Busters Chat Room Excerpts, November 12, [-1]
131   at the top?
132
133 A. That is correct. I cut and pasted the key parts into
134   a word processing document, then I added the title.
135
136 Q. Okay. But how do you know that Wade Sampson typed
137   these things?

225

138 A. First of all, Wade is Slammin Sammy, like I said.
139   Second, this post has language that sounds just like
140   Wade.
141
142 Q. Like what?
143
144 A. He loves the phrase "weird self gratification." I
145   have never heard anyone else use that phrase. And see
146   that reference to "sweetheart" at the top? Nobody
147   calls their girlfriend that anymore, but Wade does.
148
149 Q. Who is his girlfriend, by the way?
150
151 A. Gloria Wilbur.
152
153 Q. Does she live here?
154
155 A. Yeah. Over by Midtown Park. I don't know the address,
156   but I am sure you can look it up.
157
158 Q. I will do that. Anything else that tells you Wade
159   Sampson wrote this?
160
161 A. Well, he has gone to jail twice that I know of. So he
162   got that right. And he obviously knows his daughter's
163   name, Nellie. And all of that stuff about her dying
164   in a fire is just like he has told me when he has
165   talked about it. Well, almost all of it. Before
166   this, he had always said it was an accidental fire.
167   So the stuff about him setting it and pretending to
168   be horrified is new.
169
170 Q. Leaving that out of the equation for the moment,
171   what has he told you before about this fire?
172
173 A. That there was a fire, for one. That the fire marshal
174   said it was caused by an electrical appliance. That he
175   went to the emergency room in Piney River. That they
176   took him in for observation at Springfield Hospital.
177   Of course, when he said that before, I thought he
178   really was distraught, not just faking it.
179
180 Q. Anything else?
181
182 A. Well, he really does hate his ex-wife. I can assure
183   you of that.
184
185 Q. And you are his ex-partner. Does he hate you?

186 A. Well, we aren't on the best of terms. You know how
187   it is when you are former partners. We don't exactly
188   consider ourselves best friends anymore. And we are
189   still fighting a bit over splitting up the assets.
190   But it is nothing out of the ordinary. I still wish
191   him the best. Well, I used to. Now I don't know what
192   to think.
193
194 Q. Is there anything else you want us to know?
195
196 A. Not that I can think of. Other than I really hate to
197   break the confidentiality pledge. But I had to do
198   that, because somebody has to look into this stuff.
199
200 Q. Okay, then, let's wrap this up. You understand that,
201   using our electronic transcription technology, a
202   written version of this statement will be produced,
203   and you will be asked to review it and, if it is
204   correct, sign it?
205
206 A. Yes.
207
208 Q. And you are willing to sign it, freely and volun-
209   tarily?
210
211 A. Sure. I wish I did not have to be involved in any of
212   this, but I want to do the right thing here.
213
214 Q. This will end the recorded interview of Mitch
215   Bronson.

This is to certify that I have reviewed this
transcript of my recorded interview on November 13,
[-1], and that the transcript accurately states the
questions asked and the answers given.

Mitch Bronson
Mitch Bronson

227

Transcript of Interview of Gloria Wilbur
on November 15, [-1]

at Buffalo Police Department

Statement of Gloria Wilbur, age 36, of 1428 Parkside
Road, Buffalo, regarding pending investigation
of potential homicide in Piney River, pursuant to
interview by Police Detective Shelby Moore.

1 Q. State your name and address, please.
2
3 A. Gloria Wilber. 1428 Parkside Road in Buffalo.
4
5 Q. Is that by Midtown Park?
6
7 A. Right across the street.
8
9 Q. And I introduced myself when I called you this
10   morning and again when you came to the station,
11   but just to get it on the record, you realize that
12   I am Detective Shelby Moore of the Buffalo Police
13   Department, right?
14
15 A. Yes.
16
17 Q. And you came to the police station today of your own
18   free will?
19
20 A. That is correct.
21
22 Q. You drove here yourself?
23
24 A. Yes, after you called. I am glad you did. I heard
25   rumors about that creep Mitch Bronson trying to say
26   my Wade said something about the fire that killed
27   his daughter. I hope you don't believe a word that
28   jackass Bronson has said.
29
30 Q. Let's slow down just a minute. Let me cover one
31   more preliminary item. As I explained to you
32   before we turned on the recorder, this interview
33   is being recorded. And you have agreed to answer my
34   questions while being recorded. So you know that
35   my questions and your answers are being recorded,
36   so we can produce an electronic transcript of this
37   interview.

38 A. Sure. And I am glad that you are doing that, because
39   we need to set the record straight here.
40
41 Q. Why do you say that?
42
43 A. Like I said, you should not believe a word or even a
44   syllable that comes out of the mouth of that creep
45   Bronson.
46
47 Q. Why not?
48
49 A. He hates Wade.
50
51 Q. Because of their business?
52
53 A. Well, that is part of it. He is trying to cheat Wade
54   out of his fair share of the assets, now that Wade
55   had finally had enough of him stealing the proceeds
56   from the Fairview store.
57
58 Q. Stealing the proceeds? Didn't he own that store?
59
60 A. He owned half of it. But we found out that he
61   was taking about half of the cash from the cash
62   register from that store almost every day and
63   pocketing it. He admitted it and said he would
64   never do it again, but then he did, so Wade told
65   him they were through.
66
67 Q. That is why Bronson hates Wade?
68
69 A. Part of it. The other part is about me, I guess.
70
71 Q. How so?
72
73 A. I am embarrassed to say this, but that creep has a
74   crush on me, I guess. Every time he gets drunk, he
75   puts his hands all over me.
76
77 Q. Have you ever done anything to encourage him?
78
79 A. Are you kidding? That creep? Never. I love Wade.
80
81 Q. By the way, does Wade have any special names for
82   you?
83
84 A. No. He just calls me his sweetheart. Isn't that cute?
85   Nobody calls anyone that anymore, but he does. He is
86   just a great guy.

87 Q. How long have you been dating him?

88

89 A. For about four years. We have been living together
90   for ten months. Well, off and on.

91

92 Q. Off and on?

93

94 A. I moved out once.

95

96 Q. Why?

97

98 A. He threatened to push me down the stairs once when
99   he was drunk. I am not going to put up with that, so
100   I moved out.

101

102 Q. So you thought he was serious?

103

104 A. When he drinks too much, sometimes he loses his
105   temper a bit. I had to have him arrested.

106

107 Q. Has he ever gone to jail on any other occasion?

108

109 A. Only one other time. For a driving while intoxicated
110   conviction a couple of years ago. See, that's the
111   whole thing. As long as he does not drink too much,
112   he is fine.

113

114 Q. When was the last time he had a drink?

115

116 A. It is not every time he drinks. Most of the time
117   he only drinks a little, and he is fine then.
118   He has not gone on a binge since the time he
119   threatened to push me down the stairs and I had
120   him arrested.

121

122 Q. So you feel safe with him now?

123

124 A. Of course I do. I would not be there if I did not
125   feel safe. I am not one of those kind, detective.
126   Wade is a kind soul. Timid, even. Which is why that
127   jerk Bronson could take advantage of him. Poor Wade
128   is so peaceful. He will do anything to avoid a fight
129   or an argument.

130

131 Q. But you did have him arrested for domestic vio-
132   lence.

133

134 A. Potential domestic violence, detective. He never
135   touched me. Looking back, I realize that was a
136   mistake by me. He was not going to do anything to
137   me. I overreacted.

138 Q. Getting back to Mr. Bronson, you think he has it in
139   for Wade?
140
141 A. I don't think so. I know so. He took advantage of
142   Wade when they had those sandwich shops. For one
143   thing, he always ran the books and the computers,
144   while Wade handled the personnel stuff and actually
145   did all the work of running the shops. I have to
146   give this to that creep, he really knows computers.
147   He can do anything with them. He even created a
148   phony set of reports from the Fairview store that
149   fooled Wade for a long time.
150
151 Q. Is there anything else you want to tell us?
152
153 A. No. Just don't believe anything that creep Mitch
154   Bronson tells you.
155
156 Q. Let's wrap this up, then. You know that I will
157   now use our electronic transcription technology to
158   produce a written version of this statement, then I
159   will ask you to review it and sign it?
160
161 A. Yes.
162
163 Q. Are you willing to sign it, freely and voluntari-
164   ly?
165
166 A. Absolutely. Everything I have said is the complete
167   truth.
168
169 Q. This is the end of the recorded interview of Gloria
170   Wilbur.

This is to certify that I have reviewed this transcript of my recorded interview on November 15, [-1], and that the transcript accurately states the questions asked and the answers given.

Gloria Wilbur

Gloria Wilbur

232

4.27 SOCIAL MEDIA POST

In each of its permutations, this problem concerns the admissibility or other use of a "status update" posted to the Mule Strong Group of SocialNet, a social media service. The November 24, [-1], status update said, "Okay, I get it. I need money and I need to get out of this dump of a town. It is time to kill too birds with one stone." The proponent of this evidence claims that Brett L. Waye wrote this status update. For each version of the problem outlined below, the proponent wishes to use this status update, along with other evidence, to convince the fact finder (usually the jury, but in some instances the judge) that Waye committed insurance fraud and arson by burning his house two days after posting the status update.

Other evidence in the case has established, will establish, or could establish, the following:

Brett L. Waye married Hannah Goings on July 21, [-12]. They have a daughter who is ten years old and a son who is eight years old.

From July, [-12], to November 26, [-1], they lived at 1917 5th Avenue in Chillicothe, Missouri, in a home that they owned (subject to 30-year mortgage). However, in September, [-1], Hannah Goings-Waye, a CPA, accepted a job as the Chief Financial Officer of the Metro Area Hospital in Kansas City, Missouri. After accepting this position, she spent Mondays through Fridays, and sometimes weekend days, in Kansas City.

From June, [-12], to May, [-1], Brett L. Waye worked as a production manager at Bushwhacker Brewery in Chillicothe. Bushwhacker declared bankruptcy in May, [-1], and shut down its plant. Because the brewery had been the largest employer in Chillicothe, its demise has had a major negative impact on that town's economy. As of the time of the trial, many homes are on the market, and those that have sold since the brewery closure have sold for less than half of their value before the closure.

Despite a constant attempt to find work, Brett Waye has been unemployed since the demise of Bushwhacker Brewery. On January 2 of this year, he and his two children moved to Kansas City. He is now looking for work in Kansas City.

On November 26, [-1], a fire that started at about 2:00 A.M. destroyed the house at 1917 5th Avenue in Chillicothe. Nobody was in the home at the time the fire destroyed it.

You will be assigned a specific context for the proposed use of the November 24 status update. Please concentrate on that specific context and ignore all other contexts. For example, in your case, perhaps only Exhibit 6 exists, so you can make no use of the other exhibits.

In each of the specific contexts below, the proponent (i.e., the person discussed in subparagraph "i") wishes to introduce or make some other use of the November 24 post, to try to convince the jury or the judge that it establishes, or helps to establish, that Waye committed insurance fraud and arson by burning his house. The proponent should focus on this task. This problem is NOT designed for a comprehensive examination of the witness by the proponent. In each instance, the opponent should object to the proponent's use of the status update or otherwise lessen its impact, perhaps (but not necessarily) via cross-examination.

(1) *Waye v. West Is Best Insurance*: In this case, Brett L. Waye has sued West Is Best Insurance to recover under the homeowner's policy for the loss of the home. West Is Best refuses to pay the claim because it asserts that Waye burned down the house and is therefore ineligible to recover, due to the arson exclusion in the homeowner's policy.

   (a) [Background for (1)(a), (b), and (c); (2)(a), (b), and (c); and (3)(a), (b), and (c):] West Is Best calls Hannah Goings-Waye as a witness. She testifies that she and Brett were under substantial financial strain after he lost his job. She also testifies that the two of them were conversing via SocialNet's private message option on November 23, [-1], because

234

Brett no longer had a cell phone. In many of her "dozens" of messages during the "back and forth" SocialNet conversation that day, she tried to convince Brett to move to Kansas City to look for work. She testifies that the last message on November 23 was from Brett to her, saying something like, "I will think it over and get back to you tomorrow." On the evening of the next day, November 24, [-1], she saw the message at issue, which Brett probably accidentally posted to the Mules Strong Group, thinking he was sending a private message to her. She is also prepared to testify that Brett often uses the expression "two birds with one stone" and, when typing or writing, often makes errors in selecting the wrong version of to/two/too.

Problem (a): If asked, Hannah would testify that the November 24 message said something like, "Okay, I get it. I need money and I need to get out of this dump of a town. It is time to kill too birds with one stone."

(i)   For West Is Best Insurance, use Hannah's testimony to prove that Brett burned his house and committed insurance fraud.

(ii) For Brett, resist the offer and, if necessary, cross-examine Hannah.

(b) [See above for Background.] When she is asked what the November 24 message said, Hannah will say "I do not remember." Your file contains Exhibit 1. It looks like a screenshot from a computer, though you have no idea how it got into your file or who put it there.

(i)   For West Is Best Insurance, use Hannah's testimony and Exhibit 1 to prove that Brett burned his house and committed insurance fraud.

(ii) For Brett, resist the offer and, if necessary, cross-examine Hannah.

(c) [See above for Background.] When she is asked what the November 24 message said, Hannah will say, "I do not remember. But I do remember that the message seemed important enough that I should talk to Brett about it when I next saw him. So I cut-and-pasted it into a word processing document, then printed it out and put the printout into my purse. I did not save the electronic version of that file, but I did save the printout." That printed page is Exhibit 6.

235

(i) For West Is Best Insurance, use Hannah's testimony and Exhibit 6 to prove that Brett burned his house and committed insurance fraud.

(ii) For Brett, resist the offer and, if necessary, cross-examine Hannah.

(d) West Is Best calls Lynn Wallenstein, who brings Exhibit 5 (and its attachments, Exhibits 1-4) to the stand. Wallenstein's testimony, if allowed, will be consistent with Exhibit 3, the report s/he drafted.

(i) For West Is Best, use Wallenstein's testimony and, if useful, some or all of Exhibits 1-5, to prove that Brett burned his house and committed insurance fraud.

(ii) For Brett, resist the offer(s) and, if necessary, cross-examine Wallenstein.

(e) West Is Best brings the original of Exhibit 5 (and its attachments, Exhibits 1-4) to court.

(i) For West Is Best Insurance, use Exhibit 5 and its attachments to prove that Brett burned his house and committed insurance fraud.

(ii) For Brett, resist the offer.

(2) *State v. Waye*: In this case, the state is prosecuting Brett for arson and insurance fraud.

(a) [See above for Background. This background should be modified only to reflect that the state calls Hannah Goings-Waye as a witness.]

If asked, Hannah would testify that the November 24 message said something like, "Okay, I get it. I need money and I need to get out of this dump of a town. It is time to kill too birds with one stone."

(i) For the state, use Hannah's testimony to prove that Brett burned his house and committed insurance fraud.

(ii) For Brett, resist the offer and, if necessary, cross-examine Hannah.

(b) [See above for Background. This background should be modified only to reflect that the state calls Hannah Goings-Waye as a witness.] When she is asked what the November 24 message said, Hannah will say, "I do not remember." Your file contains Exhibit 1. It looks like a

236

screenshot from a computer, though you have no idea how it got into your file or who put it there.

(i) For the state, use Hannah's testimony and Exhibit 1 to prove that Brett burned his house and committed insurance fraud.

(ii) For Brett, resist the offer and, if necessary, cross-examine Hannah.

(c) [See above for Background. This background should be modified only to reflect that the state calls Hannah Goings-Waye as a witness.] When she is asked what the November 24 message said, Hannah will say, "I do not remember. But I do remember that the message seemed important enough that I should talk to Brett about it when I next saw him. So I cut-and-pasted it into a word processing document, then printed it out and put the printout into my purse. I did not save the electronic version of that file, but I did save the printout." That printed page is Exhibit 6.

(i) For the state, use Hannah's testimony and Exhibit 6 to prove that Brett burned his house and committed insurance fraud.

(ii) For Brett, resist the offer and, if necessary, cross-examine Hannah.

(d) The state calls Lynn Wallenstein, who brings Exhibit 5 (and its attachments, Exhibits 1-4) to the stand. Wallenstein's testimony, if allowed, will be consistent with Exhibit 3, the report s/he drafted.

(i) For the state, use Wallenstein's testimony and, if useful, some or all of Exhibits 1-5, to prove that Brett burned his house and committed insurance fraud.

(ii) For Brett, resist the offer(s) and, if necessary, cross-examine Wallenstein.

(e) The state brings the original of Exhibit 5 (and its attachments, Exhibits 1-4) to court.

(i) For the state, use Exhibit 5 and its attachments to prove that Brett burned his house and committed insurance fraud.

(ii) For Brett, resist the offer.

(3) *Goings-Waye v. Waye*: In this case, Hannah is suing Brett for divorce and for custody of the couple's two children. She asserts that Brett's alleged

burning of the house and insurance fraud helps to prove that he is unfit to be the custodial parent.

(a) [See above for Background. This background should be modified only to reflect that Hannah Goings-Waye calls herself as a witness.]

If asked, Hannah would testify that the November 24 message said something like, "Okay, I get it. I need money and I need to get out of this dump of a town. It is time to kill too birds with one stone."

    (i) For Hannah, use her testimony to prove that Brett burned his house and committed insurance fraud.

    (ii) For Brett, resist the offer and, if necessary, cross-examine Hannah.

(b) [See above for Background. This background should be modified only to reflect that Hannah Goings-Waye calls herself as a witness.] When she is asked what the November 24 message said, Hannah will say, "I do not remember." Your file contains Exhibit 1. It looks like a screenshot from a computer, though you have no idea how it got into your file or who put it there.

    (i) For Hannah, use her testimony and Exhibit 1 to prove that Brett burned his house and committed insurance fraud.

    (ii) For Brett, resist the offer and, if necessary, cross-examine Hannah.

(c) [See above for Background. This background should be modified only to reflect that Hannah Goings-Waye calls herself as a witness.] When she is asked what the November 24 message said, Hannah will say, "I do not remember. But I do remember that the message seemed important enough that I should talk to Brett about it when I next saw him. So I cut-and-pasted it into a word processing document, then printed it out and put the printout into my purse. I did not save the electronic version of that file, but I did save the printout." That printed page is Exhibit 6.

    (i) For Hannah, use her testimony and Exhibit 6 to prove that Brett burned his house and committed insurance fraud.

    (ii) For Brett, resist the offer and, if necessary, cross-examine Hannah.

(d) Hannah calls Lynn Wallenstein, who brings Exhibit 5 (and its attachments, Exhibits 1-4) to the stand. Wallenstein's testimony, if allowed, will be consistent with Exhibit 3, the report s/he drafted.

   (i) For Hannah, use Wallenstein's testimony and, if useful, some or all of Exhibits 1-5, to prove that Brett burned his house and committed insurance fraud.

   (ii) For Brett, resist the offer(s) and, if necessary, cross-examine Wallenstein.

(e) Hannah brings the original of Exhibit 5 (and its attachments, Exhibits 1-4) to court.

   (i) For Hannah, use Exhibit 5 and its attachments to prove that Brett burned his house and committed insurance fraud.

   (ii) For Brett, resist the offer.

(4) *Sullivan v. Focks*: In this case, Brett has testified as a fact witness to a car accident, on behalf of plaintiff Sullivan.

   (a) The cross-examination of Brett is underway.

      (i) For Focks, cross-examine Brett. You have a copy of Exhibit 5 and its attachments (Exhibits 1-4).

      (ii) For Sullivan, resist the use of Exhibits 1-5 and, if necessary, conduct related redirect examination.

   (b) Plaintiff Sullivan's case, including Brett's testimony, is completed. In her case-in-chief, defendant Focks calls Hannah to the stand. If allowed to do so, she will testify in a manner consistent with version (1)(a) of the problem, *supra*.

      (i) For Focks, conduct a direct examination of Hannah to attack Brett's credibility.

      (ii) For Sullivan, object to Hannah's testimony and, if necessary, cross-examine her.

   (c) Plaintiff Sullivan's case, including Brett's testimony, is completed. In her case-in-chief, defendant Focks calls Wallenstein to the stand.

239

(i) For Focks, conduct a direct examination of Wallenstein to attack Brett's credibility. You have a copy of Exhibit 5 and its attachments (Exhibits 1-4).

(ii) For Sullivan, resist the use of Exhibits 1-5 and, if necessary, cross-examine Wallenstein.

(5) *United States v. Waye, I*: In this case, the federal government is prosecuting Brett for alleged tax fraud. The government claims that Brett overstated his charitable deductions by claiming donations that he did not make. The alleged tax fraud concerns his [-5] tax return. Brett has not, and will not, testify in the case.

(a) The government calls Hannah to the stand during its case in chief. If allowed to do so, she will testify in a manner consistent with version (1)(a) of the problem, *supra*.

(i) For the government, conduct a direct examination of Hannah.

(ii) For Brett, object to Hannah's testimony and, if necessary, cross-examine Hannah.

(b) The government calls Wallenstein to the stand during its case in chief.

(i) For the government, conduct a direct examination of Wallenstein. You have a copy of Exhibit 5 and its attachments (Exhibits 1-4).

(ii) For Brett, resist the use of Exhibits 1-5 and, if necessary, cross-examine Wallenstein.

(6) *United States v. Waye, II*: In this case, the federal government is prosecuting Brett for alleged tax fraud. The government claims that Brett overstated his charitable deductions by claiming donations that he did not make. The alleged tax fraud concerns his [-4] tax return. Brett has testified in his defense.

(a) The cross-examination of Brett is underway.

(i) For the government, cross-examine Brett. You have a copy of Exhibit 5 and its attachments (Exhibits 1-4).

(ii) For Brett, resist the use of Exhibits 1-5 and, if necessary, conduct related redirect examination.

(b) The defense has rested. In its rebuttal case, the government calls Hannah to the stand. If allowed to do so, she will testify in a manner consistent with version (1)(a) of the problem, *supra*.

    (i)   For the government, conduct a direct examination of Hannah.

    (ii) For Brett, object to Hannah's testimony and, if necessary, cross-examine Hannah.

(c) The defense has rested. In its rebuttal case, the government calls Wallenstein to the stand.

    (i)   For the government, conduct a direct examination of Wallenstein. You have a copy of Exhibit 5 and its attachments (Exhibits 1-4).

    (ii) For Brett, resist the use of Exhibits 1-5 and, if necessary, cross-examine Wallenstein.

(d) The defense has rested. In its rebuttal case, the government has offered Exhibit 5 and its attachments (Exhibits 1-4) into evidence.

    (i)   For the government, articulate the argument for admission of Exhibit 5 and its attachments.

    (ii) For Brett, resist the offer.

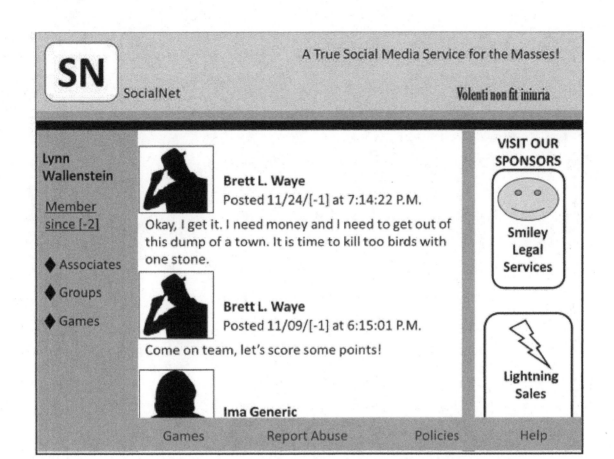

EXHIBIT
1

LSM

November 28, [-1]
Via Certified Mail

Claims Department
West Is Best Insurance
1846 Vine
Kansas City, MO

RECEIVED
Claims Dept.

11/29/[-1]

Claim#: 54A4734F

An accidental fire completely destroyed my home at 1917 5th Avenue in Chillocothe, Missouri, on November 26. I have moved with my to children into the Local Stay Motel, so the kids can stay in school here, at least for the rest of [-1]. But I expect to move, probably to Kansas City, after the first of the year.

Please let me know what I need to do to get paid for the loss to my home and for temporary living quarters here.

As you can imagine, my life is a shambles now. Please act on this immediately. Sincerely,

Brett L Waye

Brett L Waye

Local Stay Motel, 114 West Highway 36, Chillicothe, MO 64601 (660) 646-8822

EXHIBIT
2

West Is Best Insurance

To: Dale Jessen, Vice President of Claims

From:Lynn Wallenstein, Claims Adjuster II, Computer Specialist

Date: December 5, [-1]

RE: Insured Brett L. Waye, Claim No. 54A4734F, Policy G283B9Home

When I arrived back to work today after a two-week family vacation, I noticed a SocialNet status update that was apparently posted by Brett L. Waye on November 24, [-1], stating, "Okay, I get it. I need money and I need to get out of this dump of a town. It is time to kill too birds with one stone."

Brett Waye, his wife Hannah, and I were college fr classmates. We are members of the Mule Strong Group at SocialNet. That group consists largely of our classmates from the University of Central Missouri. Brett and I knew each other well in college. This helped me to sell him a homeowner's policy in Febuary of this year, when I was a sales agent.

Thus, I knew was probably our insured and I knew that any claim against his policy would hurt my loss rating from my days in sales and, therefore, reduce or eliminate my year-end bonus. I ran a quick check of the electronic file, which I am authorized to do as the Claims Department's Computer Specialist, for Brett L. Waye. In that file, I saw a letter from Waye on the stationary of the Local Stay Motel, 114 West Highway 36, Chillicothe, MO 64601, to the Claims Department, dated November 28, [-1], notifying the company of a fire at the Waye home at 1917 5th Avenue, Chillicothe, MO, on November 26, [-1]. Receipt of this letter resulted in our assignment of Claim No. 54A4734F to the claim on the homeowner's policy.

After seeing this letter, I realized that the November 24 status update could be of svalue, as it seemed to indicate that Waye was planning to start his house on fire. When I received training after transfering to the Claims Department in April of this year, company lawyers told us that one issue we face in litigation is proving that a particular person is the author of an email, social network status update, or other electronic communication, because people often claim that they did not write electronic

EXHIBIT
3

communications that others assumed were from them. Thus, I realized that it would be helpful if I could establish that Waye wrote the November 24 status update.

I am a friend of Brett Waye, but I do not condone insurance fraud. So I decided to see if I could tri entice him into disclosing his location. As you might know, at my suggestion the company paid to join a service called www.jokes and cartoons.com in October. That service, which we and other insurance companies subscribe to, helps us to find people.

At approximately 10:00 a.m. this morning, I sent a private em message replying to the November 24 message, saying "Brett: Hope all is okay. To cheer up, check this out: www.jokes and cartoons.com." Pursuant to our subscription, I sent a blind cc of my reply message too the Skip Tracing Department of www.jokes and cartoons.com.

A few Twenty minutes after I sent the private reply message, the original poster of the November 24 status update, presumably Brett Waye, clicked on www.jokes and cartoons.com. As soon as that person clicked on the www.jokes and cartoons.com website, the Skip Tracing Department at www.jokes and cartoons.com automatically sent me an email with the IP (Internet Protocol) address that was being used by that person to access the www.jokes and cartoons.com site. ꞏThe person who clicks on the www.jokes and cartoons.com site does not realize that this email with his or her IP address is being generated. That person just sees a website with jokes and cartoons.ꞏ

I copied the IP address I received via the automatic email from www.jokes and cartoons.com to my computer clipboard. Then I composed an email to FindEmNow, another computer service that we subscribe to, asking them to provide locat geographical information for the IP address, which I copied into my email.

As you may know, the IP address is associated with the internet service provider that the person using the internet is using. Thus, the IP address does not provide a precise location, such as a street address, for the person using the computer. But it does provide some information about that person's location, by providing information about the internet service provider the person was using.

Shortly after my email to FindEmNow, I received an automatic email from FindEmNow indicating that the IP address that I had provided was associated with the following geographical data:

West Is Best Insurance

<u>Sensitive Matter Report</u>

Probable State: Missouri   Probable County: Livingston

Probable City: Chillicothe Approx. Coordinates: 39.76° N, 93.56° W

I did a quick internet search for the latitude and longitude of Chilicothe, Missouri. That search revealed the coordinates to be 39.7931° north and 93.5519° west. My internet search also showed that the main highway through Chillicothe, U.S. 36, is south of the center of town. Thus, the approximate coordinates provided by FindEmNow are consistent with the probable location of the Local Stay Motel in Chillicothe. Thus, it appears that the writer of the November 24 status report was using an internet service provider, very possibly via free service provided by a motel like the Local Stay, in Chillocothe.

Because the process of locating physical addresses via IP addresses is not foolproof, one can never say with certainty that an IP address is associated with a particular physical location. However, based upon my expertise and experience, including familiarity with both the www.jokes and cartoons.com and FindEmNow services, it is my opinion that it is over 90% probable that the person who sent the November 24 status update referenced above was in Chillicothe, Missouri, probably at or near the Local Stay Motel, this morning when he linked to www.jokes and cartoons.com.com.

That person clicked the www.jokes and cartoons.com link because I sent it to him. Almost certainly, that person was Brett Waye. Waye knows me, so he trusted me when I sent him this link. Therefore, with the use of our www.jokes and cartoons.com and FindEmNow subscriptions, it is my opinion, to a level of certainty well over 90%, that we have established that the person who sent the November 24 status update was Brett L. Waye.

I hope you agree that this experience establishes the value of services like www.jokes and cartoons.com and FindEmNow. These are expensive services, to be sure. But we in the Claims Department often need to find witnesses, insureds, and others and to link emails and other electronic communications to specific persons.

Pursuant to company policy regarding sensitive matters, I have typed this report on one of the typewriters in our office, not on word processing software, and I have sent all emails regarding this

matter to the "Destroy Now" delete box, which makes them essentially untraceable (though, as we know, it is folly to ever suggest that something could never be restored). Pursuant to company policy regarding sensitive matters, I will run this manual report through the scanner, to create a pdf version that will be filed under the above-referenced matter, then place this original in your physical mailbox. I will make no paper copies.

I took a screenshot of the November 24 message and added it to the electronic file for Claim No. 54A4734F.

2345

Brett L. Waye
1917 5th Avenue
Chillicothe, MO 64601

Date _Feb 21 [-1]_

PAY
TO THE ORDER OF _West or Best Insurance Company_ $ | 982 46/100 |

Nine hundred eighty two and 46/100 ——————— DOLLARS   **FBIC**

MWE Bank of the State
101 Main St
Chillicothe, MO 64601

FOR _Annual Premium Policy #628 3139 Home_   _Brett L Waye_

⑆1234567890⑆   ⑈23 ⑊890 ⑉ 90   2345

EXHIBIT
4

Terry Sanderson, having been first duly sworn, testified as follows:

1)   I am the custodian of records at West Is Best Insurance Company of Kansas City, Missouri.

2)   In [-8], our company completed its transition to an electronic records system, whereby we retain records in electronic format, not paper. When we determine that a paper record should be maintained, we scan the document into a pdf file and retain the pdf version. In most instances, we discard the original paper version.

3)   Whenever possible, records produced by our company are created by a person who has knowledge of the information contained in the record, at or as close as reasonably possible to the time the person made the observation or received the information contained in the record.

4)   Our records are maintained and used in the ordinary course of our business, which involves marketing and issuing insurance policies and resolving claims under those policies.

5)   Today, i.e., January 4, [-0], I searched the electronic records for Claim No. 54A4734F, Policy G283B9Home, Insured: Brett L. Waye. That search revealed the following records, which are attached in printed form:

(1) Screen Shot of Social Net Post from Brett L. Waye, 11/24/[-1], 7:14:22 p.m.

(2) November 28, [-1], handwritten letter from Brett L. Waye, c/o Local Stay Motel, 114 West Highway 36, Chillicothe, MO 64601, to West Is Best Insurance

(3) West Is Best Insurance Sensitive Matter Report from Lynn Wallenstein, Claims Adjuster II, Computer Specialist, to Dale Jessen, Vice President of Claims

(4) Check for $982.46 from Brett L. Waye to West Is Best Insurance Company, dated February 21, [-1].

FURTHER AFFIANT SAYETH NOT.

DATED this the _4_ day of _January_ 20[-0]

Terry Sanderson
Terry Sanderson

SWORN to subscribed before me, this _4th_ day of _JANUARY_ 20[-0]

Pat Wozney PAT WOZNEY
NOTARY PUBLIC

My Commission Expires:

_9-16-[+4]_

NOTARY PUBLIC
NOTARY SEAL
Comm. Exp. 9/16
HOWELL COUNTY, STATE OF MISSOURI

EXHIBIT
5

257

Okay, I get it. I need money and I need to get out of this dump of a town. It is time to kill too birds with one stone.

EXHIBIT
6

V

IMPEACHMENT AND REHABILITATION

INTRODUCTION

The problems in this chapter represent cross-examination situations commonly encountered at trial. The problems principally involve impeachment with prior inconsistent statements, since these are the most common impeachment sources during trials.

For each problem assigned, you should be prepared to cross-examine or impeach the witness in a way that effectively presents the discrediting or impeaching evidence to the jury. If the witness does not admit to making an impeaching statement, be prepared to complete the impeachment by calling an appropriate prove-up witness. On redirect examination, be prepared to rehabilitate the witness by repairing or minimizing any damage done during the cross-examination.

Your instructor may modify the assignments and make specific additional assignments for these exercises.

The suggested background reading is Mauet, *Trial Techniques and Trials*, Chapter 6.

5.1 ORAL STATEMENT

This is a personal injury suit. Plaintiff, Charles Smith, charges that on June 1, [-2], the defendant, William Barnes, was driving his car in excess of the speed limit and that his speeding caused the car to leave the road, injuring Smith, who was a passenger in Barnes's car.

The case is now on trial. Plaintiff calls Rory Fletcher, a witness to the accident. Fletcher testifies that s/he had been sitting on the porch of his/her house at 4000 N. Clark Street for one hour when the Barnes car sped by. Fletcher says that the car was traveling 70 mph in a 55 mph zone. Fletcher says during that hour s/he drank a glass of iced tea, read the local newspaper, relaxed, and just watched the traffic.

You know from the police reports that a police officer, James Watson, interviewed Fletcher a few minutes after the accident. According to the report, Fletcher stated that the Barnes car was "traveling about 65 to 70 mph," and that s/he (Fletcher) "had just gone out on the porch moments before Barnes's car came by."

1.   For the defendant, cross-examine Rory Fletcher.
2.   Assume that Fletcher on cross-examination denies making the statements to Officer Watson. For the defendant, prove up the impeachment.
3.   For the plaintiff, conduct any necessary redirect examination.

5.2 ORAL STATEMENT

This is a personal injury suit. One year ago today, at 2:00 P.M., the car the defendant was driving struck a pedestrian, Mark Jones, as he was crossing Clark Street, a north-south street, at Elm Street. Jones claims that he was crossing Clark Street on the south side of Elm and was in the marked crosswalk at the time he was struck. The defendant says that Jones was outside the crosswalk.

The case is now on trial. Jones's friend, Rowan Tucker, testifies for the plaintiff on direct examination that s/he was walking directly behind Jones when the car struck Jones. Tucker says that Jones was within the crosswalk at the time of the collision.

You know from your investigation that about 20 minutes after the accident, Tucker told the investigating police officer, Sam Smith, that Mark Jones was "about five feet out of the crosswalk" at the time he was struck by the car.

1. For the defendant, cross-examine Rowan Tucker.
2. Assume that on cross-examination Rowan Tucker denies making the statement to Officer Smith. For the defendant, prove up the impeachment.
3. For the plaintiff, conduct any necessary redirect examination.

5.3   ORAL STATEMENT

This is a personal injury suit. The defendant, Alex Bevernick, struck the plaintiff, a pedestrian, with his/her car on June 15, [-1].

The case is now on trial. Bevernick testified on direct examination that s/he had the green light as s/he approached on Juniper Street and as s/he entered the intersection with Maple Street. S/he said that the light for his/her car was green when s/he struck the plaintiff. Bevernick claims the plaintiff was crossing against the red light.

You previously interviewed the owner of a hot dog stand located on the southwest corner of the intersection where the accident took place. The hot dog stand owner, Luigi Roviaro, told you that seconds after the accident, Bevernick walked over to the hot dog stand and said, "I should have stopped when the light started to change to red." Roviaro also told you that the plaintiff was sitting on a nearby curb holding his leg when Bevernick said that, but that the plaintiff was too far away to have heard the words. No one else was in the immediate vicinity.

1. For the plaintiff, cross-examine Alex Bevernick. Assume that Luigi Roviaro is available as a witness.

2. Assume that Bevernick, if asked, will deny saying those words to Roviaro. If asked what s/he did say, s/he will reply, "I told him that man was a fool to cross against the red light." For the plaintiff, cross-examine Bevernick. Prove up any impeachment.

3. For the plaintiff, cross-examine Alex Bevernick. Assume you have learned that Luigi Roviaro died one week ago.

4. For the defendant, conduct any necessary redirect examination.

5.4   WRITTEN REPORT OF ORAL STATEMENT

You represent Michael Morgan, who is accused of the murder of Bridget Wilson. On direct examination, Officer Kim O'Leary testified to an oral confession by Morgan. The officer's testimony was exactly the same as his/her report. Only O'Leary and Morgan were present at the time of the interview.

Morgan is 17 years old. This was his first arrest. He finished one year of high school before he dropped out to find work as a day laborer.

Morgan will testify later and will admit telling Officer O'Leary he went to Bridget Wilson's house and found Wilson asleep on the couch. However, he will deny saying any of the other things in the statement. Morgan will testify that he told O'Leary that when he found Wilson asleep on the couch, he turned around and walked out, going to the party by himself.

1.   For the defense, cross-examine Officer O'Leary.
2.   For the prosecution, conduct any necessary redirect examination.

INTERVIEW OF MICHAEL MORGAN

PLACE OF INTERVIEW: Homicide division
                                headquarters
                                2426 N. Damen Avenue

TIME INTERVIEW INITIATED: 2210 hours, 6/15/[-1]
TIME INTERVIEW TERMINATED: 2240 hours, 6/15/[-1]
PERSON CONDUCTING INTERVIEW: Investigator Kim O'Leary

     Subject named above was given Miranda warnings and
stated he understood and voluntarily waived his rights
and wanted to speak to reporting officer and did not
desire presence of lawyer.

     Subject then was asked extent of his knowledge
concerning death of Bridget Wilson. Subject responded by
saying he entered Bridget Wilson's home at approximately
1300 hours. By prearrangement, subject and Wilson were
to attend a party at a friend's house. When subject
arrived at Wilson's home, he found Wilson asleep on a
couch. Subject said he woke Wilson and asked her why she
was not ready for the party. He said she responded that
she was not going to the party or anywhere else with him.
Subject then became enraged and struck Wilson with an ash
tray. She fell to the floor, unconscious. When subject
observed her condition, he ran out of the house.

                              BY: *Kim O'Leary*
                              Reporting Officer

273

5.5 WRITTEN REPORT OF ORAL STATEMENT

William Hill has been charged with armed robbery. Robin Jacobs was a victim of the robbery. The case is now on trial.

On direct examination, Jacobs pointed to Hill and said, "That's the man who held us up. There's no doubt in my mind."

During direct examination, the prosecutor did not ask Jacobs about the lineup (although Helen Smith, the other victim, did testify about the lineup and her identification of the defendant). The lineup took place on May 6 of last year, the day of the robbery. Jacobs has not seen Hill since the lineup was conducted.

You have the attached FBI report about the lineup.

1. For the defense, cross-examine Robin Jacobs.
2. Should the prosecutor have asked Jacobs about the lineup on direct examination? If so, what questions should have been asked?
3. Assume that Jacobs on cross-examination denies making the statement noted in the police report. Complete the impeachment.
4. For the prosecution, conduct any necessary redirect examination.

FD-302 (10-6-[-5])

FEDERAL BUREAU OF INVESTIGATION

Date of transcription 5/6/[-1]

On 5/6/[-1] a lineup was conducted by FBI Special Agent Thomas Barnett at the Robbery headquarters building at Harrison and Kedzie, at approximately 4:00 p.m. (1600).

Individuals in the lineup were:

#1:	James Hudgins	IR# 362143
#2:	William Hill	IR# 482563
#3:	James Rhoades	IR# 482571
#4:	Frank Williams	IR# 399688
#5:	Richard Long	IR# Unknown

Viewing the lineup were Helen Smith and Robin Jacobs.

Each individual stepped forward, said the words: "This is a stickup. Don't do anything stupid," then stepped back. All five then made turns in unison.

Helen Smith and Robin Jacobs viewed the lineup through a one-way window. Immediately after the lineup each witness was interviewed separately. Smith stated that #2 was the robber. Jacobs said that #2 looked like the robber, but s/he couldn't be sure.

Investigation on 5/6/[-1]   at Robbery Headquarters Building at Harrison and Kedzie

File # 195-PX-87457-ROB   Date dictated 5/6/[-1]

By FBI Special Agent Thomas Barnett

This document contains neither recommendations nor conclusions of the FBI. It is the property of the FBI and is loaned to your agency. It and its contents are not to be distributed outside your agency.

5.6 JOB APPLICATION FORM

This is an action brought under this state's labor laws. Tracy Burke has sued TITE Security Co., Inc., claiming that s/he was unlawfully fired from his/her job because of union organizing activities.

TITE Security defends on the grounds that it fired Burke because s/he misrepresented certain material facts on his/her employment application.

It is the law of this jurisdiction that an employer may defend a wrongful discharge claim on the basis of facts unknown at the time of the discharge. However, the unknown facts must be sufficient for the trier of fact to reasonably conclude that the employee would not have been hired had the facts been known at the time of hiring. That is, the employee's misrepresentations or omissions must be material, directly related to measuring a candidate for employment, and relied on by the employer in making the hiring decision.

At trial, on cross-examination, Burke will admit the following:

(a)   S/he received a dishonorable discharge from the Marines in [-17].

(b)   While in the Marines his/her only duties were as a division clerk.

(c)   S/he was convicted of a battery charge in [-11].

Attached is the employment application form Burke submitted to TITE Security.

1.   For the defendant, cross-examine Tracy Burke.

2.   For the plaintiff, conduct any necessary redirect examination.

Tite Security, Inc.

APPLICATION FOR EMPLOYMENT

GENERAL INFORMATION

Name (Last)	(First)	(Middle Initial)	Telephone
Burke	Tracy		(555) 862-6920

Address (Mailing Address)	(City)	(State)	(Zip)	Other Telephone
1776 Reed Road	Lost Prairie	Blackacre	17742	( ) -

Previous Address (Mailing Address)	(City)	(State)	(Zip)	E-Mail
13 Maple Drive	Lost Prairie	Blackacre	17742	jarhead@www.com

POSITION

Position Desired	How did you learn about this position?
Guard	Saw Tite guards

EDUCATION AND TRAINING

High School Graduate ☐ Yes ☒ No   Name of Last High School Attended: Lost Prairie

College, Business School, Military (Most recent first)

Name and Location	Dates Attended Month/Year	Credits Earned Quarterly or Semester Hours	Other (Specify)	Graduate	Degree & Year	Major or Subject
Construction	From [-17] To			☐ Yes ☐ No		
M.P. in Marine Corps	From [-29] To [-17]			☐ Yes ☐ No		

VETERAN INFORMATION (Most recent)

Branch of Service	Date of Entry	Date of Discharge
Marine Corps	[-29]	[-17]

Highest Rank	Rank at Discharge	Special Training or Duties
PFC	PFC	M.P.

Do you receive any type of disability? If so, please describe	Type of Discharge
No	Honorable

Motor Vehicle Information

Do you have a valid driver's license? ☒ Yes ☐ No	State BLKACRE	Driver's License Number: 12-76-45-3	Expiration: [+2]

Do you own a vehicle? ☒ Yes ☐ No	Make and Year: RAV4 [-4]	Is the vehicle insured? ☒ Yes ☐ No	Type of Insurance: ☒ Collision ☒ Liability

Name of Insurance Company: EDNA Ins. Co.	Name of Insurance Agent: I.N. Shorinse

Other

Have you ever been refused a surety bond? ☐ Yes ☒ No	If yes, please provide details:
Have you ever been convicted of a crime? ☒ Yes ☐ No	If yes, please provide details: Minor traffic violations

I certify the information contained in this application is true, correct, and complete.

Signature of Applicant _Tracy Burke_   Date 7/15/[-8]

Please use the reverse side of this application to list the names of all your employers, dates of employment, and contact information of employers (you may list volunteer positions as well as paid positions, if you wish). List present or most recent employer first.

The Security, Inc.

APPLICATION FOR EMPLOYMENT

GENERAL INFORMATION

POSITION

EDUCATION AND TRAINING

VETERAN INFORMATION (If any, see p.00)

Signature of Applicant _____ Date _____

5.7 LETTER

This is a personal injury action arising out of an automobile accident that occurred on June 15 of last year at 3:00 P.M. Mackenzie Richardson, the plaintiff, sued the defendant, claiming that s/he had the green light at an intersection and that the defendant ran the red light, causing the accident.

The case is now on trial. Richardson testified on direct examination that s/he was traveling west on Maple toward the intersection with Main at 25 mph, the legal speed limit, and that the light for his/her street was green. As s/he was in the middle of the intersection s/he saw the light turn yellow. A split second later, the defendant's car, traveling southbound at a high rate of speed, crashed into the right side of his/her car.

You have subpoenaed records from the plaintiff's casualty insurance company, Acme Insurance. Among the records the company produces is a signed photocopy of the following letter to Richardson's lawyer. Richardson will admit that the signature is his/hers.

1. For the defendant, cross-examine Richardson.
2. For the plaintiff, conduct any necessary redirect examination.

July 18, [-1]

William Martin
Attorney at Law
404 Main Street

Re: Accident of 6/15/[-1]

Dear Mr. Martin:

As you requested during our previous discussions in
your office, I am writing to tell you the basic facts
surrounding the accident on June 15, [-1], in which I was
injured.

I was driving in my usual manner toward the intersection.
I was going west on Maple, approaching Main Street.
The light for me was green. I don't recall the speed I
was driving although I certainly don't make it a habit
of speeding. As I got near the intersection, the light
suddenly turned yellow. I couldn't really stop without
entering the intersection, so I kept going. The light
must still have been on yellow when the other driver
plowed into me, although I really didn't see the light
after I entered the intersection. He hit me on the right
side.

I trust when you have reviewed the matter you will file
suit against the other driver, since he refused to pay
for any of my expenses.

I am sending a copy of this letter to Elmer Jackson, my
insurance agent, since he wants to stay informed about
this.

Very truly yours,

Mackenzie Richardson

cc: Elmer Jackson
     Acme Insurance Company
     4403 Summit Ave.

285

5.8   Q AND A SIGNED STATEMENT

This is a murder prosecution. The case involves a fatal shooting that occurred on March 16 of last year at approximately 2:00 A.M., to which Angel Chaparro was a witness.

The case is now on trial. On direct examination, Angel Chaparro has testified to the following:

(a)   "One of the men who was shot was in my tavern one week before all this happened."

(b)   "I saw a man come out of the alley. He had a gun in his hand. He fired his gun at the men."

(c)   "The man who fired the gun was someone I had never seen before that night. I have not seen him since. But I had a good look at him that night."

Chaparro identifies the defendant, Julio Vega, as the shooter.

You have the attached statement of Angel Chaparro, given the same night of the shooting.

1.   For the defense, cross-examine Angel Chaparro.

2.   For the prosecution, conduct any necessary redirect examination.

Statement of Angel Chaparro, age 49, of 852 W.
Fletcher, second floor, #549-4575, Owner of the Grand
Slam tavern, 3740 W. Clark, #231-9555, relative to the
fatal shooting of Karl Ulrick, M/W age 42, of 1910 W.
Fullerton, and also the serious shooting of Wolfgang
Ulrick age 35, of 3817 N. Lakewood, incident occurred
at 3740 W. Clark St. (on Street) on 16 Mar., [-1], at
about 0200 hrs.

Typed and questioned by Inv. Richard Daletski #12123.
Statement taken at the Area #6 Homicide office, 3801
N. Damen.

1 Q. What is your name, address, occupation, and tele-
2   phone?
3
4 A. Angel Chaparro, 852 W. Fletcher, I own a tavern,
5   the Grand Slam tavern, 549-4575.
6
7 Q. Do you understand the English language?
8
9 A. I understand the language pretty well; if I don't
10   understand a word I'll ask you the meaning.
11
12 Q. How long have you owned the tavern called the Grand
13   Slam, located at 3740 W. Clark St.?
14
15 A. For six years.
16
17 Q. Do you own a gun, or keep a gun in your tavern?
18
19 A. No, sir.
20
21 Q. Do you know of any of your customers who own a
22   gun?
23
24 A. No. I wouldn't allow that. Guns make trouble. I
25   don't want no trouble with police. I have a license
26   to protect.
27
28 Q. Did anything unusual happen in your tavern tonight,
29   and can you recall how many customers were in your
30   tavern at closing time?
31
32 A. Everything was smooth; there were six customers
33   sitting at the bar.
34
35 Q. Did you know the six customers by name?
36
37 A. No. Not all of them. I knew four of them.

Continued statement of Angel Chaparro relative to
the fatal shooting of Karl Ulrick, and the serious
shooting of Wolfgang Ulrick.

1 Q. Are you referring to the four men that were taken
2   into custody by the police on the street in front
3   of your tavern?
4
5 A. Yes, Santos, Joe, Angel, and Manuel. We left the
6   tavern at the same time when I was closing.
7
8 Q. Calling your attention to the time you were
9   closing your tavern today at about 0200 hours, 16
10   Mar., [-1], did anything unusual happen outside of
11   your tavern?
12
13 A. Yes, I was putting the key in the tavern door to
14   lock it and I heard shooting, about four or five
15   shots. I then turned around and saw the blue light
16   flashing on the police cars. The police told me to
17   put my hands up, and handcuffed me. The Lieutenant
18   then came and I identified myself, and the
19   police took the handcuffs off and drove me to the
20   station.
21
22 Q. Did you see where the shots came from, and did you
23   see anyone with a gun?
24
25 A. No.
26
27 Q. Did you see the men who were shot, and if so did
28   you ever see them before tonight?
29
30 A. No, I never saw the men before.
31
32 Q. Other than hearing the four or five shots you
33   mentioned, did you see anything?
34
35 A. No, the entrance to my tavern is about four feet
36   from the sidewalk, and I could not see to either
37   side of me.
38
39 Q. Do you have any idea who might have done this
40   shooting?
41
42 A. No.

Continued statement of Angel Chaparro relative to
the fatal shooting of Karl Ulrick, and the serious
shooting of Wolfgang Ulrick.

1 Q. Are there any questions relative to this shooting
2   that I may have failed to ask you?
3
4 A. Not to my knowledge.
5
6 Q. After reading this statement, which consists of
7   three pages, and you find the statement correct as
8   you dictated, will you sign this statement?
9
10 A. Yes, I will.

_____
Angel Chaparro

5.9   DEPOSITION TRANSCRIPT

This is a negligence action. Martha Rose has sued Remy Brock for injuries she incurred when she was struck by the car Brock was driving on January 15, [-2], at the intersection of Belden Avenue and Clark Street. Belden Avenue runs east-west; Clark Street runs north-south. There are no traffic control signals or street markings at the intersection.

At trial, Rose has testified that before she stepped off the northeast corner of the intersection she looked to her left and saw no cars coming. She said she was walking slowly across Belden Avenue, moving directly south, and had reached the middle of the westbound lane when Brock's car "came out of nowhere" at a high rate of speed, hitting her and throwing her in the air about 20 feet in a due west direction.

At trial, Brock testified as follows on direct examination:

Q.   Which lane of Belden Avenue were you in?

A.   I was traveling in the westbound lane closest to the north curb of Belden Avenue. I was going about ten mph.

Q.   As you approached Clark Street, what happened?

A.   I saw the woman standing on the northeast corner of Clark and Belden. She just stood there for a few seconds. Then she suddenly ran off the curb and darted right into the path of my car. I could not avoid hitting her. There was simply no time.

Q.   What part of your car struck her?

A.   About the middle of the front.

Q.   How much time passed from the time you first saw her until you came into contact with her?

A.   It was just a few seconds.

You have the attached transcript of a deposition that Brock gave on January 15, one year ago.

1. For the plaintiff, cross-examine Brock.

2. For the defendant, conduct any necessary redirect examination.

3. Assume that Brock will not admit giving the answers contained in the deposition transcript. Prove up any impeachment.

DEPOSITION OF REMY BROCK,

Taken, under oath, on January 15, [-1], at office of
John Sawyer, 180 North LaSalle Street, Suite 630

<u>p. 16</u>

1 Q. (by John Sawyer, plaintiff's attorney) How fast
2   were you driving at the time you struck the
3   pedestrian?
4
5 A. About 20 mph.
6
7 Q. What was the highest speed you reached in the block
8   you traveled before the accident?
9
10 A. I never went more than 25 mph.
11
12 Q. When is the first time you saw the woman whom you
13   struck with your car?
14
15 A. When I hit her.
16
17 Q. Before the impact, did you ever see the woman?
18
19 A. No.
20
21 Q. (by Richard Jones, defendant's attorney) I want
22   to be sure I understand you. Did you see anything
23   before your car came into contact with the
24   plaintiff?
25
26 A. Yes, I did.
27
28 Q. I am talking about the time just before the
29   accident. What did you see?
30
31 A. I saw her come off the curb, running fast, and
      before I knew it, I hit her.

<u>p. 47</u>

I have read the questions and answers contained in
this 47-page deposition transcript and they truly
and accurately represent the questions asked and the
answers given.

Remy Brock
_____
Remy Brock

5.10 DEPOSITION TRANSCRIPT

This is a products liability action. Plaintiff is suing General Motors (GM), claiming he was injured because the hydraulic brake system on his [-7] car ruptured and failed during an emergency stop, causing an accident and resulting in injuries to himself and his car.

Plaintiff claims that the brake system on his car was defectively designed and was not the best and safest design that GM was capable of manufacturing in [-7]. GM's defense is based on "state of the art." It claims that the brake system design was the best one that GM was capable of incorporating into its [-7] production models.

The case is now on trial. The defense in its case calls as a witness Jess Reston, a GM design engineer whose principal work has been on brake systems, to testify on the design aspects of the [-7] GM brake system.

On direct, Reston testified to the following facts: GM spends millions of dollars each year on design research, its purpose being to design the most reliable and safe vehicle possible for the buying public. In its [-7] models, all GM cars had a single hydraulic brake system, using one master cylinder that connected to the brake drums on all four wheels. This design was a standard one in the industry, had been used for many years, was extremely reliable, and, viewing the brake system as a whole, was the best one readily available at that time. Through ongoing research, GM was able to modify that system to one using a dual hydraulic system, but that new system was not fully developed until the [-4] production model.

You have the attached deposition transcript of Jess Reston, given on July 14 of last year.

1. For the plaintiff, cross-examine Jess Reston.
2. For the defendant, conduct any necessary redirect examination.

Taken, under oath, on July 14, [-1],
at office of Frank Jones,
221 N. Dearborn St., #800

p. 47

1 Q. (by Frank Jones, one of plaintiff's lawyers) Mr./
2   Ms. Reston, you've been devoting your efforts to
3   brake systems designs for the past 15 years, is
4   that correct?
5
6 A. Yes.
7
8 Q. So, it's fair to say that you're familiar with the
9   progress of brake systems design at GM, as well as
10   the other manufacturers in the U.S., isn't it?
11
12 A. I like to think I am.
13
14 Q. If someone else came up with a new design or
15   system, you'd certainly consider it for use by GM,
16   wouldn't you?
17
18 A. Certainly, if it was feasible.
19
20 Q. Mr./Ms. Reston, in [-7] you knew that Alta Motors
21   had been working on a dual hydraulic brake system,
22   didn't you?
23
24 A. Yes.
25
26 Q. You were familiar with the design?
27
28 A. Yes.
29
30 Q. Its advantage is that if one of the two hydraulic
31   systems ruptures, the other one still functions,
32   doesn't it?
33
34 A. Yes.
35
36 Q. So a car can still be braked, right?
37
38 A. Yes, although obviously not as quickly or safely.
39
40 Q. Insofar as a rupture in any hydraulic brake line
41   was concerned, the dual system was a safer design
42   than GM's single brake system, wasn't it?

43 A. It was safer only in the event of a rupture in the
44   system.

   p. 48

45 Q. Well, if there was a rupture in one of the lines,
46   the Alta Motors car could still brake, while the GM
47   would have a total brake failure, wouldn't it?
48
49 A. Yes.
50
51 Q. The Alta Motors dual system, which was safer in
52   the event of a rupture, was known to you and GM in
53   [-7], right?
54
55 A. Well, we'd heard of it.
56
57 Q. Was there a reason GM didn't use the Alta Motors
58   system in [-7]?
59
60 A. We considered it, but we found that it simply
61   wasn't cost-effective.
62
63 Q. How much would it have cost to incorporate a dual
64   system in the GM cars in [-7]?
65
66 A. We estimated that it would be around $185.00 extra
67   per car.
68
69 Q. GM didn't install the dual system in its models
70   until the [-4] models, right?

   (by William Smith, one of the defendant's lawyers)
   Objection. Subsequent remedial measures are
   inadmissible.

71 Q. (by Frank Jones) Please answer the question.
72
73 A. That's correct.
74
75 Q. That was the same year the federal government first
76   required the dual system on all U.S. cars, isn't
77   it?
78
79 (by William Smith) Objection. Same basis.
80
81 Q. (by Frank Jones) Please answer.
82
83 A. Yes.

84 Q. (by William Smith, one of the defendant's lawyers)
85   What year did you first hear about the dual brake
86   system?

88 A. I think it was in [-9] or [-8].

90 Q. How long does it take GM to get a new design
91   concept actually included in a production model?

93 A. It usually takes three or four years from
94   preliminary design through inclusion in actual
95   production.

97 Q. Was cost the only reason why you didn't
98   incorporate the dual system in [-7]?

100 A. No. It just wasn't ready for production. There
101   just wasn't enough time.

_____

Jess Reston
July 28, [-1]

5.11 DEPOSITION TRANSCRIPT

This is a negligence action. Frank Johnson has sued Charles Smith for injuries he incurred when he was struck by a car driven by Smith at the intersection of State and Main Streets. Johnson, the driver of a Ford sedan, was going northbound on State Street when he collided with Smith, the driver of a Chevy sedan that was going eastbound on Main Street. The accident happened on June 1, [-2]. Plaintiff claims that defendant Smith ran the red light.

At trial Kelly Jones, a plaintiff witness, testified on direct examination as follows:

Q. Where were you standing?

A. I was on the southeast corner of State and Main, waiting for the light to change so I could cross State Street.

Q. What did you see next?

A. I saw the northbound Ford go into the intersection just as the light turned yellow for State Street. The eastbound Chevy ran the red light.

You have the attached transcript of a deposition that Jones gave on June 1, one year ago.

1. For the defendant, cross-examine Jones.

2. For the plaintiff, conduct any necessary redirect examination.

3. Assume that Jones will not admit giving the answers contained in the deposition transcript. Prove up any impeachment.

DEPOSITION OF KELLY JONES

Taken, under oath, on June 1, [-1], at office of Wilbur Harrison, 800 Congress Ave., Suite 201

<u>p. 18</u>

1 Q. (by Wilbur Harrison, defendant's attorney) Did you
2   see the two cars involved before they actually
3   collided in the intersection?
4
5 A. Yes.
6
7 Q. What did the Ford do?
8
9 A. Well, it was going northbound on State, and got to
10   about five feet before the intersection when the
11   light for State turned yellow.
12
13 Q. What did the Chevy do?
14
15 A. It was going eastbound on Main Street. It slowed
16   down as it approached the corner. It was going
17   about 20 mph when its light turned green. Then the
18   Chevy went into the intersection, and crashed into
19   the Ford.

I have read the questions and answers contained in this deposition and they accurately represent the questions asked and answers given.

_____
Kelly Jones

5.12   GRAND JURY TRANSCRIPT AND POLICE REPORT

This is a robbery prosecution. The defendant, William Hill, is charged with robbing a bank on May 2 of last year at about 9:00 A.M.

In the prosecution's case-in-chief a police investigator, Miley Byrne, testified as follows:

Q. Did you eventually arrive at William Hill's apartment on May 2?

A. Yes, sir.

Q. When did you arrive there?

A. It was about 11:30 in the morning.

Q. When you arrived at the apartment, what happened?

A. I knocked on the door. After a few seconds, Hill opened the door. He said, "What do you want?" I told him we were police officers and that he was under arrest. Then, before I had a chance to say anything else, he said, "I don't know anything about a robbery. I've been home with my brother all morning."

Q. What happened next?

A. I said, "Who said anything about this morning?" He just stared at us and didn't say anything else.

Q. Then what happened?

A. I put cuffs on him, gave him his *Miranda* rights, and took him to the station.

You have been provided with copies of the attached grand jury transcript and FBI report prior to trial.

1. For the defense, cross-examine Miley Byrne.

2. For the prosecution, conduct any necessary redirect examination.

IN RE: GRAND JURY INVESTIGATION GJ 867

MILEY BYRNE, having first been duly sworn,
testified on June 1, [-1], as follows:

<u>p.11</u>

1 Q. (by John O'Malley, Assistant District Attorney)
2   Later on, when you arrived at Hill's apartment, did
3   you have any conversation with him?
4
5 A. When he opened the door, I asked him his name, and
6   he said "William Hill." I told him he was under
7   arrest for armed robbery. He said: "Wait a minute,
8   you got the wrong guy. I've been home all morning."
9   He just kind of stared at me and wouldn't say
10   anything further.

FEDERAL BUREAU OF INVESTIGATION

Date of transcription: 5/2/[-1]

Investigator Miley Byrne was interviewed at the police headquarters and provided the following information:

After receiving the address of the car's registered owner, Byrne and his/her partner went to 6618 S. Sacramento, a three flat walk-up building, and went to the second floor. They knocked on the door and a man opened it. He was a white male, approximately 20-25, medium build. Byrne asked his name and he replied: "Billy Hill." He was advised he was under arrest for armed robbery. He replied: "You got the wrong guy. I've been here all morning with my brother." The other person having the same general description as Hill, was sitting on a sofa, but said nothing. Hill was then handcuffed, advised of his *Miranda rights*, and transported to police headquarters.

By   *Gerald Anino*
_____
Gerald Anino, FBI

5.13　POLICE REPORT

This is a murder and attempted armed robbery prosecution. Officer Terry O'Shea arrested the two defendants, Ernest Edwards and Frank Tucker. The case is now on trial.

On direct examination, O'Shea testified that s/he entered the apartment of Ernest Edwards and Frank Tucker at 405 W. Belmont Street in the late night hours of June 2 of last year. After giving *Miranda* warnings to both defendants and after receiving a statement from each defendant that he understood the warnings, O'Shea told them they were under arrest for the murder of Martha Talbert.

According to O'Shea, Tucker then said, "That dirty rat Ralston must have opened his big mouth." O'Shea then testified that s/he turned to Edwards and asked if he had anything to say. According to O'Shea, Edwards then said, "I ain't going to tell you a damned thing."

Attached is O'Shea's only police report concerning the arrests.

Assume there is no issue about the legality of the arrests, the adequacy of the *Miranda* warnings, or whether the defendants understood their rights.

1.　For the defense, cross-examine Officer O'Shea.
2.　For the prosecution, conduct any necessary redirect examination.

OFFENSE/INCIDENT REPORT

	Offense/Incident – Primary Classification					Secondary Primary Classification			Incident Code	Area of Occurrence
SCENE	Murder and Attempted Armed Robbery					Attempt Armed Robbery				12
	Address of Occurrence					Date of Occurrence (DD Month YY)			Time of Occurrence	
	117 Wilson Ave.					02 June [-1]			2200	
	Type of Location								Location Code	Unit Assigned
	☒ House/Townhome ☐ Apartment ☐ Business ☐ Other:									

All information, descriptions and statements in this entire report are approximations or summarizations unless indicated otherwise.

	Victims Name		Sex		Race		DOB	Occupation		Phone	E-Mail
VICTIM											
	Address							City		Other Contact Information	
	Parent/Guardian, if juvenile.									Phone	E-Mail

	Witness Name		Sex		Race		DOB	Occupation		Phone	E-Mail
WITNESS											
	Address							City		Other Contact Information	
	Parent/Guardian, if juvenile.									Phone	E-Mail

	Suspect #1 Name	Age	Sex	Race	Hgt	Wgt	Eyes	Hair	DOB	Phone	E-Mail
SUSPECT #1	Frank Tucker	19	M	W	5'2"	140	BR	BR	[-19]		
	Address							City		Alias or Gang Affiliation	
	405 Belmont									None	
	Parent/Guardian, if juvenile.									Phone	E-Mail

	Suspect #2 Name	Age	Sex	Race	Hgt	Wgt	Eyes	Hair	DOB	Phone	E-Mail
SUSPECT #2	Ernest Edwards	20	M	W	5'10"	200	BL	BR	[-20]		
	Address							City		Alias or Gang Affiliation	
	405 Belmont									None	
	Parent/Guardian, if juvenile.									Phone	E-Mail

	Owner of Involved Vehicle/Property	Year	Make	Style	VIN/Serial Number	Color	Lic. Plate
PROPERTY							
	Owner of Involved Vehicle/Property	Year	Make	Style	VIN/Serial Number	Color	Lic. Plate

	Narrative (Do not duplicate above information)
NARRATIVE	R/O learned through reliable informant that persons involved in murder and attempted armed robbery of Martha Talbert were Ernest Edwards and Frank Tucker, living at 405 W. Belmont. Officer O'Shea and other officers proceeded to location at 2330 hrs. Upon arriving at 405 W. Belmont the officers proceeded to the front entrance; Officer O'Shea knocked at the door and announced their presence. Upon no answer, hearing a radio in the background, the officers proceeded to force the apartment door open. Edwards and Tucker were found in their beds and were placed under arrest and given the Miranda warnings which were understood by the defendants. Upon entering the bedroom where the defendants were sleeping Officer O'Shea noticed a .38 caliber revolver serial no. 74969 in the open dresser drawer.

	First Officer on Scene		Date/Time Arrived	Time Departed	Area of Assignment
Police Personnel	O'Shea, Terry		02 June [-1]/2330		
	Officer Notifying Investigations		Date/Time Notified	Date/Time Investigations on Scene	
	Same				
	Officer Notifying Supervisor		Date/Time Notified	Date/Time Supervisor on Scene	
	Same				
	Reporting Officer's Name (PRINT)	Badge Number	Reporting Officer's Signature		
	Terry O'Shea	133	*Terry O'Shea #133*		
	Supervisor Approval Name (PRINT)	Badge Number	Supervisor Approval Signature		

FORM ID-10-T (3/[-2])

315

5.14 WRITTEN STATEMENTS

This is a personal injury and property damage action. On August 23, [-2], at about 4:00 P.M., a westbound Chevrolet driven by Sam Smith collided with a northbound Cadillac driven by George Gentry at the intersection of North Avenue, an east-west street, and Clark Street, a north-south street. Gentry sued Smith for $300,000 in damages, claiming it was Smith who went through the red light at a high rate of speed.

At the time of the collision, Jamie Taylor was waiting for a northbound bus on Clark Street. The bus stop is just off the southeast corner of the intersection. Taylor gave his/her name to the police officer who came to the scene.

The next day, Larry Long, an investigator for Smith's insurance company, went to Taylor's home, where Taylor gave the written statement that is attached. It is in Long's handwriting, except for those places where Taylor made initialed corrections and where s/he placed his/her signature.

The case is now on trial. Taylor is called as a witness by Gentry, the plaintiff. In summary, Taylor testifies that on August 23, two years ago, at about 4:00 P.M., s/he was standing at the southeast corner of North Avenue and Clark Street, waiting for a northbound Clark Street bus. S/he happened to look to the north when s/he saw a Chevrolet traveling in a westerly direction go through a red light at a high rate of speed. The Chevrolet collided with a Cadillac that was going north on Clark Street. The Cadillac had the green light.

Smith's lawyer has received credible information that two weeks before trial Taylor and his/her fiancé were seen having dinner with Gentry's lawyer, Otto Oglesby, at LeBrech, the city's most expensive restaurant. Oglesby was seen paying for the dinner. Taylor, if asked, will admit that this information is accurate.

Smith's lawyer also knows that on August 28, two years ago, Taylor made another statement to Oglesby in the presence of a stenographer. That statement, which is also attached, is entirely consistent with Taylor's trial testimony.

1   For the defendant, cross-examine Taylor.

2.   For the plaintiff, conduct any necessary redirect examination.

Statement of Jamie Taylor

I My name is Jamie A̶.̶ Taylor. ^Jt
I am 24 years old and single. I
work for General Electric as a
~~Maintenance clerk~~ ^Jt mechanic.

On August 23rd at ^about ^Jt 14pm. I
was at the corner of North
and Clark waiting for a bus to
take me to the far North side.
At that time, I was looking
toward the South for my bus
when I heard the screeching
of brakes. I looked toward the
corner, when I saw a Westbound Chevrolet collide with a
North-bound Cadillac. At the
time of the collision, the
traffic light was green for the
West-bound traffic.
        After the accident, I gave
my name and address to the
Police Officer. Signed Jamie Taylor

Witness: Larry Long Larry Long
Date: August 24 [-2]

*

319

STATEMENT OF JAMIE TAYLOR

Dated: 8/28/[-2]

1 Q. Jamie, I'm here today, August 28, [-2], to ask you
2   about the accident on August 23, [-2], involving a
3   George Gentry and a Sam Smith at the intersection
4   of North and Clark Streets. Present in your living
5   room at 857 Park Street are myself, Otto Oglesby,
6   you, Jamie Taylor, and the stenographer, Sharon
7   Dodd. Is that correct?
8
9 A. Yes.
10
11 Q. You understand that the stenographer is taking down
12   everything we say?
13
14 A. Yes.
15
16 Q. Jamie, please describe in your own words how the
17   accident happened.
18
19 A. Well, I was at North and Clark, on the southeast
20   corner, waiting for a bus. I was looking up Clark
21   Street when I noticed a Chevy, going west on North
22   Avenue, go into the intersection and ram into a
23   Cadillac going north on Clark.
24
25 Q. How fast was the Chevy going when it rammed into
26   the Cadillac?
27
28 A. The Chevy was going real fast, maybe 40 or 50 miles
29   per hour.
30
31 Q. Who had the green light when the collision
32   happened?
33
34 A. The Cadillac on Clark Street had the green light
35   when it happened.
36
37 Q. Jamie, is there anything you want to add to this
38   statement?
39
40 A. No, that's about the way it happened.

5.15 GRAND JURY TRANSCRIPT AND Q AND A SIGNED STATEMENT

This is a murder prosecution. The defendant, Ralph Tyler, is charged with the murder of a police officer on November 15, [-1].

The case is now on trial. Logan Richards is a prosecution witness. On direct examination, s/he testified that on the night of November 15, [-1], s/he was with the defendant, Ralph Tyler. Richards stated that at about 9:00 P.M. s/he and Tyler walked up to a marked police car parked on LaSalle Street, just south of Division Street, on the east side of the street. Richards stated that s/he, Richards, opened the passenger door of the squad car and that Tyler then pulled a .38 revolver from his jacket pocket, aimed it at the police officer sitting alone in the car, and fired, striking the officer in the head. Richards stated that all this was done pursuant to a conversation s/he had with Tyler about two hours before the shooting.

Richards became a state witness on December 15, one year ago, the day his/her pending armed robbery trial was scheduled to begin. S/he had been arrested for the armed robbery of a liquor store on November 29, two years ago, as s/he was running out of the store with a gun in his/her hand.

On December 15, one year ago, Richards contacted Robert Bench, the prosecutor in the pending armed robbery case, and reached the following agreement:

(a) S/he will be a prosecution witness in the murder case against Ralph Tyler.

(b) S/he will not be prosecuted for any crime relating to the murder case, so long as s/he tells the truth.

(c) S/he will be allowed to plead guilty to the lesser included offense of plain robbery in the pending case involving the liquor store.

(d) The prosecution will not recommend any specific sentence in the liquor store robbery case.

You have the attached written statement and grand jury transcript of Logan Richards. All constitutional issues concerning admissibility of the statements have been resolved in favor of the prosecution.

The prosecution has informed the defense that Richards was convicted of burglary four years ago, for which s/he served one year in the state penitentiary.

The sentence for armed robbery is 6 to 30 years. For plain robbery it is 3 to 7 years.

1. For the defense, cross-examine Logan Richards.
2. For the prosecution, conduct any necessary redirect examination.

STATEMENT OF LOGAN RICHARDS TAKEN ON
NOVEMBER 29, [-1], AT MAIN POLICE STATION

QUESTIONS ASKED BY OFFICER FRANK KELLY:

1 Q. What is your name?
2
3 A. Logan Richards.
4
5 Q. How old are you?
6
7 A. Twenty-five.
8
9 Q. I am going to ask you some questions about the
10   killing of a police officer on LaSalle and Division
11   Streets on November 15 of this year.
12
13 A. I don't know anything about that.
14
15 Q. Were you anywhere near that corner on November 15
16   of this year at about 9:00 P.M.?
17
18 A. No. I think I was at a movie on the south side with
19   my friend.
20
21 Q. Do you have any information at all about the
22   killing of a police officer on that night?
23
24 A. I didn't even know a police officer was killed
25   until you told me about it a few minutes ago.
26
27 Q. Do you have anything to add?
28
29 A. No. I have told you the absolute truth.
30
31 Q. Will you sign this statement after reading it if it
32   is true and accurate?
33
34 A. Yes.

Logan Richards
                       Logan Richards

Witnessed by:

Frank Kelly
Officer Frank Kelly

TRANSCRIPT OF TESTIMONY TAKEN DECEMBER 2, [-1]

(Reported by Claude Flynn,
Certified Shorthand Reporter)

LOGAN RICHARDS, having been first duly sworn, testified as follows:

1 Q. (by Robert Bench, Assistant County Prosecutor) What
2   is your name?
3
4 A. Logan Richards.
5
6 Q. Do you realize you are now under oath?
7
8 A. Yes, sir.
9
10 Q. I call your attention to November 15 of this
11   year, at around 9:00 P.M. Where were you at that
12   time?
13
14 A. I spent that entire evening on the south side. I
15   think I went to a movie with my friend.
16
17 Q. Were you anywhere near Division and LaSalle Streets
18   on that date?
19
20 A. No, sir. I was nowhere near that neighborhood any
21   time that day.
22
23 Q. Do you have any information about the killing of a
24   police officer at Division and LaSalle Streets on
25   November 15 of this year, or any other day?
26
27 A. No. I don't know anything about it.
28
29 Q. Have you heard anything about the killing of a
30   police officer on November 15 of this year, at
31   around Division and LaSalle Streets?
32
33 A. The first I heard of that was when the policeman
34   told me on the day I was arrested.
35
36 Q. Is there anything you wish to add?
37
38 A. No. I have told you the honest-to-God truth.

5.16   DEPOSITION TESTIMONY

This is a personal injury case. The defendant, Whitney Bell, is alleged to have struck nine-year-old Carl Heman with his car one year ago today, at 2:20 P.M., as the boy crossed Taylor Street from west to east at a point midway between Third and Fourth Avenues. The boy's mother, the named plaintiff, alleges Bell was driving his/her car at a speed well above the 25 mph speed limit on Taylor Street. Bell denies s/he was speeding and claims the accident happened because the boy ran out onto Taylor Street from between two parked cars.

At trial, on direct examination, Bell testified as follows:

Q.   How many lanes of traffic are there on Taylor Street?

A.   There is one parking lane and one traffic lane on each side, a total of four lanes.

Q.   In what direction were you going?

A.   I was going south, toward Fourth Avenue.

Q.   Were there any cars in the parking lane on the west side of Taylor Street at the time of the accident?

A.   Yes. Cars were parked all the way from Third to Fourth Avenue. That's a residential area.

Q.   When did you first see the boy you struck?

A.   When he ran in front of my car.

Q.   How fast were you going when your car struck the boy?

A.   I know I wasn't going more than 15 miles per hour.

Q.   How do you know that?

A.   Because I never go more than that on those residential streets during the day.

Q.   Did you check your speedometer?

A.   No, I don't like to take my eyes off the road in those neighborhoods.

Six months before he testified at trial, Bell's deposition was taken at the offices of plaintiff's lawyer, located at 100 South Clark Street. At the deposition, Bell testified as follows:

Q. (by plaintiff's lawyer) Mr. Bell, as you traveled south on Taylor Street toward Fourth Avenue, was anything located to your right?

A. I don't remember.

Q. How fast were you going when your car struck the boy?

A. I was going the speed limit, 25 miles per hour. I know because I checked my speedometer just after I passed Third Street.

1. For the plaintiff, cross-examine Bell.

2. For the defendant, conduct any necessary redirect examination.

5.17 DIAGRAM

This is a criminal prosecution. Arthur Martin, the defendant, is charged with the attempted murder of police officer Fran Blue.

One year ago today Officer Blue and his/her partner, Lou Redd, received a call on their police radio telling them to go to 6050 S. Woodlawn Avenue because the police had received a call that there was a man with a gun in the hallway of that building.

The officers entered the building and walked up the stairs to the second floor, where they eventually encountered Martin, who lived on that floor. Martin had a gun. There was an exchange of gunfire. Martin was shot in the shoulder. Blue was shot in the right arm just above the elbow, on the rear part of the arm. All three persons fired shots.

At the preliminary hearing, the following testimony was elicited:

Officer Blue

Q. Where was the defendant when you saw him for the first time?

A. He opened the door of his apartment. He had a gun in his hand and was aiming it at us. That's when the shooting began. Martin was right in his doorway. He never moved.

Q. How much time went by between the time you first saw the defendant and the time the shooting began?

A. Only a second or so.

Q. Where were you when the shooting began?

A. I was right in front of Martin's door, my left shoulder against the east wall, facing south and a little west, toward Martin.

Q. Where was Officer Redd at that time?

A. S/he was directly to my right, no more than two feet away.

Q. Were you two in the same place when the shooting stopped?

A. Yes, we were.

Q.   Where was the defendant when you first saw him?

A.   He had opened his apartment door. The door opens out into the hallway. He was just about in the doorway, toward the banister side of the hall. That's when I saw he was aiming at us. We all started firing.

Q.   Did the defendant ever move from the time you first saw him until the shooting ended?

A.   No.

Q.   Where were you when the shooting began?

A.   I was in the northeast corner of the hallway, opposite the defendant's door, facing the defendant.

Q.   Where was Officer Blue?

A.   S/he was directly to my right, with one foot on the first step and the other foot on the hallway floor.

Q.   Did either of you two move from the time you first saw the defendant until the time the shooting stopped?

A.   No.

The case is now on trial. The officers will testify on direct examination consistently with their preliminary hearing testimony. The attached diagram has already been admitted in evidence through the testimony of the police artist who prepared it.

1.   For the defense, cross-examine Officers Blue and Redd, using the attached diagram to demonstrate the conflict between the two officers. (If no document camera is available in the courtroom, prepare an appropriate enlarged diagram for class.)

2.   For the prosecution, conduct any necessary redirect examination of the officers.

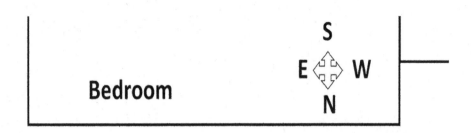

Bedroom

S

E W

N

Hall

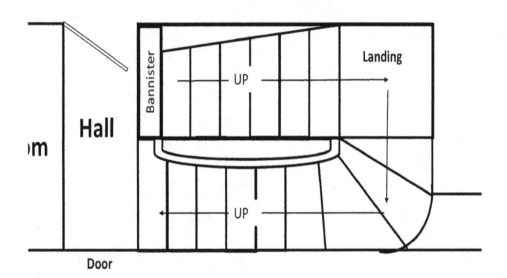

Bannister

Hall

UP

Landing

om

UP

Door

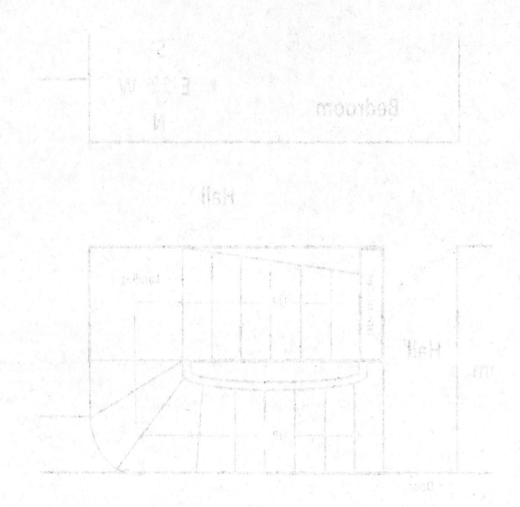

5.18   GRAND JURY TRANSCRIPT

This is a bank robbery prosecution. Haley Smith was the teller at the Maple Avenue Bank when it was robbed on May 18 of last year.

Four weeks later, on June 18, s/he testified before the grand jury. The transcript of the grand jury testimony is attached. At the time s/he testified before the grand jury, the defendant, Mark Bell, had not yet been arrested. Smith had been shown several police photographs, but none was of Bell.

Four days after the grand jury proceeding, Bell was arrested. That night, FBI Agent Sidney Goldstein called Smith. He asked him/her to appear in the preliminary hearing court the next morning. He told him/her someone had been arrested in connection with the bank robbery. The next morning, June 23, Smith and Agent Goldstein sat in the courtroom from about 9:00 A.M. until about 10:15 A.M. Five unrelated cases were called and disposed of during that time. At about 10:15 A.M., Smith heard Bell's name called by the clerk of the court and then s/he heard his/her name called. S/he looked up when his/her name was called and saw the uniformed deputy walk to a door at the side of the courtroom. When the door opened, the deputy brought Bell to the front of the judge's bench. Smith then said to Agent Goldstein, "That's the man." Then s/he and Agent Goldstein walked to the other side of the front of the judge's bench. Bell had not been shown to Smith, in person or by photograph, before his case was called. Smith will admit, if asked, that these facts are true.

Bell, the defendant, is a white male, 5' 8" tall, 31 years old, and weighs 178 pounds.

The case is now on trial. **[The instructor will provide the direct examination of Smith in class.]**

1.   For the defense, cross-examine Smith.
2.   For the prosecution, conduct any necessary redirect examination.

TRANSCRIPT OF TESTIMONY TAKEN JUNE 18, [-1]

(Reported by Genevieve Dodd,
Certified Shorthand Reporter)

HALEY SMITH, having been called as a witness and having been duly sworn, testified as follows:

1 Q. (by Gregory Jones, Assistant U.S. Attorney) Mr./Ms.
2   Smith, please describe what the man who handed you
3   the demand note looked like.
4

5 A. Well, he was a white man, maybe six feet tall, in
6   his late teens or early 20s, 180 pounds, dressed in
7   blue jeans.
8

9 Q. Did you notice anything unusual about his face or
10   appearance?
11

12 A. No, he didn't have any scars or really unusual
13   features that I noticed.
14

15 Q. Did you notice anything about his coat?
16

17 A. Well, he had his hand in his pocket and you could
18   tell he had something brown in his hand. I couldn't
19   really see what it was because his hand was over
20   it, but naturally I had to assume it was a gun.
21

22 Q. What happened next?
23

24 A. He told me to go to the back office, which I did,
25   and he told Mr. Jacobs, the branch manager, "This
26   is a stickup, don't move."
27

28 Q. Then what happened?
29

30 A. Well, he made us sit facing the wall, so we
31   couldn't see him. Mr. Jacobs kept asking him to
32   relax and not to do anything foolish.
33

34 Q. How long were you there?
35

36 A. It seemed like around five minutes or so.
37

38 Q. What happened next?
39

40 A. After a while we couldn't hear anything, so I
41   thought they had left. I then reached over to the
42   desk and triggered the alarm.

5.19 POLICE REPORT

The defendant, James Watts, is charged with the burglary of a store at the corner of LaSalle and Madison Streets. The case is now on trial. Other prosecution witnesses have testified that they saw two men run out of the burglarized store and jump into a black Chevrolet. They will say that the Chevrolet took off southbound on LaSalle at a high rate of speed, chased by a police car. They cannot identify the defendant as one of the burglars.

Officer Fran McCurry then testified on direct examination:

Q. On June 15 of last year, at about 3:30 P.M., what happened?

A. I was with my partner in our squad car. We were parked on LaSalle Street, facing south. I looked up and saw the two male whites running south on LaSalle Street, from Madison Street.

Q. What did you see the men do?

A. I saw them get into a black Chevrolet about halfway down the block, between Madison and Monroe. The car started going south.

Q. Could you see the license plate on the car?

A. Not at that time. All I could tell was that it was an Illinois plate. I did not see the plate until the arrest was made.

Q. What did you do when you saw all this?

A. We pulled up alongside the Chevrolet, and I motioned for the men to stop.

Q. Did they stop?

A. No, they sped up. We chased them in our squad car. My partner was driving. I was the passenger.

[The instructor will provide additional direct examination in class at this point.]

Q. When you left the area of 27th and State, what happened?

A. The chase continued, but we finally curbed the car at 31st and Parnell.

Q. Who was in the car at that time?

A. There was only one person in it, the defendant. We placed him under arrest.

Q. At any time during the chase were you able to see the faces of the men in the Chevrolet?

A. No, I didn't see either man's face during the chase. The first face I really saw was that of the defendant when I arrested him at 31st and Parnell.

You have Officer McCurry's signed report, which is attached. It is the only report McCurry made of the event.

1. For the defense, cross-examine Officer McCurry.

2. For the prosecution, conduct any necessary redirect examination.

ARREST REPORT

Name (Last)	(First)		(Middle)		Arrest Date			Arrest Time			Primary Arresting Officer Name / #	
Watts	James		-		15 June [-1]			1530			Fran McCurry / 1724	

Alias		Age	Sex	Race	Hgt	Wgt	Eyes	Hair	DOB	Phone	E-Mail
		19	M	W	508	140	BR	BR	15 June [-19]	Unknown	Unknown

Address of Arrest			City	SSN
31st and Parnell			Chicago	278-43-6071

Address	City	Gang Affiliation/Moniker
Unknown		None

Vehicle of Arrestee Held?	Year	Make	Style	VIN	Color	Lic. Plate
☒ Yes ☐ No	[-5]	Chevrolet	Car		Black	860-971

Victims Name	Sex	Race	DOB	Occupation	Phone	E-Mail
Marshall Co.						

Address	City	Other Contact Information
La Salle & Madison		

Parent/Guardian, if juvenile.	Phone	E-Mail

Charges

Charge Number	Statute or Warrant Number	Title or Description

Narrative
Undersigned officers assigned to area 105 observed two M/W's running from Madison on La Salle southbound. Reporting officers observed suspects get into a [-5] Chevrolet, black sedan, State License #860-971. Officers then pulled up next to the car and motioned suspects to stop. Suspects then took off at a high rate of speed. Chase proceeded south and the car was apprehended, but passenger was missing. Driver arrested, transported to station. Officer McCurry notified Jones, unit 24, in the investigations unit of the incident.

Primary Arresting Officer Name / Badge #	Area Assignment
Fran McCurry / 1724	105
Secondary Arresting Officer Name / Badge #	Area Assignment
William Simon / 276	105
Arrestee Transported to:	Receiving Officer Name / Badge #
☐ County ☒ District ☐ Southern ☐ Temp:	Skyler Tonkanita / 1032

State Warrant Check		Federal Warrant Check		Medical Staff	
Called In	Received	Called In	Received	Notified	Intake Completed

(Clearly Print Your Initials and Badge Number in the appropriate block)

FORM PD 11420 (7/[-2)

5.20 WRITTEN REPORT OF ORAL STATEMENT

This is an armed robbery prosecution. Ash Zamet was the only person in the store who saw the offender's face. Rudolph Jensen has been arrested and is on trial.

During direct examination, Zamet testified s/he was 45 years old, married, and had worked at the Schwartz Convenience Store for ten years. S/he told how a man walked into the shop, came up to the counter where s/he was standing, and pulled a revolver from his overcoat pocket. He aimed the gun at his/her stomach and said, "This is a stickup." Then he ordered him/her to open the cash register. S/he did. He told him/her to put the contents of the register in the paper bag he was carrying. S/he did. Then he turned and ran out of the store.

These questions were asked on direct examination:

Q. From the time he entered until the time he left, how long was the man in the store?

A. About two minutes. No less than that.

Q. Can you describe the man who aimed the gun at you?

[The instructor will provide additional direct examination in class at this point.]

Q. Do you see that man in court today?

A. Yes, I do. He is right over there. (The witness points to the defendant, who fits the description just given.)

Zamet will also admit the following facts if asked: S/he met with the prosecutor in his office the day s/he testified and the day before s/he testified. Four weeks ago, the defense lawyer went to Zamet's house in the company of a court reporter. S/he identified himself/herself, told him/her why s/he was there, and asked him/her questions about the robbery, which s/he refused to answer. Zamet then ordered him/her out of the house.

1. For the defense, cross-examine Zamet.

2. For the prosecution, conduct any necessary redirect examination.

3. Assume that Zamet denies or does not remember the conversation with the police officers. For the defense, call one of the officers to complete the impeachment.

OFFENSE/INCIDENT REPORT

SCENE	Offense/Incident – Primary Classification				Secondary Primary Classification		Incident Code	Area of Occurrence
								2009
	Address of Occurrence				Date of Occurrence (DD Month YY)		Time of Occurrence	
	2436 West Devon				15 Jan [-1]		1550	
	Type of Location						Location Code	Unit Assigned
	☐ House/Townhome ☐ Apartment ☐ Business ☐ Other:							

All information, descriptions and statements in this entire report are approximations or summarizations unless indicated otherwise.

VICTIM	Victims Name	Sex	Race	DOB	Occupation	Phone	E-Mail
	Schwartz Convenience Store					742-5313	
	Address			City		Other Contact Information	
	Parent/Guardian, if juvenile.					Phone	E-Mail

WITNESS	Witness Name	Home Address			Phone	E-Mail
	Ekter, Barbara	7250 North Western			973-2762	(B) 742-5313
	Witness Name	Home Address			Phone	E-Mail
	Schwartz, George	5029 North Central Park			749-4419	(B) 742-5313
	Witness Name	Home Address			Phone	E-Mail
	Zamet, Ash	4250 North Marine Drive			525-9027	(B) 742-5313

SUSPECT #1	Suspect #1 Name	Age	Sex	Race	Hgt	Wgt	Eyes	Hair	DOB	Phone	E-Mail
	Drk Overcoat - Blue & Green Shirt				600	165	Unk	Dr Brn			
	Address							City		Alias or Gang Affiliation	
	Carrying brown paper bag							Slender Build		Dk Brn Mustache	
	Parent/Guardian, if juvenile.									Phone	E-Mail
	Displayed a gun										

SUSPECT #2	Suspect #2 Name	Age	Sex	Race	Hgt	Wgt	Eyes	Hair	DOB	Phone	E-Mail
	Address							City		Alias or Gang Affiliation	
	Parent/Guardian, if juvenile.									Phone	E-Mail

PROPERTY	Owner of Involved Vehicle/Property	Year	Make	Style	VIN/Serial Number	Color	Lic. Plate
	Owner of Involved Vehicle/Property	Year	Make	Style	VIN/Serial Number	Color	Lic. Plate

NARRATIVE

Narrative (Do not duplicate above information)

P-205 sent by CC to 2435 W. Devon re: man with a gun. R/D's spoke to Schwartz, George J., the owner of Schwartz Convenience Store and two employee's #1) Ekter, Barbara and #2) Zamet, Ash. Zamet stated that the offender (description above) entered the store, walked over to Zamet, pointed a gun at Zamet's stomach and announced, "this is a stick up." The offender then ordered Zamet to open the cash register.

Police Personnel	First Officer at Scene		Date/Time Arrived	Time Departed	Area of Assignment
					2005
	Officer Notifying Investigations		Date/Time Notified	Date/Time Investigations on Scene	
	Reporting Officer's Name (PRINT)	Badge Number	Reporting Officer's Signature		Date/Time
	D. Peterson	13441			15 Jan [-1] /1610
	Reporting Officer's Name (PRINT)	Badge Number	Reporting Officer's Signature		Date/Time
	D. Shehn	5709			15 Jan [-1] /1610
	Supervisor Approval Name (PRINT)	Badge Number	Supervisor Approval Signature		Date/Time
	Gallager	5201			15 Jan [-1] /1800

FORM CDP 1113 (3/[-2)

5.21 DEPOSITION

This is a civil suit for damages arising out of allegedly negligent medical treatment rendered to 11-month-old Jonathan McKinley at the East Suburban Medical Center on March 22, [-2]. The plaintiff, Jonathan's mother, claims failure of the emergency room physician, Dr. Eric Dutton, to recognize and treat symptoms of congestive heart failure resulted in Jonathan's death. Dr. Dutton had diagnosed Jonathan as having a "touch of pneumonia." He prescribed antibiotics and sent Jonathan home, where he died of a heart attack the next morning.

Experts on both sides agree that if Jonathan had been timely and properly treated he would have lived a normal life expectancy, without disability.

Dr. Dutton brings a third-party action against Dr. Selwyn Cook, the Medical Center radiologist. Dr. Dutton claims Dr. Cook's conduct was the sole proximate cause of Jonathan's death because s/he failed to notify the emergency room staff that X-rays taken of Jonathan on March 22, [-2], showed findings of interstitial infiltrates, cardiomegaly, mild air trappings, and pleural effusion, all of which are consistent with congestive heart failure.

Dr. Cook's deposition, taken November 15, [-1], at the plaintiff's lawyer's office at 300 N. Clark Street, contains the following:

Q. Did you examine Jonathan's X-rays taken on March 22?

A. Of course.

Q. Didn't you see findings that were consistent with congestive heart failure?

A. They were consistent with congestive heart failure, but that is a condition we rarely see in a child of Jonathan's age. It was my opinion that the X-ray findings indicated viral pneumonia, although I could not rule out congestive heart failure. That's what I said in my report.

Q. Why didn't you call Dr. Dutton to report your findings?

A. I tried to call Dutton, twice in ten minutes, but I couldn't get through to the emergency room. That's when I put a copy of my report in the interdepartmental mail, which usually gets delivered within an hour.

Q. Did it get delivered within the hour?

A. I don't know. My shift was over by then, so I went home. I never saw the report again. It must have been lost. We can't find it.

At trial, Dr. Cook is called as an adverse witness by Dr. Dutton's lawyer, and testifies as follows:

Q. Dr. Cook, you examined Jonathan's X-rays, didn't you?

A. Yes.

Q. You found interstitial infiltrates, cardiomegaly, mild air trappings, and pleural effusion?

A. Yes.

[The instructor will provide additional adverse examination in class at this point.]

1. For Dr. Dutton, continue the adverse examination.
2. For Dr. Cook, conduct any necessary examination.

348

5.22   ARMED ROBBERY IDENTIFICATION

This is a criminal prosecution. Melvin Simpson is charged with the armed robbery of Campbell Burke.

As Burke walked past the alley at 6140 S. Park Street at 9:45 P.M. on February 1, [-1], a man stepped out of the alley and pointed a gun at his/her head. The man said, "Give me your wallet or I will blow your head off." Burke reached into [his back pocket]/[her purse], pulled out his/her wallet, and handed it to the man. The man took the wallet, turned, and ran into the dark alley. Burke ran to a nearby liquor store, where s/he called the police.

Detective O'Brien met Burke at the liquor store at 10:15 P.M. O'Brien interviewed Burke. The results of that interview are contained in O'Brien's report, which states, in part, the following:

> Victim related that the light from a streetlight about ten feet away allowed him/
> her to see the offender's face for three or four seconds. R/O asked victim for
> a complete description of the man who robbed him. Victim responded that
> offender was 5' 6" tall and weighed about 140 pounds. Victim described the
> gun as an automatic with a short, black barrel.

A preliminary hearing in the case was held on May 5, [-1]. Campbell Burke testified, and on cross-examination testified as follows:

Q.   You saw the face of the man who robbed you for about three or four seconds?

A.   Yes. He is sitting down right over there, at the table.

Q.   For the record, Your Honor, the witness has pointed to the defendant, Melvin Simpson. Mr./Ms. Burke, how would you describe Mr. Simpson?

A.   He is about 6' tall, heavy, maybe 200 pounds, and he has a thick mustache— the same way he looked when he robbed me.

Q.   What is your height and weight?

A.   I'm 5' 7", and I weigh about 145 pounds.

Q. Before today, were you ever asked to look at any photographs or persons to attempt to identify the man who robbed you?

A. Yes. About a month after I was robbed, Detective O'Brien came to my house and showed me a photograph. It was the guy who robbed me.

Q. How many photographs did he show you?

A. Just the one of the guy who robbed me.

Q. Did the man in the photograph have a thick mustache?

A. Yeah. Same as now.

The case is now on trial. On direct examination Burke was asked to look around the courtroom to determine if the man who robbed him was present. Burke pointed to the defendant, Melvin Simpson, who was sitting next to his lawyer at counsel table. Simpson is 6' 1" tall and weighs 210 pounds. He has a thick mustache. The prosecutor then asked:

Q. When did you first identify the defendant as the man who robbed you?

A. In early April of last year, when Detective O'Brien came to my home and showed me some photographs.

Q. How many photographs did the detective show you?

A. He showed me six or seven photographs of different men. I picked out the defendant right away. He was the only one with a mustache.

1. For the defendant, cross-examine Burke.
2. For the prosecution, conduct any necessary redirect examination.

VI

EXPERTS

VI

EXPERTS

INTRODUCTION

The problems in this chapter represent basic situations involving experts who frequently appear at trial. The problems cover expert qualifications, basic direct and cross-examination situations, impeachment with treatises, and more complex expert situations.

In addition to these problems, three of the trials in Chapter 9 contain expert witnesses who can be the bases for separate problems. Trial 9.2 has contractors, Trial 9.4 has product design experts, and Trial 9.14(C) has police use of force experts. These trials also feature opposing experts, so you will have an opportunity to see how the examinations of these experts are interrelated.

Your instructor may modify the assignments and make specific additional assignments for these exercises.

The suggested background reading is Mauet, *Trial Techniques and Trials*, Chapter 8.

6.1 MEDICAL EXPERT QUALIFICATION

This is a contested civil commitment proceeding brought by the children of Sadie Thompson, in which the children allege that their mother, because of increasing senility, is no longer able to care for either herself or her property.

Pursuant to court order, petitioners have retained Dr. Robin Schultz to conduct a psychiatric evaluation of Thompson. Along with his/her report, Dr. Schultz submits a curriculum vitae.

At the hearing on the petition, the petitioners call Dr. Schultz as a witness.

1. For the petitioner, conduct a direct examination of Dr. Schultz.
2. For the respondent, cross-examine Dr. Schultz.

Robin Schultz, M.D.
100 Main Street

November 15, [1]

Robert Kelly, Attorney at Law
42 W. Madison

Re: Sadie Thompson
     Clinical Evaluation Report

Dear Mr. Kelly:

I have examined Sadie Thompson per your request.
The examination took place November 1, [-1], in my
offices. It lasted 30 minutes, and consisted of examination and interview. I conducted the usual psychiatric
and neurological tests.

It is my opinion that Mrs. Thompson suffers from
senile dementia, moderate stage. This diagnosis reflects
a chronic organic brain syndrome associated with gener-
alized atrophy of the brain due to aging. I found elements of self centeredness and childish emotionality.

In my opinion, Sadie Thompson is unable to care for
herself or her property, which, as you informed me, is
quite extensive and varied.

My fee for services to date is $3,000. I will bill
you for any required court time at my usual rate of $800
per hour.

My curriculum vitae is enclosed.

Very truly yours,

Robin Schultz, M.D.

CURRICULUM VITAE
Robin Schultz, M.D.

Occupation: Physician, specializing in forensic psychiatry.

Present practice: Elgin Mental Health Center (assistant director), private practice, Chicago, specializing in evaluation of psychotic conditions, particularly in criminal cases.

Teaching positions: Associate clinical professor of psychiatry, Loyola University Medical School.

College: University of Chicago, B.A. degree, [-29].

Medical School: Northwestern University, M.D. degree, [-25].

Internship: Cook County Hospital, [-24] to [-23].

Residency: In psychiatry, at Bellevue Hospital, New York, [-24] to [-19].

Present Hospital Staff Positions: Northwestern University Hospital (since [-16]); Loyola University Hospital (since [-19]).

Licenses: Illinois, [-24].

Professional Associations: American Medical Association; American Psychiatric Association; American Academy of Forensic Psychiatrists (chairman, [-6] to [-3]).

Publications:

"The Folly of the Insanity Defense in Criminal Cases," *American Psychiatric Journal*, Spring, [-6], Vol. 14, pp. 122-140.
"Hoodwinking the Psychiatrist: The Malingering Defendant in Criminal Cases," *Psychiatry Quarterly*, Vol. 20, [-2], pp. 16-40.
"The Myth of the Insanity Defense," *Clinical Psychiatry*, Winter, [-1], Vol. 13 pp. 111-140.

Board Certification: American Board of Psychiatry and Neurology (Diplomate, [-10]); Committee on Certification of Mental Health Administrators (certified, [-6]).

6.2   FINGERPRINT EXPERT QUALIFICATION

This is a burglary prosecution. The case is now on trial. As part of the prosecution's case-in-chief, you intend to call Charlie Henderson, a fingerprint expert, who will testify that s/he made a comparison of a latent fingerprint found at the burglarized premises with the known fingerprints of the defendant. According to Henderson, the latent fingerprint was made by the defendant.

Henderson has previously told you that s/he graduated from high school ten years ago, attended the local community college for two years, and then joined the local police department, where s/he was assigned to the crime laboratory. S/he has been assigned to the fingerprint unit for seven years. During the first three years, s/he was assigned to the classification section (where s/he classified approximately 50 sets of fingerprints each day so that the fingerprints could be indexed in a master filing system), and thereafter began work in the identification section (where s/he compares latent fingerprints with known fingerprint cards, approximately 10 to 30 each day). S/he remains there to this day.

Henderson says s/he is a member of the American Academy of Forensic Sciences and has read the major professional literature in the field. S/he says that his/her specialty is a "learn-by-doing field, where you learn by working as an apprentice in each section for at least two years under established experts. Only then can you begin doing your work independently."

Henderson says s/he now trains new personnel at the crime lab as well as lectures on the basics of fingerprint identifications at the crime laboratory. S/he has two articles (on the iodine vapor method of raising latent fingerprints on papers and documents) published by the American Academy of Forensic Scientists in its quarterly publication. S/he was promoted to the rank of sergeant one year ago. S/he has testified for the prosecution in criminal cases about five times per year since being assigned to the identification section.

1. For the prosecution, conduct a direct examination of Henderson, limited to qualifying him/her as an expert in the appropriate field.

2. For the defense, cross-examine Henderson on his/her qualifications.

6.3 TREATING PHYSICIAN AND DIAGRAMS OF SPINE

This is a personal injury case arising out of an automobile accident. Since the date of the accident the plaintiff has been complaining of pains in his back and periodic shooting pains down his legs.

Plaintiff's treating physician, Dr. Dakota Baird, an orthopedist, has testified that as a result of his/her examinations and tests s/he determined that the plaintiff suffered a herniated disc at the L3-L4 level, which is pushing against the plaintiff's spinal cord, causing pain.

Dr. Baird has already described the basic anatomy of the back, including a description of the intervertebral discs. S/he has brought the attached anatomical charts to court.

1. For the plaintiff, continue Dr. Baird's direct examination, using the charts to illustrate the basic components of a typical lumbar vertebra and how a herniated disc can produce painful pressure on the spinal cord. (You may use any other available anatomical chart.)

2. For the defendant, oppose the introduction of the charts.

Lumbar Vertebra

(Horizontal Cross Section)

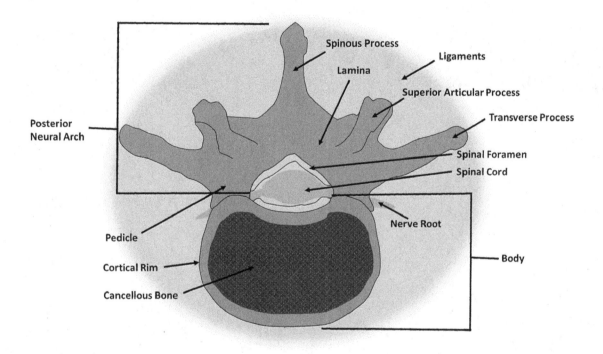

Spinous Process

Ligaments

Lamina

Superior Articular Process

Transverse Process

Posterior
Neural Arch

Spinal Foramen

Spinal Cord

Nerve Root

Pedicle

Body

Cortical Rim

Cancellous Bone

Lumbar Vertebrae

(Vertical Cross Section)

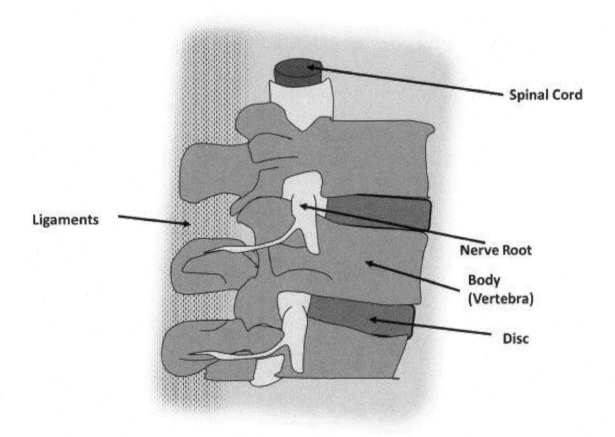

Spinal Cord

Ligaments

Nerve Root

Body
(Vertebra)

Disc

6.4   TREATING PHYSICIAN

This is a negligence action arising out of an automobile accident. Both liability and damages are in issue. The case is now on trial.

As part of her case-in-chief, plaintiff Helen Griggs calls Dr. Reilly Worthington, an orthopedist who treated her at the St. Mary's Hospital emergency room and continued treating her throughout her confinement at the hospital and as an outpatient afterward. At the conclusion of his/her services, Dr. Worthington submitted his/her bill to the plaintiff, which was paid.

Attached are the St. Mary's Hospital emergency room report and doctor's progress notes, as well as Dr. Worthington's patient history card and final bill.

Assume that Dr. Worthington has been qualified as an expert in the appropriate field.

1. For the plaintiff, conduct a direct examination of Dr. Worthington, using the attached records as you see fit.
2. For the defendant, cross-examine Dr. Worthington.

ST. MARY'S HOSPITAL
EMERGENCY ROOM / URGENT CARE

Rapid Assessment

Date/Time of Arrival	Pain Scale	Triage Category
1-15-[-1] / 3:18 P.M.	☐1 ☐2 ☐3 ☐4 ☐5 ☐6 ☐7 ☐8 ☐9 ☐10	☐I ☐II ☐III ☐IV ☐V

Patient Name	Address	Phone
Helen Griggs	1843 E. Broadway	

Chief Complaint (Subjective)

	Pt. states she was in car accident caused when other driver ran red light and crashed into the front of her car. Force of collision crushed her against steering column. Pt. wearing seatbelt at time. Pt. thinks left leg is broken.

Vitals

Temperature	Pulse	RESP/MIN	Blood Pressure
99	88	18	130 / 85

Objective Assessment

	Pallor noted, organ systems (HEENT, h/l) within normal limits. Marked tenderness and palpable swelling in distal third left lower leg with apparent subcutaneous venous oozing and crepitation of bone.

Diagnostic Workup

☐Blood Glucose	☐Creatinine test	☒X-Ray: Left lower leg lateral
☐BUN	☒EKG	☒X-Ray: A-P x-rays
☒CBC	☒Electrolytes	☐X-Ray:
☐CEA	☒SMA-12	☐X-Ray:
☒Chest X-ray	☒U/A	☐X-Ray:

Problems

Apparent fx left tibia / fibula; possible shock.

Plan

Admit, to OR.

Worthington

_____
Physicians Signature

Patient Name	
Helen Griggs	
Date	Notes
1/15/ [-1]	Report of Operation: Surgeon: Worthington Assisted by: T. Karnes Anesthesia: Sodium-pentothal Pre-op diagnosis: Fracture of left tibia/fibula Post-op diagnosis: Compound fracture, distal 1/3 left tibia, simple fracture distal 1/3 left fibula with displacement. Procedure: Patient in usual position, anesthesia given intravenously. Patient left leg x-rayed with portable unit (patient pain prevented x-ray while conscious). X-rays disclosed fracture noted. Patient left tibia and fibula manually manipulated until bones in apparent alignment (tibial fragment not sufficiently large or structural to require pins, etc.). X-ray showed alignment within normal limits. Left leg casted in plaster from toes to upper thigh in usual fashion. Patient tolerated procedure well. Vital signs stable. EBL=none. Rx 5% saline IV, Tylenol 10 mg as needed, morphine at bedtime. In: 4:30 P.M., out 5:17 P.M. **Patient to postop in good condition.** *Worthington*

Patient Name	
Helen Griggs	
Date	Notes
1/16/[-1] 9 A.M.	Patient complains of pain radiating up left leg and throbbing at fracture site. Temperature 101.8 Increased swelling. Rx Tylenol 10 mg four times a day, leg elevation, morphine at bedtime. 5% saline discontinued. *Worthington*
1/17/[-1]	Patient complains of pain. Temperature 101 Swelling stabilized. Maintain same orders, morphine discontinued. *Worthington*
1/18/[-1]	Patient complains of pain, but intermittent. Temperature 99 Pressure sensation less. Same Orders. *Worthington*
1/19/[-1]	Patient pain periodic, controlled with Tylenol. Afebrile. Swelling gone. Patient instructed to keep leg elevated as much as possible – crutches only when necessary. Will discharge with Tylenol, to return to office in 1 week. *Worthington*

REILLY WORTHINGTON, M.D.
PATIENT HISTORY CARD

Patient Name: Helen Griggs	
Address: 1843 E. Broadway	
Date	Notes
1/30/[-1]	Patient still complains of periodic pain, states swelling worse when leg not elevated – instructed to keep leg up whenever possible. Rx Tylenol only if needed. Return in 1 month.
3/3/[-1]	Cast removed, left leg x-rayed and examined. Good callus formation at fracture sites. Normal atrophy. Patient states pain gone, except for occasional throbbing or twinges at end of day. No longer uses Tylenol or aspirin. Leg re-casted, to knee. Patient instructed to exercise knee, without weight on leg, to restore full motion. Return 8 weeks.
5/1/[-1]	Cast removed, leg x-rayed and examined. Callus formation excellent. No complaints of pain. Atrophy normal. Leg wrapped in elastic bandage. Patient instructed to soak ankle and leg in hot water, twice daily, exercise ankle to restore full motion, walk without crutches, gradually putting increasing weight on leg. Return 1 month, earlier if problems.
6/3/[-1]	Patient examined. Full motion in knee, essentially full motion in ankle. Some residual swelling and puffiness in ankle. Calf and thigh still moderately atrophied. Patient walks with slight limp – should disappear in a few weeks as muscles restored to full strength. No pain, even on palpation. Patient instructed to continue physical therapy as described in booklet until recovery complete. Return only if problems.
6/30/[-1]	Bill for $12,000.00 sent – all services during course of treatment 1/15/[-1] to 6/3/[-1]
7/20/[-1]	Bill paid in full.

REILLY WORTHINGTON, M.D.

FORWARDING SERVICE REQUESTED

FOR BILLING INQUIRIES, CALL (555) 555-5555
MON-FRI 8:30 AM—4:30 PM

STATEMENT DATE	June 30, [-1]
PAY THIS AMOUNT	$12000.00

PATIENT: HELEN GRIGGS

DATE	CODE	DESCRIPTION	CHARGE	BALANCE DUE
1/15/[-1] TO 6/3/[-1]	44	PROFESSIONAL SERVICE RENDERED	12000.00	12000.00

- ✂

PATIENT: HELEN GRIGGS

MAY CHECKS PAYABLE TO:

REILLY WORTHINGTON, M.D.

FORWARDING SERVICE REQUESTED

FOR BILLING INQUIRIES, CALL (555) 555-5555
MON-FRI 8:30 AM—4:30 PM

If paying by credit card, fill out below:

CARD NUMBER	AMOUNT
SIGNATURE	EXP. DATE / CVV CODE

STATEMENT DATE	June 30, [-1]
PAY THIS AMOUNT	$12000.00

6.5 TREATING PHYSICIAN

[handwritten: cross]

[handwritten: π] *[handwritten: Δ]*

Martha Hiller is suing Thomas Randolph for personal injuries suffered in an auto accident on February 10, [-3]. Her suit asks for substantial damages. Her claim is based primarily on the pain and suffering she says have resulted from the accident.

[handwritten margin note: But wasn't seen Dr. in 2 yrs.]

The case is now on trial. Hiller will testify that her neck and head pains are as severe today as they were when she initially saw Dr. Pat Flanagan after the accident. She will say that she stopped going to the doctor because s/he was not helping her and she did not want to incur additional expense.

Hiller was not employed at the time of the accident, having retired one year earlier after 30 years of employment at Western Electric.

Aside from Dr. Flanagan's bill, her actual expenses were as follows:

St. Joseph's Hospital emergency treatment	$4,250.00
X-rays	1,300.00
Prescriptions	725.00

Dr. Flanagan is now called as a witness for the plaintiff. His/Her report and the hospital X-rays are attached. Assume that there is a stipulation that Dr. Flanagan is a qualified physician, specializing in the field of orthopedics.

1. For the plaintiff, conduct a direct examination of Dr. Flanagan.
2. For the defendant, cross-examine Dr. Flanagan.

[handwritten: Dr. specialization = orthopedics]

Pat Flanagan, M.D.
30 North Michigan Avenue

July 18, [-1]

Samuel Levin
Attorney at Law
221 N. La Salle Street

Re: Martha Hiller

Dear Mr. Levin:

I have written this report pursuant to your request
for information concerning my patient, and your client,
Martha Hiller, of 5770 N. Washtenaw. Miss Hiller has
signed the appropriate consent form for release of this
information.

Martha Hiller is a 62-year-old white female. She is
five feet, three inches in height and weighs 120 pounds.
I first saw her in the emergency room at St. Joseph's
Hospital on February 10, [-3]. She had been brought there
by a Fire Department ambulance after an auto accident
that took place at the intersection of Sheridan Road and
Surf Street.

The patient told me she was proceeding north on
Sheridan Road when a westbound car went through a red
light on Surf Street and struck her vehicle at about the
right front door. She described the impact as "heavy."
She said that on impact her body was "thrown to the left
and back again." She felt stunned and just sat behind
the wheel for a few minutes. When the police came to
the scene she asked to be transported to the hospital.
She said she never before had suffered any injuries
in an accident. She reported no prior injuries to, or
difficulties with, her neck, back, or head.

In the emergency room Miss Hiller complained of
soreness in her neck and shoulders. A visual examination *no sign of*
was made and no sign of trauma was found. X-rays were *trauma*
taken and were negative. The patient was released with *· neg. x-rays*
the suggestion she rest at home for the balance of the
day and take aspirin as needed.

I next saw Miss Hiller on Feb. 14, [-3], at my office.
She had called for an appointment that morning.

The patient reported that the pain in her neck and
shoulders had been steadily increasing. In addition, she
complained of severe headaches for the past two days. *↑ in pain*

A thorough physical examination was conducted, including the usual sensory, motor, and radiographic tests. All tests were negative for objective findings, although I noted a slight limitation in head movement. I could find no objective explanation for the pain she described, although she obviously was in discomfort.

I suggested she use an electric heating pad, take hot baths, and use aspirin as required. I asked her to see me again if the pain continued.

I saw Miss Hiller again on Feb. 21 [-3]. She told me the pain in her shoulders had diminished, but that the neck pain and the headaches had not diminished, and had, in fact, become worse.

Again, I conducted a complete physical examination, although I did not order radiographic tests. I made no objective findings. I gave her a prescription for the analgesic Emperin Compound No. 3, with codeine, and I recommended bed rest and the taking of hot baths.

I next saw Miss Hiller on March 10 [-3]. She again described continuous pain in her neck, at the base of the skull, along with severe headaches, at least once a day. I told her to continue taking the Emperin Compound, and I recommended she restrict herself to light activity and as much bed rest as possible.

The next and final time I saw Miss Hiller was April 10, [-3]. She again complained of neck pain. She said the headaches now occurred every two to three days. I renewed the prescription for the Emperin Compound, and told her to refrain from any exertion.

I have not seen or heard from Miss Hiller since that last visit.

I find it difficult to make an exact diagnosis. I believe the pain is real and that she is not malingering. Since she told me she never experienced neck or shoulder pain or anything other than an occasional mild headache before the accident, it is my opinion that Miss Hiller's condition was caused by the accident of February 10, [-3]. I would classify her condition as cervical sprain.

Since I have not seen the patient for more than two years, I have no opinion concerning her present condition.

384

My fee for services to Miss Hiller, in the hospital
and at my office, was a total of $3,300. Those bills were
paid. My fee for preparing this report is an additional
$2,000. If I am called upon to testify in this case, I,
of course, expect to be paid for my time.

                              Very truly yours,

                              Pat Flanagan
                              Pat Flanagan, M.D.

CURRICULUM VITAE

Pat Flanagan, M.D.

30 N. Michigan Avenue

Occupation

Physician, private practice limited to orthopedics since
[-8]

Education, Training & Licenses

B.A., Northwestern University, [-20]
M.D., Johns Hopkins, [-16]
Internship, Bellevue Hosp., New York City, [-16] - [-15]
Medical licenses, NY [-16], IL [-15]
Residency in orthopedics, Loyola University Hospital,
     Chicago, [-15] - [-11]
Board certified, [-8], American College of Orthopedic
     Surgeons

Employment

Northwestern University Hospital, Chicago, staff
     physician, [-11] - [-8]
Chicago Orthopedic Surgeons, member of group practice,
     since [-8]

Professional Associations

American Medical Association, since [-16]
Illinois State Medical Society, since [-15]
Cook County Medical Society, since [-15]

Publications

"Whiplash," *American Medical Association Journal*, June,
     [-10]
"Cervical Trauma," *Journal of Orthopedics*, January, [-5]

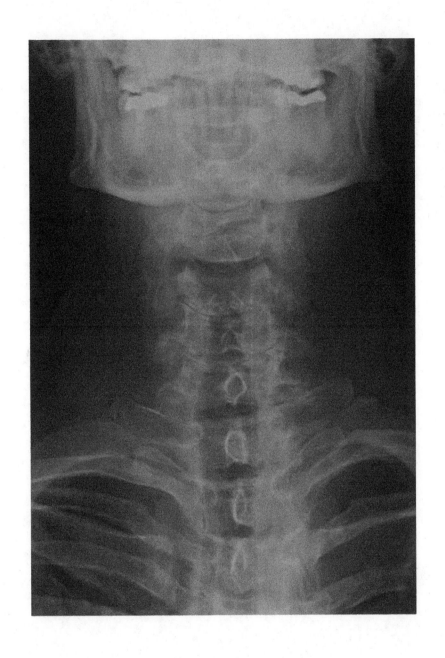

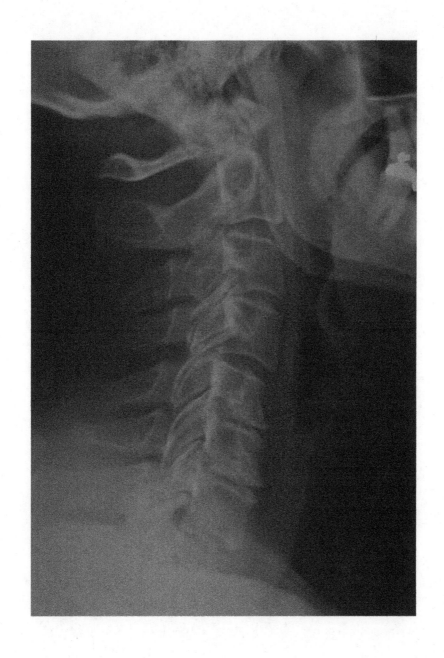

6.6 ECONOMIST

Two years ago today Richard Schiller was killed while working for the U.S. Steel Corporation. A steam boiler manufactured by the Gorp Corporation exploded, killing Schiller instantly. The explosion was caused by a faulty weld in the boiler. Pre-trial investigation has developed the following information:

Richard Schiller

Schiller was born on January 1, [-36]. Until his death he was in good health. He weighed 185 pounds and was six feet tall. He played basketball for his high school team but turned down an athletic scholarship at Notre Dame to enter the Marine Corps. He served in the Marines for three years, two of them in the Middle East, where he won the Distinguished Service Medal. He was never injured and received an honorable discharge.

Following his discharge in January [-15], Schiller went to work for U.S. Steel. He began as a steam boiler mechanic and kept that job until he was killed. His starting wage was $44,000 a year. He received wage increases of 5 percent each year until the year of his fatal accident. He had no other income.

Schiller was active in church affairs. He was a deacon at the First Activist Church. At the church he taught basketball to teenage children, including his son Mickey.

Harriet Schiller

Harriet was Richard's wife at the time of his death. She was born on January 1, [-33]. She has never worked outside the home before or since the accident. Harriet has spent these past two years following Richard's death raising Mickey and being active in the Ladies' Auxiliary at the church.

Harriet and Richard went steady throughout high school and kept in constant communication during the three years he was in military service. They were married the day after he was discharged from the Marines. Mickey was born ten months later.

Harriet and Richard were very close. When he was not working or at the church, he was at home with her. He would help with the needed repairs on their house and with the yard and house work.

Harriet has not remarried, nor has she dated anyone since Richard's death.

Mickey Schiller

Mickey was born on January 1, [-14]. He and his father were very close and did many things together, such as playing checkers and going to sporting events. Mickey is the star center on the church basketball team and learned everything he knows about basketball from his father. Mickey hopes to go to college on an athletic scholarship. He is now six feet tall and weighs 150 pounds.

Additional Information

1. Under Schiller's union contract the mandatory retirement age is 62. Pensions vest after 20 years. There is no ceiling on a permissible rate of wage increases. After 30 years of employment, the full pension is 50 percent of the employee's highest annual wage prior to retirement.

2. Schiller smoked one-half pack of cigarettes each day. He drank beer socially but not hard liquor.

3. Schiller drove the only family car, a six-year-old Kia, to work each day. He bought the house his widow still lives in for $100,000 in January [-14]. The amount of $55,000 was owed on the mortgage at the time of this trial.

4. Schiller bought a new suit each spring, as well as a few pants, shirts, and other usual clothing items each year. He spent about $125 each week on personal items such as food and other incidentals.

The administrator of the estate of Richard Schiller has brought a wrongful death action against Gorp Corporation. The complaint is based on a strict liability theory. The defendant in its answer admitted liability, so the only issue remaining is damages. The case is being tried in your state, and your jurisdiction's tort law applies. Assume that the plaintiff has presented evidence in his case-in-chief that proves the facts stated above.

Plaintiff now calls Morgan Mason, an economist, as his last witness. Mason's résumé is attached.

1. For the plaintiff, conduct a direct examination of Mason to prove the economic loss to the survivors caused by Schiller's death. Assume that you are in federal court.

2. Use the same information as in No. 1, but assume that you are in a state jurisdiction that requires the use of a hypothetical question.

3. For the defense, cross-examine Mason.

Résumé
Morgan Mason, Ph.D.
200 Maple Lane

Occupation:

Economist, self-employed consultant.

Education:

1)   University of Wisconsin, B.A. in economics, [-15].
2)   University of Wisconsin, M.A. in economics, [-13].
3)   Purdue University, Ph.D. in economics, [-10].

Employment:

1)   Metropolitan Insurance Co., [-9] to [-6], actuary and risk analyst.
2)   Allstate Insurance Co., [-6] to [-4], actuary.
3)   Self-employed economist since [-4], specializing in actuarial and economic loss analysis in personal injury cases. I have done economic loss analysis in about 200 cases, including approximately 40 death cases. In about 80 percent of them I was retained by the plaintiff's lawyer. I have testified at trials as an economic expert eight times, six for plaintiffs and two for defendants. I charge $400 an hour for deposition and court time, and $300 an hour for review, preparation, and consultation.

Publications:

1)   Ph.D. thesis: "The Effect of Taxes and Inflation in Present Cash Value Analysis."

2)   "Loss of Future Income in Wrongful Death Cases,"
     [-4], *The Economist*.

3)   "Predicting Future Income," [-2], *Economics Review*.

Teaching:

1)   Teaching Assistant, Purdue University, [-13] to
     [-10].

2)   Assistant Professor, Purdue University, [-10] to
     [-9].

Professional Association:

American Economics Association, since [-13].

6.7 IMPEACHMENT WITH TREATISE: FINGERPRINT EXPERT

This is a burglary prosecution of James Evens. The case is now on trial. Previous witnesses have testified to locating and removing a latent print at the crime scene and taking the defendant's fingerprints on a standard fingerprint card following his arrest. These witnesses have also testified that they personally delivered the latent print and the fingerprint card to Freddy Bolger, a fingerprint expert employed by the police department. No computer analysis was available due to equipment malfunction.

The prosecution then calls Bolger as a witness. After being qualified as an expert in fingerprint comparisons, s/he testifies that s/he personally received the latent print and the fingerprint card and that s/he made a comparison between them.

Bolger testifies that s/he found seven identical friction ridge characteristics in the latent print and one of the fingerprints on the card, and on that quantitative basis only concluded that the latent print was made by the same person whose fingerprints are on the card.

You have the attached excerpt from Moenssens, Starrs, Henderson, and Inbau, *Scientific Evidence in Civil and Criminal Cases* (4th ed. 1995), pp. 513-516, one of the standard works in the field.

1. For the defense, cross-examine Bolger.
2. For the prosecution, conduct any necessary redirect examination.

§8.08 Fingerprint Identification

To compare an unknown latent impression with an inked impression of known origin with the aim of determining whether both were made by the same finger, the technician looks for four different elements: The likeness of the general pattern type (or, if the type cannot be determined because the questioned pattern is incomplete, for a general similarity in flow of the ridges); the qualitative likeness of the friction ridge characteristics; the quantitative likeness of the friction ridge characteristics; and the likeness of location of the characteristics.

Many latent impressions developed at crime scenes are badly blurred or smudged, or consist of partially superimposed impressions of different fingers. As long as a sufficiently large area of friction skin is available which is not blurred, smudged, or rendered useless through superimposition, identity can be established. . . . The size of area required varies according to the number of individual ridge characteristics discovered and the frequency of their appearance in a given area. This relates to the element of quantitative likeness in that it requires that a sufficient number of characteristics be found to match in both prints, without unexplained dissimilarities. By tradition, though not by empirical studies, latent print examiners in the United States have required a matching of at least eight characteristics *not good for me* in both prints for identity, though most experts prefer at least 10-12 concordances. In England, 14 to 16 matches are required for court testimony. The qualitative comparison of the friction ridge characteristics refers to whether or not the characteristics (bifurcations, ridge endings, enclosures, ridge dots, etc.) are the same in both prints. The likeness of location of the friction ridge characteristics refers to the relationship with one another within the contours of the pattern. In other words, identity can be established if the ridge characteristics are in the same relative position to one another in both prints, with the same number of intervening ridges in both.

401

Because of criticism that had been leveled against the fingerprint examiners for failing to agree on a rule setting the minimum number of ridge characteristics that must establish a match between two prints before they can be said to be from the same digit, the International Association for Identification, a professional body composed primarily of fingerprint identification specialists, created in 1970 a Standardization Committee. The Committee consisted of 11 members whose aggregate experience in the identification field amounted to roughly 250 years. The group was charged with several mandates, one of which was to recommend adoption of a minimum standard for matching characteristics, if feasible. After a concentrated study of nearly three years' duration, the committee concluded that there exists no valid basis, at this time, for requiring a predetermined minimum number of friction ridge characteristics in two impressions in order to establish positive identification. The decision on whether two prints under examination are made by the same digit is one that must be made, the committee concluded, on the basis of the expert's experience and background, taking into account, along with the number of matching characteristics, other factors such as clarity of the impressions, types of characteristics found, location of the characteristics in relation to the core or delta, etc. The committee's formal report was unanimously approved by the association's general membership at the 58th annual conference of the IAI in 1973.

In extensive testing and research with tens of thousands of "similar," though not identical prints, experts have been unable to find more than four *clearly defined* characteristics that are quantitatively and qualitatively the same in two prints known to be from different fingers. By adhering to the old-time tradition in the profession that at least eight matching characteristics be found in both the known and the unknown print before identity is established, a degree of certainty of identification is introduced which accounts for the fact that there is very seldom a "battle of opposing experts" in fingerprint cases. Yet, in a great number of criminal cases an expert or consultant on fingerprints for the defense has been instrumental in seriously undermining the state's case by demonstrating faulty procedures used by the state's witnesses or by simply showing human errors in the use of fingerprint evidence.

402

6.8 IMPEACHMENT WITH TREATISE: MICROANALYST

This is a sexual assault prosecution. You represent the defendant, John Finley. The defendant has denied having any contact with the victim. His defense is based on a claim of mistaken identification.

The prosecution calls Dr. Riley Jones, a microanalyst for the police department crime laboratory.

On direct examination, Dr. Jones testifies that s/he received from the Lutheran-General Hospital a year ago today a slide prepared by means of a swab of the victim's vaginal pool. The slide was prepared one hour after the rape. With it was a request by investigating police officer Martin Casey, who asked the laboratory to determine whether human spermatozoa were present.

Dr. Jones testifies that s/he performed the appropriate microbiological analysis on the slide. In his/her opinion, human spermatozoa were present. No DNA test was performed due to lack of funding.

You have the attached excerpt from Moenssens, Inbau, and Starrs, *Scientific Evidence in Criminal Cases* (3d ed. 1986), pp. 342-347.

1. For the defense, cross-examine Dr. Jones.
2. For the prosecution, conduct any necessary redirect examination.

§6.11 Identification of Human Blood Types

After determining that the blood is of human origin, the blood is further classified as to blood group. Blood analysis and group determination is based on antigen antibody reactions or by enzyme system tests. The most frequently used antigen systems are the *ABO*, the *M, N, mn, Rh,* and *Gm* systems.

It is beyond the scope of this chapter to explain, in detail, each and every blood grouping system. By way of example, the basic and oldest blood grouping method—the *ABO* system—is explained here as representative of the antigen systems.

Blood grouping into types, *A, B, AB,* and *O* (really meaning zero) may be used as positive or negative evidence in a criminal prosecution. A person's blood group remains constant throughout life notwithstanding age, disease, or medication. The types are named according to the presence or absence of the *A* or *B* agglutinogen in the red blood cell. Roughly 40 percent of the population in the United States is type *A*, 43 percent is type *O*, 14 percent is type *B*, and 3 percent is type *AB*.

In 1900 Landsteiner established that the serum of one individual would clump (agglutinate) the red blood cells of another individual. The explanation for this was that red blood cells contain a substance known as an antigen and the serum of the blood contains antibodies. The two antigens in the *ABO* blood system are the antigens *A* and *B*; the two antibodies in the *ABO* blood system are anti *A* (alpha) and anti *B* (beta). In the red blood cells of a human being there will be either the *A* antigen, the *B* antigen, both the *A* and *B* antigens, or neither *A* nor *B* antigens.

These antigens may also be referred to as blood group factors; therefore, a person having *A* antigen in his red blood cells has group *A* blood, a person having *B* antigen has group *B* blood, a person having both *A* and *B* has group *AB* blood, and a person who has neither *A* nor *B* antigens in his red blood cells has group *O* blood. If a person has *A* antigen in his red blood cells he cannot have an anti *A* antibody in his serum, for this would agglutinate (clump) his own cells. The same is true of an individual having *B* antigen in his blood cells; he cannot have anti *B* antibody in his serum. It follows that a person with

405

both *A* and *B* antigens in his blood cells can have neither anti *A* nor anti *B* antibodies in his serum. However, a person who has neither antigen *A* nor *B* in his red blood cells (Group *O*) has both antibodies, anti *A* and anti *B* in his serum.

In addition to the *ABO* system of grouping blood, there are also other systems which can be used, such as *MN* blood groups, *Rh* blood groups, and others.

Blood group substances are not only present in blood. Approximately 80-85 percent of the population, known as secretors, have blood group substances in their saliva, tears, perspiration, semen, vaginal fluids, mucus, gastric contents, etc. The ability to secrete is an inherited dominant trait; the genes responsible for it are not linked to the *ABO* genes. If a person carries the secretor gene (*Se*), the *H* substances genes are identifiable by the use of anti *H* sera. If a person carries the nonsecretor gene (*se*), the *H* substance does not react to any antigen. In essence, a nonsecretor is a person with no secretor gene in his body fluid, his *H* substance is alcohol soluble, so does not mix with body fluids. By contrast, in a secretor the *H* substance is water soluble and therefore extracted in the body fluids so that the antigens are subject to detection by the use of anti sera.

6.9   IMPEACHMENT WITH TREATISE: PHYSICIAN

This is a medical malpractice action. The defendant, Dale Rosen, M.D., an obstetrician, delivered an infant, Michael Healy, at St. Mary's Hospital. Michael's parents have brought this action, alleging that Michael's retardation was caused when he experienced respiratory distress immediately following delivery and the doctor and attending nurses failed to use all the necessary standard procedures and techniques to properly ventilate and oxygenate the infant after birth.

At trial Dr. Rosen testified on direct examination that after an uneventful delivery, the infant, who was born full-term, immediately experienced respiratory distress. He was not breathing regularly or adequately, and his hands and feet were pale and blue, indicating oxygen deprivation—that is, central cyanosis.

Dr. Rosen stated that s/he immediately had the nurses suction the infant's airway while s/he stimulated his feet. When this failed to induce normal breathing, the doctor inserted a 3.5-mm endotracheal tube into the infant's trachea to ensure an airway. The infant was given an oxygen mask that was connected to pure oxygen, but no positive pressure ventilation was provided.

Dr. Rosen stated that the infant's cardiac output and acid-base status appeared normal. Accordingly, the infant was thoroughly dried and wrapped in blankets and was taken to the infant nursery about 20 minutes after delivery. The infant's extremities turned pink within 30 minutes following delivery, so the doctor removed the endotracheal tube but kept the oxygen going for approximately two more hours.

You have *The Merck Manual of Diagnosis and Therapy* (13th ed. 1977). Pages 985 to 988, which are attached, are taken from chapter 10 (Pediatrics), section 2 (The Newborn).

The *Merck Manual* is a standard reference text for nurses and hospital staffs. It deals with the diagnosis and treatment of common, recurring medical problems. Dr. Rosen will acknowledge that it is a standard authority, insofar as it describes the standard prevailing procedures for treating common medical situations.

1. For the plaintiff, cross-examine Dr. Rosen.

2. For the defendant, conduct any necessary redirect examination.

DISTURBANCES OF THE NEWBORN
ASPHYXIA AND RESUSCITATION
(Asphyxia Neonatorum)

An infant who does not breathe spontaneously at birth, or who has acute blood loss, requires resuscitation to minimize the possibility of brain damage, as well as to prevent death. Although instituting adequate ventilation usually is the main concern in newborn resuscitation, the rapid replacement of blood lost by hemorrhage during delivery is equally critical.

Treatment

Step 1. Airway: The airway should first be quickly cleared of secretions, fluid, or blood by suctioning the pharynx and nostrils with a soft catheter. Suctioning must be gentle and limited to 5 to 10 seconds, since prolonged vigorous suctioning may cause apnea or bradycardia through the vagal reflex.

The infant depressed by anesthetic agents may be stimulated repeatedly for as long as 2 min. by a method such as slapping the feet, before other efforts at resuscitation are begun. However, if central cyanosis or bradycardia develops, positive pressure ventilation (see Ventilation, below) must begin immediately. For an infant meconium-covered and depressed at birth, it is essential to visualize the vocal cords directly using a laryngoscope and to perform endotracheal suction repeatedly until the airway is clear of aspirated meconium. Instilling small amounts of saline into the trachea may help to loosen the meconium and to make aspiration easier. An endotracheal tube with the largest possible diameter should be used: a 3.5 mm tube can usually be used for full-term infants, a 3 mm tube for infants under 1.5 kg, and a 2.5 mm tube for infants of 1 kg or less. The trachea may be effectively suctioned by a mouth-to-tube technique (with intervening face mask). These procedures must be performed quickly and followed by positive pressure ventilation with O_2 in order to prevent severe anoxia.

Step 2. Ventilation: Positive pressure ventilation is effectively provided by mouth-to-mouth or bag and mask resuscitation with the infant's head in the neutral position and the jaw raised slightly to ensure a clear airway. Endotracheal intubation should be used only by experienced personnel who are comfortable at rapid intubation. Ventilation should be instituted at a rate of about 40/min.; the effectiveness is judged by upper chest movement, since hearing-transmitted breath sound is not always a reliable indicator of adequate ventilation in the new born.

. . .

Step 6. Temperature: Maintaining the infant's temperature during resuscitation is essential and is often overlooked. Cooling increases the infant's metabolic rate 2 or 3 times above the basal rate, increasing O_2 requirements. In the face of O_2 lack, the infant more rapidly develops severe O_2 debt, which can result in neurologic damage or death. After the baby is dried thoroughly, use of a radiant heater is recommended, rather than blankets, since it permits continuous observation of the infant's color and activity during resuscitation.

6.10 MEDICAL EXAMINER IN MURDER CASE

The defendant, Horace Johnson, is charged with the murder of Alma Lee Bradshaw. During discovery, the defendant stated that his defense will be that Bradshaw might have died as a result of the alcohol consumed on the day of her death and not as a result of any act he performed.

An autopsy and blood-alcohol test were performed on Bradshaw at the County Morgue.

The file contains Dr. Keegan Tapp's pathological report, the toxicological report, and statements of witnesses. It also contains a report to the defense from Dr. Ralph Schultz, a forensic pathologist. The State has a copy of the report.

Both sides have stipulated that the Cozy Tavern is located six blocks from Rose Prince's apartment.

1. For the State, conduct a direct examination of Dr. Tapp.
2. For the defense, cross-examine Dr. Tapp.

PATHOLOGICAL REPORT AND PROTOCOL

County Medical Examiner's Office
Edward Tapp

#25 of August, [-1]

Name Alma Bradshaw   Date of Death August 4th, [-1]

Address 515 W. 63rd Street   Exam. at County Morgue

Identification_____   Date Examined August 5th, [-1]

Address_____   Examined by Keegan Tapp, M.D.

External Examination:

    Race_____   Sex Female   Age 37   Length 5'2"

    Weight 80 lbs   Hair____   Iris____   Sclera_____

    Musculature   Skeleton: Slender
    Pigmentation   Medium
    Edema   Powerful
    Docubitus   Deformed
                                          Amputations

Signs of Death:

    Cornea Cloudy-Turbid Decomposition: Skin-Slip
          Dry Shrunk   Tissue Gas
    Body Heat   Discoloration
    Lividity   Dehydration
    Rigor Mortis   Putrefaction

History of Cause of Death

    Place removed from: 6136 S. Princeton. The character
of this place is an apartment. Pronounced dead at
Provident Hospital on August 4th, [-1], at 4:15 p.m.
The diagnosis is supposed assault. The body was
brought to the morgue August 4th, [-1] at 5:00 p.m. by
police.

External Examination

The body was that of a well developed undernourished female
who measured 5'2" and weighed about 80 lbs. The scalp is
covered with black hair. In the left lateral forehead over

413

the posterior 3rd of the left eyebrow there is an oblique laceration measuring 2 cm. The margins are red brown abraded. The laceration is 2 cm. in depth and tore the aponeurosis covering the inferior border of the left roof of the brain. Below the inferior border of this laceration there is a pale brown abrasion measuring 1 cm. There is greenish discoloration of the external angle of the left eye. There is a faint violaceous red discoloration of the left eyelid. There is swelling associated with no abrasion and swelling of the right eyelid which are discolored dark violaceous red. There are eggs of maggots present in the mouth. There is ecchymosis of the sclera and conjunctiva of the right eye. The irises are brown. Pupils equal 0.3 cm. in diameter. The lower gum is dentate. The upper gum sustained a frontal partial denture. There are 2 linear abrasions of the inferior aspect of the right side of the face. One is located midway below the right side of the body of the mandible and measured 0.5 cm. The other extends into the left of the inferior aspect of the chin located 0.5 cm. in front of the neck. It is interrupted and measured 4-1/2 cm. There is an old scar linear of the anterior aspect of the neck located in the thyroid cartilage and it measured 6 cm. It is located 3 cm. above the superior end of the sternum. This scar is 1 cm. to the right of the midline and extends into the left side of the neck. The chest is symmetrical. The breasts are unremarkable. The abdomen is scaphoid. The external genitalia are those of a normal female. Extending from the left inguinal region into the lateral aspect of the left thigh down to the lower 3rd including the upper half of the posterior aspect of the left thigh and extending into the external portion of the left buttock there is an area of diffuse contusion consisting of violaceous red discoloration. There is swelling of the left knee and violaceous red discoloration of both knees. There are multiple dark red abrasions of the anterior aspect of the knees measuring up to 3 cm. There are 2 dark red brown abrasions of the medial aspect of the right ankle measuring up to 1-1/2 cm. Seven dark red brown abrasions varying from 0.3 cm. to 2 cm. in longest diameter are noted in the anterior aspect of the left ankle and dorsum of the left foot. Rigor mortis is moderately present. Extending from the left interscapular dorso-vertebral region there is an old surgical scar for a left thoracotomy which measured 23-1/2 cm. and ends in a point located 7 cm. below the left nipple and 3 cm. to the left of this nipple. Dependent lividity is present in the back. There is a contusion of the dorsum of the right hand associated with multiple dark red abrasions. There is violaceous red discoloration of the dorsum of the right hand. These abrasions measure up to 1 cm. The right side of the right thigh showed diffuse contusions, swelling and violaceous red discoloration. There are multiple red brown abrasions in number of 5 of the lumbar region measuring up to 1 cm.

414

HEAD: The scalp was reflected and the soft tissue covering the inferior portion of the right occipital region
showed minimal hemorrhage in a patch measuring 3 cm. There
is minimal hemorrhage of the inferior 3rd of the latero-
anterior aspect of the right forehead. There is also
minimal hemorrhage of the soft tissue covering the left
superior orbital bridge. There are about a few cc of bright
clotted blood in the subdural space of the left occipital
lobe which is associated with contusion 0.4 cm. in length,
dark red of the inferior medial surface of the left occipital lobe. There were no fractures of the skull. The brain
was edematous. The vessels of the surface of the brain were
engorged. The brain weighed 1085 grams. There was diffuse
congestion of the inner area of the cerebral cortex.
Petechial hemorrhages were seen in the white matter. The
ventricular system contained clear fluid. There were no contusions or lacerations of the spinal cord or inter-vertebra
discs of the cervical vertebral column nor in the remainder
of the vertebral column; however, the cervical vertebral
column was supple.

BODY: The body was opened with a Y incision to reveal the
subcutaneous tissue in the midline to measure 2 cm. The left
lung was missing and replaced by dense fibrous adhesions.
There were old sutures in the left hilar region. The right
lung was attached to the chest wall by multiple fibrous
adhesions. The amount of blood in the body was reduced.
There was scoliosis of the dorsal vertebral column with the
concavity pointing toward the left. The left leaf of the
diaphragm was at the left 6th intercostal space while
the right leaf was at the 12th intercostal space. Both were
in the posterior portion. The internal genitalia were unremarkable.

RESPIRATORY SYSTEM: The right lung weighed 400 grams. The
right lung showed obstructive emphysema and the traceo-
bronchial tree contained tenacious mucous tinged with blood.
There was a bleb formation of the areas of the lung. The
exterior was reddish gray mottled with black. The cut surface was pale red brown and oozed frothy fluid. The lung was
partly hypercrepitant and partly hypocrepitant.

CARDIOVASCULAR SYSTEM: The heart weighed 220 grams. The apex
was formed by both ventricles. The epicardium was smooth.
The myocardium was pale brown and showed a slight infiltra-
tion of the right anterior ventricle. The endocardium was
smooth. The mitral valve showed thickening of the free edge.
The coronary arteries and aorta showed minimal arterio-
sclerotic changes. The spleen weighed 55 grams. The edges
were sharp. The capsule was wrinkled and gray. The cut
surface was pale red brown. The architecture was intact.

GASTROINTESTINAL SYSTEM: The liver weighed 1075 grams. The leading edge was blunt. The capsule was transparent. The cut surface was diffusely yellow and showed occasional patches measuring up to 1 cm. of hemorrhage. The liver was markedly pliable and the superior and inferior aspect could be placed together. The remainder of this tract was unremarkable. The stomach contained mucous in an amount of 25 cc.

GENITOURINARY SYSTEM: The kidneys together weighed 250 grams. The capsule stripped with ease to reveal a smooth pale brown external surface. The cortex and medulla were in their normal ratio. The cortico medullary markings were distinct. The exterior of the kidneys was noted with spiders. The urinary bladder was empty. The remainder of this tract was unremarkable.

ANATOMICAL DIAGNOSIS

1. Edema of brain
2. Multiple internal injuries and fatty liver
3. Contusion laceration and abrasion of the left eyebrow
4. Minimal contusion of brain
5. Minimal left subdural hemorrhage
6. Contusions of thighs
7. Contusions of eyelids

TOXICOLOGIST'S REPORT

Analysis of the blood showed the presence of three-hundred seventy-eight (378) mg. percent alcohol.

IN MY OPINION THE SAID ____ Alma Lee Bradshaw ____ death was

Part I - Death was caused by (enter only one cause per line
for (a), (b), and (c))

        Immediate Cause (a) ____ Edema of brain ____

        due to (b) ____ multiple internal injuries ____

        due to (c) _____

Part II - Other significant conditions contributing to death
but not related to the terminal condition given in
Part I (a).

        ____ fatty liver ____

        _____

Date ____ 8/11/[-1] ____   Signed   *Keegan Tapp*

                              Keegan Tapp, M.D.

Résumé

Keegan Tapp, M.D.
100 Elm Street

Occupation:

Physician, specializing in pathology.

Education:

University of Florida, B.S. in chemistry, [-10]
Loyola University, M.D. [-7]

Training:

Internship, Cook County Hospital, Chicago, [-6] to [-5]
Residency in pathology, Loyola University Hospital,
Chicago, [-5] to [-2]

Employment:

County Medical Examiner's Office [-2] to present. I
perform autopsies to determine the causes of death. Over
the past two years, I have performed approximately 500
such autopsies. I testify regularly in homicide cases on
causes of death, and have done so in over 25 cases to
date.

Licenses:

Illinois, [-6]; this state, [-2]; board certified,
American College of Pathology, [-1]

Publications:

"Coup-Contre-Coup: Death on the Streets," *Journal of the
American Medical Association*, Fall, [-2]

Professional Associations:

American Medical Association
American College of Pathology
American Association of Forensic Pathologists

County Medical Examiner's Office

Phillip Smith, M.D.

<u>TOXICOLOGIST'S REPORT</u>

Your case No. <u>25 of Aug., [-1]</u> Date Material received <u>Aug. 5, [-1]</u>

Toxicology case No. <u> 835 </u> Date of this report <u>Aug. 9, [-1] </u>

To Dr. <u> Tapp </u> Deputy <u> </u>

    Analysis of the specimens submitted and recorded by you as pertaining to the dead body of <u> Alma Lee Bradshaw </u>, and on which you requested an analysis by the Toxicologist for <u> alcohol </u>.

<u>Analysis of the blood showed the presence of three-hundred</u>

<u>seventy-eight (378) mg. percent alcohol. ****</u>

                                          Joseph E. Ksiazek, Chemist

STATEMENT OF ROSE PRINCE

Typed and questioned by Inv. Frank Schmidt at
police headquarters. Also present is Inv. Sam
Caldwell. Statement taken August 4, [-1], at 8:15 P.M.

1 Q. What is your name, address, and occupation?
2
3 A. Rose Prince. I live at 6136 S. Princeton in a
4   third-floor walkup apartment. I am not presently
5   employed.
6
7 Q. With whom do you live at 6136 S. Princeton?
8
9 A. I live alone.
10
11 Q. What is your education?
12
13 A. I graduated from high school.
14
15 Q. Do you know Horace Johnson?
16
17 A. No. But I know Alma lived with him on 63rd
18   Street.
19
20 Q. How well did you know Alma Bradshaw?
21
22 A. She was my cousin. We grew up together.
23
24 Q. Did you see Alma Bradshaw earlier today?
25
26 A. Yes. At about 3:00 P.M. She knocked on my door.
27
28 Q. Tell us in your own words what happened when she
29   knocked on your door.
30
31 A. Well, I opened the door and she kind of stumbled
32   into the apartment. Her eyes looked funny and she
33   smelled like she had been drinking. She looked
34   terrible. She kind of staggered around for a couple
35   of minutes. I asked her what the matter was, but
36   I could not understand her when she answered. She
37   just mumbled. I couldn't make out the words. Then
38   she just collapsed on the floor. That's when I
39   called the police.
40
41 Q. When is the last time before today that you had
42   seen Alma?

```
43  A.  I hadn't seen her for about six months. She sure
44      looked different when I saw her today. She had lost
45      a lot of weight and her knees looked all scraped
46      up. She kept holding her head with her hands.
47
48  Q.  Are there any questions about this incident that I
49      may have failed to ask you?
50
51  A.  Not to my knowledge.
52
53  Q.  After reading this statement, if you find the
54      statement correct as typed, will you sign the
55      statement?
56
57  A.  Yes.
```

SIGNED *Rose Prince*
Rose Prince

Typed and Questioned by Inv. Frank Schmidt at police headquarters. Also present is Inv. Sam Caldwell. Statement taken August 4, [-1], at 8:54 P.M.

1 Q. What is your name, address, and occupation?
2
3 A. I am Arthur Kent. I live at 515 W. 63rd Street, in
4   Apartment 203. I am presently unemployed.
5
6 Q. How long have you lived in that apartment?
7
8 A. About three years.
9
10 Q. Do you know Horace Johnson and Alma Bradshaw?
11
12 A. Sure. They lived next door to me for a year now.
13
14 Q. Did you see either one of them today?
15
16 A. I saw them both. But first I heard them.
17
18 Q. What time did you hear something?
19
20 A. It was about 10:00 or 10:30 this morning.
21
22 Q. What did you hear?
23
24 A. Well, the walls are thin. I heard both their
25   voices. They were loud. It sounded like an
26   argument. It must have gone on about 15 minutes.
27
28 Q. Could you hear what was being said?
29
30 A. Well, I heard Alma crying. Then I heard Horace say:
31   "I've had enough of you. You're finished. I don't
32   care how sick you are." At least it was something
33   like that. Horace sounded real mad. That's all I
34   remember hearing.
35
36 Q. What happened next?
37
38 A. Well, I heard their apartment door open, and then
39   I heard running sounds in the hall. And they both
40   were yelling. I went to my door and opened it.
41
42 Q. What did you see?

43 A. I saw Johnson chasing Alma down the hall. He
44   was swinging a board at her and they both were
45   yelling.
46
47 Q. How big was the board?
48
49 A. It looked real big, about three feet long. He was
50   holding it in one hand, like a club.
51
52 Q. Did he hit her with the board?
53
54 A. He sure did.
55
56 Q. How many times did he hit her?
57
58 A. I would say twice, maybe three times.
59
60 Q. What part of her body did he hit?
61
62 A. I know he hit her on the head at least once. I
63   can't say what part of her head.
64
65 Q. What happened next?
66
67 A. Well, she ran down the stairs, but he didn't go
68   after her. He went back into the apartment.
69
70 Q. Did you see what he did with the board?
71
72 A. He took it back into the apartment with him.
73
74 Q. Did you see either one of them again?
75
76 A. Yes. Right after that I went to the Cozy Tavern to
77   get some cigarettes. Alma was in there. She was
78   sitting at a table and she had a glass and a bottle
79   of gin in front of her. She was alone.
80
81 Q. Did you see her again?
82
83 A. Well, I walked past the tavern about two hours
84   later. When I looked in I saw she was still there
85   at the same table. That was about 1:00. She was
86   sitting with her head in her arms.
87
88 Q. Do you have anything else to add?
89
90 A. No, except that they were always arguing and
91   carrying on.

426

```
92  Q. Are there any questions about this incident that I
93     may have failed to ask you?
94
95  A. I don't think so.
96
97  Q. After reading this statement, if you find the
98     statement is correct as typed, will you sign the
99     statement?
100
101 A. Yes.
```

Signed: *Arthur Kent*
Arthur Kent

Typed and questioned by Inv. Frank Schmidt at police headquarters. Also present is Inv. Sam Caldwell.

Statement taken August 4, [-1], at 9:15 P.M.

1 Q. What is your name, address, and occupation?
2
3 A. Horace Johnson. I live at 515 W. 63rd Street,
4   Apartment 202. I work at United States Steel.
5
6 Q. Do you understand that you are being charged with
7   the murder of Alma Bradshaw?
8
9 A. Yes, I do.
10
11 Q. You have been told that you do not have to say
12   anything without a lawyer being present, and that
13   if you do say anything it will be used against you
14   in a court of law. If you can't afford a lawyer,
15   one will be appointed for you. Do you understand
16   your rights?
17
18 A. Yes. I don't want a lawyer. I want to tell you what
19   happened.
20
21 Q. Do you know Alma Bradshaw?
22
23 A. Of course. Alma and I lived together for the past
24   year. We were going to get married.
25
26 Q. How did you get along with her?
27
28 A. We had our differences, like anyone else. But we
29   always made up.
30
31 Q. What happened between you and Alma earlier today?
32
33 A. It was about 10:00 or so. I was dressing to go to
34   work at U.S. Steel. I was going to work from noon
35   to five. Alma was putting her clothes on. I asked
36   her where she was going. She said she was going
37   to the Cozy Tavern on the corner for something
38   to drink. I told her it was too early to start
39   drinking. She started yelling at me and swearing at
40   me. We argued back and forth for a while. Then she
41   opened the door and said she was going to the Cozy
42   and I could go to hell. I got mad and picked up a
43   board that we use to prop the door closed.

```
44    It's about two feet long and three inches wide,
45    maybe an inch thick.
46
47 Q. What happened next?
48
49 A. She ran out the door and I ran after her.
50
51 Q. Did you hit her with the board?
52
53 A. I think I touched her lightly on the rear end, but
54    that's all.
55
56 Q. Did you hit her on the head?
57
58 A. Absolutely not. I didn't want to hurt her.
59
60 Q. Go ahead.
61
62 A. She ran to the landing and down the stairs. I
63    stopped at the head of the stairs. I knew I had to
64    get to work and I didn't want to fight anymore. So
65    I went back to the apartment, finished dressing,
66    and went to work.
67
68 Q. What did you do with the board?
69
70 A. I must have thrown it down the hallway. I know I
71    didn't take it back to the apartment. I don't know
72    where it is.
73
74 Q. Did you see Alma again?
75
76 A. No. The next thing I know is that I saw you in the
77    hallway outside my door.
78
79 Q. Have you ever been convicted of a crime?
80
81 A. Yes. I was convicted of aggravated assault five
82    years ago. They told me it was a felony, but I
83    received three years probation. It was just a fight
84    in a bar. I had to use a bottle.
85
86 Q. Is there anything else you want to say?
87
88 A. No, only that I loved Alma. I would never hurt her.
89
90 Q. After reading this statement, if you find the
91    statement correct as typed, will you sign the
92    statement?
93
94 A. Yes
```

Horace Johnson
Horace Johnson

430

Memorandum to Defense Counsel

Re: Death of Alma Bradshaw

   As you requested, I have examined Dr. Tapp's report
and the toxicologist's report. I do not understand
how Dr. Tapp could have concluded Bradshaw died of a
trauma-induced edema of the brain. Given the deceased's
height, weight, and physical condition it seems obvious
to me that it is just as likely that she died of
acute alcoholic poisoning. Her liver was in terrible
shape. She had ingested an enormous amount of alcohol.
Evidence concerning trauma indicates she did not
receive any severe blows. In addition, the amount of
time and distance between the receiving of the blows
and Bradshaw's collapse leads me to believe the trauma
had very little to do with her death. As you know, an
extremely high dose of alcohol taken by a person with
one lung can cause asphyxiation, and thus a resulting
edema of the brain. You should also understand that
alcoholics bruise easily, and they are known to walk
into objects and to fall frequently when intoxicated.
These possibilities should be explored in this case.
The bruises Dr. Tapp found could have been caused when
Bradshaw collapsed in Mrs. Prince's apartment.

   Please call me if you would like further details
concerning my findings and opinions.

_____
          Ralph Schultz, M.D.

Curriculum Vitae

Ralph Schultz, M.D.
100 Franklin Street

Occupation:

M.D., forensic pathologist

Education:

Harvard University, B.S. in biology, [-30]
John Hopkins University, M.D., [-26]

Training:

Internship, Massachusetts General Hospital, Boston, [-26]
    to [-25]
Residency in pathology, Harvard University Hospital,
    Cambridge, [-25] to [-22]

Employment:

New York County (Manhattan) Medical Examiner's Office,
    deputy coroner, [-22] to [-16]
University Hospital, clinical assistant professor of
    pathology, [-16] to [-10]
Private practice in pathology, [-16] to [-10]
University Hospital, professor of forensic pathology,
    [-10] to present. I have been the pathology
    department head since [-3].

Licenses:

New York, [-22]; this state, [-16]; board certified,
    American College of Pathology, [-14]

Publications:

I have published 12 articles to date, all dealing with
    various aspects of forensic pathology, in the
    AMA Journal, *New England Journal of Medicine*, and
    pathology journals.

Professional Associations:

American Medical Association
American College of Pathology
American Association of Forensic Pathologists

I have testified more than 100 times as an expert in forensic pathology. I testified on behalf of the defense about half the time. My fee for writing a report is $3,000. My fee for a court appearance is $5,000, plus expenses.

6.11   PSYCHIATRIST TESTIMONY IN MURDER CASE

The defendant, Ronald Wasserman, is charged with murder. He does not deny committing the acts that resulted in his mother's death. He asserts the affirmative defense of insanity (or not guilty by reason of mental disease or defect, if that is the terminology used in your jurisdiction).

You have in the file a psychologist's report and the report of the witness, Dr. Reese Hopkins, who conducted an independent, court-ordered examination. In addition, you have a summary of the statements of various witnesses to relevant events. That summary was made available to Dr. Hopkins after s/he filed his/her report.

Dr. Hopkins is called as a witness for the defense.

Your state's substantive law concerning the insanity (or mental disease or defect) defense will apply. Among the references to be used is the *Diagnostic and Statistical Manual of Mental Disorders*, American Psychiatric Association.

1.   For the defendant, conduct a direct examination of Dr. Hopkins.

2.   For the State, cross-examine Dr. Hopkins.

Ronald Wasserman was 23 years old when he shot and killed his mother on August 8, [-1].

Wasserman was born and raised in this city. During last year he was in his final year at the State University Circle Campus. Throughout grade school, high school, and college he was very affectionate with his mother. His love and affection toward her became even greater during the time that he was 20, 21, 22, and 23.

Until sometime in May of last year, Wasserman was described by people who knew him well as very outgoing, friendly, and interested in other people. Wasserman would ask questions and make jokes and was always smiling. He would always answer when spoken to and he was communicative with others. He appeared to be a young man normal in every way. Before May of last year, Wasserman would take part with his father in such activities as hunting, fishing, and going to parks and zoos. Wasserman was congenial, friendly, and easy to communicate with in his relations with other young men and women of his own age group, as well as with members of his family and friends of his parents.

In the last days of May, last year, Wasserman was informed by his father, Arthur, that his mother was in the final stage of a terminal disease, namely, leukemia, and that there was no hope that she would survive. When Wasserman was informed of his mother's condition, he began to cry in the company of his father and when he was alone. From that time on a change in Wasserman's personality and demeanor began to take place.

Wasserman became withdrawn, melancholy, moody, dejected, and uncommunicative. He would stare at the floor constantly. He would not take part in conversations in the presence of others, and when asked questions at times he would not respond and other times his responses were brief.

Wasserman's speech was forced, in phrases, but was not gibberish. He would stare off into space and at times put his hands to his eyes after staring into space.

Wasserman, with his father, was at his mother's Southeast Memorial Hospital bedside on June 3, last year, when his mother told a family friend, Estelle London, that she had leukemia and that she felt horrible. Then his mother said, "If this is the way I have to feel the rest of my life, I would rather be dead; I am not going to make it." At the time Wasserman appeared to be in a complete fog, he just stood and did not move. When a family friend who had known him since his birth tried to talk to him in the hospital room, he would not say a word.

On the following day at his mother's hospital bedside, he was present, with his father, when his mother said, "I feel miserable, I would rather be dead," and he was present when his father told the family friend who asked about his mother's condition, "There is no hope." At that time, Wasserman said nothing and is described by his father as looking like the whole world had come to an end for him.

In early June, last year, Wasserman was seen by his father looking at books connected with his university work, and in the early days of June, last year, he took his final examinations. Wasserman took four courses: One he did not finish, and in the other three his grades were two Cs and one D. He thereafter enrolled in summer school to complete one course needed for graduation. Before last year, Wasserman had a B+ grade average at the university.

In late June, at the Wasserman home and in his and his father's presence, his mother told a family friend, Irene Doss, that she was "much worse," that "the pain is unbearable." Wasserman and his father were present when the friend asked his mother if she had told the doctor, and his mother answered, "There is nothing he can do. If I have to go back to the hospital, I will kill myself." The family friend described Wasserman at that time as sitting still, like a stone, with no visible reaction.

On June 30, Wasserman purchased a .22 caliber automatic pistol at the Stein gun shop, and he furnished his correct name, date of birth, and his address, etc. In early July, in Wasserman's presence, his father asked his mother how she felt and she said, "If it is possible to be in more pain, this is it. If I have to come back here again, I will kill myself." His father described Wasserman as quiet, staring down to the floor, then up to his mother and back to the floor, and as not answering when his father tried to talk to him.

During early July, last year, at the Southeastern Memorial Hospital where Wasserman's mother again was hospitalized, she told Wasserman and his father that she was "getting worse. There is great pain, I don't think I will live to come out of it."

On another occasion at that hospital, in Wasserman's presence, she said to his father she felt "very bad; if I have to come back to the hospital I will kill myself." At that time Wasserman walked out of the room and when his father tried to talk to him, he would not respond. He is described by his father at that time as a completely different person, one who was becoming more dejected. On another occasion, in early July, last year, at the family home, his father told him that his mother was despondent and that she had asked his father "to kill her, to get her out of her misery." At that time Wasserman cried and said he wished he could have the pain instead of her.

In late July, at the family home and in his presence and in his father's presence, his mother said she was in pain and then said, "Please won't one of you kill me and put me out of my misery?" At that time Wasserman said nothing and walked out of the room.

During the months of June and July, last year, Wasserman's mother underwent physical outward changes—that is to say her face was distorted and had a flattened appearance, there appeared on her extremities an open rash, her feet were swollen, and she had open sores on her hands.

In early August, last year, at the family home at a time when his mother was weak, with her face swollen and the rash all over her body, she said to Wasserman and his father that she was in great pain and she said, "Please won't you kill me and put me out of my misery?" At that time Wasserman lowered his head, stood still for a moment, and walked out of the room. He was in tears. When his father tried to talk to him he would not talk.

Mrs. Wasserman was readmitted to the hospital on August 4.

On August 5, Wasserman was visiting the home of a young woman, Irene Doss, whom he had known since grade school days and with whom he had visited two or three times a month prior to May of last year. During June and July, after learning of his mother's illness at the end of May, Wasserman visited her home once a week. Wasserman told the young woman that his mother was slipping fast and that she was pleading with him to put her out of her misery. At that time he stared off into space and put his hands to his eyes. His eyes seemed blank. He would not look at her.

On August 7, Wasserman visited briefly with his mother at the hospital. Her condition was unchanged.

On the next day, August 8, Wasserman entered his mother's room. Only he and his mother were in the room. His father had brought him to the hospital, but sat in the visitor's waiting room when Ronald went to see his mother.

Mrs. Wasserman was sleeping. Ronald took the .22 automatic out of his pocket. He fired three shots into his mother's head. After a few seconds, he turned and walked out of the room. He walked to where the attending nurse, Harriett Stone, was sitting.

Miss Stone had been the attending nurse when Wasserman visited his mother on the earlier occasions. She is 34 years old, single, and lives two blocks from the hospital. She had been a registered nurse for eight years. For the first two years she moved through various departments at Southeastern, but has spent the past six years on the floor where Mrs. Wasserman's room is located. That floor is set aside for terminally ill patients, many of them suffering from cancer.

During the time Mrs. Wasserman was in the hospital, Nurse Stone came to know Ronald, mostly through informal conversations, either while Ronald was waiting to get into his mother's room or after he had paid a visit to his mother. They talked about Mrs. Wasserman and about other things, such as sports and his school classes.

When Ronald came to the floor on August 8, she greeted him, but his only response was a nod. Nurse Stone sat at her desk, opposite Mrs. Wasserman's room, when Ronald went inside. She noticed nothing unusual about him. She was working at the desk when she heard three shots. She immediately looked up and saw Ronald standing next to his mother's bed. He was pointing the gun at his mother's head. He then turned, came out of the room, and walked the few feet to the desk where Nurse Stone was sitting.

She saw Wasserman remove the clip from the gun. He placed the clip and the gun on Nurse Stone's desk.

Wasserman said to the nurse: "Please see if my mother is dead." The nurse went into the hospital room, where she determined that Mrs. Wasserman was dead. There were three bullet wounds in her head.

The nurse then came back to the desk, where Ronald was standing. Nurse Stone said: "She is dead. Why did you do it?" Ronald answered: "She begged me to do it."

Ronald then lit a cigarette and said he wanted to go out and tell his father what he had done. He walked into the visitor waiting room, where his father sat. He told his father: "Mother won't have to suffer anymore. I put her out of her misery. I just shot her."

Police officers, answering Nurse Stone's call, arrived a few minutes later and placed Ronald under arrest. He was charged with murder. Pursuant to court orders, Ronald was examined by Dr. Arturo Guzman, a psychologist, on August 13, and by Dr. Reese Hopkins, a psychiatrist, on September 14, [-1].

Nurse Stone told the police that shortly before Ronald arrived, she had made her rounds and had given Mrs. Wasserman a sedative to allow her to sleep. In her opinion, Ronald was sane on the day he shot his mother. She told police Ronald obviously was grieving over his mother's condition, but that was not an unusual occurrence among family members of patients suffering from cancer.

Subject: Ronald Wasserman

Date: August 13, [-1]

Location: Interview and Testing Room, County Jail

Findings:

Subject was friendly and cooperative on a
superficial level.

In the field of intelligence Subject's performance
was adequate and his intellectual level was in the
bright-normal range. The test for personality functioning
suggested that in the area of reality orientation
Subject's ability to perceive reality adequately was
sufficient and adequate under essentially neutral
conditions, but under stress his reality contact tended
to become tenuous, that is, impaired. His emotional
functioning at the time was labile, that is, unstable,
vulnerable.

He did not maintain adequate emotional control over
his intellectual and social functioning in the testing
situation.

His emotions showed signs of immaturity and
impulsivity. That is, he did not have his emotions under
good control.

His fantasy life was not particularly good and it
showed signs of vulnerability, and under stress showed
signs of some bizarre and some emotionally unstable
functioning.

The Rorschach, T.A.T., and draw-a-person tests also
showed Subject's intellectual control over his emotional
function was not adequate under stress; that on the
surface without the situation of stress, an emotional
response would come to the surface, along with some

confusion. Underlying confusional reasoning may come to the fore.

Under situations without stress, Subject maintains adequate controls and could function in situations where there was not great emotional stress and upheaval put upon him.

There were no major signs of organic brain damage.

Although it is not unusual for people to have some impairment of reality perception under stress, the degree of impairment in this case was very considerable.

Although it is not unusual within limits for persons to lose some emotional stability under stress, the test showed Subject's loss of emotional stability was beyond the usual limits.

Arturo Guzman, PhD
30 N. Michigan

Reese Hopkins, M.D.
112 N. State Street

September 16, [-1]

The Honorable _____

Court Center

RE: RONALD WASSERMAN

Dear Judge _____

The following psychiatric report is subsequent to your
order requesting psychiatric evaluation of the defendant
Ronald Wasserman. The evaluation was requested concerning
criminal responsibility at the time of the alleged
offense.

SUMMARY:

    Mr. Ronald Wasserman is a 23-year-old single white
male who is presently in confinement at the County Jail
House of Corrections. His charge is murder, based on an
incident which occurred on August 8, [-1].

    CURRENT CHARGE:

    In his interview with this examiner, the defendant
was extremely reluctant to discuss the events leading
up to and including his mother's death. He stated that
his memory of the event was somewhat foggy and confused,
and that only a few incidents were clear to him during
this period of time. He recalled that he first learned
of his mother's illness from his father in May and
stated that he reacted with shock, because his mother
had seemed perfectly healthy to him. He had thought
that his mother had never been ill before, as far as
he knew. While at first he visited his mother in the
hospital voluntarily, he soon found himself finding
the visits very troubling, so that he tended to avoid
visiting her whenever possible. Sometime in early
June, according to the defendant, he began experiencing
difficulty falling asleep at night; this progressed to

the point where he was unable to fall asleep before 3:00 or 5:00 in the morning. He was also awakened by recurrent frightening dreams about animal corpses, to which he gave little thought. He did not, however, feel tired during the daytime, and did not attempt to nap; but he did experience a change in his activity and interest pattern. He visited his friends and girlfriend much less frequently, stopped playing tennis, and did not — during the entire summer of these events — go swimming or to the beach or participate in dances or parties of any kind. He felt himself somewhat cut off from other people, experienced things as somewhat dream-like or unreal, although he could not clarify this further. Regarding schoolwork, he found himself rereading pages or paragraphs and then not recalling what he had just read; after some time he gave up trying to read completely. He did believe that he was doing well in school nevertheless, and expected to receive good grades. He was baffled by the Cs and Ds he reportedly achieved in his examinations. He also recalled having been late to class several times, or even walking into a wrong classroom before realizing he had done so. He recalled having difficulty making decisions and, for example, wore the same clothes repeatedly on different days because of this inability to make decisions. His personal grooming and dressing habits deteriorated, and he had to be reminded to shower and shave. He also reported having difficulty driving his car, in that he frequently was honked at by other drivers because he was driving too slowly. On one occasion, he had a minor car accident by rear-ending another car, but no injuries resulted. He also reported mild confusion in his thinking processes, which he described as "being slowed." He experienced difficulty starting to talk and found himself talking a lot less than usual. He experienced subjectively a lack of energy, difficulty getting out of bed in the morning, as well as a marked decrease in appetite, so that he lost 20 pounds from his already thin body. In general, he described his feeling as being "numbed" or "I lost my feelings entirely," but there is no distinct depressive mood noted or reported. There were also small fluctuations from day to day or within the day, as to his mood. During this period of time, he denied suicidal ideation, anxiety symptoms, somatic symptoms, unusual use of alcohol or drugs, experiences of thought broadcasting or thought insertion, or frank hallucinations. He recalled experiencing some persistent rumbling noises and sometimes wondered if, somehow, his thoughts had been withdrawn from his head because his mind seemed so blank much of the time. He stated that it did not occur to him to seek professional help at any time, nor did he think that anything was wrong with him during that period. When he was asked in particular why he had purchased the handgun on June 30, he was unable to account for this. He stated that he did not, however, carry this gun around with him until the day on which he used it. He was also unable to account for why he shot his mother, although he commented somewhat vaguely that he was unable to tolerate his mother's suffering.

PAST RELEVANT HISTORY:

The defendant did not have a previous psychiatric history of any kind. He has not been in psychiatric treatment, and on review of systems, denied notable psychiatric or psychological dysfunction. There was also no previous involvement with alcohol or drugs, and no involvement in the Criminal Justice system. He was never involved in gang activities, and had only a very rare boyhood fistfight. He tended to describe himself as efficient, independent, contented, and likable — but also gave some indication of being a loner.

Personal history indicates that he was an only child to his parents, with whom he lived until he was 20 years of age, when he entered college. At age 20 he moved into an apartment with a roommate, with whom he has continued to live over the last three years. Even though he left his parents' home, he continued to see his parents on a regular, almost weekly basis. He described his mother as loving and generous; he described his father as somewhat distant and hardworking. There are no family disruptions

447

of any kind, and no reported family history of mental disorder, substance abuse, or sociopathy. The defendant has always been in good medical health, and has never had a hospitalization for any reason.

CURRENT MENTAL STATUS:

The undersigned psychiatrist performed a psychiatric interview on the defendant on September 14. The interview lasted for two hours and was conducted at the undersigned's office. The defendant was initially informed of the non-confidentiality of the interview.

The defendant appeared as a very thin, pale, college-age young man, who appeared somewhat younger than his stated age. He was groomed somewhat sloppily, and shook the examiner's hand somewhat limply. He immediately gave an impression of being troubled by something without being able to understand or explain it very well. His speech was slow and generally coherent. There were no neologisms and no formal thought disorder, but his speech tended to be vague, sparse, and metaphorical at times, making precise understanding difficult. His speech was not spontaneous, and he responded only when spoken to. No clear-cut delusional thought content was observed. No signs of hallucinations were observed, and no hallucinations were admitted. Throughout the interview he appeared withdrawn, with a distinctly saddened affect which was, however, sometimes labile. His eyes became wet on several occasions, but he was unaware of this, he claimed, until it had been pointed out to him. He never smiled or laughed during the interview. As noted above, it was difficult to get him to talk about the events leading up to the current charge. No clear-cut guilt or remorse was identified. There was moderate psycho-motor retardation, but without mutism, posturing, waxy-flexibility, or negativism. Suicidal ideation was denied. He was oriented to place, but was off by three days on the day of the week, and four dates on the place in the month. He could state the name of the U.S. president and the governor of Illinois. He was only able to recite four digits forward and three digits in reverse. He made several mistakes on Serial Seven Subtractions before abandoning the task prematurely. When asked to interpret the proverb, "Don't count your chickens . . . " he responded, "A cat has nine lives", but was unable to explain what he meant by this.

DIAGNOSIS:

According to the most recent edition of the *Diagnostic Manual* published by the American Psychiatric Association, the patient can be diagnosed as Major Depressive Disorder.

CONCLUSION:

Criminal Responsibility: This young man had no prior psychiatric disturbance of any kind prior to his current episode of a major depressive disorder, which has been characterized by: distinct and persistent mood change, loss of interest and pleasure in activities, withdrawal, loss of appetite and weight, initial insomnia, nightmares, difficulty thinking and concentrating, difficulty making decisions, and subjective loss of energy. No signs of catatonia were noted. The defendant became apparently preoccupied with the issues surrounding his mother's severe illness and was unable to attend to his other activities and responsibilities during this interim. While there were no gross, florid psychotic symptoms (such as frank delusions or hallucinations), the patient reported derealization, memory loss, subjective experiences of confusion, thought withdrawal, vague rumbling noises or sounds. Additionally, on interview, I observed moderate but subtle alterations in speech and thinking — all of which suggest some definite impairment in his reality testing processes — which persists even unto the present, about five weeks after the admitted homicide. In my opinion, Ronald Wasserman was suffering from mental disease or defect at the time he killed his mother. Further, it is my opinion that as a result of that mental disease or defect Ronald Wasserman lacked

449

the substantial capacity to conform his conduct to the requirements of the law.

Very truly yours,

Reese Hopkins, M.D.

Reese Hopkins, M.D.

450

Curriculum Vitae:

Reese Hopkins, M.D.   Office Address:
                                       112 N. State

Education:
    University of Illinois, Urbana-Champaign:
        B.S. Psychology, [-14]
        M.D. Medicine, [-11]
    Rotating Internship, Cook County Hospital,
        [-11 to -10]
    Residency in Psychiatry, Cook County Hospital,
        [-10 to -9]
    Post-Doctorate Fellowship, University of Chicago,
        Research in Major Depression, [-8]

Specialization of Practice:
    General Practice of Psychiatry, [-8 to present]
    Adjunct Clinical Professor of Psychiatry, University
        of Illinois-Chicago Circle, [-8 to present]

Licensure:
    State of Illinois Board of Physicians, [-11]
    Illinois Board of Psychiatry, [-7]
    Board Certified by American Board of Psychiatry and
        Neurology, [-7]
    Certified, American Board of Forensic Psychiatry, [-5]

Professional Organizations:
    Member American Psychiatric Association, [-7 to
        present]
    Member of A.P.A. National Psychiatric Trauma Task
        Force, [-7 to present]
    American Medical Association, [-9 to present]

Articles Published:
    Post Traumatic Stress Disorder - Distinguishing the
        Myth from Reality, 74 A.M.A. *Journal of Psychiatry*
        36, 7/15/[-7]
    Bereavement from the Loss of a Loved One in a
        Traumatic Accident, 83 A.M.A. *Journal of Psychiatry*
        129, 7/15/[-5]
    Co-Author, [-5] A.P.A. National Psychiatric Trauma Task
        Force Guidelines for Treatment of Trauma Victims
    The Insanity Defense in Criminal Cases, 87 A.M.A.
        Journal of Psychiatry 72, 9/15/[-5]

6.12 PSYCHIATRIST TESTIMONY IN CIVIL CASE

This is a personal injury case. On January 9, [-3], the plaintiff, Rachel Tyson, was a passenger on the City Transit Authority (CTA) elevated subway system, which is owned by the city. The subway car in which Tyson was sitting was stopped when it was hit from the rear by another subway train. Several persons were killed in the crash. Tyson was pinned in the subway car. She was eventually removed by rescue workers and taken to a nearby hospital. At the hospital Tyson was treated by Dr. Ramon Suarez and later released.

In February [-2], Tyson was seen by a psychiatrist, Dr. Arthur Shapiro. Dr. Shapiro died three weeks before this trial takes place. Each side immediately hired a psychiatrist to examine the Suarez and Shapiro reports and reach an opinion based on the facts and findings in those reports. Neither expert has personally examined the plaintiff, and neither expert prepared a written report of his opinion.

The plaintiff's expert, Dr. Leslie Horvath, has said s/he believes that Tyson is suffering from post-traumatic stress disorder. S/he believes that the disorder and the symptoms described in Dr. Shapiro's report were caused by the accident. The defendant's expert, Dr. Damien Fuller, has reached a diagnosis of compensation neurosis and/or complicated bereavement and/or malingering. The defense has also located a man named Timothy Swenson. At one time he was a social friend of Tyson. His deposition was taken last year.

Since the accident, Tyson has not returned to her job at the City Electric Company. Her gross salary at the time of the accident was $1,500 per week. Tyson's medical expenses, including the hospital bill of $16,000, Dr. Suarez's bill of $3,000, and Dr. Shapiro's bill of $5,500, have not been paid.

Tyson is suing the CTA for negligently causing the collision. The CTA has admitted liability. The only issue is the amount of damages that will reasonably and fairly compensate the plaintiff for her injuries. The case is being tried in your state and your jurisdiction's tort law applies.

You have in the file the reports of Dr. Suarez and Dr. Shapiro, Tyson's deposition, Swenson's deposition, and the résumés of the plaintiff's expert, Dr. Leslie Horvath, and the defendant's expert, Dr. Damien Fuller.

The parties have already stipulated to the admissibility of Tyson's medical expenses. The plaintiff now calls Dr. Horvath. (You should consult the *Diagnostic and Statistical Manual of Mental Disorders*, American Psychiatric Association, and other relevant sources, to prepare for the examinations.)

1. For the plaintiff, conduct a direct examination of Dr. Horvath.
2. For the defendant, cross-examine Dr. Horvath.

DR. RAMON SUAREZ

111 West Washington

MEDICAL REPORT — January 12, [-3]

NAME OF PATIENT: Rachel Tyson

HISTORY: Patient was seen for first time on January 9, [-3], in emergency room of the Northwestern Memorial Hospital. She was brought there by Fire Department ambulance from scene of CTA elevated train crash. She complained of pain in chest and head and of dizziness. There were mild bruises on the mid-sternal areas of the chest. She said she was struck on the head and suffered momentary loss of consciousness, with amnesia two or three minutes after impact. Patient was hospitalized for three days.

SUBJECTIVE SYMPTOMS: In addition to above, patient complained of headaches, nausea, and dizziness.

OBJECTIVE FINDINGS: X-rays were negative. Electroencephalogram was negative. No sign of internal injuries. With exception of mild bruises on the mid-sternal areas of the chest, no objective symptoms were observed.

TREATMENT: During hospitalization, patient was observed. Bed rest. Analgesics prescribed. Cervical collar prescribed.

DIAGNOSIS: Post-concussion syndrome. Severe whiplash of cervical spine.

<u>PROGNOSIS</u>: Uncertain. Patient still complains of headaches, nausea, and dizziness. Discharged from hospital this date with instructions to wear a cervical collar for one month and take analgesics as needed.

Ramon Suarez, M.D.

ARTHUR SHAPIRO, M.D.

500 N. Michigan

REPORT CONCERNING RACHEL TYSON, Re: Tyson v. CTA

The plaintiff is a 50-year-old white female who was in good physical and emotional health prior to the January 9, [-3], CTA elevated train crash that occurred in the downtown area of the city. The plaintiff, who had no previous psychiatric history of any kind, and whose past medical history included removal of a benign breast mass in [-18], and a partial thyroidectomy for hyper-thyroidism in [-6], was facing forward in the last car of a four-car CTA subway train, which was heading east aboveground. The train in which the plaintiff was riding was at a complete stop when it was hit by another CTA train from the rear, moving at about 25-30 miles per hour. The plaintiff was pinned in her seat, wedged between it and the metal railing in front of her surrounding the middle exit of the CTA car.

She sustained mild contusions of the mid-sternal areas of the chest and a blow to the head, which resulted in momentary loss of consciousness with amnesia two to three minutes after impact. Immediate medical evaluation, including hospitalization for three days, included negative X-rays, negative electroencephalogram, and no signs of internal injuries. Post-concussion syndrome was diagnosed as the patient presented with headaches, nausea, and dizziness.

She was discharged with instructions to wear a cervical collar for one month and take analgesics as needed. It was also noted that plaintiff had a severe whiplash injury during the accident. Her headaches, nausea, dizziness, and periods of irritability persisted through about four months following the injury, during which she was not able to return to work. Her employer offered to assign her to a less stressful job, but she refused this. She has not yet returned to any type of work. She said she is living on the proceeds of her mother's $250,000 life insurance policy.

Approximately seven months after the accident, she began to have feelings of depression, unexplainable startle reactions, tearing whenever she heard of accidents of any kind in the city, and nightmares in which she would relive aspects of the above-described accident. She continued her inability to return to work, suffered a decreased interest in dating and sexual activity, and had less contact with her close friends.

Approximately one year after the accident her attorney, who represents her in her case against the CTA, referred her to the undersigned for psychiatric assessment because of her continuing dreams, crying spells, and symptoms of anxiety and depression. It should also be noted that three passengers of the CTA car, seated within 15 feet of her, were killed in that train crash. She watched them die. Apparently it was a gory scene. Injured people in the car were screaming and crying, and there was much blood. I saw her for the first time on Feb. 5, [-2].

Prior to the injury, the plaintiff was socially active and had a number of mature heterosexual relationships, none of which eventuated in marriage. She described herself as outgoing, popular, and an active dancer and bowler. She had an outstanding job record with the City Electric Company, though on several occasions had turned down promotions to the supervisory level. She was her parents' only child, her father having died of carcinoma 20 years before the accident. The plaintiff was the sole provider for her elderly mother until her mother's death, which occurred approximately three months prior to the accident. The patient had lived with her mother all of her life until her mother's death.

When I asked her how she felt about her mother's death, she said she loved her mother very much, but that it wasn't until after the accident that she really felt the loss. It wasn't until then that she was able to cry about the death of her mother. She said she didn't really "feel depressed" about her mother's death until after the accident.

There is no history of prior psychiatric difficulties or psychiatric treatment for the patient or her family. At age 25, she had been involved in an automobile accident in which she was rear-ended. She suffered a mild whiplash injury, without neurological or orthopedic sequelae. An out-of-court settlement awarding her $5,000 was reached.

My physical evaluation in February [-2] demonstrated a completely normal physical examination. Neurological examination was similarly without evidence of organic dysfunction. Skull X-rays, cervical neck X-rays, and an EEG were again reported to be within normal limits. Mental status examination revealed a moderately depressed 50-year-old white female, who was preoccupied with the impact of the aforementioned injury on her subsequent life. She blames the injury for every event in her life, including her inability to date, inability to return to work, her inability to "enjoy life," and the recurrent physical discomforts described above. She reported a disturbed sleep pattern; more frequent dreams of the accident; tearing easily when describing the events, both during and after the accident; and expressed considerable anger at her physicians, her employer, and her attorney, whom she felt was not acting rapidly enough with the resolution of her physical problems or her legal case against the CTA.

She clearly understood the personal injury lawsuit pending against the CTA, and stated that she sought damages both for physical injuries and "emotional trauma."

The undersigned recommended to patient that she begin a course of psychiatric treatment. Her attendance was extremely erratic and, after a few months, she stopped completely.

SIGNED: _Arthur Shapiro_
ARTHUR SHAPIRO, M.D.

DATE OF REPORT: <u>NOV. 1, [-1]</u>

DEPOSITION OF RACHEL TYSON

on December 20, [-1]

at offices of defendant's attorney

RACHEL TYSON, having been first duly sworn, testified as follows:

1 Q. (by defendant's attorney) What is your name?
2
3 A. Rachel Tyson.
4
5 Q. Are you currently employed?
6
7 A. No. I have not been able to work since the crash.
8
9 Q. Have you read the report Dr. Shapiro wrote to your
10 lawyer?
11
12 A. Yes, I have. Several times.
13
14 Q. Does that report accurately reflect the things you
15 said to Dr. Shapiro?
16
17 A. Yes. It is very accurate.
18
19 Q. Does that report leave out anything you told Dr.
20 Shapiro?
21
22 A. Not that I can remember at this time.
23
24 Q. Why did you stop the course of psychiatric
25 treatment Dr. Shapiro prescribed?
26
27 A. I just couldn't stand talking about the crash.
28 That's all they wanted to talk about.
29
30 Q. Why haven't you returned to work?
31
32 A. Everything I do reminds me of the crash. I can't
33 stand the loud noises when I go outside. I can't
34 travel. It was so difficult for me to get here
35 today.
36
37 Q. What is your educational level?
38
39 A. I graduated from high school. I never went to
40 college, but I have educated myself. I read a lot
41 of everything.

42 Q. Why did you bring this lawsuit?
43
44 A. My life has been destroyed. Someone has to pay for
45   that.

This is to certify that I have read the transcript
of my deposition taken on the 20th day of December,
[-1], and that the transcript accurately states the
questions asked and the answers given.

Rachel Tyson
Rachel Tyson

Subscribed and sworn to before
me this 20th day of December, [-1]

Felix Jasmon
Notary Public

DEPOSITION OF TIMOTHY SWENSON

on December 15, [-1]

at offices of plaintiff's attorney,

TIMOTHY SWENSON, having been first duly sworn,
testified as follows:

1 Q. (by plaintiff's attorney) Please state your name.
2
3 A. Timothy Swenson.
4
5 Q. Where are you now employed?
6
7 A. I am a teller at the First Mutual Bank. I have been
8   there for about ten years.
9
10 Q. How old are you?
11
12 A. I'll be 55 on my next birthday.
13
14 Q. Are you married?
15
16 A. No. Never married.
17
18 Q. Do you know a woman named Rachel Tyson?
19
20 A. Yes.
21
22 Q. When did you first meet her?
23
24 A. It was just before Christmas of [-3]. We met at a
25   party given by some mutual friends.
26
27 Q. Would you mind describing your relationship with
28   Miss Tyson?
29
30 A. Well, we went out seven or eight times, dinner,
31   bowling, movies, things like that.
32
33 Q. You were social friends?
34
35 A. Yeah. But she would never let it be more than just
36   friends. I mean she wouldn't invite me to her
37   apartment. And she wouldn't come to mine. We just
38   went out.
39
40 Q. For how long a period of time did you go out with
41   her?

42 A. It was over a period of about three months.
43
44 Q. During that time, did you notice anything unusual
45   about her?
46
47 A. What do you mean?
48
49 Q. Well, did she ever complain of headaches or any
50   kind of pain?
51
52 A. No. Not that I can recall.
53
54 Q. Did she ever seem depressed, or sad?
55
56 A. No, every time I was with her she seemed happy. She
57   was always smiling and making little jokes. And she
58   laughed at my jokes. I can't remember a time when
59   she seemed sad.
60
61 Q. Did she ever cry in your presence?
62
63 A. Never. I would remember that.
64
65 Q. What kind of things would you do on your dates with
66   Miss Tyson?
67
68 A. Well, we would have dinner, maybe go dancing. She
69   loved to dance. She also liked to go bowling. We
70   went once, but I wasn't much good at it.
71
72 Q. Did she ever talk about her mother?
73
74 A. No, the subject never came up.
75
76 Q. Did you know she had been in a CTA accident the
77   January before you met?
78
79 A. No. The first I heard of it was when the train
80   company's lawyer called me. She never mentioned
81   it.
82
83 Q. Was there a reason why you stopped seeing Miss
84   Tyson?
85
86 A. Well, we had kind of difference of opinion about
87   where our relationship was going. She started
88   hinting about marriage and I wasn't interested in
89   that. I told her I just wanted to have a good time.
90   We agreed to disagree, if you know what I mean.
91   I just didn't call her again. She didn't call me
92   either.

464

This is to certify that I have read the transcript of my deposition taken on the 15th day of December, [-1], and that the transcript accurately states the questions asked and the answers given.

_____
Timothy Swenson

Subscribed and sworn to before
me this 20th day of December, [-1]

_____
Notary Public

CURRICULUM VITAE

LESLIE HORVATH, M.D.

Education:

Northwestern School of Medicine
    - degree M.D. [-15]
    - residency in psychiatry [-15] - [-13]
    - fellowship: stress related disorders
      [-13] - [-11]

Professional:

    - Rush Hospital
    * attending physician [-11] - present
    * associate professor, Rush University College
      of Medicine, Department of Psychiary
      [-10] - present
    - Private Practice
    * office located at 444 N. Michigan Avenue

Publications:

    - *Malingering*, New England Journal of Medicine,
      Vol. 10, [-5]
    - *Post Traumatic Stress Disorder: Fact or Fiction*,
      University of Chicago Press, [-3]

Memberships:

    * American College of Psychiatrists
      member - Committee on Stress Related Disorders
    * American Medical Association

Licenses:

    * Illinois [-15]
    * Michigan [-10]
    * Board eligible

CURRICULUM VITAE

DAMIEN FULLER, M.D.

EMPLOYMENT

- Private Practice [-13] - present. Provide direct patient care to private patients.
- Teaching [-7] - present. Psychiatry and Medicine, University of Chicago. Course includes a general overview of topics of current interest on the relationship between physical and mental health.

EDUCATION

- B.S. University of Wisconsin, Madison, [-24]
- M.S. University of Chicago, [-23]
- M.D. University of Chicago, [-20]
- Residency, University of Chicago, Billings Hospital, [-19]
- Post-Doctorate Fellowship, University of Chicago, Billings Hospital. Providing direct patient care to students and staff of the University. Research in depression.

LICENSES

- Illinois Board of Physicians, [-20]
- Illinois Board of Psychiatrists, [-19]
- Board Certified in Depressive Disorders by the American Board of Psychiatry and Neurology, [-18]

ORGANIZATIONS

- American Psychiatric Association

PUBLICATIONS

- The Etiology of Affective Disorders, *American Journal of Psychiatry*, Fall, [-7]
- Situational Depression: Sadness Is Not a Disease, *American Journal of Psychiatry*, Spring, [-5]

6.13   HEARING REGARDING ADMISSIBILITY OF EXPERT OPINION

Rose Kowalski has filed a products liability complaint against Nuevas Pharmaceuticals, Inc., manufacturer of a drug called Parlux. The drug is prescribed for prevention of postpartum physiological lactation following childbirth. Mrs. Kowalski contends the drug caused her to suffer an intracerebral hemorrhage (stroke) on day 13 of a 14-day course of Parlux following the birth of her child. Nuevas denies that its product can cause or did cause the stroke.

The plaintiff's proposed expert witness is Dr. Alexis Salkov. The defendant has moved to bar Dr. Salkov's testimony, citing FRE 702, *Daubert v. Merrell Dow Pharmaceuticals*, 509 U.S. 579 (1993), and *General Electric v. Joiner*, 522 U.S. 136 (1997). The trial court has agreed to conduct a FRE 104(a) hearing into the admissibility of the expert testimony.

The trial court has announced the hearing will be confined to Dr. Salkov's testimony. The court has ruled that Dr. Salkov is qualified to render opinions in medicine and vascular neurology, in general, but has not determined whether the proposed testimony will be allowed in the case at hand.

You have Dr. Salkov's deposition, which is consistent with the doctor's FRCP Rule 26(b) report, and you have Dr. Salkov's Curriculum Vitae. The case is being tried in a jurisdiction that has adopted the Federal Rules of Evidence that relate to expert testimony.

(1)   For the plaintiff, conduct a direct examination of Dr. Salkov at the pretrial hearing and argue for admission of his/her proposed testimony.

(2)   For the defendant, conduct a cross-examination of Dr. Salkov at the pretrial hearing and argue against admission of his/her proposed testimony.

(3)   Be prepared to address the following questions:

   (a)   Which side has the burden of production regarding the admissibility of Dr. Salkov's testimony (i.e., the burden of presenting evidence to raise an issue for the court's consideration)?

(b) Which side has the burden of persuasion regarding whether Dr. Salkov's testimony is admissible or inadmissible?

(4) Would the procedure be any different if the case were being tried in a *Frye* jurisdiction?

ALEXIS SALKOV, having been first duly sworn, testified
as follows:

1 Q. Please state your name and spell it for the
2   record?
3
4 A. Yes. I am Dr. Alexis Salkov, A-L-E-X-I-S, S-A-L-K-O-V.
5
6 Q. Thank you. Dr. Salkov, I have here your
7   Curriculum Vitae. Is this a true and accurate
8   account of your qualifications?
9
10 A. Yes.
11
12 Q. Turning to the events surrounding Mrs. Kowalski's
13   stroke, what medication was Mrs. Kowalski using
14   postpartum?
15
16 A. Mrs. Kowalski was given Parlux, a Nuevas
17   Pharmaceuticals product, to prevent lactation
18   postpartum. She took it orally for 13 days fol-
19   lowing delivery by Caesarian section.
20
21 Q. Please describe what happened while she was
22   taking Parlux.
23
24 A. On day 13 of her 14-day course of Parlux, she
25   presented at the hospital complaining of an
26   excruciating headache. A CT scan revealed an
27   intracerebral hemorrhage — blood in the brain
28   tissue. Although surgery was performed immediate-
29   ly to evacuate the blood and to repair the
30   damaged artery, the ICH caused permanent motor
31   paralysis and speech difficulty.
32
33 Q. Do you believe that Parlux can cause intracere-
34   bral hemorrhage, or ICH?
35
36 A. Yes, I do.
37
38 Q. How do you determine whether a drug can cause an
39   adverse reaction?
40
41 A. Researchers and physicians use several methods.
42   You can do a differential diagnosis and look at
43   case reports. You also learn about the drug in
44   question — for example, you can find out about

45 known side effects of the drug and the drug family
46 from textbooks and articles. You look at
47 dechallenge/rechallenge reports, which are often
48 found in case reports. Epidemiological studies,
49 if they exist, are important. Clinical trials
50 and animal studies are also important.
51
52 Q. Do you believe Parlux caused Mrs. Kowalski's
53   ICH?
54
55 A. Yes, I do. I have concluded that she suffered
56   from a bleeding-type stroke caused by her ingestion
57   of Parlux.
58
59 Q. Please explain what you mean by a bleeding-type
60   stroke?
61
62 A. Yes. A CT scan revealed blood in the brain tissue.
63   Surgery later revealed that an artery had
64   burst. So this was a bleeding-type stroke, as
65   opposed to a "dry stroke" or ischemic-type
66   stroke, in which blood flow is stopped due to a
67   clot that has formed elsewhere in the body and
68   has traveled to the brain, but the clot does not
69   cause blood to enter the brain tissue.
70
71 Q. What methodology did you use to identify Parlux
72   as the cause of Mrs. Kowalski's ICH?
73
74 A. I used the differential diagnosis method.
75   Differential diagnosis is a patient-specific
76   process of elimination that medical practition-
77   ers use to identify the most likely cause of a
78   set of signs and symptoms from a list of possi-
79   ble causes. Basically, you learn what you can
80   about the patient, then you learn what you can
81   about the drug in question, and then you put all
82   that information together and ask the question:
83   Was the drug in question the cause of an adverse
84   drug reaction?
85
86 Q. Is this a common method of analysis?
87
88 A. This is basically the scientific method for
89   analyzing adverse drug reactions in a particular
90   person. It does not address causation as a general
91   matter.
92
93 Q. Where did you learn this method?
94
95 A. I've talked to many people. I've heard many
96   lectures on the subject. I've read textbooks on

474

```
 97    this. And I've used it hundreds of times in my
 98    own practice.
 99
100 Q. Is this method reliable and widely used?
101
102 A. This is what is done on a daily basis by physi-
103    cians, scientists, regulatory agencies, and
104    drug manufacturers, and I believe that this is
105    the approach that was used by Nuevas itself in
106    analyzing cases of possible adverse drug reactions
107    reported to it at their Drug Monitoring Center in
108    Basel, Switzerland.
109
110 Q. How did you apply it to Mrs. Kowalski's case?
111
112 A. I looked at possible other causes of her ICH. To
113    begin, I reviewed her medical records. Normally,
114    if you have the patient in front of you, you
115    would do a history and physical, or an H and P.
116    And you would ask many questions about their
117    past history, what drugs they've been on in the
118    past, what drugs they're on now. Are there any
119    risk factors for stroke? If it's a stroke
120    patient, was there a family history of stroke?
121    Do they have hypertension? Et cetera. In this case
122    I wasn't able to interview the patient because
123    the stroke had affected her ability to speak,
124    but her medical records showed that she had none
125    of these factors. The CT scan, an angiogram,
126    her blood work, and other tests showed she had
127    no other condition that would lead to a stroke
128    — no head injury, no anatomical defect in the
129    brain, no blood clotting disorder, no heart
130    abnormalities. No brain tumor, no evidence of
131    treatment for hypertension. She was overweight,
132    but not clinically obese. Her cholesterol was
133    only minimally elevated. She did have a history
134    of smoking, about a pack a day, but at the end
135    of the differential diagnosis process it doesn't
136    change the result.
137
138 Q. Why not?
139
140 A. Although she had a pretty heavy habit, and I think
141    nicotine can cause some vasoconstriction, her
142    smoking history is short — only six years. I think
143    it did not cause her stroke because there was no
144    evidence for atherosclerosis, or hardening of the
145    arteries, on her angiogram, which is one of the
146    reasons smoking may be associated with stroke to
147    begin with. Her blood vessels
```

148 were clean. There is a distinct difference between
149 risk factor and cause.
150
151 Q. Isn't advanced maternal age also a risk factor for
152 intracerebral hemorrhage?
153
154 A. Barely, in this case — she was only 36.
155
156 Q. Mrs. Kowalski also had a history of headaches.
157
158 A. She does have a five-year history of intermit-
159 tent vertex throbbing headaches. However, migraine
160 headaches do not cause bleeding-type strokes.
161 There is evidence that migraine headaches can
162 cause ischemic strokes where blood vessels can
163 clamp down so that brain tissues no longer receive
164 blood, but that is different than hemorrhagic
165 stroke.
166
167 Q. Can differential diagnosis establish general
168 causation of a disease by a drug?
169
170 A. Well, it's not designed to do that. Differential
171 diagnosis is designed to be used for a specific
172 patient, which is not what general causation
173 concerns.
174
175 Q. You mentioned other case reports.
176
177 A. Yes. These are important. The two cases that I
178 am aware of are the basis for an article I pub-
179 lished on the relationship between Parlux and
180 headaches attributable to vasospasm.
181
182 Q. Tell me about the first case.
183
184 A. The first woman I saw was a postpartum patient
185 taking Parlux for lactation suppression. She
186 developed a very bad headache while taking the
187 drug. The hospital gave her Midrin, which is a
188 common headache medication, and released her.
189 She returned in critical condition, in ventricu-
190 lar tachycardia. She apparently did not suffer a
191 myocardial infarction, but she was in preinfarc-
192 tion condition.
193
194 Q. And the second case?
195
196 A. The neurologist who was involved in treating the
197 first woman related a second case history to me.

198 The second woman was also taking Parlux for lac-
199 tation suppression when she developed a
200 headache. She was also given headache medica-
201 tion. The second patient actually suffered a
202 stroke. The day after her stroke, she had an
203 angiogram, which showed widespread diffuse
204 vasospasm on the angiogram. A repeat angiogram
205 performed several months later was normal.
206
207 Q. Is there evidence that Parlux causes vasospasm?
208
209 A. There is some evidence to indicate that it does.
210 It was my belief that Parlux, with or without the
211 other drug, was clearly causing spasm and the
212 subsequent stroke.
213
214 Q. Do these case reports establish causation—that
215 Parlux can cause an intracerebral hemorrhage?
216
217 A. No, case reports by themselves do not prove
218 causation and I would never attempt to do so.
219 Case reports are traditionally viewed as the
220 least vigorous form of proof of a hypothesis or
221 validation of a theory, particularly single case
222 reports, which are not controlled. You can't
223 establish relative risk factors from a single
224 case.
225
226 Q. What evidence leads you to believe that Parlux
227 causes vasospasm?
228
229 A. Looking at the family of drugs from which the
230 drug originated is important. If you know the
231 side effect of aspirin, for example, and there's
232 a drug that is an aspirin derivative, one might
233 conclude that you would expect the side effects
234 of that derivative to be like aspirin. It may or
235 may not be true, but it's a good place to
236 start. That doesn't tell you automatically that
237 the drug must act like other family members,
238 but it gives you an idea of what the expected
239 side effects might be. Parlux shares some common
240 properties with pergolide and with the parent
241 family of ergot compounds. Ergots can cause
242 digital vasospasm; Parlux itself is on the differ-
243 ential diagnosis for myocardial infarction. It
244 contains bromocriptine, the active ingredient in
245 Parlux.

246 Q. So because Parlux is an ergot alkaloid it causes
247   vasoconstriction?
248
249 A. Not necessarily. However, because there is clear
250   myocardial infarction, it appears that Parlux
251   possibly could cause stroke as well because the
252   physiologic mechanism is identified. You would
253   have to have some evidence, as well, but again,
254   you're looking at a toxicologic syndrome of
255   ergotism where these things happen together from
256   the same drug.
257
258 Q. Do you have an opinion as to the specific
259   biological or pathological mechanism by which
260   Parlux causes the vasoconstriction in humans?
261
262 A. I've given multiple possibilities as to what
263   the cellular pharmacologic receptor mechanism
264   could be for that vasoconstriction, but I am
265   not able to say that there is one that is more
266   likely than not the mechanism. But if one ergot
267   alkaloid can be proven to a reasonable degree of
268   medical certainty to cause a vasoconstriction, for
269   example, by one mechanism, I think that is likely
270   to be the mechanism of the others as well, but
271   that is not necessarily the case.
272
273 Q. So you cannot testify to the mechanism to a
274   reasonable degree of medical probability?
275
276 A. No, I cannot.
277
278 Q. Are you aware of Dr. Ellenhorn's treatise, in
279   which he reported that the vasoconstrictive
280   property for Parlux is zero?
281
282 A. Yes, I am aware of it, but I disagree with that
283   conclusion.
284
285 Q. Have any animal studies shown that Parlux can
286   cause intracerebral hemorrhage?
287
288 A. There have been hundreds of animal studies
289   on Parlux relating to humans. These studies,
290   particularly the "hindlimb" study, show that Parlux
291   can cause vasoconstriction and hypertension.
292
293 Q. Did any of the studies on animal models show a
294   relationship with Parlux causing intracerebral
295   hemorrhage?

296 A. No. They weren't designed to do so. I am not aware
297   of any studies involving intact animals showing
298   that Parlux causes high blood pressure
299   or any other injury secondary to cerebral
300   vasospasm. I think we would be able to say that
301   the animal study shows Parlux is a vasoconstric-
302   tor.
303
304 Q. Is there a preferred animal model to rely upon
305   to study potential effects of the blood pressure
306   system in man?
307
308 A. I believe that most primates metabolize drugs
309   similarly, but what happens isn't entirely
310   known. Humans may metabolize Parlux differently
311   from other primates. With respect to the
312   "hindlimb" study, comparing a mongrel ten-kilo-
313   gram dog to a pregnant woman I would say is a
314   stretch.
315
316 Q. So what happens in animal studies generally with
317   regard to animals would not necessarily happen to
318   humans.
319
320 A. Correct.
321
322 Q. On a more general level, can a cause-and-effect
323   relationship be established for a common disease
324   without showing an association through a con-
325   trolled epidemiological study?
326
327 A. It can be difficult, but not impossible. A con-
328   trolled study alone is not enough. Clinical tri-
329   als are just one component of the entire list of
330   evidence that I would consider — clinical trials
331   in isolation don't necessarily prove anything.
332
333 Q. How would the scientific method be applied in a
334   clinical study?
335
336 A. Scientific methodology today is based on gener-
337   ating hypotheses and testing them to see if they
338   can be falsified. For example, double-blind ran-
339   domized placebo controlled studies are the way to
340   use the scientific method to determine whether
341   substance A causes effect B.
342
343 Q. Are there any studies that show that Parlux can
344   cause intracerebral hemorrhage in postpartum
345   women?
346
347 A. There are no such studies where the authors

479

348 state that Parlux probably caused intracerebral
349 hemorrhage in postpartum women, but it's impor-
350 tant to keep in mind that when a drug comes to
351 market, there may have only been a few hundred
352 or at most a few thousand patients who have
353 received that drug in clinical trials, meaning
354 premarket trials where the drug is being tested
355 to see if it's effective and if it's safe. If
356 the adverse effect in question is very rare, if it
357 only occurs in one in 5,000 patients, it
358 would be unusual to see it in the clinical
359 trials.
360
361 Q. Is it fair to say, to say to a reasonable degree
362   of medical probability, that drugs that cause
363   vasospasm or vasoconstriction are also drugs that
364   cause stroke?
365
366 A. I try not to be that general. That's language I
367   would not want to use.
368
369 Q. You mentioned rechallenge/dechallenge as being
370   another significant form of medical evidence. What
371   are "rechallenges" and "dechallenges"?
372
373 A. Dechallenge is removing the drug exposure to
374   determine if an adverse event abates while
375   rechallenge involves re-exposing a patient to the
376   drug in order to ascertain whether the adverse
377   event reappears. If you have a given case where
378   the patient develops an adverse drug reaction,
379   they get better when the drug is withdrawn, and
380   they're rechallenged with the same drug and they
381   develop the exact same phenomenon that can be
382   objectively measured, that's critical to the
383   thinking that the drug was the cause of the
384   reaction in that particular patient.
385
386 Q. Have dechallenges/rechallenges been used to
387   examine Parlux?
388
389 A. There have been three human dechallenge/rechal-
390   lenge studies involving Parlux that show evi-
391   dence of coronary artery spasm and myocardial
392   infarction.
393
394 Q. Any involving ICH?
395
395 A. No.

396 Q. Are rechallenges and dechallenges "experiments" in
397   the strict sense of the word?
398
399 A. They are more like case studies, not experi-
400   ments, strictly speaking, because they aren't
401   controlled for other factors. It's not proof
402   necessarily, but it's powerful evidence, and
403   regulatory agencies, as well as manufacturers,
404   place a very heavy emphasis on rechallenge
405   information. These cases tend to indicate that
406   Parlux possesses the vasoconstrictive processes of
407   ergot derivatives.
408
409 Q. You also mentioned epidemiology. Are you familiar
410   with the Kittner study, published in the New
411   England Journal of Medicine in 1996?
412
413 A. Yes. The authors reported that the relative risk
414   of intracerebral hemorrhage at a point during the
415   six-week period after delivery was more than
416   28 times the risk for a woman not in the post-
417   partum period. The paper concluded that a causal
418   role for a preeclampsia and eclampsia, seizures
419   associated with hypertension, could not fully
420   explain the much stronger associations with stroke
421   found for the postpartum state than for pregnancy
422   itself.
423
424 Q. Does Parlux cause preeclampsia or eclampsia?
425
426 A. Parlux does not cause preeclampsia or eclampsia or
427   eclampsia stroke or eclampsia seizure.
428
429 Q. Is there any epidemiology for Parlux?
430
431 A. Not with respect to postpartum stroke. It's
432   unusual for there to be epidemiology involving
433   adverse drug reactions. One must examine that
434   scientifically to determine if it's valid epi-
435   demiology and if the conclusions are supported
436   by the data presented. I don't recall any sta-
437   tistically significant studies demonstrating an
438   association between ergot and stroke. Epidemiol-
439   ogy is generally helpful, but because stroke in
440   the postpartum period is not a common event,
441   the small sample sizes of these studies makes
442   it difficult to draw conclusions. A much larger
443   sample size is really needed to tell us more. Of
444   course, I recognize that pregnancy and delivery
445   can be risk factors for development of a stroke,
446   but I don't believe that is what happened to
447   Mrs. Kowalski.

481

448 Q. Do you have any other support for your opinion
449   that Parlux caused Mrs. Kowalski's stroke?
450
451 A. There is one thing. The FDA has published a
452   finding that bromocriptin — the major ingredient
453   in Parlux — has been related to some serious
454   adverse experiences, like hypertension, seizures,
455   and CVAs when the drug is used to prevent
456   lactation in new mothers.
457
458 Q. Did the FDA say Parlux caused those adverse
459   reactions?
460
461 A. No, just that bromocriptine seems to be a risk
462   factor, but the FDA no longer approves of using
463   Parlux to prevent lactation, although Parlux
464   still is approved for other conditions, such
465   as Parkinson's therapy and some cases of female
466   infertility.
467
468 Q. How do you evaluate all the various forms of
469   medical evidence when you are drawing a conclu-
470   sion about cause and effect?
471
472 A. You attribute an appropriate weight to the vari-
473   ous components of the medical evidence. The med-
474   ical evidence could include, involving the drug
475   Parlux, is Parlux a vasoconstrictor? Does Parlux
476   cause vasospasm? Has Parlux been associated with
477   stroke in human beings? Is there animal evidence
478   that Parlux is a vasospastic agent? Do the phar-
479   macokinetics of the drug lend themselves to say-
480   ing it makes sense, that it's plausible the drug
481   was the cause? And again, I'm not saying that
482   any of these components individually leads one to
483   draw that conclusion, but in compilation of all
484   of the evidence involving all of these com-
485   ponents, one should be able to reach such a con-
486   clusion.

This is to certify that I have read the transcript
of my deposition taken on the 14th day of February,
[-1], and that the transcript accurately states the
questions asked and the answers given.

Alexis Salka
Alexis Salkav
February 24, [-1]

CURRICULUM VITAE
Alexis Salkov, M.D.
800 North Michigan Avenue

Education

[-12]   Post-Doctorate Fellowship in Vascular
        Neurology, Milton S. Hershey Medical Center
[-13]   Residency in Neurology, Northwestern University
        Feinberg School of Medicine
[-14]   Residency in Internal Medicine, Northwestern
        University Feinberg School of Medicine
[-16]   Rotating Internship, University of Chicago
        Hospitals
[-17]   M.D. in Medicine, Harvard Medical School [-21]
        B.S. in Chemistry, Cornell University

Licensing and Board Certification

[-13 to   Licensed to practice medicine in the State of
present] Pennsylvania
[-16 to   Licensed to practice medicine in the State of
present] Illinois
[-7 to   Diplomate in Neurology, Subspecialty Vascular
present] Neurology, American Board of Psychiatry and
          Neurology
[-8 to   Diplomate in Neurology, American Board of
present] Psychiatry and Neurology

Employment

[-12 to   Private practice in neurology, specializing in
present] vascular neurology
[-12 to   Adjunct Clinical Professor of Neurology,
present] Northwestern University, Feinberg School of
          Medicine

Professional Organizations

[-12 to   American Medical Association
present] American College of Neurology

Publications

[-3]   Case Notes on Intracerebral Hemorrhage
        Associated with Pregnancy, 87 *New England
        Journal of Medicine* 140

[-12]   Causes of Ischemic Stroke Revisited, 87 *A.M.A.
        Journal of Neurology* 223

VII

ADVANCED DIRECT AND CROSS-EXAMINATION

INTRODUCTION

The cases in this chapter represent a bridge between Chapter 3, involving discrete, self-contained witness problems, and Chapter 9, involving full trials. The chapter consists of twelve cases, five civil and seven criminal. Each case in this chapter has two witnesses, one for the plaintiff or prosecutor, the other for the defendant.

These cases, of varying levels of sophistication and complexity, require more case analysis, since the direct examination of one witness must be coordinated with the cross-examination of the other. The direct and cross-examinations must serve your overall theory of the case, be consistent with your themes, and carry out your trial strategy.

You should prepare your specific assignments as though the case were actually on trial. Accordingly, you should determine whether any admissibility issues exist and anticipate objections and arguments your opponent is likely to make. In addition, you should plan and execute your direct and cross-examinations so that you will effectively present the witnesses' testimony to the jury in a way that supports your theory of the case and your trial strategy.

NOTE: The parties must stipulate to the authenticity of all reports, transcripts, records, memos, letters, and other documents in the files. The documents may be admitted, in whole or in part, without further foundation where relevant and admissible according to the rules of evidence.

Some of the witnesses do not have background information. Be prepared to develop realistic, credible backgrounds for them.

Your instructor may modify the assignments and make specific additional assignments for these cases.

The suggested background reading is Mauet, *Trial Techniques and Trials*, Chapters 5, 6, and 7.

7.1 VEHICLE COLLISION CASE

JORDAN GABLE

v.

DYLAN CANNON

This case involves an accident that occurred on June 6, [-2], at the intersection of Main and Elm Streets in this city. Jordan Gable, the plaintiff, was driving southbound on Main, at its intersection with Elm. Dylan Cannon, the defendant, had been driving northbound on Main and was in the process of turning left onto Elm when the collision took place.

Gable suffered a broken collarbone in the collision. S/he is suing for money damages. The jury is being asked to decide only the issue of liability.

Both Main and Elm Streets are two-way streets, with one moving lane in each direction and one parking lane on each side. The traffic signals show green, yellow, and red, but no turn signal. The parties agree that the traffic signal has a three-second yellow light.

It is the law of this jurisdiction that the driver of a vehicle intending to turn to the left within an intersection shall yield the right-of-way to any vehicle approaching from the opposite direction when that oncoming vehicle is so close as to constitute an immediate hazard. Further, a car may enter an intersection when the light is yellow for that car if the driver reasonably believes s/he can do so with safety.

You have the partial depositions of Gable and Cannon, a police report by the investigating officer, a photograph of Cannon's car (Pl. Ex. 1), a photograph of Gable's car (Pl. Ex. 2), and a non-scale drawing of the intersection.

1. For the plaintiff, conduct a direct examination of Gable and cross-examine Cannon.

2. For the defendant, conduct a direct examination of Cannon and cross-examine Gable.

CITY POLICE DEPARTMENT

Accident Investigation Report

Date: 6/6/[-2]

Location: Main & Elm (each has one lane of traffic
                    and one parking lane for both directions)

Witnesses: Jordan Gable, driver, #1 car

                    Dylan Cannon, driver, #2 car

Conditions: Daylight, clear, roadway dry; 30 MPH speed
                    limit in area

Traffic Controls: One traffic light over center of
                    intersection, 3 sec yellow

On 6/6/[-2] at approximately 1430 hours the undersigned
on routine patrol was at intersection of Main and Elm,
noticed accident between two vehicles. #1, a [-3]
Honda Accord, license plate #246-LKZ, was stopped in
the intersection, near the northwest corner facing
approximately south, slightly to west. #2, a [-3] Toyota
RAV4, license plate #713-ES7, was stopped in front of #1
in contact with right rear side of #2. Driver of #1 car,
Jordan Gable, appeared injured; radioed ambulance. Gable
sitting in his/her vehicle.

Damage to #1: front bumper and grill with substantial
damage, hood pushed in and no longer closeable, and
damage to left front light. Damage to #2: right rear
pillar area pushed in, with damage to bumper and rear
gate.

Above witnesses were interviewed.

Jordan Gable provided the following information:
S/he was driving southbound in #1 car on Main Street
toward Elm Street at about 30 mph. As s/he approached Elm
Street the light turned yellow. S/he was about 30 feet
from the intersection at that time. S/he continued into
the intersection on the yellow light, when a car facing
north in the intersection suddenly made a sharp left turn
directly in front of him/her. S/he could not stop in time
and ran into the right rear side of the turning vehicle.

Dylan Cannon provided the following information:
S/he was driving with his/her husband/wife northbound in
car #2 on Main Street, intending to turn left on Elm. The
light turned to yellow as s/he entered the intersection.

491

S/he came to a complete stop because s/he saw car #1 coming southbound on Main Street. Car #1 seemed to slow down as it reached the intersection, so s/he began the turn. By then the light had changed to red. As s/he completed his/her turn s/he heard the screech of brakes and the next thing s/he knew car #1 had crashed into his/her right rear. S/he could not estimate the speed of car #1 at the time of the collision.

Marley Cannon, passenger in Car #2, could not be interviewed as s/he was feeling sick and did not want to talk to RO.

No traffic citations were issued.

University Ambulance arrived, treated Gable, took him/her to University Hospital. Mr. and Ms. Cannon declined medical treatment. Vehicle #1 towed from the scene by Ace Auto Repair. Vehicle #2 operable and driven from scene by owner.

Dale Peterson
Dale Peterson   #5462
Patrolman, City P.D.

DEPOSITION OF JORDAN GABLE

On November 1, [-1]

at offices of defendant's attorney
100 Clark Street

JORDAN GABLE, having been first duly sworn, testified as follows:

p. 4

1 Q. (by defendant's attorney) What time did the
2 accident take place?
3
4 A. It was 2:20 P.M.
5
6 Q. How are you so sure of the time?
7
8 A. I had a 2:00 P.M. appointment with a potential
9 client. I am a self-employed architect with offices
10 at 400 S. Main, about three blocks south of Elm,
11 and I had looked at the clock on the dashboard
12 about 30 seconds before the crash.
13
14 Q. How fast were you going when you reached a point
15 about 30 feet from the intersection?
16
17 A. About 25 miles an hour. I never went faster than
18 that.
19
20 Q. Tell us what happened as you approached Elm Street?
21
22 A. Well, when I was about ten feet from the inter-
23 section I saw the light change from green to
24 yellow. I just kept going, at the same speed,
25 because I knew I had plenty of time to clear the
26 intersection. When I got a few feet into the
27 intersection the Toyota RAV4 that was waiting to
28 turn suddenly veered in front of me. I jammed
29 on my brakes, but it was too late. The front
30 of my Accord hit his/her right side. (Identifies
31 Pl. Ex. 2 as his/her car, Pl. Ex. 1 as defendant's
32 car.)
33
34 Q. What color was the light when you collided with the
35 other car?
36
37 A. It was still yellow. I saw the light a split-second
38 before the crash.

```
39 Q.  Did the defendant's car have its left turn signal
40      on?
41
42 A.  Yes. But it wasn't moving. I assumed the driver
43      would wait until I cleared the intersection. S/he
44      must have been in a big hurry.
```

       This is to certify that I have read the transcript of my deposition taken on November 1, [-1], and that the transcript accurately states the questions asked and the answers given.

Jordan Gable

                              Jordan Gable

Subscribed and sworn to
before me this 30th day of
November, [-1].

Rebecca Jones

Notary Public   ss

DEPOSITION OF DYLAN CANNON

on November 2, [-1]

at offices of plaintiff's attorney

200 E. Broadway

DYLAN CANNON, having been first duly sworn, testified as follows:

p. 3

1 Q. (by plaintiff's attorney) Mr./Ms. Cannon, where
2   were you going at the time of the collision?
3
4 A. My husband/wife and I had left our home at 1400
5   Carlton Street, about two miles from Main and Elm,
6   and we were going to the doctor's office at 1200
7   W. Elm, about a mile west from the place where
8   the crash took place. My husband/wife needed to
9   get to the doctor, because s/he had a bad case of
10   bronchitis.
11
12 Q. What time was your appointment?
13
14 A. About 3:00. We had plenty of time.
15
16 Q. Tell us what happened as you approached the
17   intersection?
18
19 A. Well, I was going north on Main, and I was going to
20   turn left on Elm. I was going about 10 or 15 miles
21   per hour as I reached Elm. The light turned to
22   yellow just as I entered Elm Street. I stopped in
23   my lane, at about the middle of the intersection,
24   because I saw a car coming south on Main. It was
25   Gable's car. S/he slowed down and seemed to be
26   stopping as the light turned from yellow to red.
27   When I saw the light change to red, and when I saw
28   Gable's car stopping, I began to complete my turn.
29   That's when s/he suddenly sped up and crashed right
30   into me. I don't know why s/he did that. I had my
31   turn signal on and s/he had plenty of time to stop
32   for the red light.
33
34 Q. Did Gable's car come to a complete stop when it
35   reached the intersection?
36
37 A. It looked like it did.

38 Q. How fast was Gable's car going at the time of the
39   collision?
40
41 A. I don't know. All I can say is s/he came at me real
42   fast. S/he must have been trying to beat the light.
43   (Identifies Pl. Ex 2 as Gable's Honda Accord and
44   Pl. Ex 1 as his/her Toyota RAV4.)

This is to certify that I have read the transcript of my deposition taken on November 2, [-1], and that the transcript accurately states the questions asked and the answers given.

_____
Dylan Cannon

Subscribed and sworn to
before me this 15th day of
December, [-1].

_____
Notary Public   ss

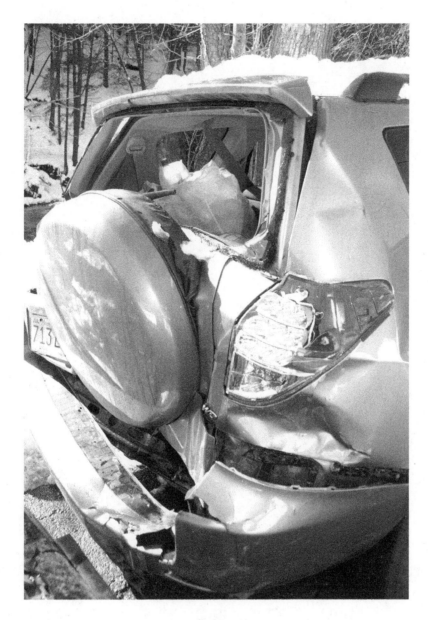

Pl. Ex. 1

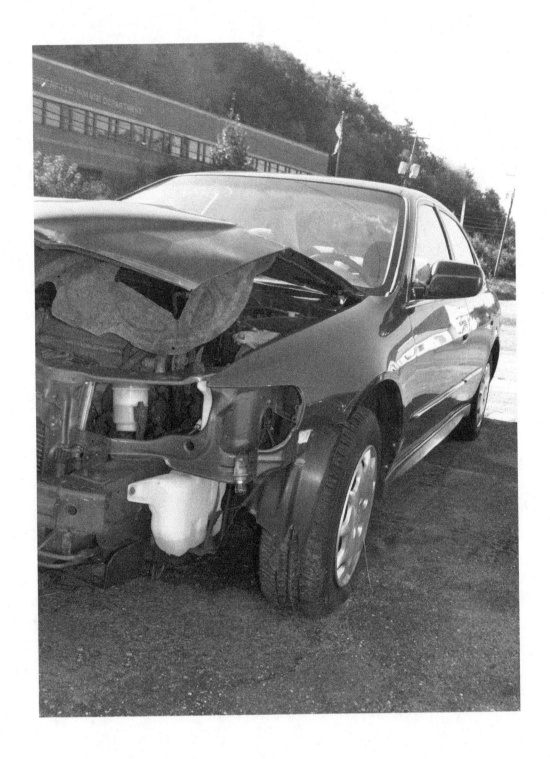

Pl. Ex. 2

Pl. IX. 2

400

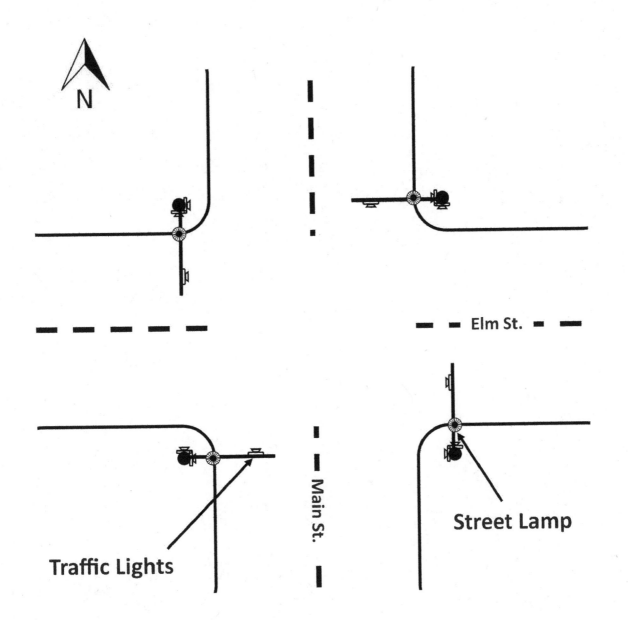

Elm St.

Main St.

Traffic Lights

Street Lamp

7.2 CIVIL RIGHTS CASE

ESTATE OF JOSE GARCIA
v.
PAT RICHARDS

The mother of Jose Garcia brings this 42 U.S.C. § 1983 action against City Police Officer Pat Richards. She claims that Officer Richards, while on duty, intentionally shot and killed Jose Garcia on May 2, [-2]. The shooting took place in the parking lot of Jack's Restaurant. Richards was there because Stacey Major informed him/her that s/he had received a call from a man wh̲o̲ ̲s̲aid ̲h̲e̲ would sell back Major's stolen Cadillac.

The Court has _____ priately brought under plaintiff's claim that the _____ mendment right not to be subjected to un_____rested. The law also provides that in mak_____use such force as is necessary under the c_____nal discussion of the law, including restric_____ce Department General Order No. 24 belo_____t in this case was unreasonable or *I* excessiv_____ccurs when there is a termination of freedo___

Th_____ discovery depositions of Stacey Major and _____epartment General Order 24, Richards's Firearms Discharge R_____ ⎯ Plaintiff's Interrogatory Number 7.

The parties have reached the following stipulations:

(a) The Chief Medical Examiner of the County believes that the decedent was *Garcia* shot from a distance of less than five feet but probably not closer than two feet. The *was shot* fatal bullet entered the decedent's back 16 inches below the top of the head in about the *in the back* middle of the back. The path was slightly upward.

503

(b) The fatal bullet was fired from Officer Richards's .357 magnum caliber Smith & Wesson revolver.

1. For the plaintiff, conduct a direct examination of Major and cross-examine Officer Richards.
2. For the defendant, conduct a direct examination of Officer Richards and cross-examine Major.

DEPOSITION OF STACEY MAJOR

on June 1, [-1]

at offices of defendant's attorney

134 N. Clark Street

STACEY MAJOR, having been first duly sworn, testified as follows:

p. 4

1 Q. (by defendant's attorney) Mr./Ms. Major, tell us
2   how this whole thing began on May 2, [-2].
3
4 A. Well, about 2:00 in the afternoon, I received a
5   call from a man who said he had my Cadillac. The
6   car had been stolen the week before. The man said
7   if I wanted it back in one piece I should bring
8     $1,000 to the parking lot at Jack's Restaurant at
9   Jackson and Kedzie at 5:00. He said if I called the
10   cops there would be trouble. I told him I would be
11   there with the money.
12
13 Q. What did you do then?
14
15 A. Then I called the officer who was assigned to the
16   theft investigation, Officer Richards. I told
17   him/her what the guy said. Richards told me s/he
18   didn't want me to go alone. We arranged to go there
19   together and I would introduce him/her to the man
20   as my brother/sister.
21
22 Q. Did you go to Jack's Restaurant?
23
24 A. Yes. Officer Richards came to my house at about 4:15,
25   and we went in his/her car to Jack's. S/he drove.
26
27 Q. What happened when you got there?
28
29 A. We pulled into the lot and sat there. About 15
30   minutes later this guy walked into the lot. He
31   was young, about 21, maybe 5'8", slender build.
32   He was wearing a blue jacket. He came up to my
33   side of the car and said, "Are you here about the
34   Cadillac?" I said we were. He said, "I told you
35   to come alone. There's no deal." Then he started
36   walking away.
37
38 Q. What happened next?

505

Garcia was walking away when Richards pulled his gun w/ finger on trigger

39 A. When he started walking away, Richards got out of
40   the car and walked after him. As s/he walked I saw
41   him/her take his gun from inside his/her pants.
42

43 Q. How was s/he holding the gun?
44

45 A. S/he was holding it with his/her right hand,
46   pointing it straight up. It looked like his/her
47   finger was on the trigger.
48

49 Q. What happened next?
50

Richards grabbed Garcia & Garcia started to run

51 A. Officer Richards approached the man from behind
52   and grabbed his shoulder with his/her left hand. I
53   heard Richards say, "I am a police officer. You
54   are under arrest." The man broke loose and
55   jumped over a guardrail that was between the
56   parking lot and an alley. Richards started to go
57   after him, but it looked like s/he tripped on the
58   guardrail. I could not see exactly. Then the gun
59   went off and the guy fell to the ground. I could
60   not see the gun at the moment it went off.
61

Witness couldn't see the gun

62 Q. Did you see the man hit, strike, or touch Officer
63   Richards at any time?   Garcia never touched officer
64

65 A. Not that I saw. He just tried to get away. But it
66   all happened very fast.
67

68 Q. Did you hear the man say anything after he left the
69   car?
70

71 A. No. He didn't say anything else.
72

73 Q. Did you ever see any kind of weapon in the man's
74   possession?
75

Unarmed— Garcia didn't have a weapon

76 A. No. There was nothing in his hands.

          This is to certify that I have read the
transcript of my deposition taken on June 1, [-1], and
that the transcript accurately states the questions
asked and the answers given.

Subscribed and sworn to
before me this 15th day of   _Stacey Major_
June, [-1].   Stacey Major

Jen Medryk
Notary Public   ss

506

DEPOSITION OF PAT RICHARDS
on June 15, [-1]

at offices of plaintiff's attorney

111 W. Washington Street

PAT RICHARDS, having been first duly sworn,
testified as follows:

p. 2

1 Q. (by plaintiff's attorney) Officer Richards, what is
2   your current assignment?
3
4 A. I am a detective with the City Police Department,
5   and I have been assigned to the Auto Theft Unit for
6   the past seven years. I have been a police officer
7   for 12 years, my first 5 as a patrol officer. I
8   have received three Department Commendations,
9   and three years ago I was given the City Police
10 Department Award of Valor after a shootout with two
11 armed robbers.
12
13 Q. Were you assigned to investigate the theft of a
14   Cadillac from Stacey Major?
15
16 A. Yes. That was my case.
17
18 Q. We understand that on May 2, [-2], you went to the
19   parking lot of Jack's Restaurant at Jackson and
20   Kedzie. Tell us how that came about?
21
22 A. Well, about 1430 hours on that day the victim of
23   the theft called me at the station. S/he informed
24   me a man had called him/her and offered to sell
25   back his/her Cadillac for $1,000 at 1700 hours at
26   Jack's. I told him/her I did not want him/her to go
27   there alone and that I would accompany him/her.
28
29 Q. Why did you say that?
30
31 A. Because it could have been a rip-off. I mean, I
32   have seen cases where a similar deal is made and
33   the subject takes the money by force and never
34   returns the stolen property. I thought it might be
35   dangerous for Mr./Ms. Major. So I arranged to go
36   with him/her, and I asked for backup to meet me at
37   the parking lot.

Garcia never took anything by force — he walked away [handwritten marginal note]

507

38 Q. I assume you weren't in uniform. Did you have a
39   weapon?
40
41 A. As a detective, I wear plain clothes. I had my .357
42   Magnum in a holster on my right side. I wore a
43   jacket to cover it.
44
45 Q. What happened when you arrived at the parking
46   lot?
47
48 A. We arrived at the lot at 1650 hours. We pulled
49   into the rear portion of the lot, near the alley.
50   I looked around for my backup, but I didn't
51   see anybody. Then the subject walked up to the
52   passenger side of the car, where Mr./Ms. Major was
53   sitting. The subject was in his early 20s, slender,
54   about 5'9", wearing jeans and a bulky blue jacket.
55   He asked Mr./Ms. Major if s/he was there about
56   the Cadillac. When Mr./Ms. Major said s/he was,
57   the subject said something I could not hear, then
58   he said, "No deal," and he started walking away,
59   toward the alley.
60
61 Q. What did you do?
62
63 A. I decided to stop the subject and question him
64   about the stolen car and his extortion attempt. So,
65   I got out of the car, drew my weapon and held it
66   down at my side, and approached the subject from
67   the rear.
68
69 Q. Why did you draw your weapon?
70
71 A. I suspected he was armed in some way. He had this
72   bulky jacket on. I feared for my safety.
73
74 Q. What happened next?
75
76 A. I reached the subject just before he got to the
77   guardrail that separates the lot from the alley.
78   With my gun pointing down at my right side, I put
79   my left hand on his shoulder, announced my office,
80   and told him he was under arrest.
81
82 Q. Did Mr. Garcia do anything when you said that?
83
84 A. He sure did. He kind of half-turned toward me,
85   and he said: "Bullshit, you're not taking me
86   anywhere." Then he swung back with his right
87   elbow two times, striking me in the chest and the
88   forehead. I let go of his shoulder and he
89   jumped over the guardrail into the alley.

508

Handwritten margin notes:

(left margin, near lines 48-53): He could have waited for back-up

(left margin, near lines 63-71): Stacy said he held it straight up

(right margin, near lines 80-82): Stacy didn't hear anything

(left margin, near lines 84-89): Witness didn't see Garcia do anything or hear anything

90 Q. What did you do then?
91
92 A. I started to go after him. But when I tried to
93   jump over the guardrail my foot hit the top of
94   it and I stumbled. My right hand hit the rail.
95   That's when the gun went off. I must have had my
96   finger on the trigger, although I do not remember
97   doing that at any time. I know that I did not
98   intentionally fire that gun, even though the
99   subject had just attacked me. When the gun went
100   off the subject took a few steps, then fell to the
101   ground.
102
103 Q. Was Mr. Garcia armed with any weapon?
104
105 A. It turned out that he was not, but I could not
106   know that. After all, he was a fleeing felon who
107   had just committed a violent attack on a police
108   officer. I did my duty.

        This is to certify that I have read the transcript
of my deposition taken on June 15, [-1], and that the
transcript accurately states the questions asked and
the answers given.

(handwritten margin note: witness saw his finger on trigger seb/chard)

(handwritten margin note: Garcia not armed)

(signature) _____
                                    Pat Richards

Subscribed and sworn to
before me this 29th day
of June, [-1].

(signature) Linda Richmond
Notary Public   ss

509

FIREARMS DISCHARGE REPORT

From: Detective Pat Richards, # 7080

To: Commanding Officer

Re: Discharge of firearm

    On May 2, [-2], at approximately 1700 hours, RO was at parking lot of Jack's Restaurant, Jackson and Kedzie Streets, in company of theft victim Stacey Major. RO was at scene as part of investigation into extortion attempt by male caller. Subject approached Mr./Ms. Major at parking lot, then attempted to flee scene when he observed RO. RO then exited vehicle in attempt to apprehend subject for offenses of Auto Theft and Attempted Extortion. RO drew weapon and held it down at side. RO feared subject might be armed. When RO told subject he was under arrest, subject pulled away from RO and attempted to flee. As RO pursued subject, RO tripped over a guard rail and weapon accidentally discharged. RO did not intentionally fire weapon. Subject was fatally wounded when gun discharged.

    RO's weapon has been submitted to Weapons Section for testing.

    Further, RO notes that when subject was told he was under arrest, he responded: "Bullshit. I am not going anywhere with you."

Pat Richards

511

CITY POLICE DEPARTMENT

GENERAL ORDER NO. 24

ISSUED JULY 1, [-4]
Effective Immediately

To all police personnel:

If a sworn officer at any time discharges a firearm for any reason that officer shall then complete a Firearm Discharge Report. The Report shall set out the reasons for the discharge of the firearm.

It is the law of this State that a peace officer is justified in using deadly force when he reasonably believes such force is necessary to prevent death or great bodily harm to himself or another, or when he reasonably believes:

(a) Such force is necessary to prevent the arrest from being defeated by resistance or escape, AND

(b) The person to be arrested has committed or has attempted to commit a forcible felony or is attempting to escape by use of a deadly weapon.

It is the policy of this Department to encourage firearm safety. All weapons should be kept holstered at all times except for inspection, cleaning, or when circumstances indicate the weapon may be used. An officer may draw a weapon whenever its use is a reasonable possibility, but the weapon should not be fired unless and until an adversary has committed some overt act that clearly indicates immediate danger of death or great bodily harm to the officer.

Generally speaking, rules of firearm safety require that an officer not place his finger on the trigger guard of a weapon unless he intends to pull the trigger. This policy recognizes there can be situations when exceptions to the general rule may be present. At all times, peace officers should act reasonably and with a view toward preserving public safety.

[handwritten margin notes:]
Garcia was running away
gun shouldn't've been holstered unless overt act ↓ signals immediate danger
shouldn't have placed finger on trigger

513

CIRCUIT COURT
Trial Division

Plaintiff's Interrogatory Number 7:

Please state any and all offense(s) that this
defendant believed the decedent had committed, was
committing, or was about to commit prior to and at the
time of the discharge of defendant's firearm.

ANSWER: Auto Theft, Attempted Extortion, Resisting???
Arrest.

_____
                                      Pat Richards

Subscribed and Sworn to before
me this 15th day of December, [-1].

_____
Notary Public

Alley

Alley

^ Guardrail: 22" tall by 3" wide ^

Neighboring Business

Parking Lot Entrance

Parking Lot Exit

Street

Sidewalk

JACK'S RESTAURANT

Entrance

Sidewalk

Sidewalk

Sidewalk

7.3 THEFT OF TRADE SECRETS CASE

MID-CONTINENT, INC.

v.

C.W. BLOCK AND TRACK OIL COMPANY, INC.

This is a civil theft of trade secrets case brought by Mid-Continent, Inc., against C.W. Block and Track Oil Company, Inc. Mid-Continent sells a gas additive, "STP," and Track Oil sells a competing gas additive, "PSSST." The case is brought in federal district court.

Mid-Continent claims that Block, a former employee, stole the formula for the gasoline additive that Mid-Continent had developed and sold the formula to his/her new employer, Track Oil, in violation of Block's written agreement not to disclose Mid-Continent's trade secrets to a competitor. Mid-Continent further claims that Track Oil conspired with Block to steal the formula.

Both defendants deny that Block stole the formula for the gasoline additive or sold it to Track Oil.

A trade secret consists of any valuable formula, process, or other information that is held in secret, is used in a business, and gives the owner of the secret a competitive advantage over others who do not know the secret.

A theft of a trade secret occurred if Mid-Continent possessed a trade secret, a confidential relationship existed between Mid-Continent and Block, Block acquired the trade secret and gave it to Track Oil, Track Oil used the trade secret in violation of the confidential relationship, and Track Oil's use of the trade secret caused damage to Mid-Continent.

The federal district court has bifurcated the issues of liability and damages. Consequently, the present trial is on the issue of liability only.

You have the depositions and affidavit of the parties and other employees of the parties. You also have the attached documents, which were obtained during discovery.

1. For the plaintiff, conduct a direct examination of Block (as an adverse witness) and cross-examine Robbie McCoy of Track Oil.

2. For the defendant, conduct whatever further examination of Block you deem appropriate and a direct examination of McCoy.

Deposition of C.W. Block

on November 10, [-1]

at offices of plaintiff's attorney

C.W. Block, having first been duly sworn,
testified as follows:

1 Q. (by plaintiff's attorney) Please state your name.
2
3 A. C.W. Block.
4
5 Q. Where are you currently employed?
6
7 A. Track Oil Company.
8
9 Q. What is your position there?
10
11 A. Vice President in charge of Sales and Marketing.
12
13 Q. Is your education background in the area of sales
14   or marketing?
15
16 A. No, I have a B.S. in chemistry, but I have a
17   good deal of work experience in marketing and
18   sales.
19
20 Q. When did you begin to work for Track Oil?
21
22 A. In July of [-3].
23
24 Q. And what was your position then?
25
26 A. The same as now.
27
28 Q. When did you first begin to negotiate with Track
29   for this position?
30
31 A. Well, that's hard to say. I interviewed at Track
32   for a slot in their Marketing Department in [-5].
33   They weren't willing to pay me what I was worth,
34   so nothing ever came of it. Then in January or
35   February of [-3] I was contacted by Mr./Ms. McCoy
36   of Track and s/he and I began negotiations for a
37   position in marketing and sales.
38
39 Q. When you began at Track in [-3] what was your
40   starting salary?
41
42 A. I think it was $75,000 a year.

43 Q. What is your current salary?
44
45 A. Is that really relevant?
46
47 Q. If it weren't, your attorney would have objected.
48   Please answer my question.
49
50 A. $150,000.
51
52 Q. How many personal bank accounts do you have?
53
54 A. One account, at Second National Bank.
55
56 Q. What are your duties at Track Oil?
57
58 A. General supervisor of the marketing and sales
59   division.
60
61 Q. Before your employment at Track did you ever
62   receive any money from Track Oil?
63
64 A. No.
65
66 Q. What was your salary at Mid-Continent when you
67   left?
68
69 A. I don't recall.
70
71 Q. Was it more or less than $75,000?
72
73 A. Less, about $50,000.
74
75 Q. Why did you leave Mid-Continent in July of [-3]?
76
77 A. I felt I had reached my limit of upward mobility
78   there. I wanted to devote my time exclusively to
79   marketing, but they wanted me to stay close to the
80   chemistry aspect of the job. I was tired of R & D
81   and lab work and I wanted to really learn something
82   about marketing.
83
84 Q. Mr./Ms. Block, I am now showing you exhibits A and
85   B to the Complaint. Exhibit A is the Memorandum of
86   Employee's Agreement. Exhibit B is the Statement of
87   Policy on Conflict of Interest. Do you recognize
88   them?
89
90 A. Yes.
91
92 Q. Is that your signature on both exhibits?
93
94 A. Yes.

95 Q. Mr./Ms. Block, in April of [-4] you were told
96   about the alcohol-based gas additive that Mid-
97   Continent was planning to market, were you not?
98
99 A. Yes. Part of my job was to sell the chemistry and
100   package the results of R & D.
101
102 Q. Were you told the exact chemical formula for the
103   additive?
104
105 A. Of course. I would have to understand the chemical
106   aspects to perform my job as a liaison between the
107   two divisions.
108
109 Q. Your bank account at Second National reflects
110   cash deposits of $10,000 in June [-4], January
111   [-3], and June [-3]. What was the source of
112   those funds?
113
114 A. Repayment of a loan I made to a friend. He died
115   last year.
116
117 Q. Have you any documents on that?
118
119 A. No. We did it on a handshake and I agreed to
120   repayment in three installments if he could manage
121   it.
122
123 Q. What had been your source of funds for the loan?
124
125 A. Personal savings, money I had saved for years.
126
127 Q. Did you know Mr./Ms. McCoy of Track prior to July,
128   [-3]?
129
130 A. Yes, I had spoken with him/her briefly the first
131   time I interviewed at Track in [-5].
132
133 Q. Did you ever have a conversation with Mr.
134   Hatfield, your boss at Mid-Continent, about the
135   need for secrecy with respect to your job —
136   specifically with respect to trade secrets?
137
138 A. Yes, sometime in early [-3], when Mr. Hatfield
139   was in town. He told me I was coming right along
140   in the company. We talked then about raiding and
141   industrial espionage.
142
143 Q. At that time were you negotiating with Track for
144   the position you got in July [-3]?

145 A. I believe I was, yes.
146
147 Q. Did you tell Mr. Hatfield that you were
148   negotiating with Track?
149
150 A. No.
151
152 Q. Did he ask you specifically if you were seeking
153   other employment?
154
155 A. There was some discussion about that, yes. I don't
156   remember what was said. It was very brief.
157
158 Q. (by defendant Block's attorney) Mr./Ms. Block,
159   could any competent chemist determine the chemical
160   formula for STP gas additive by conducting a few
161   simple experiments?
162
163 A. In my personal opinion, yes.
164
165 Q. Did you ever disclose the formula for STP gas
166   additive to anyone outside Mid-Continent?
167
168 A. No.
169
170 Q. Have you ever intentionally acted in a way
171   detrimental to Mid-Continent's interests?
172
173 A. No.

    This is to certify that I have read the transcript
of my deposition taken on the 10th day of November, [-1],
and that the transcript accurately states the questions
asked and the answers given.

                                    C. W. Block
                                    C. W. Block

Subscribed and sworn to
before me this 6th
day of December, [-1].

Sharon D. Pew
    Notary Public

Deposition of Robbie McCoy

on November 20, [-1]

at offices of plaintiff's attorney

Robbie McCoy, having first been duly sworn, testified as follows:

1 Q. (by plaintiff's attorney) State your name please.
2
3 A. Robbie McCoy.
4
5 Q. Where are you employed?
6
7 A. I am the President of Track Oil Company, located in
8   this city.
9
10 Q. How long have you held that position?
11
12 A. About 15 years.
13
14 Q. Is Track Oil publicly or privately held?
15
16 A. Privately held.
17
18 Q. Do you have an ownership interest in Track?
19
20 A. Yes, about 60 percent.
21
22 Q. Do you know C.W. Block?
23
24 A. Yes, I first met him/her in [-5]. And I have gotten
25   to know him/her better since July of [-3] when s/he
26   came on board with us.
27
28 Q. Did you have any communication with Block in
29   [-4]?
30
31 A. Well, I know s/he was with Mid-Continent then so I
32   would say no. Not while s/he was at Mid-Continent.
33   In fact, I did not speak to him/her at all until
34   s/he joined our firm in [-3].
35
36 Q. Could any large payments of money be made by Track
37   without your knowledge?
38
39 A. No. I have to authorize any expenditure over
40    $1,000.

```
41 Q.  Did you authorize any such expenditure of money for
42      C.W. Block prior to his/her employment at Track?
43
44 A.  Of course not.
45
46 Q.  Were you aware, sir, that when Block came to
47      work for you s/he would be laboring under the
48      restrictions of a non-disclosure of trade secrets
49      agreement?
50
51 A.  Well, yes, I was. I received a letter from Hatfield
52      saying just that, but I don't think I could put
53      my hands on it now. These types of agreements are
54      common in the trade, although I don't use them
55      myself here at Track.
56
57 Q.  Who was in charge of your company's benzopyrene
58      purchases in [-4]?
59
60 A.  I was. Sharon Martin told me what was needed and I
61      placed the orders.
```

This is to certify that I have read the transcript of my deposition taken on the 20th day of November, [-1], and that the transcript accurately states the questions asked and the answers given.

Robbie McCoy

Robbie McCoy

Subscribed and sworn to
before me this 20th
day of December, [-1].

Melissa Grace
Notary public

526

AFFIDAVIT OF R.S. HATFIELD

R.S. Hatfield, being first duly sworn, states the following:

1. I am the president of Mid-Continent, Inc., and have been for the past 25 years. I have seen this company grow to be a $10 million corporation. I was the president of the company in [-16], when we registered STP as a trademark.

2. I am very proud that my company is the first in the field with this kind of gas additive. Other companies market gas additives, but none had our formula until Track Oil came out with its product. No one's product ever worked as well as ours. No one ever thought about using benzopyrene. That's why we always treated our research project as top secret, to maintain the competitive advantage. We spent about $1.5 million developing our product. It really galls me to see someone come along and get it for whatever it cost to buy C.W. Block.

3. Track Oil, which sells PSSST, is really our chief competitor. They are always sniping at us, trying to get some unfair advantage. Block is the first employee we ever lost to Track. The only explanation for that is they are paying him/her more than s/he is worth.

4. I met Block several times while s/he worked for us. We never had very much to say, but I remember one time in late March of [-3]. We were in a company cocktail party. I was talking about the future of the company. I remember saying raiding and industrial espionage are among the deadly dangers of our industry. Block agreed. S/he said that was why s/he was happy to sign the confidentiality agreement.

5. I told him/her it was important to me that our employees be loyal. S/he said I had nothing to worry about with him/her, and s/he said, "This is my home. I intend to stay here for the rest of my career." I'll never forget those words.

6. When Block left, I wrote Track because I was concerned about Block's knowledge of our trade secrets. I have attached that letter to this affidavit. I also attached the Conflict of Interest and Confidentiality agreement Block signed.

R. S. Hatfield

R. S. Hatfield

Subscribed and sworn to
before me this 4th day
of November, [-1].

Condance Stenerson

Notary Public

Deposition of Claude Adkins

on September 20, [-1]

at offices of defendant's attorney

CLAUDE ADKINS, having first been duly sworn, testified as follows:

1 Q. (by attorney for defendant Track Oil) Would you
2   state your name, please?
3
4 A. Claude Adkins.
5
6 Q. Where are you currently employed?
7
8 A. Mid-Continent, here in town.
9
10 Q. How long have you been employed there?
11
12 A. Altogether about 14 years, both here and in New
13   York.
14
15 Q. What is your current position at Mid-Continent?
16
17 A. Well, my title is Chief Chemical Engineer and
18   Research Analyst, but that just means I supervise
19   the lab personnel and make decisions about
20   continuing or abandoning certain areas of research
21   and development. To be honest about it, I sometimes
22   just tinker myself with some ideas because I get
23   bored with the paper part of the job.
24
25 Q. Was this the nature of your employment in [-5] and
26   [-4]?
27
28 A. Yes.
29
30 Q. What is your educational background?
31
32 A. B.S. in chemical engineering. I've done some post-
33   graduate work, but no degree.
34
35 Q. Do you know C.W. Block?
36
37 A. Yes.

38 Q. How did you come to know him/her?
39
40 A. In the Spring of [-5] Block started as a chemical
41   engineer with Mid-Continent. In no time at all,
42   s/he was hobnobbing with the brass and kicking
43   around ideas about products and sales techniques.
44   Sometime in [-5] s/he was switched from straight
45   lab work to what we call an interface for R &
46   D and marketing. S/he knew chemistry, and the
47   marketing department thought s/he knew marketing,
48   so s/he took our ideas and turned them into
49   marketable products.
50
51 Q. Did you work in close contact with him/her?
52
53 A. Not really, once s/he moved to the marketing
54   aspect.
55
56 Q. Did you ever tell anybody you thought Block was
57   acting strangely or unusual in the Spring or
58   Summer of [-4]?
59
60 A. I may have, but I don't recall.
61
62 Q. Your company makes a gas additive called STP?
63
64 A. Yes.
65
66 Q. Were you involved in the development of STP?
67
68 A. Yes, I was part of the process, if that's what
69   you mean. Some of my lab people had been at it
70   for a long time. It was difficult to make a
71   good catalyst to improve gas mileage in a cost
72   efficient way. The product always cost more
73   than the gas it saved. But we kept trying it
74   off and on, and in January, [-4], we hit on a
75   concentration that seemed to work and was fairly
76   cheap. Some of my people did the quantitative
77   analysis and I just threw out some suggestions. So
78   I guess I was part of it, but I can't really take
79   the credit.
80
81 Q. Based on your tests, what is the effect of the
82   additive?
83
84 A. It improves gas mileage by about 30 percent when
85   added to a tank filled with regular or premium
86   gas.
87
88 Q. To manufacture this additive, this claimed trade
89   secret, do you use any secret ingredients?

530

90 A. No.

91

92 Q. What chemicals do you use?

93

94 A. I understand our exact formula is subject to some
95   kind of agreement between you lawyers, so I would
96   just as soon not go into it.

97

98 Q. Well, let me ask you this, the additive is alcohol
99   based, is it not?

100

101 A. Yes.

102

103 Q. Is there anything unusual about alcohol in a
104   chemistry lab?

105

106 A. Well, no.

107

108 Q. In fact, aren't all the chemicals in the Mid-
109   Continent formula just those one would expect in a
110   typical additive?

111

112 A. Well, that's true, except for the benzopyrene.
113   No one ever used it before. It's the addition of
114   benzopyrene that made our formula work. We found
115   just the right amount.

116

117 Q. Mr. Adkins, couldn't any qualified chemist buy a
118   can of the gas treatment and break it down to the
119   exact components with several hours' work?

120

121 A. You mean reverse engineering?

122

123 Q. Exactly.

124

125 A. Well, I honestly can't say. I've only made it
126   from start to finish. I haven't tried from finish
127   to start. One thing, though, about this reverse
128   engineering. You can't always break down a
129   system to learn its components because sometimes
130   the testing can destroy the equilibrium of the
131   system and the whole solution can be permanently
132   altered.

133

134 Q. Is your alcohol-based gas additive one of those
135   delicate systems?

136

137 A. I believe it is.

138

139 Q. Where do you purchase most of the chemicals you
140   use in the R & D lab?

141 A. All over.

142

143 Q. Where do you purchase benzopyrene?

144

145 A. I don't know. You'd have to check with
146   Purchasing.

147

148 Q. (by plaintiff's attorney) When you are working on
149   an idea in the R & D lab, do you keep notes?

150

151 A. Oh, yes, and we're extremely careful of them.
152   Can't afford to have loose papers around the
153   lab. It would be absolute chaos. Each technician
154   is given a notebook with numbered pages, and
155   all notes, results, ideas, and formulas must
156   be written down. Then at the end of each day
157   a supervisor countersigns it and dates it. The
158   technician, or really any chemist in R & D, then
159   keeps the notebook in his or her bench drawer.
160   When the book is filled, it is locked in the
161   custodian's vault.

162

163 Q. What is the purpose of this secrecy?

164

165 A. It protects Mid-Continent's trade secrets and it
166   protects the intellectual property of an inventor,
167   so it's best for all parties concerned.

168

169 Q. Could C.W. Block have had access to any of these
170   notebooks?

171

172 A. Of course. They really aren't under lock and key
173   until they're complete.

174

175 Q. Did you ever tell Block the trade secret involved
176   in this litigation?

177

178 A. Yes, I had to. It was his/her job to take the
179   chemistry and make it salable and marketable.

180

181 Q. When you first came to Mid-Continent 14 years ago,
182   did you sign any trade secret agreements like
183   these on the complaint marked A & B?

184

185 A. Yes, I think they were identical.

186

187 Q. Do you know where those agreements are now?

188

189 A. Yes, in my permanent file in personnel.

190

191 Q. During [-4] did you ever see C.W. Block with an
192   officer or employee of Track Oil?

532

```
193  A. No, I never saw him/her with anyone, but I heard
194     him/her talking to someone.
195
196  Q. When and where was that?
197
198  A. One night in the early summer of [-4] I walked
199     into Block's office and s/he looked like s/he was
200     trying to hang up the phone so that I wouldn't
201     know what s/he was doing. I heard him/her say,
202     "Okay, McCoy, I gotta go. I've done my part."
203
204  Q. At that time did you know who McCoy was?
205
206  A. Well, I knew s/he was the competition, if that's
207     what you mean.
```

        This is to certify that I have read the
transcript of my deposition taken on the 20th day of
September [-1], and that the transcript accurately
states the questions asked and the answers given.

_____
                Claude Adkins

Subscribed and sworn to
before me this 10th
day of October, [-1].

_____
        Notary Public

Deposition of Sharon Martin

on November 17, [-1]

at offices of plaintiff's attorney

 SHARON MARTIN, having first been duly sworn,
testified as follows:

1 Q. (by plaintiff's attorney) Please state your name.
2
3 A. Sharon Martin.
4
5 Q. Where are you employed?
6
7 A. Track Oil.
8
9 Q. How long have you been employed there?
10
11 A. A little over eight years.
12
13 Q. What is your position?
14
15 A. Assistant Supervisor, Research and Development
16   section.
17
18 Q. What are your duties?
19
20 A. In general, I function as the senior chemical
21   engineer in this area, and I direct our resources
22   into those areas that are important and promis-
23   ing.
24
25 Q. What is your educational background?
26
27 A. I got my B.S. and Masters in Chemistry from
28   Cornell. I have done some work toward my doctor-
29   ate.
30
31 Q. Since you have been associated with Track, has the
32   R & D section been working toward developing a gas
33   additive to increase mileage?
34
35 A. Yes, in the years when the energy crisis was just
36   gaining recognition, Track started working with the
37   idea. It wasn't very feasible when gas was cheap,
38   since our costs outweighed the gas savings. We
39   abandoned it until mid-[-4] when I read an article
40   in the Chemical and Engineering News that got me
41   thinking that alcohol might be a good base to work
42   from, using it with benzopyrene.

43 Q. Do you recall the title of the article that started
44   this process for you?
45
46 A. No.
47
48 Q. Do you recall the issue?
49
50 A. No.
51
52 Q. Would you be able to locate it?
53
54 A. Maybe, but not easily. I don't keep back issues.
55
56 Q. Did the article actually suggest alcohol and
57   benzopyrene as a gas additive or catalyst?
58
59 A. Oh, no, it just started me thinking that way.
60
61 Q. Do you have any notes of your development of this
62   concept in [-4]?
63
64 A. I had my notes, of course.
65
66 Q. Do you have them here today?
67
68 A. No, my files were stolen from my car last year.
69   I made a report about it to the police. You can
70   check.
71
72 Q. Can you tell us who prepared those notes?
73
74 A. Yes, I did. Those were the notes of my own
75   experiments and I took them from my own bench
76   book. I worked on this project myself, and the
77   amount of work required for something like this
78   is enormous. Now, all the notes are gone. So is
79   the book.
80
81 Q. Can your product PSSST be reverse engineered, or
82   broken down to determine the chemical
83   composition?
84
85 A. Most solutions or compounds can unless there is
86   something delicate in the equilibrium system that
87   will break down.
88
89 Q. Is an alcohol-based gas additive such a solu-
90   tion?
91
92 A. Our product is because of the benzopyrene.

```
93   Q. You indicated that it took some time to develop
94      the PSSST formula. Why is that?
95
96   A. Well, the formula itself is quite straightforward,
97      but determining the relative concentrations of
98      all the chemicals to maximize the combustion
99      reaction in the engine yet remain cost efficient
100     for our production was the difficulty. We found
101     alcohol and benzopyrene to be the optimum media
102     to work with, but it took some time to get the
103     proportions acceptable for our purposes. We
104     finally did it.
105
106  Q. In [-4] where did Track purchase its chemicals?
107
108  A. All over.
109
110  Q. Where did Track purchase benzopyrene in [-4]?
111
112  A. I think from General Chemical Company.
113
114  Q. When was Track's PSSST formula forwarded from R &
115     D to marketing?
116
117  A. The Fall of [-4] — probably October.
118
119  Q. Do you know when Track first marketed PSSST?
120
121  A. January, [-3], as I recall.
122
123  Q. I have nothing further.
```

This is to certify that I have read the transcript of my deposition taken on the 17th day of November, [-1], and that the transcript accurately states the questions asked and the answers given.

_____
                    Sharon Martin

Subscribed and sworn to
before me this 10th
day of December, [-1].

_____
        Notary Public

537

Mid-Continent, Inc.

July 21, [-3]

Mr./Ms. Robbie McCoy
Track Oil Company

Dear Mr./Ms. McCoy:

Mr./Ms. C.W. Block, an employee of Mid-Continent, Inc.
since March, [-5] has informed us that s/he has accepted
employment with your company.

Mr./Ms. Block has been a trusted employee of our Company
for several years and, during the course of his/her
employment with us, Mr./Ms. Block has been entrusted
with, or exposed to, confidential information that is the
property of Mid-Continent, Inc., and which constitutes
valuable trade secrets.

In your employment of Mr./Ms. Block, we are certain
that you, as well as ourselves, will expect him/her to
honor his/her legal obligation to refrain from, directly
or indirectly, disclosing or using any Mid-Continent
confidential information that s/he has gained and was
entrusted with during his/her Mid-Continent employment.
For your information, we have attached a copy of the
secrecy and patent agreement Mr./Ms. Block signed when
s/he entered our employ.

Yours very truly,

R.S. Hatfield
President, Mid-Continent, Inc.

cc: C.W. Block

539

MID-CONTINENT COMPANY, INC.

MEMORANDUM OF EMPLOYEE'S AGREEMENT

IN CONSIDERATION OF MY EMPLOYMENT by MID-CONTINENT COMPANY, INC., and/or the continuance of such employment:

1. I recognize that the technology, methods, processes, and formulas used by the Company in its business constitute valuable trade secrets that are the property of the Company and I agree not to reveal or use the same other than in the business of the Company.

2. I agree to disclose to and assign to MID-CONTINENT COMPANY, INC. all inventions made by me during the term of such employment and relating to any business in which the Company is engaged, whether made during usual working hours or otherwise, and whether alone or jointly with others, and to execute such instruments and do all other things necessary or desirable in order to obtain and maintain U.S. and foreign patents on such inventions in the Company's name.

THIS AGREEMENT does not, of course, bind either party to any specific period of employment.

C. W. Block	*3/3/[-5]*	*C. W. Block*
(Name of Employee-Type or Print)	Date	Signature of Employee

MID-CONTINENT, INC.

STATEMENT OF POLICY ON CONFLICT OF INTEREST

The ethical conduct of all of our officers, executives, and employees in all transactions affecting the Company is a matter of vital importance. The best interests of the Company must be the only consideration and the interests of individual employees cannot be permitted to play any part in such transactions.

In order that conflicts of interests may be avoided, each employee who is in a position to influence or control decisions affecting the Company's interests must observe the following:

1. Maintain constantly a high standard of conduct and disqualify himself or herself from exerting influence in any transaction where s/he finds his/her own interests may conflict with the best interests of the Company, or where s/he may gain any financial benefit.

2. Report any financial interest that s/he or any member of his/her family may have in any concern doing business with the Company. Stock ownership of less than 5 percent in any publicly owned corporation need not be reported. (A publicly owned corporation is any corporation required to file reports with the Securities and Exchange Commission.)

3. Report promptly to his/her superior any remuneration s/he receives from any individual or concern with whom the Company does business.

4. Accept no cash and no merchandise of significant value ($25.00 or more) from anyone who has a business relationship with the Company.

5. Refrain from lending money to, borrowing money from, or having loans guaranteed by anyone doing business with the Company, except that an employee may borrow from a financial institution with which the Company does business.

6. Refrain from using information or knowledge acquired by virtue of his/her position in the Company for any personal gain or advantage, or divulging such

knowledge or information to anyone who would use it in any manner detrimental to the interests of the Company or its stockholders, or to gain any personal advantage not available to our stockholders.

7. Report to the Company any knowledge of the existence of a violation of the above conflict of interest policy.

Please sign one copy of this Statement, and feel free to make comments or to raise any questions you wish. The questionnaire should then be returned in the enclosed envelope to the Industrial Relations Department of your division.

R.S. HATFIELD
Chairman of the Board
and President

I have read the above policy, have not violated it, and agree to abide by it fully.

Date <u>March 3, [-5]</u>   Name <u>C. W. Block</u>

Comments:

Chemicals for your way of life . . .
YEAR END WAREHOUSE SUMMARY SHEETS

Year: [-4]

Client: _____ MID-CONTINENT

Client Account No: _____ 68-34921

Product: _____ Benzopyrene _____

PLEASE LIST AMOUNT IN BARRELS SHIPPED EACH MONTH:

JAN.	1,280
FEB.	1,320
MAR.	1,160
APR.	1,580
MAY	12,060
JUN.	14,831
JUL.	15,168
AUG.	16,000
SEPT.	17,821
OCT.	20,180
NOV.	26,392
DEC.	25,280

TOTAL FOR THE YEAR: 153,072

Please write legibly. Press firmly and make sure the numbers appear on all carbons.

George White
Warehouse Foreman

1-8-[3]

Chemicals for your way of life . . .
YEAR END WAREHOUSE SUMMARY SHEETS

Year: [-4]

Client: TRACK OIL
Client Account No: 74-80321

Product: Benzopyrene

PLEASE LIST AMOUNT IN BARRELS SHIPPED EACH MONTH:

JAN.	80
FEB.	20
MAR.	110
APR.	90
MAY	115
JUN.	1,160
JUL.	1,280
AUG.	1,300
SEPT.	1,468
OCT.	1,500
NOV.	1,521
DEC.	1,589

TOTAL FOR THE YEAR: 10,233

Please write legibly. Press firmly and make sure the
numbers appear on all carbons.

George White
Warehouse Foreman

1-8-[-3]

PASSBOOK ACCOUNT RECORD

SECOND NATIONAL BANK

Account Name: C. W. Block

Account# 365212

DATE	WITHDRAWAL	DEPOSIT	BALANCE	TELLER
6/4/[-5]	$2,000		$ 2,921	7A
7/25/[-5]		$ 150	3,071	7A
10/30/[-5]		100	3,171	7A
1/5/[-4]	1,000		2,171	6A
3/4/[-4]		300	2,471	6A
6/10/[-4]		10,000	12,471	Auto
7/10/[-4]	1,000		11,471	7A
8/14/[-4]	2,000		9,471	7A
9/10/[-4]	3,000		6,471	6A
10/15/[-4]	2,000		4,471	6A
12/15/[-4]	2,000		2,471	7A
1/13/[-3]		10,000	12,471	Auto
2/15/[-3]	50		12,421	7A
3/19/[-3]	100		12,321	7A
4/21/[-3]		100	12,421	7A
5/16/[-3]	4,000		8,421	7A
6/16/[-3]	4,000		4,421	7A
7/1/[-3]	2,000		2,421	6A
7/15/[-3]		10,000	12,421	6A
3/4/[-2]	2,000		10,421	6A

7.4   HOME PURCHASE CONTRACT CASE

ROBIN JOHNSON

v.

SUPERIOR HOMES, INC.

This case is a contract dispute involving the sale of a house. Robin Johnson, the plaintiff, bought the house from Superior Homes, Inc., the defendant. The house was part of a new subdivision that Superior Homes was building in town. Jerry Williams was the sales representative employed by Superior Homes who entered into the sales contract with Johnson.

After Johnson bought the house and moved in, s/he noticed that the concrete floor in the house was developing cracks. Superior Homes denied any responsibility for the cracks, and Johnson brought this lawsuit alleging breach of implied warranty of habitability and fraud. Johnson asks for all proper damages, including punitive damages.

A breach of the implied warranty of habitability occurs when a builder constructs a new house containing a substantial latent defect. A latent defect is a defect in the house that cannot be discovered by ordinary and reasonable care.

A fraud occurs when a person makes a false statement of a material fact, the person making the statement knows it is false, the statement is made with the intent to induce another person to act, the other person acts in justifiable reliance on the truth of the statement, and the relying party suffers damage as a result of the reliance. Mere puffing or expressions of opinion are not statements of material fact.

You have the depositions of Johnson, the plaintiff, and Williams, the defendant's sales representative. You also have the attached documents that were obtained during discovery.

1. For the plaintiff, conduct a direct examination of Johnson and cross-examine Williams.

2. For the defendant, conduct a direct examination of Williams and cross-examine Johnson.

DEPOSITION OF ROBIN JOHNSON

on June 1, [-1]

at offices of defendant's attorney

ROBIN JOHNSON, having been first duly sworn, testified as follows:

1 Q. (by defendant's attorney) Tell us a little about
2   yourself.
3

4 A. I'm 25 years old, I'm single, I graduated from
5   college two years ago, and I live at the Peppertree
6   Apartments on Main Street.
7

8 Q. Tell us about your current employment.
9

10 A. I work at Compact Computers as a technical sup-
11   port person.
12

13 Q. What's your current salary?
14

15 A. $52,000 per year, with a small bonus during a
16   profitable year.
17

18 Q. Mr./Ms. Johnson, had you ever purchased a house
19   before you purchased the house from Superior
20   Homes?
21

22 A. No, that was the first time.
23

24 Q. What attracted you to the Forest Hills subdivi-
25   sion?
26

27 A. I guess it was a combination of things — the
28   location, the designs of the models, and the fact
29   that they were selling directly to the buyers.
30

31 Q. When did you first go out to the subdivision?
32

33 A. I'd seen it from the main road several times, but
34   the first time I actually went in was around the
35   first of March, [-2].
36

37 Q. What happened that day?
38

39 A. I stopped at the sales office, a trailer near the
40   entrance to the subdivision. I met Jerry Williams,
41   one of the sales people, in the office.

42   We talked a bit, I picked up some sales literature
43   about the subdivision, which explained the
44   differences in the models for sale, toured the
45   subdivision with Williams, and looked inside some
46   of the completed houses.

47

48 Q. What did the subdivision look like at that time?

49

50 A. Most of the houses were already built, although
51   some were still under construction. Some of the
52   homes looked occupied.

53

54 Q. When did you go back?

55

56 A. On March 15.

57

58 Q. What happened that day?

59

60 A. I met Jerry Williams again, and we went to the
61   house I was interested in, at 123 Forest Street.
62   I walked through it, checking things out. I did
63   notice a couple of cracks in the concrete floor,
64   where it was still exposed, like in the closets.
65   I asked Williams about them, and s/he said that
66   all concrete floors develop cracks when they dry.
67   I asked him/her if I should have an independent
68   contractor check it out, and s/he said I could,
69   but that it would be a waste of money, since the
70   county had inspected the house and had issued
71   a certificate of occupancy, which meant that
72   everything was all right. So we went back to the
73   sales office, and I signed a sales contact for the
74   house and gave him/her a $5,000 check as earnest
75   money.

76

77 Q. Did you ever have an independent inspection done of
78   the house before the closing?

79

80 A. No. Based on what Williams said, I thought it was
81   unnecessary.

82

83 Q. When did you close on the house?

84

85 A. The closing was on May 1, [-2], and I moved in
86   right afterward.

87

88 Q. When did you notice anything about the cracks?

89

90 A. Within two or three months I noticed that the
91   cracks that I could see in the closets seemed to be
92   getting bigger. They weren't getting wider,

93 but one side of the cracks was higher than the
94 other side. I could feel the height difference
95 through the carpeting in the rooms.
96
97 Q. What did you do?
98
99 A. I realized that there was a real problem, so
100   I hired Sandy Henderson, a soil and masonry
101   engineer, to inspect my house. He found that there
102   were two large cracks running across the middle
103   of the house, and that the concrete was higher
104   on one side of the crack than the other. He said
105   that this was not normal, might get worse over
106   time, and said that the problem was caused by the
107   soil under the concrete slab not being properly
108   compacted before the concrete slab was poured.
109   He said that the soil had settled, and that the
110   concrete slab had cracked because the soil was not
111   supporting the slab properly.
112
113 Q. When did Henderson do the inspection?
114
115 A. I received his report sometime in September, so he
116   probably did it a few days before then.
117
118 Q. So what did you do when you received the report?
119
120 A. I called Williams, told him/her what the engineer
121   had found, and demanded that they fix the problem
122   or buy the house back.
123
124 Q. What was the response of Superior Homes?
125
126 A. There really wasn't any. Williams kept saying that
127   the cracks were nothing out of the ordinary, and
128   they refused to do anything. I then hired a lawyer
129   who brought this lawsuit.
130
131 Q. Did you see the newspaper article about the
132   problem in the Forest Hills subdivision?
133
134 A. Yes.
135
136 Q. When did you see it?
137
138 A. The day it came out in the Forest Daily, but I
139   didn't really pay much attention to it.

This is to certify that I have read the transcript of my deposition taken on June 1, [-1], and that the transcript accurately states the questions asked and the answers given.

Robin Johnson
Robin Johnson

Subscribed to and sworn to before me
on the 1st day of July, [-1].

Zelola Mummfries
Notary Public

DEPOSITION OF JERRY WILLIAMS

on June 15, [-1]

at offices of plaintiff's attorney

JERRY WILLIAMS, having been first duly sworn, testified as follows:

1 Q. (by plaintiff's attorney) Tell us about your
2   background and employment history.
3
4 A. I'm a high school grad, I'm married and have three
5   children, I worked 15 years as a car salesman, and
6   then decided to move to real estate.
7
8 Q. Mr./Ms. Williams, tell us your background in the
9   real estate business.
10
11 A. I've been a real estate agent for five years. I
12   worked for a local real estate office for about
13   four years before I took the job with Superior
14   Homes at the Forest Hills subdivision. I'm one of
15   six sales agents at the subdivision.
16
17 Q. Are you a licensed real estate broker?
18
19 A. Yes, I received my broker's license five years
20   ago.
21
22 Q. What's that involve?
23
24 A. Basically you take a written test. I studied for it
25   in my spare time.
26
27 Q. Why did you take the job as a sales representative
28   at Forest Hills?
29
30 A. It seemed like a good opportunity. I thought the
31   subdivision would sell, and if I did well there
32   Superior Homes would move me to other projects,
33   since it's a big company.
34
35 Q. Have you received any special training in building
36   construction?
37
38 A. No, other than what I've picked up on the job.
39
40 Q. Describe the Forest Hills subdivision.

557

41 A. It's a typical modern subdivision, in a hilly
42   suburban setting, with about 200 homes. There
43   are several models to choose from, although
44   lot sizes are all about a quarter acre. All the
45   units are single level, built on a concrete slab
46   foundation, which means that none of the units
47   had basements.
48
49 Q. How many homes had been sold as of March, [-2]?
50
51 A. I'd estimate about 75 had been sold by then. Most
52   of the remaining were either being built or were
53   already completed.
54
55 Q. When was the first time you met Robin Johnson?
56
57 A. On March 1, [-2], according to our records.
58
59 Q. What happened that day?
60
61 A. I remember meeting him/her at the sales office,
62   which is in a trailer near the entrance to the
63   subdivision. We talked, looked at models of the
64   various homes for sale, and drove around. I gave
65   him/her the standard information packet on the
66   subdivision. S/he seemed interested, but nothing
67   firm happened that day.
68
69 Q. What happened the next time you met?
70
71 A. S/he came back on March 15, [-2]. S/he wanted to
72   look at a particular home, the one at 123 Forest
73   Street, so we drove to it and inspected the house.
74   We then went back to the sales office and signed a
75   contract.
76
77 Q. Didn't s/he inquire about cracks in the concrete
78   floors?
79
80 A. Yes, s/he did. S/he asked about small cracks in
81   the floor, that you could see in the closets.
82   I told him/her that concrete sometimes develops
83   small cracks as it dries and hardens. I remember
84   telling him/her that all the homes are inspected
85   by the county before a certificate of occupancy
86   is issued, which had already been done for that
87   house.
88
89 Q. Didn't you tell him/her that an independent
90   inspection was unnecessary?
91
92   A. That's not true. I told him/her she could and

93   should have the place inspected by anyone at his/
94   her cost. In fact, the sales contract specifically
95   provides for inspection by the buyer. Most buyers
96   do just that — have an outsider inspect the house
97   before closing.
98
99 Q. Let's talk about the newspaper article about
100   Forest Hills. When did you see it?
101
102 A. The day it came out. September 1, [-2].
103
104 Q. What effect did the article have on sales?
105
106 A. It was a disaster. It just killed sales. Hardly
107   anyone came out to look at the models, and the
108   ones that did, all they wanted to talk about was
109   the article.
110
111 Q. Before March 15, did you know of any other homes
112   with a cracking problem in the slab foundation?
113
114 A. Not really, nothing I would call a problem. I was
115   aware of a few homes that had some cracks, but
116   that was only about five homes out of 200 in the
117   subdivision. The construction sites vary a great
118   deal, since Forest Hills is in a hilly area, so
119   there's no reason to believe that any problem at
120   a particular site would also show up at another
121   site.
122
123 Q. Did you tell Robin Johnson about these other
124   problems?
125
126 A. No, I didn't, because I wouldn't call it a
127   problem.
128
129 Q. Those other homes with foundation cracks, some of
130   them have pending lawsuits against Superior Homes,
131   right?
132
133 A. Yes.
134
135 Q. Johnson demanded that Superior Homes buy the house
136   back from her, right?
137
138 A. That's what s/he asked, but that was impossible.

     This is to certify that I have read the
transcript of my deposition taken on June 15, [-1], and

that the transcript accurately states the questions asked
and the answers given.

Jerry Williams
Jerry Williams

Subscribed to and sworn to before me
on the 15th day of July, [-1].

Dorris Chambers
Notary Public

FOREST COUNTY BUILDING DEPARTMENT

Certificate of Occupancy

Address: 123 Forest Street
                            Forest Hills subdivision
                            Forest County

Building inspector: Arthur Avery

Date of inspection: August 28, [-3]

    I, Arthur Avery, state that I have inspected the
above property and find that the property complies with
all applicable local, county, and state safety codes.
I therefore certify that the above property is safe for
human occupancy.

Arthur Avery
Arthur Avery
Forest County Building Inspector

Date of issuance of certificate:
September 1, [-3]

RESIDENTIAL REAL ESTATE PURCHASE CONTRACT

Seller: Superior Homes, Inc.
Buyer: Robin Johnson
Property: Residential home at 123 Forest Street, Forest
           Hills subdivision
Price: $200,000.00 (two hundred thousand dollars)

Buyer will take title as: sole and separate property.

Earnest money received from buyer, Robin Johnson, is in
the amount of $5,000.00 (personal check). Earnest money
shall be held by seller and is considered to be part of
the purchase price for the premises described below.

Buyer agrees to purchase, and seller agrees to sell, the
real property and all fixtures and improvements described
as: a one story residential home, of approx. 2,000 square
feet, on a parcel of approx. one/fourth acre, located at
123 Forest Street, Forest Hills subdivision.

The full purchase price of $200,000.00 shall be payable
in full at closing, minus the $5,000.00 earnest money
deposit. The remaining balance of $195,000.00 shall be
payable at closing to be held on May 1, [-2], at offices
of seller. Taxes, insurance premiums, homeowner fees, if
any, shall be prorated at the time of closing.

Buyer shall have 30 days from date of contract to obtain
mortgage commitment from a lender of buyer's choosing.
If buyer fails to obtain such commitment, this contract
shall be null and void.

Seller warrants that it has title to the property and
will obtain a preliminary title report and shall furnish
to buyer, at closing and at seller's expense, a standard
owner's title insurance policy in the full amount of the
purchase price showing good and marketable title to the
property, subject only to zoning regulations, easements,
rights-of-way, and current taxes.

Seller warrants that it shall maintain the premises
so that at the closing the premises shall be in
substantially the same condition as on the effective date
of this contract. Seller grants buyer reasonable access
to enter and inspect the premises. Seller warrants that
it has disclosed to buyer all material latent defects
concerning the premises that are known to seller.

Seller warrants that it has disclosed to the buyer any information, except opinions of value, that it possesses that materially and adversely affects the consideration to be paid by buyer.

Effective date: March 15, [-2]

Jerry Williams
Seller's agent's signature

Robin Johnson
Buyer's signature

The following article from the Forest Daily appeared on page 1 of the metro section of the newspaper on September 15, [-2].

Forest Daily

METRO

September 15, [-2]

SECTION

B

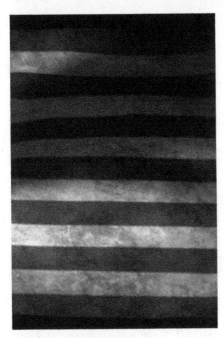

Life's Guarantees

becomes necessary for one
nich have connected them with

"Settling In" at Forest Hills

September 15, [-2]

Is there a problem at the Forest Hills subdivision on the northwest side of town?

Reliable sources report that a number of homes in the subdivision are experiencing settling problems that are causing foundation slabs to crack and displace.

Officers at Superior Homes, the developer of Forest Hills, refused to comment. In the meantime the affected homeowners complain that they "have gotten the runaround" by Superior Homes, and that nothing has been done to correct the problems in the affected homes.

METRO

"Settling In" at
Forest Hill

September 15, 1987

SUPER COMPUTER
Vancouver, BC

July 15, [-2]

Robin Johnson
123 Forest Street

Re: Application to technical support division

Dear Robin:

We apologize for not being able to make a final decision on your application, although we first received your application to work in our computer technical support division in the Vancouver, BC, office in January. Your, and other applications, were "on hold" until the company made basic decisions on the long-term future and direction of this office.

We are happy to report that the company has decided to expand operations at this office and, consequently, are just as happy to offer you a position in the computer technical support division beginning November 1, [-2]. The starting salary will be $75,000 (U.S. dollars).

However, to address our overall needs in a timely fashion, we will need your answer by October 1, [-2]. Please feel free to call me about the offer and discuss it at any time. We hope you will join the Super Computer family!

Sincerely,

Mark Woods,
Personnel supervisor

"Forest Hills"

A Superior Homes Development

Memorandum

To: Sales personnel

From: Art Smith, vice president

Date: March 1, [-2]

As you know, sales of homes at Forest Hills are averaging approximately three per week since sales began last September. At this rate, it is my expectation to have the entire subdivision sold by the early part of next year. We have closed, or have under contract, approximately 70 of the 200 homes in the subdivision. However, we will have to double our efforts to meet our goal to sell all the homes by year's end. Those of you who produce results necessary to meet this goal will be rewarded accordingly.

On a more troubling note, the purchasers of five homes have complained in recent weeks about cracks in the slab foundations of their homes. I'm sure you have heard, directly or indirectly, about this. I have examined each of these homes, and the cracks appear to be nothing more than the kind of small cracks that sometimes develop in slab foundations that settle over time. Our masonry contractor inspected those homes and came to the same conclusion.

While five homes with foundation cracks hardly suggests a larger problem, since the sites, site preparation, and models vary substantially within the subdivision, these complaints, if they become generally known, can do considerable damage to sales.

Please keep these thoughts in mind as we move ahead in the coming months.

Sandy Henderson
Soil and Masonry Testing

September 28, [-2]

Robin Johnson
123 Forest Street

Re: Soil and masonry tests at 123 Forest Street

Dear Robin:

Pursuant to your telephone request on September 16, I have inspected and tested your home at 123 Forest Street. Specifically, I have tested the concrete slab foundation, ground fill in the built-up grade, and the underlying ground by taking core samples of the slab, fill, and underlying ground. I have found the following:

1. There are two cracks running in a north-south direction across the entire slab foundation, in approximately the middle of the slab. The two cracks are approximately 2' apart, running parallel to each other, and the cracks appear to run through the entire 4" thickness of the slab. The slabs, on either side of each crack, are displaced approximately 1/8" vertically. This means that the eastern slab is approximately 1/4" higher than the western end of the slab.

2. The concrete slab foundation is a common design in this part of the country. The slab is 4" thick, made of concrete with wire mesh embedded in the concrete. Nothing abnormal was found with the slab foundation.

3. The grade under the slab foundation has been built up between 4' to 6' from the natural grade. The built-up grade is approximately 4' at the eastern end of the house, increasing to 6' at the western end of the house. The grade is built up with common gravel. Nothing abnormal was found with the gravel material used to build up the grade.

4. The underlying ground is typical for this area, being composed of rocky gravel, and is appropriate for residential construction.

Based on my examination and testing, I have concluded that the cracks in the slab foundation of your house are caused by uneven settling, or subsidence, of the gravel fill used to build up the grade under the foundation. A displacement of 1/4" between the eastern and western ends of the house, causing cracks in the foundation, should not occur in a properly constructed house.

The only explanation for this settling of the fill is that the fill was not compacted properly before the concrete slab foundation was poured. Such fill must be added in layers, watered, and compacted with proper equipment. The fill must be added not more than 12" to 18" at a time, watered, and compacted, before the next layer is added and the process is repeated, until the grade is built up to the desired level. If this process is not properly done, the fill will subside over time, causing the slab foundation to lose its support, causing cracking and displacement of the slab.

While cracks sometimes appear in concrete slabs, displacement of the slab should not occur. Any displacement of 1/8" or more in vertical direction, as is the case here, is evidence of a construction defect: improper build-up of the grade.

Since the subsidence problem is caused by improper build-up of the grade (rather than improper fill material, or hydrological problems), the subsidence will usually stop as the grade settles. Although it is impossible to say when that will occur, in my experience a grade build-up of 6' will probably settle and stabilize within one year after construction of the house.

Remedying the slab displacement problem is difficult and expensive. The usual solution is to inject material under the slab foundation to bring it into proper alignment. I estimate that this process would, in your case, cost approximately $50,000.00.

If you have any further questions, please let me know. My bill for $3,000 is enclosed with this letter.

Sincerely,

Sandy Henderson

Sandy Henderson

enc.

7.5   AGE DISCRIMINATION EMPLOYMENT CASE

FRAN BOYLE

v.

HOME MART, INC.

Fran Boyle brings this civil action in the U.S. District Court against Home Mart, Inc. S/he alleges s/he was discharged from his/her job on September 1, [-2], because of his/her age, in violation of the Age Discrimination in Employment Act (ADEA), 29 U.S.C. § 621 et seq. The ADEA prohibits employers from discriminating against employees at least 40 years old based on their age.

Boyle alleges s/he was within the protected age group, that s/he performed his/her job satisfactorily, that s/he was fired because of his/her age, and that s/he was replaced by a substantially younger employee who was otherwise similarly situated. Boyle has received a 29 U.S.C. § 626 "right to sue" letter from the Equal Employment Opportunity Commission.

Home Mart denies any age discrimination. In its affirmative defense, Home Mart alleges Boyle was fired as part of a company reorganization. It further alleges Boyle was fired because his/her job performance was not satisfactory, s/he had a negative attitude, and employee morale in the department s/he headed was so low that sales were affected. The company's answer was signed by Pat Seaborg, vice president for sales at Home Mart and general manager of the store where Boyle had been employed.

[handwritten margin note: why Home Mart says she was fired]

This is the liability stage of the trial. You have the depositions of Boyle and Seaborg, affidavits from two Home Mart employees, Boyle's last job evaluation, a corporate memo to Seaborg, and the termination letter sent to Boyle by Seaborg.

1. For the plaintiff, conduct a direct examination of Boyle and cross-examine Seaborg.

2. For the defendant, conduct a direct examination of Seaborg and cross-examine Boyle.

573

1 Q. (by defendant's attorney) Please state your full
2 name and tell us something about yourself.
3
4 A. My name is Fran Boyle. I live in this city, at
5 4812 Newton Street. I live alone. I was recently
6 divorced. I have two grown children. I am not
7 working. I have looked ever since Home Mart fired
8 me, but I can't find a job. No one wants to hire
9 anyone my age.
10
11 Q. How old are you?
12
13 A. I'll be 60 in two weeks.
14
15 Q. Tell us about the jobs you have held since you
16 graduated from high school.
17
18 A. After high school I went into the U.S. Army. That
19 was in [-42]. I came out of the army in [-39].
20 I went to work for Sears, in their hardware
21 department, and stayed there for five years. Then
22 I opened my own little hardware store, because I
23 wanted to be independent. That lasted six years,
24 but I couldn't compete with the big guys, so I
25 closed it sometime in [-28] or maybe it was
26 [-27]. I bounced from job to job for a while,
27 mostly selling hardware and home appliances, then
28 I hooked on with Home Mart in [-21]. I was there
29 for 19 years, all at the Big Tree store.
30
31 Q. What did you do at Home Mart?
32
33 A. I always was in hardware. I started as a junior
34 clerk, then a senior clerk after a few years, and
35 in [-8] I was made department manager. That's where
36 I was when they dumped me.
37
38 Q. In this lawsuit, you claim you were fired because
39 of your age. Why do you say that?
40
41 A. I know that was the reason. My department was
42 doing real well, our sales figures were holding
43 up, and I know our customers liked doing business
44 there. But I kept hearing things. After I was
45 fired one of my employees told me he heard
46 Seaborg refer to our department as the "geriatric
47 ward" and that Seaborg referred to me as an "old
48 fogey."

[handwritten margin note: She moved up through the company junior clerk to store manager]

575

49 Q. Did Seaborg talk to you about your job perfor-
50   mance?
51
52 A. Just two weeks before I was fired Seaborg called me
53   into his/her office at the store. S/he told me I
54   would have to do better, but s/he didn't say what
55   I was doing wrong. S/he just said "the old ways
56   won't work anymore," and that I "would have to
57   get up to date." When I asked him/her what
58   s/he meant, s/he just said, "I don't have the time
59   or energy to explain. You won't change anyway."
60   Then s/he told me to get out of his/her office,
61   so I left. Next thing I knew I was handed the
62   termination letter. I was gone. No notice, not even
63   a warning.
64
65 Q. Why do you think you were fired?
66
67 A. I think they were trying to save money. I earned
68    $75,000 in [-3] and was on my way to earning at
69   least that much in [-2]. I know they replaced me
70   with some 29-year-old kid for a lot less money.
71   Besides that, my pension was due to vest. Once I
72   had 20 years at the store the company would have to
73   match all my contributions and I could afford to
74   retire.
75
76 Q. Didn't Pat Seaborg tell you that you weren't
77   keeping up with modern sales technology?
78
79 A. S/he mentioned something about how the other
80   department heads were using computers to keep track
81   of inventory and sales, while I was doing it by
82   hand. But I told him/her I was willing to learn,
83   and my employees would later put the information in
84   the computers anyway.
85
86 Q. How many people worked for you in the Hardware
87   Department?
88
89 A. Six.
90
91 Q. Did you get along with all them?
92
93 A. Sure. They were loyal and supported me all the
94   way.
95
96 Q. Did you take some of the store's tools home for
97   your personal use?

brought home tools to practice w/ them
— show customers how they worked

98 A. Yeah, I brought some home from time to time. I
99   wanted to be sure I knew how they worked. You
100   can't sell something unless you know what you
101   are talking about. I didn't intend to keep them.
102   In all, they can't be worth more than $100,
103   retail.
104
105 Q. I understand you were going through a difficult
106   divorce during the year before you were
107   terminated. Did that affect your job performance?
108
109 A. It was more than difficult, it was painful. I had
110   been married to the same man/woman for 38 years.
111   Sure, I may have been a little cranky because of
112   it, but it didn't affect the way I did my job.
113   Besides, it was all over and settled a month
114   before I was fired.

divorce was over a month before she was fired

   I have read the questions and answers contained
in this transcript and they accurately represent the
questions asked and answers given.

                                Fran Boyle
                                 Fran Boyle

Signed and sworn to before me
on December 20, [-1]

Michael Josephs
Notary Public

DEPOSITION OF PAT SEABORG

on December 12, [-1]

at plaintiff's lawyer's office

1 Q. (by plaintiff's lawyer) Please tell me your full
2   name and your occupation.
3
4 A. I am Pat Seaborg. I am vice president for sales at
5   Home Mart, Incorporated, and general sales manager
6   of the store in this city.
7
8 Q. How many stores does Home Mart have?
9
10 A. Three. One in this city, at 1200 Big Tree Avenue,
11   and two others in this state. The one I run,
12   called "Big Tree," is the largest.
13
14 Q. Tell me something about your background, including
15   your age and your employment history.
16
17 A. I live with my husband/wife and infant son at 1424
18   Briar Street in this city. I am 36 years old. I
19   have a Bachelor's degree in liberal arts and a
20   Master's degree in business administration, both
21   from Harvard. I received the Master's degree in
22   [-5] and the Bachelor's in [-7]. I went to work
23   at Home Mart after receiving the Master's degree.
24   They hired me to work in their sales department. I
25   became vice president for sales in [-4]. Then, in
26   early [-2], when they realized the Big Tree store
27   was in trouble, I also became general manager of
28   that store. I still hold both positions.
29
30 Q. Were you the person at Home Mart who made the
31   decision to fire Fran Boyle?
32
33 A. Yes.
34
35 Q. Why did you make that decision?
36
37 A. Despite Fran's years of faithful service to the
38   store, s/he just was not doing the job. His/Her
39   sales figures were going down. Employees in his/her
40   department were complaining that s/he was short-
41   tempered and hard to get along with. They told us
42   s/he even was arguing with customers. And s/he
43   refused to adapt to modern methods. For instance,
44   s/he never learned the computer system we installed

45   for recording inventory and sales. S/he still did
46   all that by hand. His/Her job evaluation by the
47   store manager who served directly under me was
48   barely satisfactory. We knew we had to reorganize
49   the store. I was under orders to cut costs.
50
51 Q. How did you reorganize and cut costs?
52
53 A. Well, before [-2] we had 210 employees in that
54   store, with ten departments and ten department
55   managers. We merged into seven departments. That
56   meant we had to fire three managers. Boyle was one
57   of them.
58
59 Q. Did you abolish the hardware department as a
60   separate entity?
61
62 A. No. That is one department we kept intact.
63   Customers expect a department that has hardware and
64   nothing else.
65
66 Q. What were the last job evaluations of the other two
67   managers who were fired?
68
69 A. Both had received "poor" evaluations for the past
70   two years.
71
72 Q. How old were those two fired managers?
73
74 A. One was 55, the other 56. Each had been at the
75   store about fifteen years.
76
77 Q. Tell me about the seven department managers who
78   were not fired. How old were they and what were
79   their last job evaluations?
80
81 A. They ranged in age from 32 to 44. Four of them
82   had "superior" evaluations and three of them were
83   "satisfactory."
84
85 Q. Who is running the hardware department now?
86
87 A. A young woman named Freda Harbaugh. She had
88   applied for a job in early [-2], but we did
89   not decide to hire her until a month after we
90   let Boyle go. She's only 30 years old, but she
91   really knows modern sales techniques. She's an
92   expert when it comes to using computers. And I
93   understand everyone in the department likes and
94   respects her.
95
96 Q. How much does Freda Harbaugh earn?

580

97 A. She gets $45,000 a year now, but we are thinking
98   about giving her a bonus at the end of this year.
99   The fact that she makes less than Boyle did had
100   nothing to do with our decision to discharge
101   Boyle.
102
103 Q. Has there been any change in the gross sales
104   figures for the hardware department since Boyle
105   was fired?
106
107 A. They are up 5 percent since Freda came on board
108   with us in October of [-2]. We have high hopes
109   they will keep going up.
110
111 Q. Isn't it true that in [-3] the gross sales figures
112   were down substantially in six other store
113   departments, while Boyle's sales figures were down
114   only slightly?
115
116 A. That's true if you call a 3 percent decrease
117   slight, but I don't. We expect more from hardware
118   than we do from some of the other departments.
119   Hardware sales had never gone down before [-3].
120   And you should know that the sales figures for the
121   first six months of [-2] were down 5 percent from
122   the first six months of [-3].
123
124 Q. When Boyle was at the store, did you ever refer to
125   the hardware department as the "geriatric ward" or
126   to Fran Boyle as "that old fogey"?
127
128 A. No, never. I don't use words like that. All I
129   ever said was that the department was not keeping
130   up with the times, that it needed to modernize.
131   That's what I told Boyle when s/he came to my
132   office in mid-August of last year, but s/he
133   wouldn't listen. S/he walked out of my office
134   and slammed the door behind him/her. That's
135   when I made the decision to let him/her go. That
136   decision had nothing to do with his/her age, or
137   his/her salary, or his/her pension benefits. It
138   was a wise economic decision.
139
140 Q. Isn't it true that if Boyle were employed until
141   his/her pension vested, the company would have
142   to fund half of that pension payout when s/he
143   retired?
144
145 A. I suppose that's true, but that had nothing to do
146   with his/her being fired.

147 Q. Did you have any other reason for firing Boyle
148   that you have not yet told me about?
149
150 A. Well, after this lawsuit was filed I found out
151   s/he had been taking tools home for his/her personal
152   use. That alone would be a reason for firing him.

        I have read the questions and answers contained
in this deposition and they accurately represent the
questions asked and answers given.

                                    Pat Seaborg
                                    Pat Seaborg

Signed and sworn to before me
on December 30, [-1]

Angie Healy
Notary Public

MEMORANDUM

Date: July 1, [-2]

To: Pat Seaborg, General Manager, Big Tree store

From: Wilhelm Pratt, CEO, Home Mart, Inc.

Re: Required economic measures

Pat, I realize you have not been at the Big Tree store very long, but you have to do something pretty fast. Our overall gross sales figures are down at all the stores, probably a reflection of a slow retail economy all over the country. I am relying on you to do some cost-cutting at the Big Tree store. Do what you have to do, but do it. Get rid of the deadwood, keep the team players, modernize, if you know what I mean. I will expect a turnaround by the end of the year. Don't disappoint me.

heard Pat Seaborg calling Fran Boyle "old fogey" + geriatric ward

AFFIDAVIT OF PAUL KELLER

I, Paul Keller, being duly sworn on November 21, [1], state:

1. For the past five years I have been employed by Home Mart, Inc., the defendant in Boyle vs. Home Mart, at the Big Tree store in this city. I have been employed as a salesman in the hardware department during that time. My supervisor was my friend Fran Boyle until September 1, [-2].

2. In the last week of July, [-2], I was walking past Pat Seaborg's office at the store. His/Her door was wide open. I saw that s/he was on the phone. I don't know who s/he was talking to but I heard him/her say that s/he didn't know what s/he was going to do about "that old fogey" in the hardware department. S/he said something about hardware being the "geriatric ward" in the store, and s/he said "no wonder our sales figures are in the ditch."

3. That's all I remember hearing, except s/he was saying something like the store's well-being was his/her first priority.

4. After I heard that Fran was being fired, I called him/her at home and told him/her what I heard Seaborg say.

5. I am willing to testify at the trial concerning Fran's firing.

Paul Keller

Paul Keller

Signed and sworn to before me
on November 21, [-1]

Jennifer Duguio

Notary Public

anti-Boyle

AFFIDAVIT OF LONNY SKELLY

I, Lonny Skelly, being duly sworn on October 25, [1], state:

1. For the past four years I have been employed in the Hardware department of the Home Mart store on Big Tree. My direct supervisor until September 1, [-2], was Fran Boyle.

2. On a day in the middle of July, [-2], I went to the office of Pat Seaborg, general manager of our store. I went there to complain about the behavior of Fran Boyle.

3. On the aforesaid date, I told Seaborg that Boyle was very difficult to get along with. I told him/her how Boyle would shout at me and other employees of the department for every little thing. S/he always seemed angry about something. It got to a point where none of us wanted to talk to Boyle about anything. I also told Seaborg how Boyle acted this way with some customers, too.

4. I related this information to Seaborg because I think Home Mart is a great store and I enjoy working there. I think Boyle's behavior is affecting our ability to do our jobs and to sell our products to customers. We just don't seem to be working as a team anymore.

5. I am willing to testify to the contents of this affidavit at any trial relating to the discharge of Fran Boyle.

Lonny Skelly
Lonny Skelly

Signed and sworn to before me
on October 25, [-1]

Emily Isacc
Notary Public

589

TERMINATION NOTICE

To: Fran Boyle

From: Pat Seaborg, General Manager

Date: August 16, [-2]

This is to notify you that as of September 1, [-2], your employment with this company will be terminated. In accord with company policy, you will receive a severance check representing two weeks of salary. Please be sure to remove all personal items from your locker and from the store premises. Turn in your keys and your employee identification card to store security before September 1.

Thank you for your years of service to this company.

Pat Seaborg
Pat Seaborg

7.6 MURDER CASE

STATE

v.

DARLENE LINZY

This is a murder case brought against the defendant, Darlene Linzy. Linzy is charged with the murder of Linda Goodrom on January 1 of last year.

A police officer, Avery Jordan, will testify for the prosecution. His/Her grand jury testimony is attached. Also attached is Officer Jordan's report of his/her post-arrest interview with the defendant.

Darlene Linzy will testify on her own behalf. **[The defense attorney should ask the instructor for a copy of the former defense lawyer's memo. The prosecution will not have access to that memo.]**

1. For the prosecution, conduct a direct examination of Officer Jordan and cross-examine Linzy.

2. For the defense, conduct a direct examination of Linzy and cross-examine Officer Jordan.

HOMICIDE INVESTIGATION REPORT

TO: Commanding Officer, Homicide Division

FROM: Investigator Avery Jordan

RE: Shooting death of Linda Goodrom

On January 1, [-1], reporting officer was assigned to the shooting death of Linda Goodrom. Victim had been shot while in the doorway to Easy Life Tavern, at 817 E. 43rd Street. Witnesses said victim was shot by a young female who immediately after the shooting left in a green car with license number 1237.

Check of license plate showed it belonged to Darlene Linzy, 1214 E. 43rd Street. Reporting Officer went to Linzy's address, where Linzy was placed under arrest. When Linzy responded to reporting officer's knock on door, a .38 caliber revolver was seen in plain view on hallway table. Revolver was sent to crime lab section for analysis.

At the North Avenue Station, RO advised Linzy of her constitutional rights. She said she wanted to tell what happened and was willing to waive her rights.

Her account follows:

I went to the Easy Life to meet a girlfriend to celebrate New Year's Eve. I had my gun in my purse because that is a dangerous neighborhood. After about an hour, near midnight, a woman was dancing near my table. She threw a lighted cigarette in my drink. I asked her why she did that. She said something like, "Well, since I didn't burn your clothing or you, I suggest you back off." We said some things to each other, but I thought that was the end of it. I ordered another vodka martini, my third and last of the night. About an hour later, around 1:00 A.M., I got up to leave. As I neared the door, in a small hallway, that same woman blocked my way. She said she wanted to knock my head off, or something like that. I said I didn't want to fight. That's when she slapped me. Then she stepped toward me, and when she was right up to me, she reached into her pocket. I thought she was going to kill me. So I reached into my purse and took out my .38. I wasn't going to wait to see if she had a knife or something. So I fired my gun, one time. People started coming toward me, so I ran out and got into my car and drove away. Then I just went home and waited for the police.

595

RO asked Linzy if she would give a written statement, but she declined. She was formally charged with the murder of Linda Goodrom.

_____

Reporting Officer

1/1/[-1], approx. 1400 hours
Time and Date of Report

Before the Grand Jury of This County, February 15,
[-1]

Re: State v. Darlene Linzy

Transcript of the sworn testimony of Avery Jordan,
taken in the above-entitled matter on January 29, [-1].

1 Q. (by John O'Malley, assistant county prosecutor)
2   Please state your full name and assignment.
3
4 A. Avery Jordan, I'm a homicide investigator with the
5   city police department.
6
7 Q. How long have you been so employed?
8
9 A. I was a patrol officer for five years, then a
10   homicide investigator for the past three years.
11
12 Q. On January 1 of this year, were you assigned to
13   investigate the death of Linda Goodrom?
14
15 A. Yes.
16
17 Q. Could you relate to the Grand Jury how, when, and
18   where the victim's body was found?
19
20 A. On that date I received an assignment that there
21   had been a shooting at 817 East 43rd Street. I
22   was further informed that the female victim had
23   been taken to the Michael Reese Hospital, where
24   she was pronounced dead. I went to Michael Reese
25   Hospital and I viewed the body of the deceased and
26   during the observation I saw a gunshot wound to the
27   victim's left chest. Victim was 5'7", weighed about
28   150 pounds, and was 27 years old. I then went to
29   817 East 43rd Street where I received information
30   that the person responsible for the shooting was
31   a female who had left in her automobile, license
32   plate number 1237.
33
34 Q. What did you do next?
35
36 A. We checked out the license plate number and learned
37   that it belonged to a Darlene Linzy at 1214 E. 43rd
38   Street.
39
40 Q. What did you do then?
41
42 A. We went to Ms. Linzy's home at about 2:00 P.M. on
43   January 1. We placed her under arrest. We seized
44   a gun that was in open view on the table in her

45 hallway. Ballistics tests later showed that was the
46 gun that killed Linda Goodrom. We then brought her
47 to the North Avenue Police Station, where we spoke
48 to her about the shooting.
49
50 Q. What did she say about the shooting?
51
52 A. After advising her of her constitutional rights,
53 Ms. Linzy indicated she had gone to the tavern
54 to meet a girlfriend. At the tavern, the victim
55 was dancing on the floor and had thrown a lighted
56 cigarette onto the table where Linzy was
57 seated. After the dance was completed, Linzy
58 stated she asked the victim, "Why did you throw
59 the cigarette on the table," and the victim
60 replied, "Well, since I didn't burn your
61 clothing or you, I suggest you back off." Several
62 words were passed in the tavern according to
63 Linzy, and approximately an hour after the first
64 contact, Linzy stated she got up to leave and at
65 that time the victim approached her, offered to
66 fight. She declined to fight. At that point, Linzy
67 indicated the victim slapped her. According to
68 Linzy, the victim then made a step toward her
69 and it was at that point that Linzy reached into
70 her purse, pulled out her gun, and shot the
71 victim.
72
73 Q. Was that a written statement?
74
75 A. No. It was an oral statement. She refused to
76 give a written statement. I took notes as she
77 spoke, then destroyed the notes after I wrote my
78 report. The report accurately reflects what she
79 told me.
80
81 Q. Did Darlene Linzy tell you why she shot the
82 woman?
83
84 A. No.
85
86 Q. Did she tell you how far the victim was from her
87 when she fired the shot?
88
89 A. No.
90
91 Q. Did the victim have any weapon in her posses-
92 sion?
93
94 A. None that we found.

95 Q. Did Darlene Linzy tell you anything else about the
96   shooting?
97
98 A. Not that I recall.
99
100 Q. Thank you, Officer. That will be all.

EASY LIFE TAVERN

Entry

Alley

Men's Room

Women's Room

Storage Cooler

Delivery Door

Door

Door

Access Door

Table

Table

Bar

Stage for DJ

Dance Floor

Table

Table

Table

Pool Table

Table

Fire Exit

LASXLIRE TAVERN

Alley — Entry

Storage Cooler

Delivery Door

Women's Room   Men's Room

Access Door   Door   Pool

Table   Table

Bar   Dance Floor   Stage for D...

Table   Table   Table

Table   Pool Table

Fire Exit

7.7 DRUG ENTRAPMENT CASE

STATE

v.

MICKEY DRANE

The defendant, Mickey Drane, is charged with Unlawful Delivery of a Controlled Substance, that is, cocaine. S/he admits making the delivery, but asserts the affirmative defense of entrapment.

In this state, "A person is not guilty of an offense if his conduct is incited or induced by a public officer or employee, or agent of either, for the purpose of obtaining evidence for the prosecution of such person. However, this section does not apply if a public officer or employee, or agent of either, merely affords to such person the opportunity or facility for committing an offense in furtherance of a criminal purpose which such person has originated."

This case was tried once before, one year ago today. The defendant was found guilty by a jury, but the conviction was reversed on appeal because of faulty jury instructions. It is being retried. You have the partial trial transcripts of the key prosecution witness, Leigh Schindler, and the defendant, Mickey Drane. You also have an excerpt from the report of Detective Martha Arnold of the State Police Narcotics Task Force.

Assume that Detective Martha Arnold is a 20-year law enforcement veteran. After she was hired in [-20], she worked for ten years as a patrol officer before being promoted to detective. She was assigned to the Narcotics Task Force in [-5]. Before joining the Task Force, she was assigned to investigate burglaries and other felonies. **[Note: The defense attorney should ask the instructor for a memo to the file written by the defense attorney's private investigator.]**

1. For the prosecution, conduct a direct examination of Schindler and cross-examine Drane.

2. For the defense, conduct a direct examination of Drane and cross-examine Schindler.

LEIGH SCHINDLER, being first duly sworn,
testified as follows:

1 Q. (by prosecuting attorney) Please tell the jury your
2   name and where you live.
3
4 A. My name is Leigh Schindler, and I live at 4433 W.
5   Harrison Street. I live there with my two little
6   girls, ages five and seven. There's just the three
7   of us.
8
9 Q. Do you know the defendant, Mickey Drane?
10
11 A. Sure. We worked together at the Ford assembly plant
12   in this city for about five years.
13
14 Q. Did you have occasion to see the defendant on
15   February 7, [-2]?
16
17 A. Yes.
18
19 Q. When and where did you see him/her?
20
21 A. At Anne's Truck Stop, at Maple and Route 45, about
22   6:00 at night.
23
24 Q. Was that a chance meeting, or was it arranged?
25
26 A. It was arranged. I had called him/her at his/her
27   home about 4:00 that afternoon.
28
29 Q. Tell us about that conversation?
30
31 A. Well, I asked Mickey if s/he had any coke s/he
32   could sell me. S/he said s/he could get some if I
33   was sure I wanted it. I told him/her I was sure.
34   S/he said, "Okay, meet me at Anne's at 6:00 tonight
35   and bring $100." I said I would and that was about
36   it.
37
38 Q. Then what did you do?
39
40 A. I called Agent Arnold of the Task Force and told
41   her the deal was on. She said to go ahead with it,
42   that she would set up a surveillance. Earlier that
43   day she had given me five $20 bills. I guess they
44   were marked or something.
45
46 Q. What happened at 6:00 at Anne's?
47
48 A. I pulled into the parking lot in the back of the
49   truck stop. A few minutes later, Mickey Drane

605

50 pulled up next to me. Then s/he got out of the
51 car and came up to my car. S/he asked me if I had
52 the money. I gave it to him/her and s/he gave me
53 a plastic bag with white powder in it. (St. Ex. 1,
54 stipulated to be cocaine.) As s/he started to walk
55 away Agent Arnold and six other officers moved in
56 and arrested Mickey. They found the money in his/
57 her pocket.
58
59 Q. When Drane walked up to your car, did s/he say
60   anything else?
61
62 A. No. S/he just asked for the money and kind of
63   shook his/her head. That was it.
64
65 Q. No further questions.
66
67 Q. (by defense attorney) Mr./Ms. Schindler, when did
68   you become an informant for the Task Force?
69
70 A. It was the middle of January, [-2].
71
72 Q. Was that because you had been arrested for selling
73   a $20 bag of cocaine to a man named Harry
74   Wendell?
75
76 A. That was a reason, but it wasn't the main reason.
77   I was just sick and tired of what that coke was
78   doing to me, and I wanted to make this community a
79   better place for my kids.
80
81 Q. Did you sell cocaine to people before you were
82   arrested for selling it to Harry Wendell?
83
84 A. Yes. I sold small amounts to people at work for
85   a few years. I even sold to Mickey Drane a few
86   times.
87
88 Q. Had Mickey Drane ever sold cocaine to you before
89   February 7, [-2]?
90
91 A. No, s/he just bought.
92
93 Q. In fact, you asked Mickey Drane for cocaine at
94   least five times before February 7, and each time
95   s/he turned you down, isn't that true?
96
97 A. It was only two or three times. But s/he did turn
98   me down.
99
100 Q. You and Mickey Drane were friends before February
101   7, weren't you?

102 A. Just at work. We used to talk and joke a lot. I
103   guess we met for a beer every once in a while. But
104   that was it.
105
106 Q. Have you made any other buys of cocaine since you
107   began working for the Task Force?
108
109 A. Yes, about six of them.
110
111 Q. Do you get paid for that?
112
113 A. They give me $100 each time I set up an arrest.
114
115 Q. Isn't it a fact that when you were arrested in
116   mid-January, you were afraid that the police would
117   take your children away from you?
118
119 A. No, that is not true. Of course, I was concerned
120   about what would happen to my kids, but the police
121   never said anything about it.
122
123 Q. When you called Mickey Drane on February 7, didn't
124   you tell him/her you were sick and needed some
125   coke to get to work the next day?
126
127 A. I don't remember saying that. I told you what we
128   said.
129
130 Q. No further questions.

MICKEY DRANE, being first duly sworn, testified as follows:

1 Q. (by defense attorney) State your name and where you
2   live.
3

4 A. Mickey Drane. I live at 415 Hiawatha, in the
5   city. I live there with my husband/wife and three
6   children, ages 7, 9, and 12.
7

8 Q. Are you employed?
9

10 A. I worked at the Ford assembly plant in this city
11   for 14 years, but I was placed on suspension when I
12   was arrested in this case.
13

14 Q. Had you ever before been arrested?
15

16 A. No, never.
17

18 Q. Do you know Leigh Schindler?
19

20 A. Yes. We were on the same assembly line at Ford for
21   five years. We got to be good friends. We would
22   take our coffee breaks together, go bowling, have
23   dinner on occasion. S/he would tell me his/her
24   troubles and I would tell him/her mine.
25

26 Q. Did you ever buy cocaine from him/her?
27

28 A. Yes, a few times. Small amounts. I never used
29   it much. Leigh sold it to lots of people at the
30   plant. But I stopped using it in the winter of
31   [-3]. It cost too much, and I knew people who got
32   hooked on it. I didn't want anything to do with
33   it.
34

35 Q. After you stopped using it, did you talk to Leigh
36   about cocaine?
37

38 A. Yes. Sometime after the first of [-2] s/he started
39   coming up to me at breaks and asking if I could
40   get him/her some cocaine. S/he must have asked
41   five different times during the last two weeks of
42   January. S/he said s/he really needed it, but I
43   told him/her I didn't know how to get cocaine.
44

45 Q. What happened on February 7, [-2]?
46

47 A. Leigh called me at home in the afternoon. S/he was
48   crying and sounded sick. S/he told me s/he needed
49   cocaine desperately. S/he said s/he couldn't take

50 care of his/her children or even get to work the
51 next day unless s/he had some coke to keep him/her
52 going. I told him/her I would see what I could do.
53
54 Q. What did you do?
55
56 A. I called this guy from work who I knew used
57 coke. His name is Harry. I asked him if he
58 would sell me some coke. He said he would for
59 $100. So I picked it up from him, and then I
60 called Leigh and told him/her to meet me at Anne's
61 Truck Stop at 6:00 P.M.
62
63 Q. Did you meet him/her at 6:00 P.M.?
64
65 A. Yes. We both pulled into the parking lot at
66 Anne's. I got out and walked up to her car.
67
68 Q. What did you do at his/her car?
69
70 A. I told him/her I had the coke, but that I would
71 rather throw it away than see him/her use it. S/he
72 started crying again and told me s/he had to have
73 it or s/he could not go on living. So I gave it
74 to him/her. S/he gave me the money and I started
75 walking away. Next thing I knew there were cops
76 all over the place and I was being arrested.
77
78 Q. Did you make any money on that sale?
79
80 A. Not a cent.
81
82 Q. Had you ever before sold any cocaine to anyone?
83
84 A. Absolutely not.
85
86 Q. No further questions.
87
88 Q. (by prosecuting attorney) Mr. Drane, you knew
89 cocaine was an illegal drug?
90
91 A. Of course.
92
93 Q. You knew selling it was illegal?
94
95 A. Yes.
96
97 Q. What is the full name of this man "Harry" who you
98 claim sold you the cocaine?
99
100 A. I don't know his last name. He disappeared right

610

```
101    after I was busted. No one knows where he is. I
102    tried to find out.
103
104 Q. Leigh Schindler was not a close friend on February
105    7, was s/he?
106
107 A. Not real close, but we talked a lot. I trusted
108    him/her. I thought s/he needed help and so I tried
109    to help him/her.
110
111 Q. Even if it meant violating the law?
112
113 A. I suppose so.
114
115 Q. No further questions.
```

POLICE
NARCOTICS TASK FORCE

Arrest Report

To: Commanding Officer Frank Murphy

From: Martha Arnold, Star #7969

Re: Arrest of Mickey Drane

At 1610 hours, [-2] undersigned RO received a call from CI #1424. CI informed RO s/he had arranged for cocaine buy from Mickey Drane, a co-worker at Ford plant. Buy was to take place at Anne's Truck Stop, Maple and Route 45 at 1800 hours. (Earlier this day RO provided CI with five pre-recorded $20 bills.) RO approved buy and began arrangements for surveillance of scene.

At 1805 hours RO, in company of six additional agents, observed CI drive into said lot, parking approximately 20 feet from CI's car. RO remained in car as subject approached CI's car. RO observed subject Mickey Drane hand packet to CI and then observed CI hand currency to subject. When subject walked away from car RO made pre-arranged signal and agents made arrest of Mickey Drane, seizing pre-recorded funds from his right pants pocket.

Subject Mickey Drane was given Miranda warnings and responded s/he understood said warnings. Subject then said: "I don't know why you are arresting me, I didn't sell any cocaine. I don't know anything about cocaine." When asked why s/he had pre-recorded funds in pocket, subject said s/he would make no further statements without presence of a lawyer. Questioning ceased, subject was transported to station where s/he was formally processed and charged with Delivery of a Controlled Substance.

Det. Martha Arnold
#7969

At 1410 hour (I-2) undersigned SO received a call
from CI #1434. CI informed PO s/he had arranged for a
cocaine buy from Mickey Dante. A co-worker of PO's gave
buy was to take place at Anne's Tavern Stage Handle and
Anne at 1600 hours. Be told this may be possible CI
with a voice recorded SO CI is I SO approved our plan
begin information on the surveillance of scene.

At 1555 hours PO, in company of our additional SO
units, observed CI drive into said bar, parking
approximately 25 feet from CI's car. SO remained in car
as subject approached CI's car. SO observed CI hand
Mickey Dante half packet to CI and then observed CI hand
currency to subject. When subject walked away from CI's
car SO approached subject and reportedly made arrest of which
drugs, anything preceded and found from currency on his
pocket.

Subject Mickey Dante was given his rights. Subject and
reported s/he understood said warnings. Subject then
said: "I don't know why you are questioning me. I didn't
sell any cocaine. I don't know anything about cocaine
when asked why s/he had pre-recorded funds in pocket
subject said s/he would make no further statements.

Without presence of a lawyer. Questioning ceased. Subject
was transported to station where s/he was formally
processed and charged with delivery of a controlled
substance.

                                   Det. Martha Arnold
                                        #7969

7.8 CRIMINAL FRAUD CASE

UNITED STATES

v.

ROBIN JONES

This is a federal criminal case. The defendant, Robin Jones, is charged in a federal mail fraud indictment with defrauding the victim, Dr. Kelly Gibson, of $50,000. The indictment charges that Jones fraudulently induced Gibson to invest the money into a new company that Jones was starting. Jones denies that s/he obtained the money from Gibson fraudulently.

You have the reports of the FBI agent that investigated the case, the Grand Jury testimony of both Gibson and the Jones, and the attached documents.

1. For the prosecution, conduct a direct examination of Gibson and cross-examine Jones.

2. For the defense, conduct a direct examination of Jones and cross-examine Gibson.

FEDERAL BUREAU OF INVESTIGATION

Form 302

Reporting agent: Lynn Palmer, Special Agent

Date of report: 11/20/[-2]

Subject: Robin Jones

The following is a summary of witness statements in connection with the investigation of allegations of mail fraud against Robin Jones, an attorney with offices at 100 Elm Lane.

Dr. Kelly Gibson was interviewed at his/her offices at 18 Washington Street on 10/20/[-2] and provided the following information:

Dr. Gibson resides locally at 4220 Maple, is single, and has been engaged in the practice of internal medicine at current office for ten years. On March 15, [-2], Dr. Gibson was in the office of his/her attorney, Robin Jones. S/he retained Jones to handle several fee collection matters. At that time, Jones proposed s/he invest $50,000 to obtain 49 percent of a business named Sellers and Buyers. The alleged business would consist of a listing service for real estate sellers, who then would be able to sell their properties without the necessity of paying broker commissions. At that time, Jones made the following representations: (1) The business would be actively running 90 days after stock was issued; (2) The business would be incorporated and stock issued by the end of May of this year; (3) Jones expected no problem getting sellers to list their properties because s/he already had spoken to several of them; and (4) Jones would pay himself/herself a reasonable salary as president. That is what Gibson could recall about representations Jones had made. Based on those representations Dr. Gibson signed an investment contract and deposited a $50,000 check to Jones in the U.S. Mail on April 2, [-2]. As far as Dr. Gibson has learned, no corporation was formed, no stock was issued, and no listings have taken place. Jones has refused to return any portion of the $50,000. Dr. Gibson now believes s/he was defrauded and there is no such business as Sellers and Buyers.

Undersigned placed a phone call to Robin Jones at his/her office on November 2, [-2]. I represented myself as a potential investor who had heard about

617

Jones's new enterprise. I said I was always looking for new investment opportunities and wondered if Jones had room for new people. Jones responded as follows: "There is always room for one more. Come in and talk. I have an exciting new business underway and you might be interested." When I asked Jones how much of a percentage of stock was available, s/he refused to answer, instead insisting that I speak to him/her in person at his/her office. That concluded the conversation.

On November 5, [-2], undersigned received a telephone call from Chris Skelly, a local real estate broker. I then interviewed Skelly that day at his home at 1620 Elm. Skelly provided the following information:

Skelly has been a real estate broker in this area for the past 15 years, with offices located at 180 Broadway. He is an officer of the local Board of Realtors. Skelly saw an ad in the Business Gazette and decided to check it out. It referred to a business called Sellers & Buyers. He became suspicious because it referred to the sale of real estate without the use of brokers. Skelly told Jones his name was Chris O'Leary and that he might be interested in investing in the business. The two met at Jones's office on October 8, [-2]. Jones told Skelly of plans to set up a catalog and website where sellers would list their properties and buyers would subscribe to the catalog and purchase a password that would allow them access to the website, thus cutting out the brokers and their fees. Jones told Skelly s/he expected to incorporate within a month and would then begin issuing shares to investors. S/he said s/he had local newspaper advertising and a first-rate catalog and website lined up and ready to go. Skelly says Jones told him all s/he needed were some investors, and s/he told him s/he would sell him a 49 percent interest in the business for $60,000, shares to be issued shortly thereafter. The deal had to be closed in five days. Skelly said he would let Jones know, then left. That was the substance of the entire conversation. Skelly called the FBI because of his belief that Sellers & Buyers was a phony enterprise.

On November 15, [-2], undersigned interviewed subject Robin Jones at his/her office at 100 Elm. Jones was told s/he was being investigated for mail fraud, specifically that s/he was being investigated for allegations that s/he defrauded Dr. Kelly Gibson of $50,000. Jones was read the Miranda rights, said s/he understood them, agreed to waive his/her rights, and stated the following:

Jones is engaged in a civil law practice, specializing in representing debtors and creditors, mostly creditors. S/he has maintained his/her office at 100 Elm Lane for 12 years. S/he is divorced and his/her former husband/wife has custody of their 16-year-old son. On graduation from State University Law School in [-14] s/he was employed by the County Public Defender, but left after two years because "I couldn't stand the scum I had to represent." Jones was having problems getting Sellers & Buyers started. S/he needed more capital to produce the necessary catalog, begin the newspaper ad campaign, and create the website. That is why s/he placed the investment opportunity ad in the Business Gazette on February 28, [-2], to begin running on March 18 and thereafter. S/he denied ever deceiving anyone. S/he said s/he did his/her best to get the business off the ground, but "it takes money to make money. Any new business is a risk, even doctors should know that." When undersigned asked Jones what s/he did with the $50,000 from Dr. Gibson, s/he said: "Well, I have to live. S/he would have got it all back, with a big profit, if s/he wasn't so impatient." When undersigned asked Jones for the names of people who could support his/her claim of efforts to start the business, Jones referred to Mary Johnson, a loan officer of the First National Bank, and Sandy Williams, advertising manager of the Daily News Publications Company. When asked for additional names or documents, Jones became agitated and said s/he didn't want to answer any more questions. Interview was terminated.

Mary Johnson was interviewed at her office at First National Bank, 220 Financial Way, on November 17, [-2]. She provided the following information:

Robin Jones submitted a business loan application for $50,000 on 3/1/[-2]. The loan application was for a proposed business called "Sellers & Buyers." Jones said s/he had a plan to put real estate buyers and sellers together and cut out the real estate brokers and their high commissions. Jones said s/he was planning on advertising the business in the newspaper to attract both sellers and prospective buyers. Sellers would pay to list their properties and buyers would subscribe to the listings. Jones said s/he planned to publish a monthly publication of available listings, as well as a website. It was immediately obvious that any loan application was premature, and that Jones had done little hard, concrete planning to implement his/her idea. Jones did not fill out the business plan section of the application or attach any documentation to the application. Johnson told Jones that s/he should first incorporate the business, then prepare a detailed business plan itemizing the projected income and expenses for the first year of operation, such as anticipated revenue from sellers and buyers, costs of advertising, costs of publication, website costs, personnel expenses, office and office equipment expenses, and so on. Finally, Johnson told Jones that $50,000 was far too little capital for the business, and s/he would probably need at least $100,000 and more likely $150,000 just to begin operating and survive the first year. Johnson told Jones that if s/he took these preliminary steps s/he might reapply for a loan in the future, and the application would then be given serious consideration. To date Jones has not reapplied for a loan or made any further contact with the bank. I obtained a copy of Jones' loan application and Ms. Johnson's letter rejecting Jones' loan application.

On November 19, [-2], undersigned interviewed Sandy Williams, advertising manager of the Daily News Publications Company, at his office at 411 Grand Avenue. Williams provided the following information:

Williams has been employed by the Daily News Publishing Company for 16 years. He began as a copywriter in the advertising department, became assistant manager in [-6], and manager in [-3]. He is a graduate of State University, where he received his degree in advertising in [-17]. His duties include supervision of all advertising in the various Daily News Company publications. On March 20, [-2], Robin Jones met with Williams at the Daily News Office. Jones said s/he wanted to set up a business that would bring real estate buyers and sellers together, eliminating the broker's fee. Williams advised Jones of the cost of such a campaign, including newspaper advertising and catalog production and distribution. Williams advised Jones the ad campaign cost would be about $5,000 per month and the initial catalog cost would be about $5,000. Williams also told Jones that website development would probably cost an additional $10,000 or so, but that this was simply an educated guess on his part because this was outside his expertise and experience. Williams describes Jones as vague about his/her plans and lacking eagerness to proceed. Williams urged Jones to proceed with the ad campaign, the catalog, and the website at the same time. While the two had some telephone contact in the next several months, they did not discuss the matter again until October 10, [-2]. On that day Jones came to Williams' office. Williams told Jones of his company's willingness to proceed with the ad campaign and catalog, but would require a deposit of $15,000. Jones declined to proceed under those terms and left. There was no further contact.

The summaries set out above were prepared from notes taken at the time of the interviews. The notes were accurately transcribed as part of this report. Then, pursuant to office practice, the notes were destroyed.

It is the undersigned's opinion that Robin Jones engaged in a scheme to defraud Dr. Gibson of $50,000 and that s/he used the U.S. mail to further that scheme. The undersigned will submit this report to the U.S. Attorney with the recommendation that a grand jury be convened to investigate this matter and return the appropriate indictment. No further interviews are contemplated at this time.

Lynn Palmer
Lynn Palmer, Special Agent

FEDERAL BUREAU OF INVESTIGATION

Form 302

Reporting agent: Lynn Palmer, Special Agent

Date of report: 10/25/[-2]

Subject: Robin Jones and "Sellers & Buyers"

On this date checked with the Secretary of State/ Corporation Commission, which reported that "Sellers & Buyers" was not a registered corporation in this state, and that no corporation showing a Robin Jones of this city as either president, officer, or incorporator was registered in this state. Ordered certified copy of records.

Also checked with the Securities and Exchange Commission in Washington, DC, which reported that "Sellers & Buyers" was not registered with the SEC and that no registration statement had been filed for that entity.

Also checked title of Jones's residence at 100 Elm. Jones is a renter of premises, managed by City Rental Company. Contacted company, manager reported that Robin Jones had rented the home on 1/5/[-2] for a term of one year, paid $2,400 for the security deposit and first month's rent, and paid the monthly rent of $1,200 by checks drawn on the First National Bank. Rent includes all utilities. Jones always paid promptly, has been model renter.

By: _Lynn Palmer_
Lynn Palmer, FBI

      Kelly Gibson, having been first duly sworn,
testified as follows:

1 Q. (by assistant U.S. Attorney) Dr. Gibson, how did
2   the discussion about investing in "Sellers &
3   Buyers" come about?
4
5 A. I was in Jones's office to talk about my cases. I
6   had hired him/her to go after my patients who had
7   refused to pay their bills for medical services. I
8   had just given him/her a $5,000 check to cover his/
9   her retainer and court costs. We were talking about
10   how tight the economy seems to be these days when
11   s/he asked me if I would be interested in investing
12   in his/her new business.
13
14 Q. When was this?
15
16 A. It was March 15 of this year, in his/her office. I
17   know the date because it is on the retainer
18   check.
19
20 Q. What was said?
21
22 A. Well, I remember saying something about how unhappy
23   I was with the low interest the banks and money
24   markets were paying. That's when s/he told me there
25   were other ways to make money in this economy. I
26   asked him/her what s/he meant. S/he said s/he was
27   starting up this new business that could not miss.
28   S/he told me I could get in on the ground floor, if
29   I was interested.
30
31 Q. What did you tell him/her?
32
33 A. I told him/her I would like to hear more about it.
34
35 Q. Did you hear more about it?
36
37 A. I certainly did. I didn't really understand all
38   of it, but s/he had this plan for cutting out the
39   real estate brokers and their fat commissions by
40   bringing buyers and sellers together. S/he would
41   charge a fee for doing that. It sounded attractive,
42   and it seemed like a good idea. S/he was going to
43   use the newspapers and a website to advertise, and
44   s/he said overhead would be low because s/he would
45   run the business out of his/her office and his/her

46   home. S/he said s/he was going to devote as much
47   time as necessary actively running the business.
48   S/he told me s/he expected to expand to other
49   cities, perhaps by franchising. S/he said this
50   opportunity was more exciting than practicing law.
51

52 Q. What did s/he want you to do?
53

54 A. Well, s/he said s/he didn't have enough capital to
55   get the company off the ground. S/he said it would
56   take around $50,000 more to get it going. So s/he
57   offered me 49 percent of the stock of the company
58   for $50,000.
59

60 Q. Did s/he say what you would get for that $50,000?
61

62 A. Yes. S/he said I would be a 49 percent owner of
63   the corporation. S/he was going to incorporate the
64   company and issue stock by the end of May, this
65   year. Advertising would begin at that time, and
66   s/he said the website and the business would be up
67   and running within three months of the day I came
68   on board, by signing a contract. S/he said s/he did
69   not anticipate any problem getting the listings,
70   since s/he already had several sellers lined up.
71

72 Q. Were those his/her exact words?
73

74 A. That's exactly what s/he said about having sellers
75   lined up. I know I would not have been interested
76   unless s/he told me that. I can't say the rest of
77   it is in his/her exact words, but that is the gist
78   of what s/he said. S/he was very persuasive. S/he
79   expected to charge sellers $1,000 to be listed.
80   S/he said I would be getting dividends by the end
81   of the year.
82

83 Q. What else did s/he say?
84

85 A. S/he told me s/he would put the catalog on a Web
86   page on the Internet, so that s/he would be able to
87   reach potential buyers who were moving here.
88

89 Q. What did you do?
90

91 A. I thought about it for a few days, then I
92   decided to make the investment. We arranged to
93   meet at his/her office on April 1. We signed the
94   contract on that day. I remember s/he told me I
95   was making the smartest financial decision of my

```
96   life. I put the $50,000 check to him/her in the
97   mail the next day.
98
99  Q. What happened next?
100
101 A. Nothing happened. I called him/her several times
102    in April, May, and June, and s/he kept telling
103    me that his/her plans were coming along and
104    that things were on schedule. But I still hadn't
105    received any stock and I couldn't tell if the
106    business was moving ahead. I never did see any
107    advertisements about the business in the newspaper
108    or anything about it on the Internet. Starting in
109    July, I called more often, asking questions about
110    the business. S/he seemed to be putting me off,
111    and by mid-September s/he wasn't even returning
112    my calls. That's when I wrote him/her a letter
113    demanding my money back and telling him/her s/he
114    was no longer my attorney.
115
116 Q. Did s/he ever respond to that letter?
117
118 A. S/he sent me a letter that contained nothing but
119    a lot of double-talk. S/he never returned a penny
120    of the retainer. I realized I had been taken, so I
121    called the police on October 10. I told them what
122    happened. They sent the case to the FBI. Looking
123    back at it now, I can't believe I was so gullible.
124    But, after all, s/he was my lawyer.
```

ROBIN JONES, being first duly sworn, testified as follows:

1 Q. (by assistant U.S. Attorney) Mr./Ms. Jones, you are
2   under subpoena to be here today, are you not?
3
4 A. Yes, but I would have come voluntarily. I want to
5   clear this thing up.
6
7 Q. Do you understand that you have the right to remain
8   silent and not answer any questions?
9
10 A. Yes.
11
12 Q. Do you understand anything you say can and will be
13   used against you in a court of law?
14
15 A. Yes.
16
17 Q. Do you understand you have the right to consult
18   with a lawyer at any time during questioning, and
19   that if you cannot afford a lawyer one will be
20   appointed for you by a court at no cost to you?
21
22 A. Yes. I understand all that. I waive my rights and
23   stand ready to answer any questions you have.
24
25 Q. The grand jury wants to ask you about a company
26   named Sellers & Buyers. Is that your company?
27
28 A. Yes. I conceived the idea for Sellers & Buyers
29   and it was my intent to turn it into a successful
30   enterprise.
31
32 Q. What is the business of Sellers & Buyers?
33
34 A. It is a listing service for buyers and sellers
35   of real estate. Our purpose is to eliminate the
36   excessive commission fees of brokers. Sellers would
37   list their properties in our catalog, in newspaper
38   ads, and on our website. They would pay a fee for
39   that, $1,000. That would bring buyers and sellers
40   together. They didn't need brokers. The catalogs
41   would show the property and list everything the buyer
42   needed to know. Buyers would subscribe to the catalog
43   for $20.00 each month. That payment would also get
44   them access to our website, via a password.

45 Q. What did you need to start a business like that?
46
47 A. Capital. I needed capital. And other kinds of
48   financing. That's why I gave Dr. Gibson the
49   opportunity to invest. And that is why I went to
50   the bank for a loan. I needed funds to get the
51   advertising, the catalog, and the website off the
52   ground.
53
54 Q. What gave you the idea for a business like Sellers
55   & Buyers?
56
57 A. It came to me when I received a letter from a
58   client about the high broker commissions on
59   real estate sales. His letter got me thinking.
60   I remembered seeing apartment building guides
61   for rental listings, and I thought with a little
62   creative thinking and some energy the same thing
63   could be done for real estate sales.
64
65 Q. When did you go to the bank for the loan?
66
67 A. It was March 1, [-2]. I spoke to Mary Johnson, a
68   loan officer at First National. I filled out a loan
69   application that day. All I wanted was $50,000, but
70   you would have thought I was asking for the keys
71   to the vault. She wanted all sorts of paperwork and
72   budget information I didn't have. So she turned me
73   down, but she said I could come back when I had more
74   information. She sent me a letter telling me that.
75
76 Q. Did you go back?
77
78 A. Not yet. I haven't had the time.
79
80 Q. What did you do about listing properties in a
81   catalog and in newspaper ads?
82
83 A. I worked real hard on that. I went to see Sandy
84   Williams at the Daily News Publication Company.
85   That's the company that publishes the local daily
86   newspaper, and they have a catalog division that
87   does real good work. He's the advertising manager.
88
89 Q. When did you see Sandy Williams?
90
91 A. First time was a couple weeks after I went to the
92   bank. I wanted to get an idea about the kind of
93   cost I was looking at. I also wanted to see what
94   kind of ideas Williams had for presenting the
      listings.

95 Q. What happened that first time you met Sandy
96   Williams?
97
98 A. He told me what I would need to put the ads and
99   listings together. I didn't understand everything
100   he said, but I could see a lot of work had to be
101   done. I know he said the ad campaign alone would
102   cost $5,000 a month, and that I would need another
103   $5,000 just for the first catalog. The catalog
104   would have to be different every month, because
105   the listings would change. He wanted a $15,000
106   deposit. I asked if he would get started for
107   $1,000, but he refused. I said I would get back to
108   him.
109
110 Q. Did you ever get back to him?
111
112 A. Sure. I called him at his office several times
113   in the next few months, but it seemed like every
114   time we talked the price of things would go up.
115   He didn't seem eager for my business. I talked to
116   him in person this past October at his office. I
117   told him I wanted to get started by the first of
118   the year, and that I would have the money he was
119   asking for. He said he would get started as soon
120   as the money arrived, but then this investigation
121   came up, so I put everything on hold.
122
123 Q. What progress did you make on developing your
124   website?
125
126 A. I did some Internet searches looking for website
127   developers. I have not contacted any of them yet.
128
129 Q. Mr./Ms. Jones, when you spoke to Dr. Gibson in
130   March and April of [-2] did you tell him/her you
131   were going to incorporate the business by the end
132   of May of that year?
133
134 A. No. I said I would incorporate, but I never said
135   when it would be done.
136
137 Q. Did you tell him/her the business would be up and
138   running within three months of the day s/he signed
139   the contract?
140
141 A. Absolutely not.
142
143 Q. Did you tell him/her you already had several
144   sellers lined up?

631

145 A. No. I said I didn't expect to have any difficulty
146   lining up sellers.
147
148 Q. Did you promise to put the catalogs on the
149   Internet?
150
151 A. No. I don't know much about the Internet.
152
153 Q. What else did you do to plan for this business
154   before you spoke to Dr. Gibson?
155
156 A. I reviewed the Business Gazette for property sales
157   activity, I went over to the Board of Realtors and
158   picked up whatever catalogs they had, and I looked
159   up the law involving real estate brokers.
160
161 Q. Did you ever actually line up any sellers?
162
163 A. I talked to a number of people, although I can't
164   remember their names now. I didn't have any lined
165   up on paper, but I had plenty of promises.
166
167 Q. Did you talk to a potential investor named Chris
168   O'Leary in your office on October 8, [-2]?
169
170 A. I met with a man named O'Leary sometime around
171   there.
172
173 Q. Did you offer Mr. O'Leary a 49 percent interest in
174   the Sellers & Buyers business for $60,000?
175
176 A. No. I talked to him about a $60,000 investment,
177   but told him I wanted a loan from his group. I
178   never said anything about any ownership interest.
179   How could I? Dr. Gibson already had a 49 percent
180   interest. I wasn't going to give up control over
181   my own business.
182
183 Q. Did you tell O'Leary you had sellers lined up?
184
185 A. No. I told him the same thing I told Dr. Gibson.
186   I didn't expect any difficulties getting sellers.
187   It was a very short conversation. I never saw or
188   talked to him again.
189
190 Q. Did you ever form a corporation or issue any
191   stock?
192
193 A. No. I never had the chance.
194
195 Q. Did you use some of Dr. Gibson's investment money
196   for your personal expenses?

632

197 A. I had a right to use that money. I was entitled
198   to fair compensation for my efforts on behalf
199   of the business. I was using the office and my
200   home for that business. Because of all the time
201   I was putting in on Sellers & Buyers my practice
202   was suffering. I didn't use all the money, but
203   it looks like I might have to, to defend myself
204   against these untrue charges Dr. Gibson has made
205   against me. I wish s/he had never asked me for
206   investment ideas.
207
208 Q. Are you saying s/he brought up the matter of
209   investments?
210
211 A. Sure. I was his/her lawyer, not his/her investment
212   counselor. I wouldn't bring it up. When I told
213   him/her about my idea, s/he got all excited. It
214   was a good idea, and it still is.
215
216 Q. Did you really believe property owners would pay
217    $1,000 to be listed in your catalog?
218
219 A. Sure. $1,000 is a lot cheaper than the 7 percent
220   commission those real estate people charge. Once
221   the word got out about the money they would be
222   saving, they would wait in line to get in the
223   catalog and onto the website.

FIRST NATIONAL BANK

FDIC Insured

BUSINESS LOAN APPLICATION

Date: 3/1/[-2]

Applicant: Robin Jones, president of Sellers &
                    Buyers, Inc.

Address: 100 Elm Lane

Amount sought: $50,000

Terms sought: 5-yr note, 8%/yr interest

Loan purpose: Start up new business called Sellers &
                    Buyers

Assets: Cash on hand approximately $13,000, this
                    bank

Liabilities: None

Business plan   (attach all appropriate documentation):

Warning: It is a violation of 18 U.S.C. § 1014 to make a
false statement in connection with a loan application to
a federally insured bank.

Yours Sincerely,

Robin Jones, Esq.

FIRST NATIONAL BANK

FDIC insured

March 1, [-2]

Robin Jones, Attorney at Law

100 Elm Lane

Re: 3/1/[-2] loan application for "Sellers & Buyers"

Dear Robin:

As I told you orally today, we are denying your application for a $50,000 loan.

In order for this bank to reconsider your loan application, you will need to take the following steps. First, you should immediately incorporate the business. Since you are a lawyer, this should present little difficulty. Second, you should prepare a detailed business plan itemizing the projected income and expenses for the first year of operation, such as anticipated revenue from sellers and buyers, costs of advertising, costs of publication, website costs, personnel expenses, office and office equipment expenses, and so on. The bank simply cannot consider a business loan application seriously without these steps being first implemented. You may wish to employ an experienced accountant or business planner to assist you in preparing the business plan.

Finally, I must note that your application for $50,000 appears unrealistically optimistic. Based on my experience with small businesses, I believe that your capital needs during the first year will be in the $100,000 range, and perhaps as high as $150,000. The biggest reason for small business failures is insufficient capitalization to carry the business during the first year.

As you develop the detailed business plan discussed in my office, please keep these considerations in mind.

We look forward to hearing from you in the future.

Sincerely,

Mary Johnson

Mary Johnson,
Loan officer

"Business Gazette"

1/4 page ad that appeared in the [-2] issues on 3/18, 4/2, 5/7, 6/4, 7/2, 8/6, 9/3, 10/1, and 11/4

INVESTMENT OPPORTUNITY!

"Sellers & Buyers," a new start-up business, is looking for investors looking for a long-term business opportunity.

"Sellers & Buyers" has developed a system for direct sales of real estate without real estate brokers. Both sellers and buyers win!

If you are a serious investor, looking for a serious business opportunity, call or write:

Robin Jones, President
"Sellers & Buyers"
100 Elm Lane
998-1234

INVESTMENT CONTRACT

The parties, "Sellers & Buyers" through its president, Robin Jones, and Kelly Gibson, M.D., hereby agree to the following:

"Sellers & Buyers" is a company established to market real estate listings that put sellers and buyers of real estate in direct contact with each other and avoid the expenses involved in using real estate brokers as intermediaries.

It is anticipated that "Sellers & Buyers" will be incorporated by and begin operations by September, [-2]. It is understood that Robin Jones is and will continue to be the president and majority owner of the company.

Kelly Gibson, M.D., agrees to invest the sum of $50,000 (fifty thousand dollars) in "Sellers & Buyers" and will remit that amount to Robin Jones on or before April 5, [-2].

"Sellers & Buyers" will issue common stock certificates to Kelly Gibson, M.D. representing 49 percent of the stock ownership of "Sellers & Buyers" within 30 days of the company's incorporation.

Other than the foregoing, no additional promises or representations have been made by either party, and this contract shall be the full extent of the agreement between the parties.

Dated: April 1, [-2]

Yours Sincerely,

Robin Jones, Esq.

Kelly Gibson, M.D.

641

                    Kelly Gibson, M.D.

                                        September 30, [-2]

Robin Jones, Esq.
100 Elm Lane

Re: My $50,000 investment in "Sellers & Buyers"

Dear Robin:

     It has been six months since I invested my $50,000
in "Sellers & Buyers." At the time we entered into our
contract, you represented that the business would be
incorporated within 60 days, and that the business would
be fully operating in six months. To date none of these
things has happened.

     Instead, you have consistently stalled off my
inquiries, and lately have refused to return my calls
altogether.

     Consequently, I have concluded that you have no
intentions, and never had any intentions, of getting this
business started. If you do not return my $50,000 by
October 10, [-2], I will refer this case to the police
and seek appropriate legal action.

     Please be further advised that as of today you are
hereby dismissed as my lawyer on my civil claims. Please
return my $5,000 retainer immediately.

                              Sincerely,

                              Kelly Gibson

                              Kelly Gibson, M.D.

September 30, 1-21-

Robin Dobas, Esq.
100 Elm Lane.

Re: My $50,000 investment in "Sellers & Buyers"

Dear Robin:

It had been six months since I invested my $50,000 in "Sellers & Buyers". At that time we entered into our contract, you represented that the business would be incorporated within 60 days, and that the business would be fully operative in six months. To date none of these things has happened.

Instead, you have completely brushed off my inquiries, and lately have refused to return my calls altogether.

Consequently, I have concluded that you have no intentions, and never had any intentions, of getting this business started. If you do not return my $50,000 by October 10, 1-21, I will refer this case to the police and seek appropriate legal action.

Please be further advised that as of today you are hereby dismissed as my lawyer on my civil claims. Please return my $50,000 retainer immediately.

Sincerely,

Kelly Gibson, M.D.

Robin Jones
Attorney at Law
100 Elm Lane

5 October [-2]

Kelly Gibson, M.D.
18 Washington
Dear Dr. Gibson:

Thank you for your letter of September 30. I can understand your frustration in how slowly "Sellers & Buyers" seems to be in getting off the ground. I share your frustration.

As you know, with a busy law practice I can only devote part of my time to this business venture. I have been working as hard as I can under the circumstances to make the business a success, but it is taking more time than I anticipated.

At the present time your funds are fully committed to the business, and our contract does not call for a refund in the event you change your mind about the desirability of your investment. However, if the cash position of the company improves in the future we can discuss buying out your investment at that time. In the meantime, since the business should be incorporated and stock issued within a few weeks, you can at that time sell your shares to any willing buyer.

I am sorry that you have decided to end our lawyer and client relationship. Of course, you have a right to do that if you wish. I will refund your retainer, minus my actual costs and the reasonable value of the time I have spent investigating and researching your various claims. My usual hourly rate is $150/hr. Since I have spent 30 hours of my professional time, and an additional $300 in costs, you are entitled to the return of $200. I will be happy to send your files to an attorney of your choosing.

Dr. Gibson, I urge you to reconsider your position on "Sellers & Buyers." Some degree of patience is required, but I assure you this remains an outstanding

business opportunity. We can be of service to this
community while earning the profits that await us in the
near future.

                              Yours Sincerely,

                              Robin Jones, Esq.

SECRETARY OF STATE/CORPORATION COMMISSION

Statement of Absence of Records

I, Louise Fletcher, an employee in the records department of the Secretary of State/Corporation Commission, state that I have searched the records of the Secretary of State/Corporation Commission, and that there are no records of the following:

1. A domestic or foreign corporation having the name "Sellers & Buyers" for the year [-2] or any other year.

2. A domestic or foreign corporation having a "Robin Jones" as an incorporator for the year [-2] or any other year.

Louise Fletcher
Louise Fletcher

Subscribed to and sworn before me on 11/5/[-2].

Patty West
Notary Public

[Seal]

7.9   ARMED ROBBERY CASE

STATE
v.
LARRY RILEY

This is an armed robbery case. Larry Riley is charged with the armed robbery of Val Potempa. The indictment charges that on December 15, [-1], Larry Riley, while armed with a handgun, took approximately $400 in U.S. currency from the person and presence of Val Potempa by the use of force or by threatening the imminent use of force.

You have police reports concerning the Potempa robbery and the Grandhoff robbery and the arrest of Riley, a court-reported statement Riley gave to a prosecutor on the night of his arrest, and the preliminary hearing testimony of Potempa.   The Grandhoff robbery has not been formally charged against Riley. **[Note: The defense attorney should ask the instructor for the memo to file written by Riley's former attorney, an assistant public defender. This memo will be available only to defense counsel.]**

1.   For the prosecution, conduct a direct examination of Potempa and cross-examine Riley.
2.   For the defense, conduct a direct examination of Riley and cross-examine Potempa.

POLICE REPORT

Date: 12/15/[-1]
Time of report: 2300 hours
Location of incident: Parking lot in back of 1214 North
                      Woods
Offense: Armed robbery
Victim: Val Potempa, 2850 Circle Drive
R/O: Inv.   Sam Polk

Narrative:

   Pursuant to armed robbery report received on 911,
R/O arrived at parking lot behind Val's Chicken House,
1214 North Woods, at approx. 2220 hours. Present and
leaning on his car was Val Potempa, owner of Val's
Chicken House, a take-out restaurant. Potempa advised
R/O that approx. 15 minutes earlier a man approached
him/her as s/he was unlocking the door to his/her car.
Potempa had the night's proceeds in his/her pants pocket,
approximately $400. The man pointed a handgun that looked
like a .38 caliber revolver at his/her head and said,
"I want your money. Give it all up or I will blow your
head off." Potempa gave the man all the money s/he had.
The man said, "Don't move for five minutes, or it will
be your last move." Then the man turned and ran. Potempa
described the robber as being about the same average
height and weight s/he is, with no unusual physical
characteristics. The man's face was not covered, but he
wore a dark cap pulled down on his forehead. S/he did
not notice any facial hair. S/he said s/he never had
seen the man before, but would recognize him if s/he saw
him again. Because Potempa appeared shaken and upset,
R/O ended the interview and told Potempa s/he would be
contacted at a later date. R/O observed that the parking
lot was well lit by a single floodlight attached to the
back of the restaurant, about 60 feet from Potempa's
parked car.

SUPPLEMENTARY POLICE REPORT

Date: 12/19/[-1]

Time of report: 1400 hours

Offense: Armed Robbery of 12/15/[-1]

Victim: Val Potempa, 2850 Circle Drive

R/O: Inv. Sam Polk

Narrative:

This is a follow-up to report on robbery of Val Potempa on 12/15/[-1] at 1214 North Woods. R/O has attempted to arrange meeting with Potempa at second District police headquarters for purpose of a photo identification procedure, but Potempa has not returned phone calls to R/O, despite R/O leaving several messages at Potempa's place of business. R/O will continue efforts to contact Potempa, as this armed robbery fits the pattern of other recent robberies in the area.

SUPPLEMENTARY POLICE REPORT

Date: 12/20/[-1]

Time of report: 1600 hours

Offense: Armed robbery of 12/15/[-1]

Victim: Val Potempa, 2850 Circle Drive

R/O: Inv. Sam Polk

Narrative:

R/O received phone call from above-named victim at 1500 hours this date. Victim advised that the man who robbed him/her had just come into his/her restaurant to place an order for a take-out chicken dinner. R/O advised victim to do nothing until officers arrived. R/O accompanied by Investigators Kelly and Goldstein immediately went to Val's Chicken House at 1214 North Woods. Upon our entering the restaurant, Potempa pointed at a man standing at the counter. Officers approached the man and placed him under arrest. A search of the arrestee revealed a knife with a five-inch blade. No other weapons. He possessed $22 in U.S. currency and 48 cents in change. He identified himself as Larry Riley. Arrestee did not resist, but demanded to know what he was being arrested for. R/O advised Riley the charge was armed robbery of the proprietor of the restaurant. R/O then read Riley the Miranda rights per a pre-printed card. Riley denied any knowledge of the robbery. Before being removed from premises, Riley pointed to Potempa and said, "Why are you doing this to me?" Potempa laughed and shook his/her head. At police station, Riley refused to answer R/O's questions, but indicated he would speak to an assistant county attorney if one was present. Riley was booked, printed, and formally charged. Bureau of Identification records reveal Riley has no previous arrests or convictions. It should be noted that Riley resides at 1418 North Woods, Apartment 4B, two blocks from Val's Chicken House. R/O will attempt to arrange lineup where victims of similar robberies will view Riley. County Attorney's office contacted.

STATEMENT OF LARRY RILEY,
MADE ON 12/20/[-1] TO ACA KARLA BRADBURN

1 Q. Mr. Riley, have you been advised of your right
2   to remain silent, your right to have an attorney
3   present for any questioning, your right to the
4   appointment of a free attorney if you are without
5   funds to hire an attorney, and the fact that
6   anything you say to me could be used against you in
7   a court of law?
8
9 A. Yeah, I know all that. I want to talk to you.
10
11 Q. Did you take part in an armed robbery of a man/
12   woman in the parking lot behind Val's Chicken House
13   on December 15, [-1]?
14
15 A. Absolutely not.
16
17 Q. Were you in that parking lot any time that day?
18
19 A. No, not that day. But I often cross through that
20   lot to get from Woods Street to the alley. I have
21   lived around there for about five years.
22
23 Q. Were you ever inside Val's Chicken House before the
24   day you were arrested?
25
26 A. Yeah, that's what I want to tell you about. I used
27   to go in there all the time. I would call the owner
28   "Val" and s/he would call me "Larry." I would order
29   the chicken dinner special every time. S/he knew
30   me.
31
32 Q. Mr./Ms. Potempa says you robbed him/her with a gun.
33   Why would s/he say that if it were not true?
34
35 A. I don't know. Maybe it's because we had an argument
36   in the chicken store just before Thanksgiving.
37
38 Q. What kind of argument?
39
40 A. It was no big deal. I thought I had given him/her a
41    $20 bill for the chicken dinner, and s/he gave me
42   change for a ten. When I complained s/he insisted
43   I gave him/her a ten. I knew s/he was wrong, but I
44   didn't want to make any more out of it. I took the
45   change s/he gave me and I left. I told him/her I
46   never was coming back. I haven't, until today.

657

47 Q. Where were you on December 15 between 10:00 and
48   10:30 in the evening?
49
50 A. I was with my girlfriend at the movies. I don't
51   remember the name of it, but it was something about
52   invaders from outer space.
53
54 Q. What is your girlfriend's name?
55
56 A. Martha Steward. She lives next door to me, in
57   Apartment 4A. Ask her.
58
59 Q. We will. By the way, are you employed?
60
61 A. I'm between jobs right now. I had been working
62   as a shipping clerk at General Motors, but I was
63   laid off a few months ago. I had been there six
64   years. I've been looking, but there isn't much
65   out there.
66
67 Q. Is there anything else you want to tell me?
68
69 A. No. Just that I didn't do any robbery. Except
70   when I was in the army, I never picked up a
71   gun.
72
73 Q. If you find my questions and your answers have been
74   accurately recorded by the stenographer, will you
75   sign this statement?
76
77 A. Sure.

signed: _____
                   Larry Riley

witnessed: _____
                   Karla Bradburn

SUPPLEMENTARY POLICE REPORT

Date: 12/20/[-1]

Time of report: 1900 hours

Subject of report: Follow-up report concerning investigation of armed robbery of Val Potempa and arrest of Larry Riley

R/O: Inv. Sam Polk

Narrative:

Pursuant to instruction from ACA Blackburn R/O interviewed Martha Steward at her apartment, number 4A, 1418 North Woods. Ms. Steward advised she has known her next-door neighbor Larry Riley for about two years. They go out together every so often, but there is nothing serious about their relationship. She knows Riley as a quiet kind of guy, something of a "loner." She remembers going to a movie with him recently. They saw "Invaders from Outer Space" at the Paradise Theater in the neighborhood. However, she is positive they went to the movie on 12/16, not 12/15. She is sure that she worked overtime on 12/15 as a nurse at Mercy Hospital and did not get home until midnight. In addition, she clearly remembers Riley took her to a fairly expensive restaurant before the movie. He said he was celebrating the fact that he had won $400 at the casino on the previous day. Ms. Steward said she would be available for trial if she is needed.

SUPPLEMENTARY POLICE REPORT

Date: 12/22/[-1]

Time of report: 1600 hours

Subject of report: Follow-up investigation of armed robbery of Val Potempa on 12/15/[-1] and arrest of Larry Riley

R/O: Inv. Sam Polk

Narrative:

At 1520 hours this date R/O conducted a lineup in connection with recent armed robberies in the area. Present in the lineup were Larry Riley, police officers Val Kelly and Jim Lindstrom, and prisoners Mike Smetka and Bill Hill. Each is a male white, in his early or mid-30s, and of average height and weight. The victim, Earl Grandhoff, identified Larry Riley as the man who robbed him at gunpoint just before midnight on 12/11/[-1] in an alley behind 2830 North Ashland. Location of crime is three blocks from Val's Chicken House. Victim advised R/O that Riley was wearing a dark cap pulled down over his forehead at the time of the robbery. Riley approached victim, pointed the gun at his head, and said, "Give up your money or I will blow your head off. I want all of it now." After victim gave Riley contents of his pocket, Riley said, "Don't move for five minutes." Then Riley turned and ran. R/O will file additional armed robbery charge against Riley.

TRANSCRIPT OF PRELIMINARY HEARING

Report of Proceedings, held before the Honorable Robert Fitzhugh on December 31, [-1].

VAL POTEMPA, after being first duly sworn, testified as follows:

1 Q. (by the prosecutor) Mr./Ms. Potempa, where were you
2   at about 10:00 on the night of December 15?
3

4 A. I had just closed my restaurant, Val's Chicken
5   House at 1214 North Woods, and I was going to my
6   car to go home. I had the night's proceeds in an
7   envelope in my jacket pocket.
8

9 Q. How much did you have?
10

11 A. Slightly over $400.
12

13 Q. What happened?
14

15 A. A man walked up to me. He was pointing a gun at my
16   head. He said, "I want your money. Give it all up
17   or I will blow your head off." So I gave him my
18   money. Then he said, "Don't move for five minutes,
19   or it will be your last move." Then he turned and
20   ran.
21

22 Q. What kind of gun was it?
23

24 A. It looked like a .38 caliber revolver.
25

26 Q. Had you ever seen that man before that night?
27

28 A. He looked familiar. I might have seen him in the
29   neighborhood. He might even have been in my store
30   before, but I can't say for sure. I know I saw him
31   come in the store five days after the robbery. I
32   called the police right away.
33

34 Q. Do you see that man who robbed you in this court
35   today?
36

37 A. Sure. He is sitting right over there, next to his
38   lawyer. He's wearing a blue and white shirt.
39

40 Q. Your Honor, let the record show the witness has
41   pointed to the defendant, Larry Riley. I have no
42   further questions.

43 Q. (by the defense attorney) Mr./Ms. Potempa, before
44   Larry Riley came into your store on December
45   20, had he been in your store on any previous
46   occasion?
47
48 A. Like I say, he could have been, but I don't really
49   know.
50
51 Q. Before December 20, did the police ever show you
52   any photographs?
53
54 A. No. I guess they called me to come to the police
55   station, but I just wasn't up to it.
56
57 Q. Why weren't you up to it?
58
59 A. Well, the robbery upset me. I was already being
60   treated for a nervous condition, and this made
61   matters worse. Business has been rotten enough,
62   and here this guy comes along and takes my
63   money. It's a good thing my insurance covered all
64   of it.
65
66 Q. Are you taking any medication for your nervous
67   condition?
68
69 By the prosecutor: Object. That is irrelevant.
70
71 The Court: This is just a hearing. I'll allow the
72 question. Please answer.
73
74 A. I take Thorazine, 200 milligrams a day.
75
76 Q. What did you mean when you said business was
77   rotten?
78
79 A. I mean just that. I was barely able to make my
80   expenses. My suppliers were hounding me for payment
81   of their bills.
82
83 Q. How long was the robber in the parking lot on
84   December 15?
85
86 A. The whole thing took less than a minute.
87
88 Q. Were you ever asked to look at a lineup before or
89   after December 20 in connection with the
90   robbery?
91
92 A. No.
93
94 Q. Were you ever placed in a lineup?

95 By the prosecutor: Objection. Irrelevant.
96
97 The Court: Sustained.
98
99 Q. Were you ever in military service?
100
101 A. Yeah, the Marines. For three months twelve years
102   ago.
103
104 Q. Why only three months?
105
106 A. I just couldn't adjust. That's where I developed
107   my nervous condition. They gave me a general
108   discharge, under honorable conditions.

Val's Chicken House

| 1210 N. Woods | Alley | Entrance 1214 N. Woods | Alley | 1218 N. Woods |

Customer Seating and Take-out Area

Service Counter

Kitchen & Storage

Order Window   Pick-up Window

Parking Lot

Alley

Not to scale

7.10 BRIBERY CASE

UNITED STATES
v.
HARLEY WIGGINS

This is a federal criminal case. Harley Wiggins is charged with bribery in violation of 18 U.S.C. § 666. The indictment charges that Wiggins received a $9,500 bribe from Pat Hanson, a real estate developer, on February 15, [-1], in return for Wiggins's promise to promote passage of a zoning change proposal brought before the County Board. Wiggins is a member of the Board and chair of its Zoning Committee.

You have the report of the FBI agent who investigated the case, an excerpt from the County Board Proceedings where the zoning change was voted on, certain bank records, and the grand jury testimony of Hanson and Wiggins.

1. For the prosecution, conduct a direct examination of Hanson and cross-examine Wiggins.

2. For the defense, conduct a direct examination of Wiggins and cross-examine Hanson.

FEDERAL BUREAU OF INVESTIGATION

Form 302

Reporting agent: Helen Randolph, Special Agent

Date of Report: 9/14/[-1]

Subject: Harley Wiggins

The following is a summary of my investigation concerning allegations of bribery against Harley Wiggins, a member of the Creek County Board.

In early July of this year, the undersigned began hearing rumors of impropriety concerning the Crest Prairie Development planned for the southeast part of Creek County. Investigation revealed that the developer is Pat Hanson. Hanson is reputed to have connections with organized crime. Bureau files revealed s/he is under current investigation for tax evasion for the years [-5] through [-2]. The U.S. Attorney's office for this District informed the undersigned that a multi-count tax evasion indictment against Hanson is imminent. Further investigation revealed that Hanson's multi-million dollar Crest Prairie Development plan had languished for two years in the Creek County Board files without being called for a vote. It appears there was a flurry of activity concerning the development in March of this year. The development plan was placed on the Board's agenda for March 16 of this year after a favorable vote by the Board's Zoning Committee one week earlier. The chair of the Zoning Committee is Harley Wiggins, an announced candidate for president of the Creek County Board in the upcoming November elections.

The undersigned interviewed Richard Parsons, clerk of the five-person Creek County Zoning Committee, on July 19 of this year. Parsons advised that the Committee's backlog of cases was substantial. He said that Hanson's development plan had not been called for a Committee vote because so many other plans were ahead of it for consideration. Committee procedure was to take up the proposed plans in the same order in which they were filed with the Committee. He said nothing had been done to keep the plan from a vote. He was surprised, however, when the Hanson plan appeared on the Committee agenda on March 9, since there were several matters ahead of it for consideration. The agenda was the chair's prerogative. He did not ask Wiggins why the Crest Prairie Development plan was being taken out of order. That had happened

671

several times in the past and there was no cause for suspicion. There was no transcript made of the Committee session. The only minutes taken simply reflect the vote. The Committee voted five to nothing to recommend passage of the plan to the full Board. Parsons does not recall that anything out of the ordinary happened at the meeting.

An examination of the transcript of the March 16, [-1], County Board meeting reveals that the vote on the Development was seven votes in favor and four opposed. Members voted in alphabetical order, Wiggins being the last. Wiggins abstained from voting on the Development plan. S/he gave no reason for his/her abstention.

The undersigned interviewed Pat Hanson at his/her office at 400 Lark Street, Creek City, on July 28 of this year. After advising him/her of my office, and telling him/her the purpose of my visit, Hanson stated the following:

S/he has been a real estate developer in this community for the past ten years. Most of his/her projects are commercial and of varying sizes. The Crest Prairie Development was his/her biggest yet. It would cover 200 acres and be like a self-contained community. Almost all of the land had already been bought, using bank loans that totaled $10,000,000. S/he estimated the project would cost more than $60,000,000 before it was finished. S/he had been faced with foreclosure threats from banks holding his/her loans. The loans had been extended in [-3] and [-2] and early [-1], but it was clear s/he could not hold the banks off much longer with promises that the project soon would get off the ground. All of his/her assets were tied up in the project. S/he was facing bankruptcy. In early February of this year s/he learned Wiggins was planning to run for president of the County Board. On February 15, s/he went to Wiggins's office at the Wiggins Hardware Company at 1200 Lake Street in Creek City. S/he brought an envelope with $9,500 in cash in it, and left the envelope with Wiggins's administrative assistant. In the envelope, on a piece of blank paper, s/he left a note that said, "Good luck in your upcoming campaign. We need people like you, Pat." S/he did not speak to Wiggins about the contribution that day or any other day. It was not intended to influence the Zoning Committee or the County Board, although s/he was "pleasantly surprised" when the development plan was approved by the Zoning Committee and the County Board. Hanson denied any connections with organized crime. When the undersigned observed that

672

Hanson currently was being investigated for possible income tax offenses, Hanson terminated the interview. (It should be noted that Hanson filed for personal bankruptcy on August 18 of this year.)

On August 5 of this year the undersigned went to the Wiggins Hardware Company at 1200 Lake Street, Creek City, for the purpose of interviewing Harley Wiggins about the $9,500 payment. When the undersigned announced her office and told Wiggins the purpose of the interview, Wiggins said, "I don't have to explain my actions to anybody. I always do the right thing. There isn't enough money in the world to buy my vote. I am not going to say anything more without my lawyer." The undersigned then terminated the interview.

On August 10 of this year Hanson and his/her attorney, Rudolph Gibbons, met with Assistant U.S. Attorney Edwin Reinheimer at the Federal Building. The next day, pursuant to a plea agreement, Hanson testified before a federal grand jury.

Pursuant to instruction from Assistant U.S. Attorney Reinheimer, the undersigned served a subpoena on Harley Wiggins. It called for him/her to appear before the federal grand jury on August 28.

Helen Randolph, SA

Pat Hanson, being first duly sworn, testified as follows:

1 Q. (by Assistant United States Attorney) Mr./Ms.
2   Hanson, are you testifying here today subject to a
3   plea agreement with the government?
4
5 A. Yes.
6
7 Q. What do you understand that plea agreement to be?
8
9 A. In return for my truthful testimony about my
10   dealings with Harley Wiggins, I will not be
11   charged with bribery. Also, I will be allowed to
12   plead guilty to one count of tax evasion for the
13   year [-2]. The government will tell the sentencing
14   judge about my cooperation in the case
15   against Wiggins. I understand I will be fined the
16   amount of money I should have paid in [-2], about
17    $40,000. The tax payments for the other years, for
18   [-5], [-4], and [-3], will be forgiven and I
19   will not be criminally charged for those years.
20   There will be no civil action against me by the
21   IRS. I won't be sentenced until after I testify
22   against Wiggins.
23
24 Q. Mr./Ms. Hanson, please tell the grand jury
25   something about yourself.
26
27 A. I am 50 years old. I have lived in Creek City
28   all my life. I am married and have two teenage
29   boys. I have spent most of my life in sales. I
30   sold used and new cars for about ten years, and
31   then went into real estate. I am not a licensed
32   broker anymore. About ten years ago I began
33   developing properties in this area. First, it was
34   just small commercial properties, but then I had
35   the idea of a large planned development, kind of
36   a small city. That was the Crest Prairie
37   Development.
38
39 Q. Tell us about that development.
40
41 A. It was my dream. I wanted to build a place where
42   people could get away from urban blight, could
43   raise their kids safely. So I began buying land in
44   the southeastern part of the county. I've got

45　　about 200 acres now. I used bank loans totaling
46　　$10,000,000 for most of it. As I would buy a parcel
47　　of land, I would pledge it for another loan. I
48　　also used all of my own money. That's why I had to
49　　fudge the numbers on my tax returns for the past
50　　four years. It was the only way I could keep the
51　　development going.
52
53 Q. When did you meet Harley Wiggins?
54
55 A. When I realized my development wasn't getting out
56　　of the County Board Zoning Committee, even after it
57　　sat there for two years, I went to see him/her at
58　　his/her hardware store. That was early in February
59　　of this year, maybe the first week of the month.
60　　We were alone in his/her office. I told him/her the
61　　delay was killing me, that the bankers were going
62　　to call in their loans and the whole plan would go
63　　down the drain.
64
65 Q. What did s/he say?
66
67 A. S/he said the plan would have to wait its turn with
68　　all the others, that it could take another six to
69　　eight months before s/he called it for a committee
70　　vote. That's when I asked him/her if I could do
71　　anything to speed things up.
72
73 Q. What did s/he say?
74
75 A. S/he said that I had been around long enough to
76　　know how things work. I asked him/her how much
77　　it would take. S/he told me s/he wanted $9,500
78　　in cash. S/he said that would be just under the
79　　$10,000 point where banks have to report cash
80　　deposits to the government. I told him/her I would
81　　be back in a week.
82
83 Q. Did you go back?
84
85 A. Yes. On February 15 I went back to his/her store. I
86　　had an envelope with $9,500 in it. I had kept the
87　　cash in my safety deposit box. Those were my last
88　　dollars. When I walked into his/her office
89　　s/he didn't say anything. S/he just pointed to his/
90　　her desk. I put the envelope on his/her desk and
91　　I left. I never spoke to him/her again. In about
92　　a month the County Board approved my project. It
93　　turned out that I wasted the money. The banks
94　　called in my loans five days ago. They'll take
95　　everything. The project will never get off the
96　　ground. I'll have to declare bankruptcy.

676

```
 97  Q. Did you give Mr./Ms. Wiggins the money for his/her
 98      upcoming campaign?
 99
100  A. No. I just said that to the FBI agent so she would
101      leave me alone. Wiggins and I never discussed his/
102      her campaign.
103
104  Q. Have you ever been charged with a crime before
105      today?
106
107  A. No. The closest I ever came was about 12 years
108      ago when I was hauled in front of the State Real
109      Estate Board. I was accused of misrepresenting
110      the appraisal value of a house so I could
111      make a sale. I didn't fight the charge. They
112      revoked my broker's license and I never got
113      it back.
```

Harley Wiggins, being first duly sworn, testified
as follows:

1 Q. (by Assistant United States Attorney) Mr./Ms.
2   Wiggins, do you understand that you have signed a
3   waiver of your rights?
4
5 A. Yes. I am testifying here voluntarily. I want to
6   clear this up.
7
8 Q. Please tell the grand jury something about
9   yourself.
10
11 A. I am 48 years old. I have lived in Creek City all
12   my life. I live with my husband/wife and three
13   children. I have owned the Wiggins Hardware Store
14   since I inherited it from my father. After high
15   school I went to work in the store and I never left
16   it.
17
18 Q. Do you hold any public office?
19
20 A. I am a member of the Creek County Board, and I am
21   chair of the Board's Zoning Committee. Those are
22   unpaid positions.
23
24 Q. What is the procedure when someone applies for the
25   Board's approval of a development plan?
26
27 A. We get all the information we can, along with an
28   evaluation from our experts. Then, when it comes up
29   on the Committee agenda, we hold a hearing.
30
31 Q. Tell us how Pat Hanson's Crest Prairie Development
32   plan was handled.
33
34 A. Just like any other request for approval. It had to
35   wait its turn, then we voted on it in committee,
36   then at the full board meeting.
37
38 Q. We have been told that at your March committee
39   meeting the Crest Prairie Development plan was
40   considered ahead of some older petitions. Is that
41   true?
42
43 A. I don't remember anything like that. It has
44   happened in the past, though. I do remember I liked

45   Hanson's plan. It had playgrounds and schools. I
46   thought it would be good for the county.
47
48 Q. Did you receive $9,500 in cash from Pat Hanson?
49
50 A. Yes, I did. S/he sent the money to me in an
51   envelope. There was a note inside saying it was
52   for my board president campaign. I thought that
53   was very nice of him/her. S/he never asked me for
54   anything and if I thought s/he was looking for
55   special treatment I would have sent the money back
56   to him/her.
57
58 Q. What happened to the note that was inside the
59   envelope?
60
61 A. I don't know. I probably threw it away.
62
63 Q. What did you do with the money?
64
65 A. First, I deposited it in the hardware store
66   account. Later, I put it in my campaign account.
67
68 Q. When did you put the money in your campaign
69   account?
70
71 A. My records show it was August 8.
72
73 Q. Why did you wait so long before putting the money
74   in your campaign account?
75
76 A. Campaigns around here don't really begin until the
77   September before the November election. I didn't
78   even open up the campaign account until August 1.
79   There was no need to do it earlier.
80
81 Q. How did Hanson know you were running for board
82   president?
83
84 A. I don't know. I never told him/her. In fact, I
85   don't remember ever having a conversation with
86   Hanson, other than "Hello, how are you?", that kind
87   of thing. I knew him/her, of course. S/he was born
88   and raised in Creek City. But there was no secret
89   about my candidacy. I had announced it publicly in
90   January of this year.
91
92 Q. Did you ever talk to Hanson at your hardware
93   store at any time before the board vote on his/her
94   plan?

680

```
 95 A. Absolutely not. In fact, I don't recall ever
 96    seeing him/her in my store.
 97
 98 Q. Why did you abstain from voting on Hanson's
 99    development when it came before the county board?
100
101 A. S/he had given me that campaign money. I did not
102    think it would be right to vote on his/her plan.
103    People might get the wrong impression. I thought
104    it was important to protect my reputation.
105
106 Q. Did you vote on the plan when it was before your
107    committee?
108
109 A. I don't remember.
```

EXCERPTS FROM TRANSCRIPT OF
MINUTES OF CREEK COUNTY BOARD MEETING
ON MARCH 16, [-1]

President Bates: The question before the Board is whether it will accept the recommendation of the Zoning Committee that the Crest Prairie Development plan be approved as submitted. The clerk will call the roll.

Clerk: Mr. Carter? Yes. Ms. Diamond? No. Ms. Fletcher? Yes. Mr. Garvas? Yes. Ms. Hammond? No. Mr. Jackson? Yes. Mr. Long? No. Mr. Nash? Yes. Ms. Osmond? No. Mr. Peters? Yes. Mr. Phillips? Yes. Mr./Ms. Wiggins? I abstain.

Clerk: Mr. President, the vote is seven yeas, four nays, and one abstention. The motion to approve carries.

Savings Deposit Slip

For deposit to the account of:

Wiggins Hardware Store
1200 Lake Street
Creek City

Date: _2|16|[□]_

First National Bank
Creek City

1221 4282 2330 6853

Cash: _$9,500.00_

Checks: _____

_____

_____

_____

Total: _$9,500.00_

Savings Withdrawal Slip

For withdrawal from the account of:

Wiggins Hardware Store
1200 Lake Street
Creek City

Date: _8|8|[□]_

First National Bank
Creek City

1221 4282 2330 6853

Cash: _$9,500.00_

Checks: _____

_____

_____

_____

Total: _$9,500.00_

Checking Deposit Slip

For deposit to the account of:

Wiggins for Board President
1200 Lake Street
Creek City

Date: _8|8|[□]_

First National Bank
Creek City

1221 4282 2330 8721

Cash: _$9,500.00_

Checks: _____

_____

_____

_____

Total: _$9,500.00_

First National Bank
Creek City

Monthly Account Summary
Statement period: August 1 through August 31, [-1]

Account	Date opened	Account Number	Ending Balance
1. maximum savings	6/1/[-14]	2330 6853	$ 2,633.90
2. checking	8/6/[-1]	2330 8721	$ 9,600.00

Your maximum savings account #2330 6853 - Wiggins Hardware Co.
Beginning balance on 8/1/[-1]:	$	12,121.17
Total deposits:	0	
Total withdrawals:	1	$ 9,500.00
Interest paid:		$ 12.73
Ending balance on 8/31/[-1]:		$ 2,633.90

Your checking account #2330 8721 - Wiggins for Board President
Beginning balance on 8/6/[-1]:		$ 100.00
Total deposits:	2	$ 9,500.00
Total withdrawals:	0	
Ending balance on 8/31/[-1]:		$ 9,600.00

7.11 INSIDER TRADING CASE

UNITED STATES
v.
RYLEE SANBORN

This is a federal criminal case. Rylee Sanborn is charged with insider trading in violation of 15 U.S.C. §§ 78j and 78ff, and making a false statement to the Securities and Exchange Commission (SEC) investigators in violation of 18 U.S.C. § 1001. The indictment charges that Sanborn used inside information to earn a profit on corporate stock s/he bought and sold, then lied about it to the SEC.

You have the indictment against Sanborn and the depositions of Devyn Martin, chief financial officer for the corporation, and Sanborn. You also have two e-mails written by Martin and one e-mail written by Sanborn.

1. For the prosecution, conduct a direct examination of Martin and cross-examine Sanborn.

2. For the defense, conduct a direct examination of Sanborn and cross-examine Martin

UNITED STATES DISTRICT COURT

UNITED STATES OF AMERICA)

)   <u>INDICTMENT</u>

v.   )

)   Cr. H-05-01

RYLEE SANBORN,   )

    Defendant.   )

The Grand Jury charges:

At all times relevant to this indictment

1. Vid-Blittz Corporation ("Vid-Blittz") was a Delaware corporation with its headquarters in Illinois. Vid-Blittz was engaged in the manufacture of computer graphic components and graphics systems.

2. Vid-Blittz was a publicly traded company whose shares are listed on the New York Stock Exchange. Vid-Blittz and its directors, officers, and employees were required to comply with regulations of the U.S. Securities and Exchange Commission ("SEC").

3. Defendant RYLEE SANBORN was employed by Vid-Blittz beginning in [-8] as a software engineer.

4. On or about March 5, [-2], in a company-wide confidential e-mail, Chief Financial Officer DEVYN MARTIN announced the details of a profitable contract awarded to Vid-Blittz by Applux to produce graphics processors for a game console called the "A-Station." The e-mail announced that Applux would "prepay" Vid-Blittz $200 million and predicted that "if A-Station becomes as big as the leading Playstation, we generate about $2 Billion in sales over five years."

5. On or about March 6, [-2], SANBORN gained nonpublic information concerning the value of Vid-Blittz shares when s/he read the confidential company-wide e-mails announcing the A-Station contract awarded by Applux.

6. On or about March 6, [-2], SANBORN purchased 1,000 shares of Vid-Blittz stock for $61 a share.

7. On or about March 10, [-2], Vid-Blittz and Applux publicly announced the A-Station contract.

8. On or about March 15, [-2], SANBORN sold his/her 1,000 shares of Vid-Blittz stock for $110 a share. S/he made a profit of $49,000.

9. On or about August 1, [-1], RYLEE SANBORN was interviewed in Chicago, Illinois, by the SEC.

COUNT ONE
(Insider trading)

10. The allegations in paragraphs 1 through 9 are realleged as if fully set forth here.

11. Defendant RYLEE SANBORN engaged in securities fraud when s/he (1) purchased 1,000 shares of Vid-Blittz Corporation stock on March 6, [-2], while knowingly possessing material, nonpublic information concerning the value of those stocks, and when s/he (2) profited from the sale of those stocks, in violation of 15 U.S.C. §§ 78j and 78ff, and 17 C.F.R. § 240.10b-5.

COUNT TWO
(False statement)

12. The allegations in paragraphs 1 through 9 are realleged as if fully set forth here.

13. On or about August 1, [-1], SANBORN made a materially false statement to SEC investigators, in violation of 18 U.S.C. § 1001. SANBORN made a false statement when s/he denied that his/her decision to purchase one thousand shares of Vid-Blittz stock was based on possession of material, nonpublic information. In response to the question, "Had you become aware of the contract by any means before you purchased the stock?" SANBORN responded "No." That statement was false, as SANBORN had read confidential company-wide e-mails sent on or about March 5 and March 6, [-1], which announced the details of a profitable contract awarded to Vid-Blittz by Applux.

_____
Grand Jury Foreperson

692

```
To:        All employees - CONFIDENTIAL
From:      Devyn Martin
Subject:   A-Station deal is closed!
Date:      March 5, [-2]
Time:      11:04 P.M.
```

At the very last moment, Applux was able to recognize that we are the only company that can help transform it into a consumer electronics giant.

The deal is pretty simple—we build a custom chip by combining VB20 and Cruise1, called VB2X. We sell them VC2X and MFC (multimedia peripherals chip-southbridge) for the game console market. We collaborate with WebTV to build set top boxes based on A-Station. Applux "prepays" us $200 million (that's right—$200,000,000) as their commitment to the program. If A-Station becomes as big as Playstation, we generate about $2 billion in sales over five years.

But what's really important is the magnitude of the program. This is a big project. We are going to be on a world stage competing against the giants. We have to succeed—we have to execute.

So, I need all of you to hyper focus and deliver. We now have the opportunity to take Vid-Blittz to the next level. Let's seize the moment.

Winning A-Station is an incredible achievement. You should all be very proud. Please note: It is essential that no one outside the company learns about the contract until a public announcement is made.

        Devyn Martin
        Senior Vice President for Corporate Development
        Vid-Blittz Corporation

****

This electronic mail transmission may contain confidential or privileged information. If you believe that you have received this message in error, please notify the sender by reply transmission and delete the message without copying or disclosing it.

****

```
To:       All employees
From:     Devyn Martin
Subject:  A-Station shhhhh . . .
Date:     March 6, [-2]
Time:     9:15 A.M.
```

I'd like to remind everyone to keep the A-Station news quiet. Not a word to anyone outside of our walls.

Effective today, the trading window is closed due to the A-Station contract. The window will stay closed until the third trading day after this announcement is made public via press release (by Applux or Vid-Blittz). The fact that the window is closed is also confidential information—not to be disclosed outside Vid-Blittz.

Anybody who has placed an order for Vid-Blittz stock should cancel that order.

Let's let the news roll out in a controlled way. Applux plans to make the news public this Friday. But anything can happen; let's not jinx it! Thanks!

> Devyn Martin
> Senior Vice President for Corporate Development
> Vid-Blittz Corporation

****

****

To: Rylee Sanborn
From: k001-cHipz@hotmail.com Subject: Note to self
Date: March 6, [-2]
Time: 9:27 A.M.

Buy stock at lunch today

DEPOSITION OF DEVYN MARTIN
on August 1, [-1]
at the offices of the Securities and
Exchange Commission
175 W. Jackson Boulevard, Suite 900
Chicago, IL 60604

DEVYN MARTIN, having been first duly sworn,
testified as follows:

1 Q. (by an SEC investigator) Please state your name
2   and spell it for the record.
3
4 A. Devyn Martin. D-e-v-y-n M-a-r-t-i-n.
5
6 Q. What is your occupation?
7
8 A. I am the chief financial officer of Vid-Blittz
9   Corporation, a publicly traded company.
10
11 Q. What is Vid-Blittz's primary business?
12
13 A. We specialize in programmable graphics processors
14   and graphics systems.
15
16 Q. Before we discuss what happened with regards to
17   Rylee Sanborn, let's talk about your qualifications
18   as an expert in the fields of finance, economics,
19   and technology industries. What is your educational
20   background?
21
22 A. I graduated from the U.C. Berkeley in [-21] with
23   a Bachelor of Arts in economics. After gradua-
24   tion, I worked as a research fellow for the
25   Institute for Economics and Liberty. I studied
26   the regulatory reform of the banking and securi-
27   ties industries. In my time there, I published
28   two scholarly articles on regulatory reform. I
29   also contributed to the development of three
30   position papers on issues relating to the finan-
31   cial industries. After my fellowship I attended
32   the Wharton School of Business. I received my
33   M.B.A. in [-17].
34
35 Q. What was your work experience after graduation?
36
37 A. From [-16] to [-13], I served as corporate vice-
38   president for Governmental Relations with

39   Mototech Industries. From [-13] to [-6], I
40   served as a corporate vice-president with the
41   Biometric Security Section. In late [-6] I was
42   invited to join the Securities and Exchange
43   Commission as an economic fellow in the Office
44   of Economic Analysis. I held that position until
45   March 1,[-3], when I was hired by Vid-Blittz
46   Corporation as senior vice president for corpo-
47   rate development. On September 1, [-3], I
48   assumed the position of chief financial officer.
49   Our former CFO retired June 30, [-3].
50
51 Q. Were you involved with the bid for the Applux
52   contract?
53
54 A. Yes I was. We entered into discussions with
55   Applux in October of [-3]. We made an initial
56   bid in January of [-2]. After that, we continued
57   negotiations.
58
59 Q. What agreement did you reach?
60
61 A. Vid-Blittz was tapped to develop a custom graph-
62   ics processor chip for the A-Station game con-
63   sole, designed to work with WebTV. We were also
64   selected as the exclusive supplier of this chip.
65   Applux prepaid us $200,000 to help cover the
66   initial development costs. Of course we still
67   had to pay the bulk of development costs, but we
68   hoped to generate $2 billion in sales over a
69   five-year period, if the A-Station became com-
70   petitive with the Sonjax Playstation.
71
72 Q. When did you first notify the employees of Vid-
73   Blittz that you had entered into a contract to
74   produce the graphics chip for the A-Station game
75   console?
76
77 A. I sent out a company-wide e-mail announcing the
78   deal on Sunday night.
79
80 Q. I have here an e-mail sent by you on March 5,
81   [-2] at 11:04 P.M. Is this the e-mail you are
82   referring to?
83
84 A. Yes.
85
86 Q. I also have here a second e-mail, sent March 6,
87   [-2], at 9:15 A.M. Do you recognize the March
88   6th e-mail?

89 A. Yes, that's the one I sent on March 6.
90
91 Q. Why did you send the second e-mail?
92
93 Q. I was concerned that the first e-mail was not
94   explicit enough about the need for confidential-
95   ity. I sent the second to clarify this point and
96   to prevent inadvertent insider trading.
97
98 Q. On Monday, March 6, did you notice Vid-Blittz
99   employees discussing the A-Station contract?
100
101 A. Yes. When I came to work at 9:00 A.M. Everybody was
102   talking about it. The company was humming with the
103   news.
104
105 Q. Do you know Rylee Sanborn?
106
107 A. Yes, I do. His/Her cubicle is near my office.
108
109 Q. Did you witness any conversations between Rylee
110   Sanborn and other employees on the morning of
111   March 6?
112
113 A. No. When I came in s/he had not yet arrived.
114   I went to my office and spent the rest of the
115   morning there with the door closed, making calls.
116
117 Q. Tell me about the rise in price of Vid-Blittz's
118   stock?
119
120 A. At the close of the market on Friday, March 3,
121   Vid-Blittz was trading at $58 a share. At the
122   close on Monday, March 6, it was trading at $68.
123   On the morning of March 7, it went to $70. On
124   March 8, it closed at $72. Then, when the mar-
125   ket closed on March 9 it was up to $76. After
126   our announcement on the morning of March 10, it
127   shot up — $101 at the close of that day; $104 at
128   the close the following Monday; and $110 at the
129   close Tuesday. It closed at $111 on
130   Wednesday, March 15, the day Rylee Sanborn sold
131   his/her stock.
132
133 Q. On Thursday, March 9, Standard & Poor's made the
134   announcement that Vid-Blittz would be listed in
135   the mid-cap 400 index.
136
137 A. Yes, I was quite pleased with that development.

138 Q. Following the S & P announcement, Vid-Blittz's
139   stock price increased. It rose from the closing
140   price on Wednesday of $72 per share to $110 by
141   the time Sanborn sold his/her stock on Wednesday,
142   March 15.
143
144 Q. Could that be due to the new listing by Standard &
145   Poor's?
146
147 A. No, I don't believe so.
148
149 Q. Can a new listing lead to a substantial increase
150   in value?
151
152 A. Yes, a study I performed while working at the SEC
153   showed that technology-based stocks often increase
154   10 percent in value following listing. However,
155   that 10 percent gain is usually more gradual, an
156   aggregate gain over a period of anywhere from a
157   few days to several weeks. In this case, the price
158   jumped sharply between our contract announcement
159   on Friday March 10 and closing on March 14.
160
161 Q. Are you reasonably certain that the increase in
162   value cannot be attributed to the Standard &
163   Poor's listing?
164
165 A. Yes, I'm quite certain. It is extremely unlikely
166   that the listing led to such a sharp rise in
167   value. Listings generally do not have an immedi-
168   ate impact on the market.
169
170 Q. Could market fluctuations combined with the
171   listing have caused the sharp rise in value?
172
173 A. No, that is unlikely as well.
174
175 Q. To what do you attribute the rise in value?
176
177 A. I believe the sudden increase is attributable
178   first to rumors concerning Vid-Blittz's contract
179   with Applux, which were pushing up the price from
180   Monday afternoon through Thursday, and, second,
181   to the effect of the official announcement of the
182   contract on Friday.
183
184 Q. Are you aware of any specific rumors that Vid-
185   Blittz was going to be awarded the contract?

186 A. No, but early Monday morning we scheduled a press
187   conference for Friday, March 10, to make the
188   announcement. I'm sure the rumors started to fly.

Devyn Martin
_____
                        Devyn Martin
                     August 15, [-1]

DEPOSITION OF RYLEE SANBORN
on August 1, [-1]
at the offices of the Securities and Exchange
Commission
175 W. Jackson Boulevard, Suite 900
Chicago, IL 60604

RYLEE SANBORN, having been first duly sworn, testified as follows:

1 Q. (by an SEC investigator) Please state your name
2 and spell it for the record.
3
4 A. Rylee Sanborn. R-y-l-e-e S-a-n-b-o-r-n.
5
6 Q. What is your occupation?
7
8 A. I am a software engineer for Vid-Blittz
9 Productions. We make OEM video graphics cards and
10 complete graphics systems. At the moment, I am
11 the lead programmer for a contract to produce
12 graphics cards for the next generation of Navy
13 flight simulators.
14
15 Q. How long have you been employed by Vid-Blittz?
16
17 A. I started with the company as a software engineer
18 in [-8].
19
20 Q. Did you purchase shares of Vid-Bittz stock at
21 11:35 A.M. on Monday, March 6, [-2]?
22
23 A. Yes I did. I placed my order on my lunch hour,
24 from work.
25
26 Q. How many shares did you purchase?
27
28 A. One thousand shares.
29
30 Q. What price did you pay?
31
32 A. $61.00 a share, $61,000 in all.
33
34 Q. When did you sell those shares?
35
36 A. Wednesday of the following week, on March 15,
37 [-2].
38
39 Q. How much did you profit from the transaction?

40 A. Let's see, I sold them for $110.00 a share, so
41   I made a profit of $49.00 a share. I made a
42   profit of $49,000 altogether.
43
44 Q. I have here an e-mail dated March 5th, [-2], at
45   11:04 P.M., announcing the award of the A-
46   Station contract to Vid-Blittz. Do you remember
47   this e-mail?
48
49 A. Yes, I do.
50
51 Q. Did you base your decision to purchase Vid-
52   Blittz stock on the information you read in
53   this e-mail?
54
55 A. No, I hadn't read the e-mail yet when I placed
56   my order.
57
58 Q. When did you read the e-mail?
59
60 A. About 1:00 P.M. on Monday, March 6, [-2].
61
62 Q. I have here a second e-mail, sent on March 6,
63   [-2], at 9:15 A.M., from Devyn Martin. Did you
64   read this second e-mail before making your pur-
65   chase?
66
67 A. No.
68
69 Q. When did you read it?
70
71 A. Right after I read the first e-mail, shortly
72   after 1:00 P.M.
73
74 Q. What did you understand it to say?
75
76 A. It said to keep the news about the contract
77   quiet until the news was made public on Friday,
78   March 10. It also said not to buy any Vid-Blittz
79   stock until three trading days after the
80   announcement and to cancel any orders already
81   placed.
82
83 Q. Did you cancel your order?
84
85 A. No, it was too late. I called the broker back,
86   but he said that the order had already gone
87   through.
88
89 Q. Which branch of your brokerage firm did you
90   call?

706

91 A. I don't remember.
92
93 Q. Do you remember the name of the person you spoke
94   with?
95
96 A. No, I don't know who it was.
97
98 Q. Was it a man or a woman?
99
100 A. I can't remember.
101
102 Q. Did you talk to the broker about selling your
103   stock?
104
105 A. Not until the following week, on Wednesday,
106   March 15.
107
108 Q. What time did you come into work on March 6,
109   [-2]?
110
111 A. I came in about 10:00 A.M. We have flexible work
112   hours at Vid-Blittz.
113
114 Q. Do you recognize this e-mail dated on March 6,
115   [-2], at 9:27 A.M., with the subject line "Note
116   to self"?
117
118 A. Yes, I sent that from home to remind myself to
119   buy the stock at lunch and not to wait.
120
121 Q. Did you read either of Mr./Ms. Martin's e-mails
122   before 1:00 P.M.?
123
124 A. No. I didn't read any e-mail before 1:00 P.M.
125
126 Q. Was your computer on that morning?
127
128 A. Yes, I just didn't look at my e-mails.
129
130 Q. What were you doing between 10:00 A.M. and 1:00
131   P.M.?
132
133 A. I was taking care of personal business on-line,
134   like looking at homes in the area.
135
136 Q. Do you typically spend the morning on personal
137   business?
138
139 A. Not every day, but I do once in a while. Vid-
140   Blittz is really laid back about it. We have
141   flex-time and the company lets us use our Internet
142   connection any way we like.

143 Q. Were you using your Internet connection that
144   morning?
145
146 A. Yes, I was checking out the home listings online.
147
148 Q. Do you frequently wait three hours to check your
149   e-mail, after you arrive at work?
150
151 A. Yes, I often wait until after lunch to look at my
152   e-mail. It gives me a chance to get something done
153   in the morning before I start responding to peo-
154   ple's questions.
155
156 Q. Can anybody verify your work habits?
157
158 A. Look at my e-mail outbox, you'll see that on a lot
159   of days I haven't sent any e-mails out before 1:00
160   P.M.
161
162 Q. How did you become aware that Vid-Blittz had
163   actually been chosen to supply graphics proces-
164   sors for the A-Station?
165
166 A. At 1:00 P.M. on Monday when I read the e-mail
167   announcements from Devyn Martin.
168
169 Q. Did you talk to anyone who was aware of the
170   contract before you made your purchase?
171
172 A. No, at least not about the contract. I said "good
173   morning" to a couple people on the way to my desk.
174
175 Q. Had you become aware of the contract by any means
176   before you purchased the stock?
177
178 A. No.
179
180 Q. On March 6, [-2], was the office abuzz with the
181   news that Vid-Blittz had been awarded the con-
182   tract?
183
184 A. Yes, in the afternoon they were very excited.
185
186 Q. Did you hear any conversations concerning the
187   contract before you made your trade?
188
189 A. Not that I know of. I mean, there is always a
190   conversation going on somewhere that you can hear,
191   but I wasn't paying attention. I didn't hear any
192   conversation in particular.

193 Q. How is your office laid out?
194
195 A. The executives have actual offices with walls,
196   doors, and windows, along the perimeter of the
197   building. Executive administrative assistants
198   have their own offices as well, outside the
199   executive offices. Everybody else—engineers,
200   project managers, programmers, and all the other
201   employees—they all work in cubicles with five-
202   foot-high walls. The cubicles occupy the center
203   space of the building.
204
205 Q. And where is your cubicle in relation to other
206   cubicles?
207
208 A. Mine is one of a block of four. I am located at
209   the west end of the building, next to a vice-
210   president's office. There are six units of four
211   cubicles on my floor.
212
213 Q. Is your cubicle close to the main entrance to the
214   floor?
215
216 A. No, the elevators and restrooms are at the east
217   end of the building. It's kind of far from the
218   facilities, but at least there's not a lot of
219   traffic by my desk.
220
221 Q. Can you overhear conversations in other cubicles
222   while you work?
223
224 A. Yes, but I generally don't listen. Some people
225   listen. I wouldn't say anything there that I
226   wanted to keep private.
227
228 Q. Are you aware of conversations as you walk by
229   other people's cubicles?
230
231 A. Yes, but like I said, I didn't notice anything in
232   particular that day.
233
234 Q. Do employees leave their cubicles to talk to other
235   employees?
236
237 A. Yes, it's an easygoing atmosphere. You can stop
238   by and talk to people pretty much whenever you
239   want, as long as you get your work done. People
240   also socialize in the cafeteria or outside the
241   building where the smokers hang out.

242 Q. Did you leave your cubicle to speak with anyone
243   the morning of March 6, [-2]?
244
245 A. No, I didn't leave my desk except to go eat lunch
246   in the cafeteria.
247
248 Q. Did you speak to any of your coworkers before 1:00
249   P.M.?
250
251 A. Not except to say "good morning."
252
253 Q. When did you decide to purchase stock in Vid-
254   Blittz?
255
256 A. Monday morning, on March 6.
257
258 Q. Why did you decide to purchase Vid-Blittz stock?
259
260 A. I'd been keeping an eye on the stock because Vid-
261   Blittz had excellent earnings in February—its
262   stock had gone from $30 to $60 a share. There
263   was a raging bull market going on at the time,
264   and people were snapping up hot stocks like
265   Vid-Blittz. But the main reason I acted when I
266   did was because I saw on TV, on the Financial
267   News Network, breaking news that Vid-Blittz was
268   negotiating for the contract for the A-Station
269   console. The price was already heading upward
270   from the Friday close by the time I saw the
271   announcement.
272
273 Q. Were you aware of Applux's plans for a new game
274   console, the A-Station?
275
276 A. Yes, generally. There was a lot of industry buzz.
277   Its graphics capabilities were supposed to be
278   really advanced—even better than Micromo's Xbox
279   and Sonjax's Playstation. Everyone was waiting for
280   it. My boss saw the announcement at the Summer
281   [-3] Electronic Entertainment Expo in Los Angeles.
282   But I wasn't personally involved with the contract
283   or anything. Management doesn't include me in
284   those discussions.
285
286 Q. Prior to March 5, [-2], did you know that Vid-
287   Blittz was bidding on a contract to be the sole
288   supplier of graphics processors for the new game
289   console?
300
301 A. Well, I read in the Wall Street Journal that
302   Applux was considering using us, among other
303   companies. But industry gossip had been that

710

304   Applux was going to go with a small startup com-
305   pany bidding for the project, DigiGig.
306
307 Q. Had you ever purchased stock prior to March 6, [-2]?
308
309 A. Yes, I'd been playing the market over the past
310   several years. I'd been pretty active buying stock
311   in technology companies—Sun Microsystems, OSI
312   Systems, Altera, Puma Technology—then selling it
313   off quick for a profit.
314
315 Q. Have you made such a large purchase before?
316
317 A. Not quite. My largest trade before that was
318     $10,000 worth of shares in Altera, which I bought
319   in early February, [-2] and sold on the Friday
320   before I bought the Vid-Blittz stock.
321
322 Q. When did Vid-Blittz and Applux publicly announce
323   the A-Station contract?
324
325 A. They made the announcement on Friday morning, on
326   March 10th, just before the markets opened.
327
328 Q. Why didn't you sell your stock before the official
329   announcement of the A-Station contract?
330
331 A. The damage was already done—I'd already bought
332   the stock. Besides, I didn't do anything wrong.
333   I didn't know the contract had been signed when I
334   placed my order.
335
336 Q. Did you ask any Vid-Blittz employees or execu-
337   tives for advice about selling the stock?
337
338 A. No.
339
340 Q. Why did you sell when you did?
341
342 A. I knew I could make a substantial profit.
343   The value was skyrocketing even before the
344   announcment. I didn't think there was much more
345   room for upward movement, so I sold as soon as the
346   blackout period for trading was over.

Rylee Sanborn
Rylee Sanborn
August 15, [-1]

7.12 CELL PHONE FROM SEARCH INCIDENT TO ARREST CASE

STATE

v.

DUSTIN SCOTT

This is a criminal case against Dustin Scott for possession of cocaine with intent to distribute, i.e., drug dealing, on January 10, [-0]. On that date, Police Officer Kelly Anderson arrested Scott outside the local basketball arena, shortly before a Thankful Cadavers rock concert at the arena. The Thankful Cadavers are a tribute band honoring the Grateful Dead.

After Officer Anderson arrested Scott, s/he conducted a search incident to arrest. During that search, Anderson found fourteen fifty-dollar bills, twelve twenty-dollar bills, three ten-dollar bills, six one-dollar bills, and 78 cents in coins. S/he also found four "8-ball"–sized packages containing a powdery substance, plus a cell phone. Immediately after taking possession of the cell phone, s/he removed its battery, then gave it to a fellow officer who placed the cell phone in a bag designed to block signals sent by another cell phone or other device.

On January 11, [-0], Officer Anderson drafted and signed, in the presence of the Police Department's Notary Public, an affidavit, then filed it with the court. Before the magistrate could decide whether to grant the search warrant, Scott appeared at an arraignment on January 11, [-0]. He was represented by private counsel at the arraignment. Pursuant to his attorney's instructions, he entered a "not guilty" plea.

At the arraignment, defense counsel stated, "Your Honor, I would like to put the court on notice that I will be filing a motion to suppress all of the items the officer found when s/he conducted an illegal search of my client—the money, the small bags, and the cell phone. I plan to file this motion within the next two days. Also, based upon my experience in these cases, I assume that the police will seek a search warrant to allow them to examine the contents of the cell phone. While we understand that the

713

court usually decides whether to issue search warrants in ex parte proceedings, we request the right to be heard before the court reaches a decision on the search warrant request. After all, we will be raising the same issues if the court does grant the search warrant, in yet another motion to suppress."

The magistrate responded by saying, "I think you raise a good point. I will schedule one hearing where I will consider your motion to suppress the fruits of the search and consider the police department's request, if any, for a search warrant authorizing examination of the contents of the cell phone."

You are now appearing at that hearing. At the hearing, the state will call Officer Anderson. The defendant will call Dakota Sorensen.

The defendant has filed a motion to suppress all items found in the search incident to Officer Anderson's arrest of Dustin Scott, on the grounds that Officer Anderson did not have probable cause to make a warrantless arrest. The state has responded to this motion by arguing that Officer Anderson had sufficient information, including information provided by a confidential informant, to constitute probable cause that Scott was selling cocaine.

The state had filed Officer Anderson's affidavit with the court at the same time as Scott was being arraigned. The state is seeking a search warrant to examine the contents of the cell phone and to chemically test the powder inside the four small packages to determine if it is cocaine.

You have Officer Anderson's affidavit, which s/he wrote with the expectation that, as in most cases, the court would consider the request for a search warrant in an ex parte proceeding.

You also have an e-mail that Dakota Sorensen sent to the Police Department. The prosecutor sent a copy of this e-mail to defense counsel, under its *Brady v. Maryland*, 373 U.S. 83 (1963), and Model Rule 3.8(d) duty to provide potentially exculpatory information to the defendant. You also have a copy of the arrest records for Dustin Scott and Dakota Sorensen.

You should assume that a state statute makes it an infraction to "sell a ticket to any entertainment event for more than the face value of the ticket." As a narcotics officer, Officer Anderson has never arrested or ticketed anyone for violation of this anti-scalping statute.

1. For the prosecution, conduct a direct examination of Officer Anderson and cross-examine Sorensen.

2. For the defense, conduct a direct examination of Sorensen and cross-examine Anderson.

Affidavit of Officer Kelly Anderson

1.   Your affiant has been a member of the Police Department since [-8]. From March 18, [-8], to October 29, [-2], your affiant was a patrol officer. On October 29, [-2], your affiant was promoted to the Narcotics Unit. Your affiant has served continuously as a narcotics officer since October 29, [-2].

2.   Your affiant graduated from the basic six-week officer training course at the State Law Enforcement Academy in March, [-8]. Since joining the Narcotics Unit in [-2], your affiant has attended three full-day training sessions for narcotics officers as well as several shorter training sessions for narcotics officers.

3.   Your affiant has participated in several dozen arrests for narcotics offenses since October 29, [-2]. Many of these arrests have come after your affiant has observed persons participating in suspicious narcotics-related activities.

4.   On January 10, [-0], at approximately 18:24, your affiant received a telephone call from a confidential informant advising your affiant that "a white guy, about five foot, ten inches tall with dark hair, wearing a hooded grey sweatshirt that says something about how drugs are a good thing is selling coke outside the main entrance to the Thankful Cadaver concert."

5.   This confidential informant has provided similar information about the sales of narcotics to your affiant on four previous occasions. On three of those occasions, that information resulted in your affiant's arrest of a person that fit the confidential informant's description for possession of narcotics with intent to distribute, after your affiant observed each of those persons engaging in suspicious activity. On the other occasion, your affiant arrived at the location described by the confidential informant and saw a person matching the description provided by the confidential information, but your affiant did not observe suspicious activity by that person, so your affiant did not make an arrest.

6.   This confidential informant is a paid informant. On each of the three previous occasions when the information provided by the confidential informant resulted in an arrest, your affiant paid the confidential informant two hundred dollars. On the other occasion, when no arrest resulted, the confidential informant received no payment from the Police Department. Your affiant will pay the confidential informant

717

two hundred dollars for the information he or she provided in this investigation, because that information resulted in an arrest.

7.   After receiving the telephone call described above, your affiant drove his/her unmarked vehicle to the parking lot outside the basketball arena's main entrance.

8.   After arriving at the parking lot outside the main entrance at 18:36, your affiant observed the words "Thankful Cadavers live at 7:00 P.M. TODAY" on the basketball arena's marquee sign over the main entrance.

9.   While inside the parked, unmarked vehicle, your affiant observed a Caucasian or mostly Caucasian male, possibly of slightly mixed ancestry, in a grey hooded sweatshirt milling about the area near the main entrance to the basketball arena. The male appeared to be of medium build, probably between 5' 8" and 5' 11" tall. Because the male was wearing the hood of his jacket up, it was difficult to determine the precise color of his hair, but his eyebrows were dark, not blonde or red.

10.   Using binoculars, your affiant observed that the grey hooded sweatshirt worn by the man milling about the arena had the words, "Reality is just a cop out for those who can't handle drugs," printed on its front.

11.   At 18:47, your affiant observed the man in the grey hooded sweatshirt come face to face with a person who was either male or female, with a separation of approximately two feet. It was difficult to determine the sex of this person, because this person, too, was wearing a hooded sweatshirt with the hood up.

12.   When they were approximately two feet apart, the person of indeterminate gender handed the man in the "Reality is just a cop out for those who can't handle drugs" sweatshirt something that appeared to be paper money.

13.   The man in the "Reality is just a cop out for those who can't handle drugs" sweatshirt then reached into his right front pants pocket and retrieved a small item that your affiant could not precisely identify because the man's hand blocked your affiant's view. The man then handed this item to the person of indeterminate gender. The person of indeterminate gender then placed the item in the pouch on the front of his or her sweatshirt and walked away.

14.   Your affiant then used his/her police communications system to call for backup to report to the main entrance of the basketball arena.

15. At 18:48, your affiant exited the parked vehicle and began walking in the direction of the man in the "Reality is just a cop out for those who can't handle drugs" sweatshirt.

16. While walking toward this man, your affiant lost sight of him, due to the large crowd outside the main entrance to the basketball arena.

17. At approximately 18:52, your affiant again observed the man in the "Reality is just a cop out for those who can't handle drugs" sweatshirt at a distance of approximately twenty feet.

18. At approximately 18:53, your affiant grabbed the hands of the man in the previously described hooded sweatshirt, pulled them behind his back, and told him, "You are under arrest for possession of cocaine with intent to distribute." Then your affiant recited the *Miranda* warnings to the arrestee.

19. Shortly after making the arrest, your affiant then observed two black and white police cruisers arrive just outside the main entrance to the basketball arena. Patrol Officer Wendy Wilson exited one vehicle and Patrol Officer Terry McKay exited the other vehicle. Both officers approached the arrestee and your affiant with their firearms drawn and pointed to the arrestee and your affiant.

20. Your affiant then conducted a pat-down search incident of the arrestee.

21. While patting the outside of the right front pants pocket of the arrestee, your affiant felt soft objects. Your affiant reached inside the pocket and found fourteen fifty-dollar bills, twelve twenty-dollar bills, three ten-dollar bills, six one-dollar bills, and 78 cents in coins, as well as four small plastic bags.

22. Each of the four small bags appeared to have been made from white kitchen garbage bags or some similar substance. Each was tied with dental floss. From feeling the outside of each bag, your affiant believed that each contained a powdery substance.

23. Based upon your affiant's experience as a narcotics officer, your affiant believed each bag contained approximately one-eighth of an ounce of powder cocaine, of unknown purity. In your affiant's experience, this is a common quantity for street sales of cocaine. Depending upon purity, location, market conditions, and other factors, the street value of an "8-ball" of cocaine is between $80 and $250, under most circumstances.

24.   While patting down the outside left front pants pocket of the arrestee, your affiant felt a hard object. Your affiant reached inside the pants pocket and found a cell phone. Pursuant to your affiant's training, your affiant immediately removed the battery from inside the cell phone. Then your affiant gave the cell phone to Officer Wilson and asked Officer Wilson to place it inside a signal-blocking bag. Officer Wilson did so, then later returned the bag to your affiant.

25.   Officer McKay handcuffed the arrestee, placed him into a black and white patrol car, and transported him to the county jail for booking. Based upon fingerprints taken during the booking process, the booking officer determined that the arrestee was Dustin Scott.

26.   Upon returning to Police Department headquarters, your affiant placed the following items into a large, clear bag:

    a.   Fourteen fifty-dollar bills, twelve twenty-dollar bills, three ten-dollar bills, six one-dollar bills, and 78 cents in coins.

    b.   Four small plastic bags containing a powdery substance.

    c.   Cell phone, in signal-blocking bag.

    d.   Battery from cell phone.

    e.   3" by 5" card with the following typed information: Officer: Kelly Anderson. Date: 1/10/[-0]. Suspect: Dustin Scott.

Your affiant then placed the bag into the evidence locker assigned to your affiant, then locked the evidence locker.

27.   It is the conclusion of your affiant that Dustin Scott was involved in the sales of cocaine outside the main entrance to the basketball arena, the location of the Thankful Cadavers concert. Your affiant has been advised, at law enforcement meetings and training sessions, that Thankful Cadavers concerts attract many concert attendees who are users of narcotics and, therefore, also attract sellers of narcotics. The activities of the man your affiant now knows as Dustin Scott, including milling among those arriving for the concert and exchanging a small object for cash, are consistent with selling narcotics. These acts are also consistent with the information provided by the reliable confidential informant.

28.   The items found in the search incident to arrest are also consistent with your affiant's conclusion that Dustin Scott was engaged in the sale of cocaine. The

contents of the four small bags have not yet been chemically tested, but bags of this size rarely contain anything other than cocaine. The large quantity of cash found on Dustin Scott is consistent with narcotics trafficking at the street level, outside a rock concert. Narcotics traffickers almost always carry cell phones.

29.   Based upon your affiant's training and experience as a narcotics officer, it is your affiant's opinion that the cell phone probably contains evidence of narcotics trafficking, such as text messages related to narcotics transactions, phone numbers of known and suspected narcotics traffickers and consumers, records of phone calls to known and suspected narcotics traffickers and consumers, e-mails to and from known and suspected narcotics traffickers, Internet searches related to narcotics trafficking, and notes regarding narcotics trafficking.

30.   Your affiant requests the issuance of a search warrant authorizing the chemical testing of the contents of the four small bags and examination of the contents of the cell phone.

FURTHER AFFIANT SAYETH NOT.

Kelly Anderson
Officer Kelly Anderson

SWORN to subscribed before me, this _11_ day of _Jan_ 20[-0]

Lola Granola
NOTARY PUBLIC

My Commission Expires:

July 10, 20 (+3)

721

From: Dakota Sorensen
Sent: January 14, [-0], 6:56 PM
To: Police Department Comment Line
Subject: Police misconduct at Thankful Cadavers Concert

Dear Perpetrators of the Police State:

You did it again. You will never be happy until you
destroy every fiber of freedom in this community, will
you? Shame on you!

A few days ago the Thankful Cadavers held a concert at
the basketball arena. It was a nice event, or at least I
thought it was until I heard the news that you fascists
arrested Dustin Scott. Were there people there who were
using substances you hate, that should be legal anyway?
Probably. But what is the big deal? Why do you have to
ruin every event like this by staking out the parking lot
and arresting everyone who does not look like you think
they should look?

I have known Dustin Scott for a long time. Long enough
to know that he has to put up with almost constant
harassment from you. You ought to be ashamed of
yourselves.

Despite what you seem to think, Dustin is a great guy.
When he found himself with an extra ticket to the
concert, he called to ask me if I wanted it. Wanted it? I
sure did. I tried to get a ticket myself, but they sold
out in a couple of hours. Dustin told me the face value
of his ticket was $38.00, so I told him I would give
him $40, since he had the hassle of getting it, which
probably meant he had to pay some sort of service charge.

We arranged to meet outside the main entrance a little
bit before the concert. He told me he would be in a grey
hooded sweatshirt. When I got there, there were lots
of people in hooded sweatshirts, especially grey ones,
including me, because it was one of those nights that was
chilly, but not freezing cold. So it took me a while to
spot him.

When I did see him, I noticed that his sweatshirt said
"some people just can't handle drugs" or something like
that. While I gave him the forty bucks and got the
ticket, I told him he was going to get into trouble
wearing a shirt like that at a Thankful Cadavers concert.
It was a joke, just like Dustin's sweatshirt. He laughed.

Then it turns out he did get into trouble. Did one of
your gestapo boys go to the concert looking for people to
hassle, then found somebody because of their **sweatshirt**?
Have you ever heard of the First Amendment? Why don't you
just leave us alone? We are not causing any trouble.
I have had it with you and your bullying. I will do
anything I can to make life difficult for the Police
Department, especially narcs, in this town. Why don't you
"serve and protect," like it says on your fancy cop cars,
instead of hassling the innocent?
Thanks a lot, heroes,

Dakota Sorensen
Defender of Freedom

ABS NO: 99 1231234 1
LAST NAME: SCOTT
FIRST NAME: DUSTIN
CURRENT ADDRESS: UNKNOWN
CITY/STATE/ZIP: UNKNOWN
DOB: 09/03/[-29]
SID: 123456789
DOC: 978645312
LAST ACTION: 02/04/[-1]

CRIMINAL HISTORY:

ARRESTED OR RECEIVED 06/06/[-5] 23:48
    AGENCY – LOCAL PD (LOPD1000)
        AGENCY CASE – [-5]008456
        CHARGE 1 – WRONGFUL POSSESSION OF ILLEGAL SUBSTANCE
        NON FELONY
    COURT –
        CHARGE 1 – DRUG POSSESSION
        PLEAD GUILTY
        SENTENCE- 08/09/[-5]
        6 MONTHS PROBATION

ARRESTED OR RECEIVED 02/08/[-4] 22:15
    AGENCY – LOCAL PD (LOPD1000)
        AGENCY CASE – [-4]000111
        CHARGE 1 – WRONGFUL POSSESSION OF SCHED 2 DRUG WITH INTENT
    COURT –
        CHARGE 1 – POSSESSION OF METH W/ INTENT TO DISTRIBUTE
        PLEAD GUILTY
        SENTENCE- 03/09/[-4]
        6 MONTHS PROBATION

ARRESTED OR RECEIVED 05/28/[-3] 16:20
    AGENCY – FAIRFIELD PD (FFPD7700)
        AGENCY CASE – [-3]0000234
        CHARGE 1 – WRONGFUL POSSESSION OF SCHED 1 DRUG WITH INTENT
        NOTE –
        ARREST IN PUBLIC PLACE: RIVERSIDE PARK
    COURT –
        CHARGE 1 – POSSESSION OF METH W/ INTENT TO DISTRIBUTE
        PLEAD GUILTY
        SENTENCE- 07/12/[-3]
        30 DAYS JAIL, 6 MONTHS PROBATION

ARRESTED OR RECEIVED 02/04/[-1] 12:00
     AGENCY – LOCAL PD (LOPD1000)
          AGENCY CASE – [-1]0000876
          CHARGE 1 – WRONGFUL POSSESSION OF SCHED 2 DRUG
          NON FELONY
COURT –
          CHARGE 1 – WRONGFUL POSSESSION OF COCAINE
          PLEAD GUILTY – NON FELONY
          SENTENCE- 03/04/[-1]
          30 DAYS JAIL, 6 MONTHS PROBATION

ABS NO: 43 4321321 9
LAST NAME: SORENSEN
FIRST NAME: DAKOTA
CURRENT ADDRESS: UNKNOWN
CITY/STATE/ZIP: UNKNOWN
DOB: 03/09/[-26]
SID: 987654321
DOC: 132465798
LAST ACTION: 04/02/[-1]

CRIMINAL HISTORY:

ARRESTED OR RECEIVED 05/28/[-3] 16:20
    AGENCY – FAIRFIELD PD (FFPD7700)
           AGENCY CASE – [-3]0000234
           CHARGE 1 – WRONGFUL POSSESSION OF SCHED 1 DRUG WITH INTENT
           NOTE –
           ARREST IN PUBLIC PLACE: RIVERSIDE PARK
    COURT –
           CHARGE 1 – POSSESSION OF METH W/ INTENT TO DISTRIBUTE
           PLEAD GUILTY
           SENTENCE- 07/12/[-3]
           6 MONTHS PROBATION

ARRESTED OR RECEIVED 08/09/[-2] 08:59
    AGENCY – LOCAL PD (LOPD1000)
           AGENCY CASE – [-2]012345
           CHARGE 1 – TRAFFIC INFRACTION – ILLEGAL UTURN
           TRAFFIC
    COURT –
           CHARGE 1 – TRAFFIC INFRACTION – ILLEGAL UTURN
           PLEAD GUILTY
           SENTENCE- 09/09/[-2]
           FINE $95, 0 POINTS

ARRESTED OR RECEIVED 04/02/[-1] 21:18
    AGENCY – LOCAL PD (LOPD1000)
           AGENCY CASE – [-1]004567
           CHARGE 1 – BATTERY (DOMESTIC VIOLENCE)
           FELONY
    COURT –
           CHARGE 1 –
           SENTENCE-

OFFICER: Kelly Anderson

DATE: 1/10/[-0]

SUSPECT: Dustin Scott

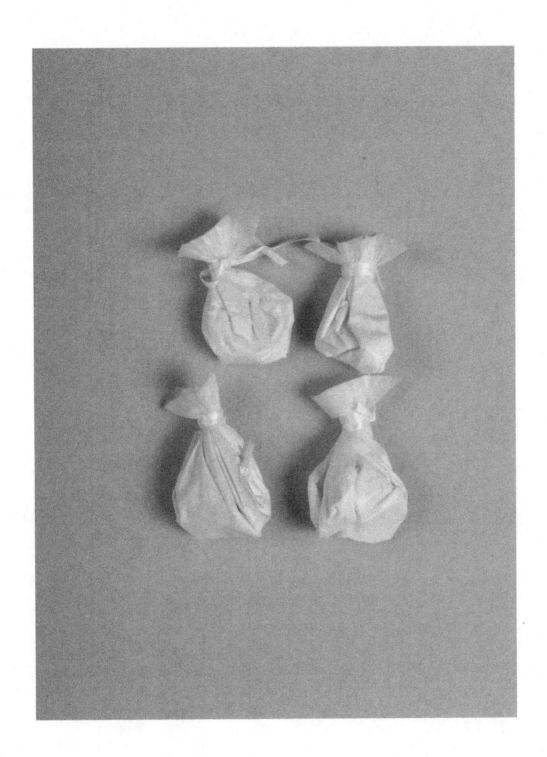

VIII

CLOSING ARGUMENTS

VIII

INTRODUCTION

The cases in Chapter 9, prepared as full trials, may also be used in this chapter as representative civil and criminal cases on which to base separate closing argument assignments. In addition, the two-witness cases in Chapter 7 may be used for additional closing argument assignments. This chapter contains six problems that involve commonly encountered situations in which effective closing arguments may be particularly important. For each problem assigned, you should be prepared to present an effectively organized and persuasively delivered closing argument to the jury.

In preparing your closing arguments, be prepared to tell the jury not only what the evidence is, but what the evidence means and why it should compel the jury to decide the case your way. Use jury instructions, analogies, and other techniques to construct a persuasive argument.

Your instructor may modify the assignments and make specific additional assignments for these exercises.

The suggested background reading is Mauet, *Trial Techniques and Trials*, Chapter 9.

8.1 LIABILITY ARGUMENT IN CONTRACT ACTION

This is a suit for breach of contract. Kane Construction Company entered into an agreement with the Glen County Highway Department to build a road extending five miles from River Bend to Tall Trees. The contract price was $7,500,000 and the contract was awarded to Kane as low bidder among ten construction companies. The other bids ranged from $8,000,000 to $10,000,000.

The contract provided for partial progress payments for "work actually completed." Kane contends that the phrase "work actually completed" includes any work done, such as excavating and grading, but the department contends that the phrase applies only to the actually completed paved road. Since the contract is ambiguous on that point, the jury will determine what the parties intended when they used that phrase.

At the end of the first 30 days, Kane submitted a bill for partial payment. At that point, only preliminary excavating and grading work had been done. No paved portion of the highway had been completed. The department refused to pay.

When the department refused to make the progress payment, Kane walked off the job, notifying the department that it would not continue the work because the contract had been breached. Kane then filed this suit for breach of contract.

The judge will instruct the jury that if it finds that the phrase "work actually completed" means any work, and not just actual road completed, that would mean that the department breached the contract and Kane would be entitled to recover the amount of profit it would have earned under the contract, which Kane says is $750,000.

The department offered evidence that Kane's bid was unrealistically low, that the company was behind schedule in the work, and that it had encountered unexpected construction problems that were not the department's fault. Department witnesses said that if Kane had actually completed the work as required by the contract, the company would have lost $1,000,000.

1. For the plaintiff, ask the jury for damages of $750,000. Stress the reasons why this or any other contract should be enforced.

2. For the defendant, tell the jury it should not award damages to the plaintiff. Stress the reasons why the plaintiff actually walked off the job.

3. For the plaintiff, rebut the defendant's argument.

8.2 DAMAGES ARGUMENT IN NEGLIGENCE ACTION

Three years ago today, Margaret Bone was struck by the defendant Ray Kelly's car as she was crossing Bell Street in a marked crosswalk. The car struck her on the left side, throwing her onto the pavement. She was taken to and examined at a nearby hospital and was released the same day. All X-rays were negative. Her emergency room bill was $1,800.

Miss Bone has testified to suffering continuous back and leg pain since the accident. She testified that the pain, which she described as periodic stabbing or shooting pain down her back and left leg, prevents her from doing activities such as house cleaning and gardening. She has difficulty sleeping and doing other everyday activities. However, Dr. Peter Greenberg, her treating physician, stated at trial that he could find no objective medical findings other than some bruises he noticed on her left leg during the three days following the accident, although he believed then and continues to believe now that her complaints of pain are genuine and were caused by the accident. He has not seen Bone for two and one-half years. He saw Bone in his office five times, and his bill for these services was $2,250.

Bone was not employed at the time of the accident, nor has she since sought employment. She is 63 years old and unmarried. She lives alone.

Six months before trial, Bone was examined by the defendant's specialist, Dr. Andrew Silver. He testified at trial that he also could find no objective medical findings for her complaints of pain and was unable to determine any basis for the complaints.

1. For the plaintiff, ask the jury for substantial money damages. Assume that the defendant is not contesting liability.
2. For the defendant, argue the issue of damages.
3. For the plaintiff, rebut the defendant's argument.

8.3 DAMAGES ARGUMENT IN PRODUCTS LIABILITY ACTION

This is a products liability case. Four years ago the plaintiff, Mark Venner, suffering from mild acne, began taking a drug manufactured by the defendant, Cursory Corporation. The drug, called Kleptocin, was prescribed by Venner's doctor. He did so after reading Cursory's literature that touted the drug for "infections" but said nothing about using it for minor viral or infection problems. The drug had received approval by the Food and Drug Administration (FDA) after testing showed it was effective in fighting severe infections.

The literature contained the following statement:

CAUTION: Reports of paralysis have been received from a small percentage of users after heavy and prolonged use of drug.

INDICATED USE: This drug has proved effective in cases of infection.

The doctor had not passed on the warning to Venner. Only the Cursory Company is being sued. It is the law of this jurisdiction that the manufacturer's duty to make and distribute a reasonably safe product cannot be delegated to another.

Venner claims that after taking the drug for three months he became paralyzed in both legs. Doctors have testified that he never will walk again. The plaintiff's expert witnesses have testified that Kleptocin was the proximate cause of the paralysis. They told the jury that the drug was useful in cases of severe infection, but that it never should have been used for something like mild acne. The plaintiff's theory of liability centers on the failure of Cursory to warn users that the drug should be used only in cases of severe infection.

The plaintiff also presented evidence to support his claim that Cursory engaged in the minimum testing possible under FDA guidelines and that the competing company, Klurg Pharmaceutical, was testing a new antibiotic at about the same time Kleptocin was being tested. The defense presented witnesses who said that Cursory acted reasonably and in accord with the state of scientific knowledge at the time of ingestion. Kleptocin was a new drug when Venner used it.

The plaintiff is now 20 years old, is single, has only a high school diploma, and is unable to find work.

Cursory is a Fortune 500 company traded on the New York Stock Exchange, with a net worth of $100 million.

1. For the plaintiff, tell the jury why it should award substantial compensatory and punitive damages to the plaintiff.

2. For the defendant, tell the jury why a verdict should not be brought against the company.

3. For the plaintiff, rebut the defendant's argument.

8.4 IDENTIFICATION ARGUMENT IN ROBBERY CASE

Six months ago today, at approximately 10:00 P.M., William Jones was robbed at knifepoint in an alley in the 600 block of Congress Street. The defendant, Frank Smith, has been charged with the robbery, and the case is now on trial.

Jones testified during the trial that he had been in a local tavern, the Blarney Stone, for about one hour just before the robbery occurred. He admitted to drinking "about two beers" while there. He was taking a shortcut to his parked car when the robbery occurred.

Jones testified that he was walking down the alley and was about 50 feet from Congress when a man suddenly came from nowhere and blocked his path, held a knife in his face, told him not to move, and with his other hand reached into Jones's pocket and removed his wallet. The man also took Jones's wristwatch, then ran down the alley away from Congress and disappeared.

Jones stated that the entire episode took about 30 seconds. There was a streetlight on Congress at the entrance to the alley but no lights in the alley itself. Jones described the robber to the police as a "white male, 18 to 25 years old, 5' 9" to 6' tall, medium build, wearing blue jeans and jacket, with no unusual characteristics." Jones described the knife as a "long hunting-style knife, with a blade about 6" long, sharpened on one edge only, with a bone handle."

The morning after the robbery Jones went to the police station, where a robbery detective asked him to look through a mug book to see if he could recognize anyone as the man who had robbed him the night before. The mug book contained about 200 photographs, each photograph being the face and shoulders of a different white male between the ages of 18 and 30 of varying heights and weights. After Jones had looked at about 50 photographs, he pointed to a photograph of Frank Smith, the defendant, and said, "that looks like him," but that he "wanted to see him in person to be sure."

One week later, following Smith's arrest, Jones was again asked to return to the station to view a lineup. When he arrived, the police had already placed five men, one of whom was the defendant, in a lineup. Each man in the lineup was a white male between 18 and 25 years old, between 5' 8" and 6' 2" tall, and weighing between 150 and 190 pounds. The detective asked Jones if he recognized anyone, and Jones stated that he recognized the defendant as the man who had robbed him the previous week. No photograph was taken of the lineup. None of the other men in the lineup was included in the photographs shown to Jones at the police station.

At trial, Smith testified on his own behalf. He denied committing the robbery. He stated that he was 19 years old, was 5' 9" tall, and weighed 150 pounds. He said his mug shot had been taken when he was arrested for possession of marijuana when he was 18 years old. He pleaded guilty to that charge and was placed on one year's probation.

1. For the prosecution, tell the jury why Jones's identification of Smith is credible and is sufficient to convict him of the robbery charge.
2. For the defense, argue the identification issue.
3. For the prosecution, rebut the defendant's argument.

8.5 IDENTIFICATION AND ALIBI ARGUMENT IN ROBBERY CASE

This is an armed robbery case. The defense is mistaken identification and alibi. The only identification witness, Rita Brown, saw a man who robbed her at gunpoint for about 60 seconds. She was held up six months ago at 2:00 P.M. on Sunday on the street in front of her home. The weather was dry and clear. She called police at once but was unable to identify anyone in the photos shown to her at the police station. She says she saw the robber again three weeks later, on a Monday at 8:00 A.M., waiting for a bus one block from the scene of the robbery. She called the police. They arrived minutes later and arrested the man, Marshall Jonas, at the bus stop. He lived one-half block from the bus stop at the time. No lineup was conducted.

Testifying at the trial, Jonas said that at the time of the crime he was at his cousin's house, eating chicken with his cousin, William Marshall, and his girlfriend, Shirley Gregory. Jonas called Marshall as an alibi witness at the trial but did not call Gregory. There is nothing in the record to indicate why she was not called.

Jonas also testified that he arrived at the bus stop each weekday morning at about 8:00 A.M. He worked at a Chicken King restaurant downtown. He said that he never saw Rita Brown before the day he was arrested. He has no criminal record.

1. For the prosecution, argue the reliability of the eyewitness identification.
2. For the defense, argue the weakness and defects of eyewitness identification.
3. For the prosecution, rebut the defendant's argument.

8.6   SELF-DEFENSE ARGUMENT IN MURDER CASE

This is a murder prosecution. The defense is self-defense. The defendant, Marsha Jones, and the victim, Elmer Jones, were married and living in a one-bedroom apartment in a two-flat building. Both were 30 years old, had been married for eight years, and had no children. Elmer Jones was employed as a guard in the county jail; Marsha Jones worked as a part-time secretary.

Testifying at trial, Marsha Jones stated that on the day of the shooting, six months ago today, she was in the living room of the apartment watching television when her husband came home about 11:00 P.M. He had been drinking and promptly got into an argument with her. He was yelling that the house was a mess and that as usual she hadn't done a thing about it. She stated that she tried to calm him down, but he just got worse, started threatening her, and then began punching her in the stomach. She tried to protect herself but couldn't. In desperation, she ran to the bedroom where she knew her husband kept his revolver that he used for work at the jail. She then returned to the living room and told her husband to leave her alone. She testified that her husband laughed, told her she wouldn't use the gun, and suddenly lunged at her. She then pulled the trigger of the gun twice. Her husband then fell down in the living room.

Immediately after the shooting she called the police. When the police arrived she told them what had happened. The police did not notice any bruises on her body.

Marsha Jones also testified that her husband often came home drunk and often threatened her and beat her. She said that her husband was about 6' 2" tall and weighed about 210 pounds. She is 5' 4" tall and weighs 120 pounds.

On cross-examination, the defendant admitted she had not told the police of the earlier threats and beatings and admitted she had never called the police about them or told anyone. She said Elmer had threatened to kill her if she told anyone. She said there was a telephone in the living room and bedroom, but she never called anyone.

Ballistics evidence showed that the victim was shot from over three feet away and that his body had two bullet-entry wounds. The first bullet entered his body in the chest at the left nipple and exited his back at the same level as the entry wound. The second bullet entered his body at the left rib cage just below the armpit and exited the body below the right armpit. The expert was unable to determine which shot had been fired first.

The autopsy report also disclosed that the victim's blood contained alcohol in an amount slightly in excess of the state's presumption-of-intoxication level.

1. For the prosecution, tell the jury why it should convict the defendant and not believe the defendant's testimony.
2. For the defense, argue why the killing was justifiable self-defense.
3. For the prosecution, rebut the defendant's argument.

IX

TRIALS

Introduction

General Jury Instructions

General Civil Jury Instructions

General Criminal Jury Instructions

Suggested Verdict Forms

9.14(A) Misdemeanor Battery and Assault of a Law Enforcement Officer: State v. Todd Wearl

9.14(B) Intentional Tort (Battery): George Otta v. Todd Wearl

9.14(C) 42 U.S.C. § 1983 Suit: Todd Wearl v. Dan Kinger

INTRODUCTION

Each of the trials on the Companion Website illustrates factual situations and issues commonly found in civil and criminal trials. Their lengths make them possible to be tried effectively in three or four hours. The civil cases [9.1 to 9.5, 9.12, and 9.14(B) and (C)] and criminal cases [9.6 to 9.10, 9.13, and 9.14(A)] are arranged in approximate order of increasing complexity. The 9.11 file can be tried as either a civil or a criminal case.

Your instructor will give you specific additional instructions and ground rules for each trial. However, you should prepare your case as though it were a real case with all the formalities and procedures of an actual trial. Backgrounds of witnesses have usually been intentionally limited or omitted entirely. Be prepared to develop realistic, credible backgrounds for them. Unless instructed otherwise, you should call each witness allocated to your side. If impeachment prove up becomes necessary, call a prove up witness or prepare an appropriate stipulation.

To keep this book from becoming overly large, the trial files themselves are included on the Companion Website, and this chapter contains only brief overviews. You should use the exhibits in the case files found on the Companion Website. You may also prepare additional appropriate exhibits, such as enlargements of diagrams or anatomical drawings, or obtain suitable objects shown in photographs, such as weapons or clothing.

Prepare elements instructions for the claims and defenses, definitions of any critical concepts and terms, and verdict forms. The general jury instructions that follow may also be used. Be prepared to present your proposed jury instructions to the court before trial.

Presenting your case persuasively requires both adequate preparation and the execution of effective techniques. This is where all the specific techniques you have practiced in the preceding chapters should come together so that your side of the issues can be effectively and persuasively presented to the jury.

The suggested background reading is Mauet, *Trial Techniques and Trials*, especially Chapters 1, 2, and 11.

(for use in civil and criminal trials)

[1] Members of the jury, the evidence and arguments in this case have been completed, and I now will instruct you as to the law.

[2] The law that applies to this case is stated in these instructions and it is your duty to follow all of them. You must not single out certain instructions and disregard others.

[3] It is your duty to determine the facts and to determine them only from the evidence in this case. You are to apply the law to the facts and in this way decide the case.

[4] Neither sympathy nor prejudice should influence you. [You should not be influenced by any person's race, color, religion, or national ancestry.]

[5] From time to time it has been the duty of the court to rule on the admissibility of evidence. You should not concern yourselves with the reasons for these rulings. You should disregard questions [and exhibits] that were withdrawn or to which objections were sustained.

[6] Any evidence that was received for a limited purpose should not be considered by you for any other purpose.

[7] You should disregard testimony [and exhibits] that the court has refused or stricken.

[8] The evidence that you should consider consists only of the testimony of the witnesses [and the exhibits] that the court has received.

[9] You are the sole judges of the believability of the witnesses and of the weight to be given to the testimony of each of them. In considering the testimony of any witness, you may take into account the witness's ability and opportunity to observe, [the witness's age,] the witness's memory, the witness's manner while testifying, any interest, bias, or prejudice the witness may have, and the reasonableness of the witness's testimony considered in the light of all the evidence in the case.

[10] You should consider all the evidence in the light of your own observations and experience in life.

[11] Opening statements are made by the attorneys to acquaint you with the facts they expect to prove. Closing arguments are made by the attorneys to discuss the facts and circumstances in the case and should be confined to the evidence and to reasonable inferences to be drawn from the evidence. Neither opening statements nor closing arguments are evidence. Any statement or argument made by the attorneys that is not based on the evidence should be disregarded.

[12] Faithful performance by you of your duties as jurors is vital to the administration of justice.

[13] When you retire to your jury room at the end of the trial, you will first select one of your number to act as your presiding juror to preside over your deliberations.

[14] You will then discuss the case with your fellow jurors. Each of you must decide the case for yourself, but you should do so only after you have considered all the evidence, discussed it fully with the other jurors, and listened to the views of your fellow jurors.

[15] Your verdict[s] must be agreed to by each juror. Although the verdict must be unanimous, the verdict should be signed by your presiding juror alone.

[1]   When a party has a burden of proof on any issue, that means you must be persuaded, considering all the evidence in the case, that the issue on which the party has the burden of proof is probably more true than not true.

[2]   [(One) (Both)] of the parties in this case [(is a corporation) (are corporations)]. A corporation must be considered in the same way you would consider an individual party in this case.

[1] The defendant[s] [(is) (are)] charged with the offense[s] of _____ [which include(s) the offense(s) of _____]. The defendant[s] [(has) (have)] pleaded not guilty.

[2] The [(information) (indictment) (complaint)] in this case is the formal method of accusing the defendant[s] of an offense and placing [(him) (her) (them)] on trial. It is not any evidence against the defendant[s] and does not create any inference of guilt.

[3] [(The) (Each)] defendant is presumed to be innocent of the charge[s] against (him) (or) (her). This presumption remains with (him) (or) (her) throughout every stage of the trial and during your deliberations on the verdict, and is not overcome unless from all the evidence in the case you are convinced beyond a reasonable doubt that the defendant is guilty. All of you must agree on the verdict [for each defendant].

[4] The State has the burden of proving the guilt of the defendant beyond a reasonable doubt, and this burden remains on the State throughout the case. The defendant is not required to prove (his) (or) (her) innocence.

[5] You should give separate consideration to each defendant. Each is entitled to have his case decided on the evidence and the law that applies to (him) (or) (her).

[Any evidence that was limited to (one defendant) (some defendants) should not be considered by you as to (any) (the) other defendant(s).]

[6] The fact that [(a) (the)] defendant[s] did not testify must not be considered by you in any way in arriving at your verdict.

761

[7]   You are not to concern yourself with possible punishment or sentence for the offense charged during your deliberation. It is the function of the trial judge to determine the sentence should there be a verdict of guilty.

Suggested Verdict Forms

(Edit to suit the circumstances of each case and the law in your jurisdiction.)

[Caption]

Verdict

We, the jury in the above case, find in favor of _____
                                                          (party)

and against _____.
                        (party)

We find that plaintiff was damaged in the amount of _____ dollars.
                                                            (dollar amount)

We find _____ _____% responsible, and _____
              (party)   (percentage)   (party)

_____% responsible, for plaintiffs damages.
(percentage)

_____
                  Presiding Juror

[Caption]

Verdict

We, the jury in the above case, find defendant _____
                                                        (name of defendant)

_____ of the charge of _____.
(guilty or not guilty)   (crime charged)

_____
                  Presiding Juror

9.1 FALSE ARREST, MALICIOUS PROSECUTION, AND DEFAMATION

KAREN ADAMS

v.

CHANDLER DEPARTMENT STORE

Introduction

The Chandler Department Store is a large department store in a shopping mall in this city. It is a corporation and its only place of business is the mall store.

Karen Adams is a doctor specializing in pediatrics. She is single and lives and has her medical office in this city.

On November 1, [-2], Dr. Adams was shopping in the cosmetics department on the first floor of the Chandler Department Store. A sales clerk saw Dr. Adams put a container of Paris spray cologne in her purse and walk away from the counter. The clerk signaled a store detective, an off-duty police officer, who was standing nearby.

The detective stopped Dr. Adams by a store exit and told her she had not paid for an item from the cosmetics department. Dr. Adams denied it. The detective then escorted Dr. Adams to the store security counter, where her purse was searched, revealing the Paris spray cologne container. Dr. Adams claimed that the cologne was hers.

The store manager was called, and s/he talked to Dr. Adams in the security office. The manager then called the police. Dr. Adams was arrested and taken to the police station, where she was processed and released the next day.

Three weeks later the criminal charges against Dr. Adams were dropped by the local prosecutor's office. An account of Dr. Adams's arrest, and the later dismissal of the charges, were reported in the local newspaper.

Dr. Adams then brought this lawsuit.

Plaintiff Adams sues defendant Chandler Department Store on three theories:

1. False arrest. Plaintiff claims that the Chandler Department Store caused her to be falsely arrested because there was no reasonable basis for the arrest.

2. Malicious prosecution. Plaintiff claims that Chandler Department Store's insistence that she be arrested for shoplifting was malicious and was done because plaintiff refused to sign a waiver of liability.

3. Defamation. Plaintiff claims that she was defamed when the store's security guard called her a "shoplifter" in front of other store customers.

Plaintiff seeks all damages allowable under applicable law, including punitive damages for willful and wanton misconduct.

Defendant denies each of plaintiff's allegations. Defendant also asserts as a defense this jurisdiction's shoplifter detention statute, stating that its detention of Dr. Adams was proper under the law.

Witnesses

Plaintiff may call the following witnesses:

1. Dr. Karen Adams
2. Bailey Williams
3. Dr. Jesse Lee

Defendant may call the following witnesses:

1. Kelly Jackson
2. Kaden Flannigan
3. Pat Curran

If impeachment prove up becomes necessary, the parties must prepare an appropriate stipulation to admit the prove up evidence.

Exhibits and Materials

The following may be available:

1. *Daily Gazette* articles dated 11/2/[-2] and 11/22/[-2]
2. Misdemeanor complaint and summons
3. City Police Department general incident report dated 11/1/[-2]
4. City Police Department general incident report dated 11/2/[-2]
5. City Police Department general incident report dated 11/20/[-2]
6. Chandler Department Store shoplifting incident report
7. Sample sticker
8. Photograph of Paris spray cologne bottle prepared by plaintiff for use as a demonstrative exhibit at trial
9. Drug prescription from Dr. Lee
10. Dr. Lee's patient notes
11. Diagram of cologne counter

A statute in this jurisdiction provides as follows:

> Any retail establishment that has reasonable grounds to believe that any person has taken any item of merchandise without paying for that merchandise may detain the person for a reasonable period of time, under reasonable circumstances, to determine whether such merchandise has in fact been taken without being paid for.

The parties must stipulate to the following:

1. The city police department reports are, under FRE 803(8), certified public records.

2. The misdemeanor complaint and summons are, under FRE 803(8), certified public records.

3. The two newspaper clippings from the *Daily Gazette* on 11/2/[-2] and 11/22/[-2] are actual clippings from the newspaper on those dates.

9.2 CONTRACT

<h3 style="text-align:center">WHITNEY THOMPSON</h3>
V.
<h3 style="text-align:center">THERMORAD CORPORATION</h3>

Introduction

This case involves the adequacy of an electric baseboard heating system that was installed in plaintiff's apartments. Two years ago plaintiff Whitney Thompson was building a 50-unit apartment complex. S/he advertised for bids and contracted with defendant, Thermorad Corporation, the low bidder, to install an adequate baseboard heating system. Thermorad selected and installed its Model I system in the apartments.

The Model I failed to heat the apartments adequately when the weather turned cold. Thompson claims that Thermorad did not select an adequate system for the apartments. Thermorad claims that the problem was caused by Thompson's insulating the apartments with only 6 inches of fiberglass insulation in the ceilings, instead of 12 inches, the industry standard.

When the parties could not agree on a solution, Thompson contracted with another heating contractor, Peerless Heating, to remove the Thermorad Model I system and replace it with a Peerless system.

Pleadings

Plaintiff's suit raises two theories. First, plaintiff sues defendant for breach of contract. S/he seeks to recover the $100,000 s/he paid Thermorad, the $25,000 that represents the difference between Thermorad's price and the amount later paid Peerless, and for lost rental income.

Second, plaintiff sues defendant for misrepresentation. Plaintiff claims that defendant misrepresented the ability of the Model I system to heat the apartment units adequately, and that this was done to induce plaintiff to enter into a contract with the defendant. S/he seeks consequential and punitive damages.

Defendant claims it performed its part of the contract and owes plaintiff nothing. Defendant says plaintiff's defectively insulated building was the reason for the heating problem, and that plaintiff misrepresented the amount of insulation s/he would install in the apartment units. Defendant also claims that plaintiff failed to mitigate damages.

The case is being tried in your state and your jurisdiction's contract and tort law applies.

Witnesses

Plaintiff may call the following witnesses:

1. Whitney Thompson
2. Sandy Hatch
3. Cory Turner

Defendant may call the following witnesses:

1. Emery Jacobs
2. Jaime Woods

If impeachment prove up becomes necessary, call a prove up witness or prepare an appropriate stipulation.

Exhibits and Materials

The following may be available:

1. Excerpts from depositions of:
   (a) Whitney Thompson
   (b) Emery Jacobs
   (c) Jaime Woods

    (d)   Sandy Hatch

    (e)   Cory Turner

2. Thermorad memo dated March 15, [-2]

3. Whitney Thompson letter to John Smith

4. Advertisement for bids

5. Thermorad Model I brochure

6. Thermorad's letter response to advertisement

7. Contract

8. Other correspondence and memos of Thompson and Thermorad

9. Canceled checks to Thermorad and Peerless

10. Photograph of Thermorad Model I system

11. Blueprints of apartment unit

Assume that the trial judge will allow admission of all relevant evidence to determine the intent of the parties and the meaning of the contract. Both parties must stipulate that:

1. The apartment blueprints called for six inches of fiberglass insulation in the ceiling of each apartment.

2. The construction industry insulation standard for this area is R-19 in the walls and R-38 in the ceilings, which is six inches of fiberglass insulation in the walls, twelve inches in the ceilings.

3. There is no applicable building code requirement for any insulation in buildings.

9.3 NEGLIGENCE (CONTRIBUTION CLAIM)

JORDAN MINOR CONSTRUCTION COMPANY

v.

MID-AMERICAN CONCRETE COMPANY

Introduction

This is a contribution action. The plaintiff, Jordan Minor Construction Company, paid a sum of money to settle a negligence claim against it filed by Antonio Giovanni. Minor Construction now claims it is entitled to contribution from Mid-American Concrete Company for a percentage of the amount of money paid. The jury will be called on to determine the relative percentage of fault among Minor Construction, Mid-American, and a nonparty, Accurate Steel Company.

This case involves an 1,800-pound steel staircase that was installed between the first and second floors of the Madonna High School, part of a $40 million construction project. On June 19, [-2], the staircase fell through the floor and crashed into the basement. Antonio Giovanni, a cement finisher (employed by Steiger Construction Company, which is not a party) who was working in the basement, was pinned under the staircase and lost his arm as a result of this accident.

There are three contracts involved in this case. The first is between Madonna High School and Jordan Minor Construction Company, the general contractor on the project. The second is between Minor Construction and Mid-American Concrete Company, the manufacturer and installer of concrete flooring known as Flexistan. The third is between Minor Construction and Accurate Steel Company, the manufacturer and installer of the steel staircase. Each company is incorporated under the laws of this state.

Flexistan is a trade name for structural concrete floor blocks. Mid-American, for this project, decided to manufacture the blocks with each block having three hollow cores filled with foam. When the blocks were manufactured, the process was done in such a way that it resulted in concrete covering the outsides of the hollow cores so that the Flexistan blocks appeared to be solid. Mid-American delivered and installed the Flexistan in the staircase area of the first floor of the Madonna High School during the morning of June 16, [-2].

773

Accurate Steel delivered the steel staircase in the early afternoon of June 16, [-2]. However, contrary to plans, Accurate Steel did not manufacture or deliver a steel channel on which the bottom of the staircase was to rest. The channel is designated to distribute the weight of the staircase on the floor. The staircase was then installed with the bottom resting directly on the middle of a Flexistan block.

Three days later, on June 19, [-2], the Flexistan block on which the staircase was resting suddenly shattered, causing the staircase to fall into the basement where Giovanni was working.

Pleadings

Antonio Giovanni sued Jordan Minor Construction Company but not Mid-American Concrete Company or Accurate Steel Company. Shortly after the staircase collapse, Accurate Steel declared bankruptcy. It is without assets or insurance. Minor Construction then filed a third-party claim for contribution against Mid-American. While the case was in the discovery phase, Minor Construction settled its case with Giovanni for $1.5 million. That left Minor Construction as the plaintiff against Mid-American in the contribution action. As plaintiff, Minor Construction has the burden of proof.

Minor Construction contends Mid-American was at fault and negligently created a dangerous condition because: (1) Mid-American did not tell anyone that it was installing Flexistan blocks with hollow cores, and (2) the Flexistan blocks that Mid-American delivered to the job site contained no warnings or notice that they were hollow core.

Mid-American denied Minor Construction's allegations and denied it was negligent in any way. Further, Mid-American claims the injury to Giovanni was caused by the negligence of Minor Construction and/or the negligence of Accurate Steel.

Applicable Law (Jury Instructions) and Pretrial Rulings

It is the law of this jurisdiction that a party who has paid a sum of money for causing an injury to another may be entitled to recover a percentage of that sum from a third party. In this case, Minor Construction has paid a sum of money to Antonio Giovanni in settlement of his claims for his injuries and damages. Minor Construction

774

now claims it is entitled to contribution from Mid-American Concrete Company for a percentage of that sum paid.

To apportion damages, the jury must determine from all the evidence the relative degrees of fault of Minor Construction, Mid-American, and Accurate Steel. To make that determination, the jury should consider the duty owed by each company to Antonio Giovanni, the extent to which the conduct of each company deviated from the duty owed to Antonio Giovanni, and the extent to which the negligent conduct of each company proximately caused Antonio Giovanni's injuries and damages.

In pretrial rulings, the trial court has held:

1. The negligence, if any, of Antonio Giovanni is not relevant to this case;

2. The jury is not to be told that Accurate Steel went into bankruptcy and is without assets;

3. The jury is not to be told the dollar amount of Minor Construction's settlement with Antonio Giovanni; and

4. Antonio Giovanni is unavailable as a witness, for purposes of Rule 32 of the Rules of Civil Procedure, and all parties to this case had reasonable notice of the deposition of Giovanni (though Mid-American did not participate). Thus, the court has ruled that either or both parties to this case may present Giovanni's testimony via the reading of his deposition transcript. As with other testimony, the court will consider objections, other than Rule 32 objections and objections that are waived by virtue of not being raised at the deposition, to this testimony.

The verdict form to be given to the jury is to read as follows:

We, the jury, apportion responsibility as follows:

Minor Construction Company	_____%
Mid-American Concrete Company	_____%
Accurate Steel Company	_____%
TOTAL	0% or 100%

If you find that any of these companies was not at fault in a way that proximately caused Antonio Giovanni's personal injuries, then you should enter zero percent as to that company. The percentages you find must total 0% or 100%.

Witnesses

Minor may call the following witnesses:

1. Antonio Giovanni (by deposition)
2. Jordan Minor
3. Terry Henderson

Mid-American may call the following witnesses:

1. Harper Stark
2. Archie Tubbs

Exhibits and Materials

The following may be available:

1. Deposition of Giovanni
2. Deposition of Minor
3. Deposition of Stark
4. Deposition of Tubbs
5. Deposition of Henderson
6. Contracts
7. Memorandum of Mid-American
8. Memorandum of Accurate Steel
9. Photograph of steel channel
10. Diagram of Flexistan blocks
11. Diagram of steel staircase

9.4 PRODUCTS LIABILITY AND WRONGFUL DEATH

SHIRLEY HARTE,
Administrator of the Estate of Marion Harte, Deceased
v.
ACME MANUFACTURING CO.

Introduction

This is a wrongful death and survival action arising from a fire in Marion Harte's apartment on July 31, [-2]. The fire started when Marion Harte used a mechanical cigarette lighter, the Acme "Magic Lite." The lighter was a gift from Marion Harte's son/daughter, Shirley, who had bought it just that day at the Flint Hardware Company.

When Marion Harte attempted to light her cigarette, the lighter exploded, enveloping her in flames, causing extensive burns on her face, chest, and arms. She was taken to a hospital by paramedics, but died about one hour after the accident.

The plaintiff is Shirley Harte. S/he brings this product liability action against Acme Manufacturing Company, the maker of the Magic Lite. S/he seeks money damages for the wrongful death of his/her mother and for his/her mother's pain and suffering during the one hour she lived after the accident.

Pleadings

Plaintiff claims the Magic Lite manufactured by Acme was unreasonably dangerous because: (1) it was defectively designed; (2) warnings on the lighter were inadequate; and (3) there were no warnings or instructions in the box containing the lighter. Plaintiff proceeds solely on a strict liability theory.

Plaintiff seeks damages under the wrongful death claim for the primary loss that resulted from Marion Harte's death, which may include the loss of money, goods, services, and society. S/he seeks damages under the survival claim for any conscious pain and suffering Marion Harte experienced between the time of her injuries and her death and any medical and funeral expenses incurred as a result of her injuries and death.

Acme Manufacturing Company admits designing and manufacturing the lighter, but contends its design was not defective and that the warnings on the lighter and in the box were adequate. Acme further asserts the affirmative defenses of assumption of the risk, contributory negligence, product misuse, and other "fault" or other theories that are viable under the facts and the applicable law. In essence, the defendant contends that the fire was caused by Marion Harte's failure to follow the instructions on the lighter and in the box.

Flint Hardware Company had been named as a defendant in the original lawsuit. The plaintiff contended that Flint knew or should have known the lighter was being sold without the insert warnings in the box. The claim against Flint was settled 60 days ago. Plaintiff and Flint entered into a covenant not to sue. Under the covenant, plaintiff agreed to dismiss Flint as a defendant, and Flint agreed to pay plaintiff $25,000 and agreed that its store manager, Cassidy White, would be available to testify at trial and that his/her testimony would be consistent with his/her deposition.

The case is being tried in your state and your jurisdiction's tort law applies.

Witnesses

Plaintiff may call the following witnesses:

1. Shirley Harte
2. Fran Wilson
3. Dale Berg

Defendant may call the following witnesses:

1. Cassidy White
2. Rowan Mercer
3. Meredith Swan

If impeachment prove up becomes necessary, the parties must prepare an appropriate stipulation to admit the prove up evidence.

778

Exhibits and Materials

The following may be available:

1. City Fire Department paramedic report
2. Mercy Memorial Hospital autopsy report
3. Flint Hardware receipt
4. Two photographs of Magic Lite
5. Diagram of Magic Lite
6. Magic Lite instructions
7. Two letters to Acme Manufacturing Co.
8. Letter from Rowan Mercer to Cassidy White
9. Letter from Consumer Products Laboratory to Mercer
10. Resume of Meredith Swan
11. Memorandum to Plaintiff's Lawyer
12. Excerpts of depositions of
    (a) Shirley Harte
    (b) Fran Wilson
    (c) Cassidy White
    (d) Rowan Mercer
    (e) Meredith Swan

The parties must stipulate to the following:

1. The present life expectancy for a woman 51 years old is 30.3 years.
2. The City Fire Department Paramedic Report is a certified public record, under FRE 803(8).
3. The autopsy report from the Mercy Memorial Hospital is a business record of the hospital, under FRE 803(6).

9.5 GENDER DISCRIMINATION, WRONGFUL TERMINATION, AND DEFAMATION

SHARON DONALDSON

v.

EMPIRE CAR RENTAL COMPANY

Introduction

Empire Car Rental Company is a small car rental company that began in [-7]. It is located only in this city and presently has two offices; the downtown office, opened in [-6], and the airport office, opened in [-4].

Sharon Donaldson is a lifelong resident of this city. She graduated from the local state university in [-6] and began working for Empire, which had recently opened the downtown office. She worked as a rental agent after completing her training period.

When Empire opened the airport office in [-4], it hired Lou Smith as its manager. Donaldson was transferred to the airport office and promoted to assistant manager. A few months later Smith decided to leave Empire, and Donaldson was promoted to manager of the airport office.

In [-3] Empire created a new management position, the city manager, who would be in charge of both offices and any future ones in this city. Richard Jackson was hired as the new city manager.

Jackson and Donaldson did not work well together. The friction between the two came to a head in September [-2] when Jackson called Donaldson into his office and fired her, effective immediately. Jackson gave as his reason that Donaldson had violated company policy by authorizing the rental of a car with unlimited mileage to a personal friend.

Donaldson was out of work for approximately one year. She contacted an employment agency, Career Placements, to find her a new job. Donaldson finally received and accepted a job offer with another company, Equipment Leasing. Her salary at that job is substantially lower than her salary at Empire.

In November [-2], Donaldson filed a discrimination claim with the Equal Employment Opportunity Commission (EEOC). The EEOC investigated the claim, determined that Title VII had been violated, and issued a right to sue letter. Donaldson then brought this lawsuit.

Pleadings

Plaintiff Donaldson sues defendant Empire Car Rental Company on three theories:

1. Title VII employment discrimination. Plaintiff claims that she was subjected to disparate treatment by Empire. To prove a claim of disparate treatment under Title VII, plaintiff must prove that her gender played a motivating part in a particular employment decision. If plaintiff proves this by a preponderance of the evidence, the burden of presenting evidence shifts to the defendant, who may avoid liability only by providing a nondiscriminatory reason for the plaintiff's treatment. Plaintiff then has the burden of proving the employer's reason is pretextual.

2. Breach of contract. Plaintiff claims that the personnel manual issued by Empire was part of her employment contract and that Empire breached it by firing her without taking the procedural steps required by the manual.

3. Defamation. Plaintiff claims that Richard Jackson, Empire's city manager, defamed her when he called her "dishonest" in a letter to Career Placements.

Plaintiff seeks all damages allowed under applicable law, including lost wages and commissions, lost future income, and punitive damages.

Empire denies each of plaintiff's allegations. Empire says that the personnel manual's procedures permitted Donaldson's firing. Empire also asserts an affirmative defense to the defamation claim, stating that Jackson had a qualified privilege to repeat his evaluation of Donaldson to her employment agency and prospective future employers.

The case is being tried in the local U.S. District Court. No jurisdictional issues have been raised.

Witnesses

Plaintiff may call the following witnesses:

1. Sharon Donaldson
2. Dana Ripley
3. Sandy Hoffman

Defendant may call the following witnesses:

1. Richard Jackson
2. Chris Steele
3. John Kinney

If impeachment prove up becomes necessary, the parties must prepare an appropriate stipulation to admit the prove up evidence.

Exhibits and Materials

The following may be available:

1. EEOC investigative file, which includes:
   (a) Interviews of witnesses
   (b) Empire's records
   (c) Empire's personnel manual
   (d) EEOC right to sue and determination letters
   (e) Career Placements' records
   (f) Jackson's letter to Hoffman
2. Excerpts of depositions of:
   (a) Sharon Donaldson

(b) Richard Jackson

(c) John Kinney

(d) Dana Ripley

(e) Chris Steele

(f) Sandy Hoffman

Stipulations

The parties must stipulate to the following:

1. The EEOC witness interviews, right to sue letter, determination letter, and any other EEOC records are all certified public records, under FRE 803(8), of the EEOC.

2. The court has previously ruled as a matter of law that the Personnel Manual is a binding contract between the parties.

9.6 MURDER

STATE

v.

MERLE RAUSCH

Introduction

This case involves a shooting that occurred on June 15, [-1], on the 3300 block of North Clark Street.

The defendant, Merle Rausch, and the victim, William Jones, were in the Red Apple tavern that evening. Around 11:00 P.M. they got into an argument, which was broken up. Rausch then left the tavern, followed by Jones. The shooting occurred on the street a short while later.

Pleadings

The State has filed murder charges against Rausch. He has entered a plea of not guilty and served notice on the State of his intended defense of self-defense. The case is being tried in your state and your jurisdiction's criminal law applies, including the law on lesser-included offenses.

Witnesses

Prosecution may call the following witnesses:

1. Nicky Felton
2. Freddy Martin
3. Officer Taylor Connor
4. Dr. Sidney Burns

Defense may call the following witnesses:

1. Merle Rausch
2. Finley Williams

If impeachment prove up becomes necessary, the parties must prepare an appropriate stipulation to admit the prove up evidence.

Exhibits and Materials

The following may be available:

1. Police report
2. Preliminary hearing transcript
3. Report of interview
4. Pathologist's report
5. Diagram
6. Photo of street and sidewalk
7. Gun
8. Box containing five cartridges and one empty casing
9. Photo of five cartridges and one empty casing

Both sides must agree to the authenticity of John French's Report of Interview with Finley Williams.

9.7　MURDER AND ATTEMPTED ARMED ROBBERY

STATE

v.

JOHN HUDSON

Introduction

 This case involves an attempted robbery and shooting that occurred in Lazar's Clothing Store on February 14, [-1]. The store was owned and managed by Sidney and Sara Lazar. Mrs. Lazar was shot and killed during the attempted robbery. Two men were involved in the crime.

 After the shooting, police arrived and interviewed Mr. Lazar and a bystander, Ryan Green. That afternoon, Mr. Lazar looked through a stack of photographs and tentatively identified photographs of John Hudson and Dale Buckner as photos of the two men who had killed his wife.

 That night, after checking the two suspects' arrest records and obtaining an arrest warrant for Hudson and Buckner, the police went to their apartment and arrested them. The police also found certain physical evidence in the apartment. Outside they saw a car matching the description of the getaway car.

 The police then called Mr. Lazar and the bystander, Green. At the police station, both Lazar and Green participated in several identification procedures.

 The police records show that Hudson was convicted of aggravated assault seven years ago and was sentenced to two years in the penitentiary.

 A ballistics expert at the police crime lab examined a gun found in the apartment and concluded that it had been recently cleaned. Because of this, he was unable to determine whether it had been recently fired. The ballistics expert also examined the bullet that was removed from Sara Lazar's body. The expert concluded the bullet was a .38 caliber bullet, but because it was too damaged he could not determine if it was fired from the gun.

 A pathologist who performed the autopsy on Sara Lazar's body determined that death was caused by a single gunshot wound to her head, which entered her brain.

A custodian of the records of the state motor vehicle department looked through the records and found that a [-8] black Cadillac sedan was registered to John Hudson on February 14, [-1].

Pleadings

Hudson and Buckner were formally charged with murder and attempted armed robbery. Both entered pleas of not guilty. They were held in custody without bond. Buckner was stabbed to death in a jail fight three weeks before trial. Hudson is being tried. The case is being tried in your state, so your jurisdiction's criminal law applies. The trial court has denied all motions to suppress evidence based on constitutional grounds.

Witnesses

Prosecution may call the following witnesses:

1. Sidney Lazar
2. Ryan Green
3. Investigator Sam Reilly

Defense may call the following witnesses:

1. John Hudson
2. Whitney Barr

If impeachment prove up becomes necessary, the parties must prepare an appropriate stipulation to admit the prove up evidence. Prosecution and defense must agree to stipulations for the following:

1. Pathologist, as to the cause of Mrs. Lazar's death
2. Ballistics expert, as to the examination of the gun and bullet

3. Custodian of records, as to the vehicle registration for Hudson's car

4. The distance between Lazar's Clothing Store and Sam's Chicken Shack is five miles, and the normal driving time between them in mid-afternoon is approximately 15 minutes

5. The defendant's prior conviction (if admissible for impeachment and not admitted by the defendant)

6. Barr's time card is a business record of Lester's Auto Repair

Exhibits and Materials

The following might be available:

1. Police report

2. Transcript of preliminary hearing

3. Albert LaRue memorandum

4. Whitney Barr statement

5. Whitney Barr time card

6. Gun

7. Box for bullet

8. Bullet

9. Black leather jacket

9.8 AGGRAVATED SEXUAL ASSAULT

STATE
v.
MICHAEL MILLER

Introduction

This case involves an alleged aggravated sexual assault that occurred during the night of January 8, [-1]. The victim, Shirley Thompson, claims that the defendant, Michael Miller, abducted her at knifepoint in an alley while she was walking home from work and raped her twice. The defendant admits that he had sexual intercourse with Mrs. Thompson, but claims that it was with her consent.

Pleadings

The State has filed aggravated sexual assault charges against Miller. He has entered a plea of not guilty and served notice on the State of his intended consent defense. The case is being tried in your state and your jurisdiction's criminal law applies.

Witnesses

Prosecution may call the following witnesses:

1. Shirley Thompson
2. Ralph Thompson
3. Detective Rich
4. Dr. Reyes Perez

Defense may call the following witnesses:

1. Michael Miller
2. Sam Collins

If impeachment prove up becomes necessary, the parties must prepare an appropriate stipulation to admit the prove up evidence.

Exhibits and Materials

The following may be available:

1. Rich's report
2. Miller's statement
3. Collins's statement
4. Map
5. Dr. Perez's report
6. Grand jury transcript
7. Photographs

Both parties must agree on the following written stipulations:

1. Dr. Perez's report is a business record of the Williams Memorial Hospital, in accordance with FRE 803(6).
2. The two vehicle photographs attached to this case file are of the defendant's car and accurately show how the car looked on January 8 and 9, [-1].
3. The gas station photograph attached to this case file is of Eddie's Service Station. It accurately shows how the station looked on January 8 and 9, [-1].

9.9 MURDER

STATE

v.

FRANK FLETCHER and ARTHUR MORRIS

Introduction

This case involves a killing of a police officer on July 2, [-1]. Officer William Kane was shot while he was sitting in his parked squad car. A witness, Shelby Green, reported what s/he had seen to the police.

Two weeks later Richard Edwards was arrested for a burglary. Green identified Edwards as one of the three men who were involved in the Officer Kane shooting. At first Edwards denied being involved in the shooting, but he later changed his story following an agreement with the prosecutors. He then implicated defendants Fletcher and Morris as the other persons who committed the shooting. On July 26, the police arrested defendants Fletcher and Morris at their apartment.

Police records show that Fletcher had been convicted of armed robbery, receiving a two-year sentence, six years ago. Morris had been convicted of burglary two years ago and received one year of probation.

Edwards has been charged with the burglary, for which he was arrested, but that charge is still pending at the time of the trial in this cause. He has not been charged with the killing of Officer Kane. Police records show Edwards was convicted of burglary six years ago and served a sentence of one year in the state penitentiary.

The autopsy report from the county medical examiner's office disclosed that Officer William Kane was killed by a gunshot that entered his head at the right temple and exited his head at the left temple, lacerating the brain. The autopsy was performed on July 3, [-1], by Dr. David Dodd, a county medical examiner's pathologist. No pellet was recovered from the body.

Pleadings

The state has filed murder charges against Fletcher and Morris. Both have entered pleas of not guilty. The case is being tried in your state and your jurisdiction's criminal law applies.

Witnesses

The State may call the following witnesses:

1. Richard Edwards
2. Shelby Green
3. Investigator Quinn Kelly
4. Sergeant Lee Williams

The defense may call the following witnesses:

1. Frank Fletcher
2. Arthur Morris
3. Madison Sampson

If impeachment prove up becomes necessary, the parties must prepare an appropriate stipulation to admit the prove up evidence.

Exhibits and Materials

The following may be available:

1. Edwards's statement to Kelly
2. Edwards's grand jury testimony
3. Kelly's arrest report
4. Preliminary hearing transcript
5. Sampson's statement to Daniels
6. Ballistics report

7. Fingerprint report

8. "Off the Heat" sign

9. Photograph of the squad car

10. Diagram of intersection

11. Box of .38 caliber shells (photographs)

Both sides must agree on written stipulations for the following:

1. Cause of Officer Kane's death

2. Prior convictions of Fletcher, Morris, and Edwards (if admissible to impeach and not admitted during examination)

3. The box of .38 caliber shells in this file is the box of shells Investigator Kelly says s/he found in Morris's dresser.

4. The photograph of a police squad car in this file is a photograph of Officer Kane's car, taken by a police photographer on the day of the shooting.

5. Edwards has been in police custody since his arrest on July 16.

6. Fletcher and Morris have been in custody since their arrest on July 26.

7. The ballistics report qualifies as a Rule 803(8) public record.

8. Admissibility of the fingerprints report

Fletcher and Morris have filed a Notice of Alibi in which they state they were at their apartment watching a videotape of *Jurassic Park* at the time of the killing. No one else was present in the apartment at that time.

The trial court has denied the defendant's motions to suppress their statements and the items found in their apartment.

9.10 BRIBERY

STATE
v.
AVERY WENTWORTH and CHRIS BENSON

Introduction

This case involves an alleged bribery of two police officers following their arrest of Reed Foster for possession of heroin.

Reed Foster was stopped by the defendants, Officers Avery Wentworth and Chris Benson, on January 10, [-1], for running a red light. A subsequent search uncovered heroin. Foster was taken to the station. S/he called his/her lawyer, Taylor Johnson, who came to the station and met with one of the arresting officers.

Two days later Johnson presented a motion to suppress on Reed Foster's behalf. Officer Benson testified at the hearing. The motion was granted and the heroin charges were dismissed.

On January 23, Reed Foster went to the district attorney's office and complained that his/her lawyer, Taylor Johnson, and the two police officers, Wentworth and Benson, had shaken him/her down for money.

Taylor Johnson was called before the grand jury and initially denied Foster's charges. Following discussions with the district attorney and after receiving a grant of immunity, Johnson appeared a second time before the grand jury and changed his/her story.

On February 6, the defendants' lockers at the station were searched. At this time the defendants made statements and physical evidence was found.

Police records indicate that Reed Foster pled guilty on January 5, [-7], to burglary and was sentenced to one year in the penitentiary. On February 1 of last year, Foster was arrested on a burglary charge. That charge is still pending at the time of this trial.

The State has obtained a deposit slip from the First State Bank. It shows that Avery Wentworth deposited $400 in cash in his/her savings account on January 13 of last year.

Pleadings

Benson and Wentworth are charged with bribery. Both have entered pleas of not guilty. The case is being tried in your state and your jurisdiction's criminal law applies.

Witnesses

Prosecution may call the following witnesses:

1. Taylor Johnson
2. Reed Foster
3. Morgan Goodman

Defense may call the following witnesses:

1. Chris Benson
2. Avery Wentworth
3. Bobby Hall

If impeachment prove up becomes necessary, the parties must prepare an appropriate stipulation to admit the prove up evidence.

Exhibits and Materials

The following may be available:

1. Police report of January 10, [-1]
2. Transcript of January 12, [-1]
3. Statement of Reed Foster
4. Grand jury testimony of Taylor Johnson on January 28, [-1]
5. Immunity order
6. Grand jury testimony of Taylor Johnson on February 4, [-1]
7. Memo of Morgan Goodman

8. Interview of Bobby Hall

9. Deposit slip

10. Three $100 bills

All parties must agree on written stipulations for the following:

1. Business records foundation for the deposit slip.

2. Prior convictions of Reed Foster (if admissible to impeach and not admitted during examination).

3. Investigator Tom Johnson's report, which is an authentic and complete copy of the original, had to be disclosed by the defense to the prosecution under the applicable discovery rules.

4. There have been no disciplinary proceedings initiated by the state bar against Taylor Johnson as of this date.

9.11 CRIMINAL MAIL FRAUD OR CIVIL FRAUD

UNITED STATES OF AMERICA or ROCK INSURANCE CO.
v.
CHRIS MANNING

Introduction

This case can be used as a criminal mail fraud prosecution or as a civil fraud case with compensatory and punitive damages.

Chris Manning, a lawyer, is charged with defrauding the Rock Insurance Company by being part of a fraudulent scheme in which a car accident was staged and a false claim was submitted to Rock Insurance.

The government/plaintiff alleges that Manning organized the scheme with another person, Lynn Stone, and that Stone recruited a driver who was instructed in how to stage a rear-end collision, then claim s/he received neck and back injuries, and then go to Manning to file a claim against the other driver's insurance company. Manning would collect a contingency fee from the settlement amount and would give Stone 20 percent of his/her contingency fee as a finder's fee.

Manning denies s/he paid Stone a finder's fee and says that s/he believed each case s/he filed was a legitimate case in which his/her client had been injured and that s/he obtained a reasonable, good-faith settlement for his/her client.

Pleadings

The United States has obtained an indictment of the defendant, charging him/her with one count of mail fraud under Title 18, § 1341. The indictment alleges that Manning devised a scheme to obtain money from the Rock Insurance Company by means of false and fraudulent representations (that a legitimate accident had occurred, and that Manning's client had actually been injured and incurred substantial expenses), and that Manning knowingly used the U.S. mail system for the purpose of executing the scheme. The case is in the local U.S. District Court.

Rock Insurance Company has filed a civil fraudulent misrepresentations complaint against Manning. The complaint alleges that Manning made a claim to the Rock Insurance Company that contained intentional and material misrepresentations of facts (that a legitimate accident had occurred and that Manning's client had actually been injured and incurred substantial expenses), that Manning knew they were false when made, that Manning intended to induce the Rock Insurance Company to pay on the claim, that plaintiff reasonably relied on Manning's misrepresentations, and that plaintiff was consequently damaged. Rock Insurance Company seeks all damages allowed under applicable law, including punitive damages. Jurisdiction is based on diversity of citizenship, since Rock Insurance is an out-of-state company and Manning is a citizen of this state. The case is in the local U.S. District Court.

Defendant in the criminal case has entered a plea of not guilty. Defendant in the civil case denies the plaintiff's allegations.

When trying the criminal case, assume the civil case has been stayed until the criminal case is concluded. When trying the civil case, assume the criminal case was dismissed and never tried. All materials in this case file are available in both the criminal and civil cases.

Witnesses

Plaintiff may call the following witnesses:

1. Randy Carlson
2. Lynn Stone
3. Sandy Adams

Defendant may call the following witnesses:

1. Chris Manning
2. Sean Brent

If impeachment prove up becomes necessary, the parties must prepare an appropriate stipulation to admit the prove up evidence.

Exhibits and Materials

The following may be available:

1. City Police accident report
2. Mercy Hospital emergency room report
3. City Towing repair estimate
4. Albertson's Food Store letter
5. Super Call Telephone Company records search report
6. FBI reports
7. Manning's office records
8. Manning's checking account records
9. Dr. Sandy Adams's office records
10. Rock Insurance Company records
11. Express Money Center letter
12. Rock Insurance Company check
13. Grand jury transcripts
14. IRS memo

The parties must stipulate to the following:

1. Business records foundations for all business records.
2. All checks and deposit slips are authentic.
3. Manning's demand letters and Rock Insurance's settlement check were placed in the U.S. mail and mailed in interstate commerce.
4. The transcripts of recorded telephone conversations in the FBI reports are accurate verbatim transcripts of the conversations.

9.12 MEDICAL NEGLIGENCE

JENNIFER SMITH

v.

KELLY DAVIS, M.D.

Introduction

In February, [-2], Jennifer Smith went to Dr. Sandy Johnson, an internist, for an annual examination. Dr. Johnson recommended that Smith begin having annual mammograms and referred her to Dr. Kelly Davis, a radiologist. Dr. Davis's mammogram revealed that Smith had a small lump in her right breast, which Dr. Davis found to be consistent with a probable fibroadenoma, a non-cancerous tumor. Dr. Davis sent the report to Dr. Johnson, who discussed the report with Smith. However, Smith did not have any follow-up procedures done to verify the diagnosis or treat the tumor.

In November, [-2], Smith noticed a lump in her right breast and again saw Dr. Johnson, who referred her to Dr. Chris Tucker, another radiologist. Dr. Tucker's mammogram revealed that Smith had a larger mass in her right breast, which Dr. Tucker found highly likely to be cancerous. A later biopsy confirmed the diagnosis.

In December, [-2], Smith had a partial mastectomy of her right breast, which was followed with radiation and chemotherapy.

Pleadings

Plaintiff's suit raises one claim, medical negligence, against Dr. Johnson and Dr. Davis, for failing to properly diagnose and timely treat her breast cancer.

Before trial, Dr. Johnson settled with the plaintiff for $500,000. Plaintiff's claim against Dr. Davis is now being tried, and both liability and damages are in issue.

The case has been filed in your federal district court as a diversity action (plaintiff moved to another state before she filed the action) and your state's tort law and relevant jury instructions apply.

805

Witnesses

Plaintiff may call the following witnesses:

1. Jennifer Smith
2. Dr. Chris Tucker

Defendant may call the following witnesses:

1. Dr. Kelly Davis
2. Dr. Sandy Johnson

Your instructor may impose other requirements and limitations on the issues to be tried, the witnesses that can be called, and the evidence that can be presented.

If impeachment prove up becomes necessary, call a prove up witness or prepare an appropriate stipulation.

Exhibits

The following may be available:

1. Medical records of:
   (a) Dr. Sandy Johnson
   (b) Dr. Kelly Davis
   (c) Dr. Chris Tucker
   (d) Dr. Terry Barnes
   (e) Good Shepherd Regional Medical Center
2. American College of Radiology BIRADS Codes
3. Stages of Breast Cancer information
4. Dr. Kelly Davis expert report (including curriculum vitae)
5. Dr. Chris Tucker expert report (including curriculum vitae)
6. Settlement agreement between plaintiff and Dr. Sandy Johnson

7. Depositions of:
   (a) Jennifer Smith
   (b) Dr. Sandy Johnson
   (c) Dr. Chris Tucker
   (d) Dr. Kelly Davis

Stipulations

The parties must stipulate that:

1. The medical records of the doctors and hospital in this case file are business records under FRE 803(6).

2. The life expectancy of a 42-year-old woman in the United States is 39.1 years.

3. Plaintiff has incurred the following medical expenses to date:
   (a) Dr. Sandy Johnson: $1,200
   (b) Dr. Kelly Davis: $600
   (c) Dr. Chris Tucker: $1,400
   (d) Dr. Terry Barnes: $10,000
   (e) Good Shepherd Hospital (surgery & post-op): $30,000
   (f) Good Shepherd Hospital (chemo & radiation): $40,000

4. Dr. Chris Tucker and Dr. Kelly Davis are, through their education, training, and experience, qualified to give expert opinions concerning the radiological diagnosis, treatment, and prognosis of breast cancer.

9.13 DRIVING WHILE INTOXICATED AND CARELESS AND IMPRUDENT DRIVING

STATE

v.

BRAD SMITHTON

Introduction

This is a criminal driving while intoxicated (DWI) and careless and imprudent driving (C & I) case. The various states have assorted structures for driving while intoxicated (sometimes known as "driving under the influence" or "impaired driving") offenses. The materials in this trial use the basic structure from the state of Missouri. Therefore, the jury instructions here are based on Missouri law. Many, but by no means all, other states would have similar jury instructions. Your instructor might ask you to ignore the law outlined here and use the structure and jury instructions of your state.

In the early morning hours of July 1, [-1], Brad Smithton left a party and drove his Jeep to pick up his girlfriend, Sara Twist. After picking up Twist, Smithton took a shortcut through a remote part of the Central State University campus on a street called "Prominence Point." The northern and southern portions of this short street are paved, but the middle portion is a dirt road (i.e., essentially a pair of tire ruts). Lieutenant Rocky Roberson of the Central State University Police Department arrested Smithton on suspicion of DWI, C & I, and an alleged offense related to his vehicle license plate.

The arresting officer and another officer filled out official paperwork. That official paperwork is included in this file. [You should assume that the defense made the appropriate discovery request and that the prosecution complied by providing the materials included in this trial file.]

The instructor will give the defense attorney(s) information for the defendant, Brad Smithton. Only the defense attorney(s) and the defendant himself are allowed to see this information. The prosecutor(s) cannot.

Pleadings

The three citations ("tickets") are noted in the Exhibits and Materials listed below. The DWI and C & I citations constitute the pleadings for this case. The prosecutor dropped the third charge, regarding Smithton's alleged driving of a vehicle that did not have a front and rear license plate visible to other drivers.

Witnesses

The prosecution may call the following witnesses:

1. Lieutenant Rocky Roberson
2. Officer Bernie Fine

The defendant may call the following witnesses:

1. Defendant Brad Smithton
2. Otis Campbell (Brad Smithton's fraternity brother)

Either party may call the following witnesses:

1. Sergeant Kim Donaldson [The prosecutor(s) should find a person to play this role.]
2. Sara Twist [The defense attorney(s) should find a person to play this role.]

The witnesses are not necessarily loyal to the attorneys who call them. To recreate the dynamics that would be present in a real trial as closely as possible, the prosecutors should find volunteers to play the roles of Lieutenant Rocky Roberson, Officer Bernie Fine, and Sergeant Kim Donaldson, and the defense attorney(s) should find volunteers for the roles of Sara Twist, Brad Smithton, and Otis Campbell.

If impeachment prove up becomes necessary, the parties must prepare an appropriate stipulation to admit the prove up evidence. The parties must stipulate that the deposition transcripts and transcripts of interviews accurately reflect what was said. No witness is allowed to claim any transcription error.

Exhibits and Materials

The following items are available:

1. Lieutenant Rocky Roberson's original report (7/1/[-1]), including a hand-drawn map by Roberson

2. InfoMaster Evidence Ticket

3. 7/1/[-1] Supplemental Report by Officer Bernie Fine, with photo of Jeep

4. 7/10/[-1] Supplemental Report by Officer Bernie Fine, with Transcript of Interview of Otis Campbell

5. 9/22/[-1] letter from Scott W. Gregory, the defense attorney who previously represented Brad Smithton, with its enclosure, the affidavit of Sara Twist [The lead prosecutor did not respond to this letter. Therefore, attorney Gregory's attempts at plea negotiations were not successful.]

6. The deposition of Sergeant Kim Donaldson [This deposition was taken to preserve Donaldson's testimony, because s/he anticipated being out of the country at the time of the trial. However, his trip was cancelled, because the Central State University Police Department could not come up with the funds to pay for it. As a result, Sergeant Donaldson is available to testify at trial.]

7. Refusal to Submit to Alcohol/Drug Test Form

8. Alcohol Influence Report Form

9. DWI Citation (Count I at trial)

10. C & I Citation (Count II at trial)

11. Vehicle License Citation (dropped by prosecutor before trial)
12. Driving Record (for Brad Smithton)
13. Jury Instructions

Statutes in this jurisdiction provide for DWI and C & I offenses. The required elements are outlined in the jury instructions at the end of the set of trial materials on the Companion Website. [Note: Your instructor might ask you to craft your own set of jury instructions, based on your jurisdiction's statutes.] Another statute in this state also makes it a traffic offense to operate a vehicle without both a front and rear license plate that are visible to other drivers.

9.14(A) MISDEMEANOR BATTERY AND ASSAULT OF A LAW ENFORCEMENT OFFICER

STATE

v.

TODD WEARL

Introduction

This trial is somewhat different from traditional hypothetical trials in trial advocacy classes. Usually, witnesses are asked to read a set of instructions that tell them what they "know" and then to testify based on that knowledge. In this trial, witnesses will observe the event in question (via a video on the Internet) and then testify based on their actual observations. Thus, the witnesses will be relying on their own observations of the event and their recollections of those observations.

The events that led to this litigation occurred in your city, which will be called "University" for purposes of this trial, on August 14, [-1], just outside the Library/ Museum Building, which is also sometimes referred to by its formal name of "Hulston Hall." The diagram included in these trial materials shows the outline of the Library/ Museum Building. The outline is accurate. The north half of the building is the Museum portion. The south half is the Library portion. The door from which two of the three participants in the incident (one of the men in civilian clothing and the police officer) exited the building is between the Museum portion and the Library portion.

Two males were walking in opposite directions outside the Library/Museum building. George Otta, who was wearing a white T-shirt, was leaving the building. Todd Wearl, who was wearing a red T-shirt, was walking toward the building. They ran into each other and a disagreement ensued. A uniformed policeman, Officer Dan Kinger, saw these events from inside the Library/Museum Building, then responded. He eventually pepper sprayed Mr. Wearl.

Those playing witness roles will view a video recording of the incident. Each ordinary witness will watch a specifically designated video once, then testify based on his or her recollection of what he or she saw and heard. To give those playing the roles of the participants in the incident (George Otta, Todd Wearl, and Officer Dan Kinger) a somewhat more comprehensive perspective of what occurred, each of them will be allowed to view two videos, but they will be allowed to watch each video only once.

All participants should assume that Otta, Wearl, and Kinger had never met each other before this incident. This was a chance encounter between the three of them. They have no "history" with each other.

Special Instructions

The attorneys in this case should carefully follow these instructions:

Delivering Instructions to Witnesses. Your instructor will give you an envelope containing a set of instructions for each of your witnesses. As an attorney in the case, you are not allowed to look at these instructions at any point before trial. Instead, deliver the sealed envelope to your witness and ask him or her to read all of the enclosed instructions before watching the videotape(s) assigned to that witness.

Finding Volunteers to Serve as Witnesses. As a student attorney, you will be expected to find volunteers to play the witness roles.

The prosecutor(s) will have to find "volunteers" for

1. George Otta [Must be male.]
2. Officer Dan Kinger [Must be male.]
3. Witness 1 [Note: Witness 1 was talking on a cell phone when the incident occurred.]
4. Witness 8

The defense attorney(s) will have to find "volunteers" for

1. Todd Wearl [Must be male.]
2. Witness 4A
3. Witness 4B [Note: Witnesses 4A and 4B were standing in location 4, talking to each other, when the incident occurred. Therefore, you should

find people for these roles who would have some reason to be talking to each other. In other words, find two people who know each other.]

    4.   Witness 2

After you find persons willing to fill these roles, you should give them their witness instruction packets, as noted above. Ask them to review all of the instructions before watching the assigned videos. Then wait for them to watch the videos on their own—that is, without you being present. After this occurs, you should interview them. All of this should occur before the witnesses are deposed.

You are not required to call every witness in this case. Instead, you should choose those witnesses you wish to call. You are allowed to call witnesses who were "found" by your opponent.

Exhibits and Materials

The following may be available:

1. Diagram of Library/Museum Building [Note: This diagram is of unknown origin. Someone apparently copied the basic outline of the building from a map and inserted numbers on it. It was probably someone who worked for the University Police or for one of the law firms involved in the case, but nobody now knows who created the diagram. Some, but not necessarily all, of the numbers on the diagram show the approximate locations of witnesses. Attorneys should ignore all numbers that are not relevant to their case (and, if they plan to offer the diagram as an exhibit in some form, should probably remove some or all numbers and other writing from the diagram).]

2. University Police Uniform Incident/Offense Report (six pages, including two pages on the traditional uniform report form, two pages of typed narrative, and a two-page "Use of Force Report")

3. River City Hospital Discharge Instructions (re: George Otta)

4. River City Hospital Radiology Department Report (re: George Otta)

5. River City Hospital Emergency Department Report (re: George Otta)

6. River City Hospital Work/School Excuse (re: George Otta)

7. Jury Instructions (including Verdict Form) [Note: Your instructor might ask you to draft your own set of jury instructions, based upon the law in your jurisdiction.]

Stipulations

The parties must stipulate as follows:

1. All medical records are the originals of these records, created and kept in the regular course of business of the medical institution that created and kept them.

2. All statements of observations in medical records are accurate reflections of the observations made by the person recording the observations in the records, made at or near the time of these observations.

3. To the extent that the medical records contain opinions of medical professionals, these opinions are the conclusions of persons qualified as experts to reach those conclusions. The opinions are based upon adequate bases. The methods the experts used to reach the conclusions are sufficient under the applicable standards of the jurisdiction.

9.14(B)   INTENTIONAL TORT (BATTERY)

GEORGE OTTA

v.

TODD WEARL

Introduction

This trial is somewhat different from traditional hypothetical trials in trial advocacy classes. Usually, witnesses are asked to read a set of instructions that tell them what they "know" and then to testify based on that knowledge. In this trial, witnesses will observe the event in question (via a video on the Internet) and then testify based on their actual observations. Thus, the witnesses will be relying on their own observations of the event and their recollections of those observations.

The events that led to this litigation occurred in your city, which will be called "University" for purposes of this trial, on August 14, [-1], just outside the Library/Museum Building, which is also sometimes referred to by its formal name of "Hulston Hall." The diagram included in these trial materials shows the outline of the Library/Museum Building. The outline is accurate. The north half of the building is the Museum portion. The south half is the Library portion. The door from which two of the three participants in the incident (one of the men in civilian clothing and the police officer) exited the building is between the Museum portion and the Library portion.

Two males were walking in opposite directions outside the Library/Museum building. George Otta, who was wearing a white T-shirt, was leaving the building. Todd Wearl, who was wearing a red T-shirt, was walking toward the building. They ran into each other and a disagreement ensued. A uniformed policeman, Officer Dan Kinger, saw these events from inside the Library/Museum Building, then responded. He eventually pepper sprayed Mr. Wearl.

Those playing witness roles will view a video recording of the incident. Each ordinary witness will watch a specifically designated video once, then testify based on his or her recollection of what he or she saw and heard. To give those playing the roles of the participants in the incident (George Otta, Todd Wearl, and Officer Dan Kinger) a somewhat more comprehensive perspective of what occurred, each of them will be allowed to view two videos, but they will be allowed to watch each video only once.

All participants should assume that Otta, Wearl, and Kinger had never met each other before this incident. This was a chance encounter between the three of them. They have no "history" with each other.

Also, you should assume that the local prosecutor decided NOT to pursue the criminal case against Wearl. Thus, you should assume that this intentional tort suit for battery by Otta against Wearl is the only litigation that has arisen out of this incident.

Special Instructions

The attorneys in this case should carefully follow these instructions:

Delivering Instructions to Witnesses. Your instructor will give you an envelope containing a set of instructions for each of your witnesses. As an attorney in the case, you are not allowed to look at these instructions at any point before trial. Instead, deliver the sealed envelope to your witness and ask him or her to read all of the enclosed instructions before watching the videotape(s) assigned to that witness.

Finding Volunteers to Serve as Witnesses. As a student attorney, you will be expected to find volunteers to play the witness roles.

Plaintiff's counsel will have to find "volunteers" for

1. George Otta [Must be male.]
2. Officer Dan Kinger [Must be male.]
3. Witness 1 [Note: Witness 1 was talking on a cell phone when the incident occurred.]
4. Dr. Alex Tintinalli

The defense attorney(s) will have to find "volunteers" for

1. Todd Wearl [Must be male.]
2. Witness 4A
3. Witness 4B [Note: Witnesses 4A and 4B were standing in location 4, talking to each other, when the incident occurred. Therefore, you should find people for these roles who would have some reason to be talking to each other. In other words, find two people who know each other.]
4. Witness 2

After you find persons willing to fill these roles, you should give them their witness instruction packets, as noted above. Ask them to review all of the instructions before watching the assigned videos. Then wait for them to watch the videos on their own—that is, without you being present. After this occurs, you should interview them. All of this should occur before the witnesses are deposed.

You are not required to call every witness in this case. Instead, you should choose those witnesses you wish to call. You are allowed to call witnesses who were "found" by your opponent.

Exhibits and Materials

The following may be available:

1. Diagram of Library/Museum Building [Note: This diagram is of unknown origin. Someone apparently copied the basic outline of the building from a map and inserted numbers on it. It was probably someone who worked for the University Police or for one of the law firms involved in the case, but nobody now knows who created the diagram. Some, but not necessarily all, of the numbers on the diagram show the approximate locations of witnesses. Attorneys should ignore all numbers that are not relevant to their case (and, if they plan to offer the diagram as an exhibit in some form, should probably remove some or all numbers and other writing from the diagram).]

2. University Police Uniform Incident/Offense Report (six pages, including two pages on the traditional uniform report form, two pages of typed narrative, and a two-page "Use of Force Report")

3. River City Hospital Discharge Instructions (re: George Otta)

4. River City Hospital Radiology Department Report (re: George Otta)

5. River City Hospital Emergency Department Report (re: George Otta)

6. River City Hospital Work/School Excuse (re: George Otta)

7. Jury Instructions (including Verdict Form) [Note: Your instructor might ask you to draft your own set of jury instructions, based upon the law in your jurisdiction.]

Stipulations

The parties must stipulate as follows:

1. All medical records are the originals of these records, created and kept in the regular course of business of the medical institution that created and kept them.

2. All statements of observations in medical records are accurate reflections of the observations made by the person recording the observations in the records, made at or near the time of these observations.

9.14(C) 42 U.S.C. § 1983 SUIT

TODD WEARL
v.
DAN KINGER

Introduction

This trial is somewhat different from traditional hypothetical trials in trial advocacy classes. Usually, witnesses are asked to read a set of instructions that tell them what they "know" and then to testify based on that knowledge. In this trial, witnesses will observe the event in question (via a video on the Internet) and then testify based on their actual observations. Thus, the witnesses will be relying on their own observations of the event and their recollections of those observations.

The events that led to this litigation occurred in your city, which will be called "University" for purposes of this trial, on August 14, [-1], just outside the Library/Museum Building, which is also sometimes referred to by its formal name of "Hulston Hall." The diagram included in these trial materials shows the outline of the Library/Museum Building. The outline is accurate. The north half of the building is the Museum portion. The south half is the Library portion. The door from which two of the three participants in the incident (one of the men in civilian clothing and the police officer) exited the building is between the Museum portion and the Library portion.

Two males were walking in opposite directions outside the Library/Museum building. George Otta, who was wearing a white T-shirt, was leaving the building. Todd Wearl, who was wearing a red T-shirt, was walking toward the building. They ran into each other and a disagreement ensued. A uniformed policeman, Officer Dan Kinger, saw these events from inside the Library/Museum Building, then responded. He eventually pepper sprayed Mr. Wearl.

Those playing witness roles will view a video recording of the incident. Each ordinary witness will watch a specifically designated video once, then testify based on his or her recollection of what he or she saw and heard. To give those playing the roles of the participants in the incident (George Otta, Todd Wearl, and Officer Dan Kinger) a somewhat more comprehensive perspective of what occurred, each of them will be allowed to view two videos, but they will be allowed to watch each video only once.

All participants should assume that Otta, Wearl, and Kinger had never met each other before this incident. This was a chance encounter between the three of them. They have no "history" with each other.

Also, you should assume that the local prosecutor decided not to pursue the criminal case against Wearl. Thus, you should assume that this civil rights suit by Wearl against Officer Kinger is the only litigation that has arisen out of this incident.

Special Instructions

The attorneys in this case should carefully follow these instructions:

Delivering Instructions to Witnesses. Your instructor will give you an envelope containing a set of instructions for each of your witnesses. As an attorney in the case, you are not allowed to look at these instructions at any point before trial. Instead, deliver the sealed envelope to your witness and ask him or her to read all of the enclosed instructions before watching the videotape(s) assigned to that witness.

Finding Volunteers to Serve as Witnesses. As a student attorney, you will be expected to find volunteers to play the witness roles.

Plaintiff's counsel will have to find "volunteers" for

1. Todd Wearl [Must be male.]
2. Witness 2
3. Dr. Pat Stevens
4. Plaintiff's Liability Expert

The defense attorney(s) will have to find "volunteers" for

1. George Otta [Must be male.]
2. Officer Dan Kinger [Must be male.]

3. Witness 1 [Note: Witness 1 was talking on a cell phone when the incident occurred.]

4. Defendant's Liability Expert

After you find persons willing to fill these roles, you should give them their witness instruction packets, as noted above. Ask them to review all of the instructions before watching the assigned videos. Then wait for them to watch the videos on their own—that is, without you being present. After this occurs, you should interview them. All of this should occur before the witnesses are deposed.

You are not required to call every witness in this case. Instead, you should choose those witnesses you wish to call. You are allowed to call witnesses who were "found" by your opponent.

Exhibits and Materials

The following may be available:

1. Diagram of Library/Museum Building [Note: This diagram is of unknown origin. Someone apparently copied the basic outline of the building from a map and inserted numbers on it. It was probably someone who worked for the University Police or for one of the law firms involved in the case, but nobody now knows who created the diagram. Some, but not necessarily all, of the numbers on the diagram show the approximate locations of witnesses. Attorneys should ignore all numbers that are not relevant to their case (and, if they plan to offer the diagram as an exhibit in some form, should probably remove some or all numbers and other writing from the diagram).]

2. University Police Uniform Incident/Offense Report (six pages, including two pages on the traditional uniform report form, two pages of typed narrative, and a two-page "Use of Force Report")

3. University Eye Care Associates letter by Dr. Pat Stevens (re: Todd Wearl)

4. Excerpts from University Police Department Manual Re Use of Force
5. Jury Instructions (including Verdict Form) [Note: Your instructor might ask you to draft your own set of jury instructions.]

Stipulations

The parties must stipulate as follows:

1. All medical records are the originals of these records, created and kept in the regular course of business of the medical institution that created and kept them.
2. All statements of observations in medical records are accurate reflections of the observations made by the person recording the observations in the records, made at or near the time of these observations.